INSIGHT GUIDES
TEXAS

Contents

THE BEST OF TEXAS: TOP ATTRACTIONS

From historic monuments and world-class art collections to unmissable sights like NASA's Johnson Space Center, this vast state is home to an impressive variety of sights and attractions.

▽ **The Menil Collection and Rothko Chapel, Houston**. Passionate art collectors the Menils' personal collection of art is displayed in an intimate setting in a stunning building by Renzo Piano. The interfaith chapel contains a collection of paintings by Mark Rothko. See page 175.

△ **The Alamo, San Antonio**. The birthplace of the revolution that led to the nine-year Texas Republic in 1836, this somber Spanish mission chapel is the heart of Texas pride in exuberant San Antonio. See page 156.

▽ **The River Walk, San Antonio**. Stroll or take a boat tour along an enchanting European-style riverside promenade in downtown San Antonio that captures the lights, color, and history of the largest Hispanic city in Texas. See page 156.

▽ **Nacogdoches, East Texas**. Its Caddo Indian name betrays the ancient origins of this attractive historic town, home to a state university, nature trails, museums, antique stores, and nearby Caddo Mounds State Historic Site. See page 192.

△ **Padre Island National Seashore, the Gulf Coast**. Texas's favorite beach destination beckons vacationers with its warm Gulf Coast waters, soft white sand, sea shells, and vivid sunsets. There are also rare whooping cranes and sea turtles in wildlife refuges. See page 211.

◁ **State Capitol, Austin**. Brasher, taller, and more conservative than its Washington replica, Texas's State Capitol offers political spectacle and granite beauty, plus excellent museums on the adjoining UT campus. See page 139.

▽ **Palo Duro Canyon State Park, West Texas**. West Texas's Grand Canyon rivals Arizona's top attraction for sheer beauty and its rugged desert canyon features, colorful rocks, historic cabins, and links to famed painter Georgia O'Keeffe. See page 274.

△ **NASA's Johnson Space Center, Houston**. Mission Control for the program that trained astronauts for moon landings and space shuttle travel, the still glamorous space center explores the space race, its achievements, and today's emphasis on medical research. See page 184.

▽ **Dallas Arts District, North Texas**. The largest arts district in the US takes up nine blocks of downtown Dallas, a sensory experience that includes world-class museums, galleries, and performing arts, restaurants, and unique pocket parks. See page 102.

▽ **Big Bend National Park, West Texas**. This huge, remote park in far West Texas's Big Bend Country protects teeming wildlife, shadowed canyons, and Wild West historic sites along the Rio Grande bordering the US and Mexico. See page 253.

THE BEST OF TEXAS: EDITOR'S CHOICE

Here at a glance are our recommendations – from music festivals to quirky museums and galleries, plus the pick of the state parks and where to find the best eats.

Cadillac Ranch, Amarillo.

BEST MUSEUMS AND GALLERIES

Cadillac Ranch (Amarillo). Visit this humorous art installation featuring four partially-buried Cadillacs beside the interstate and add some graffiti of your own. See page 277.

The Orange Show Center for Visionary Art (Houston). This folk art museum is dedicated to the orange and is a community arts center supported by the likes of ZZ Top. See page 176.

Amon Carter Museum (Fort Worth). Artworks by Frederic Remington and Charles M. Russell, who specialized in depicting life on the range, are the highlights here. See page 114.

Nasher Sculpture Center (Dallas). This lovely outdoor setting in the Dallas Arts District displays artworks by Giacometti, Matisse, Miro, and other world-class sculptors. See page 103.

The Menil Collection and the Rothko Chapel (Houston). A world-class art collection combining Medieval and Byzantine art and contemporary works by Rothko. See page 175.

Museum of the Gulf Coast (Port Arthur). This museum interprets the Gulf Coast and its famed native sons and daughters, including Janis Joplin and Clarence Frogman Henry. See page 191

Bullock Texas State History Museum (Austin). Texas's colorful history – from American Indians to six different flags – comes alive in this three-story museum next to the State Capitol. See page 137.

BEST WILDLIFE WATCHING

Galveston, Mustang, Padre Islands. Three of Texas's 350-mile (560km) -long barrier islands offer history, a chance to see rare whooping cranes, beachcombing, and camping. See page 202.

The Austin Bats. Ann W. Richards Congress Avenue Bridge in the Texas capital is home to a huge colony of Mexican freetail bats, which swirls forth at dusk in a crowd-pleasing spectacle. See page 140.

Big Thicket National Preserve. Rivers, pine woods, and desert come together in this large national preserve along the Texas–Louisiana border that is home to pileated woodpeckers and common nighthawks. See page 283.

High Island, Bolivar Peninsula. Texas Audubon operates four bird sanctuaries on High Island, an oak-dense upland used by neo-tropical migrant birds during their spring migrations. See page 202.

Bats over Ann W. Richards Congress Avenue Bridge, Austin.

BEST FESTIVALS AND EVENTS

Texas wildflowers.

Cinco de Mayo and Diez y Seis. *Tejanos* (Hispanic Texans) celebrate these Mexican independence holidays on May 5 and September 16. See page 300.

Spring Wildflowers. Driving in the Hill Country to see bluebonnets and other Texas flora in spring is a time-honored Lone Star tradition. See page 150.

Austin City Limits Music Festival. Around 150 bands perform over three days each September on the shores of Town Lake in downtown Austin, the self-proclaimed "Live Music Capital of the World." See page 138.

Kerrville Folk Festival. Springtime homage to folk and acoustic music, in the heart of Texas Hill Country. See page 146.

Juneteenth. Commemorating June 19, 1865, when Texas slaves learned they were free, this is a popular Galveston Festival. See page 202.

Willie Nelson's 4th of July Picnic. Fireworks, hot sun, cold beer, hours of music, and Willie Nelson make for an only-in-Texas blowout. Various locations. See page 77.

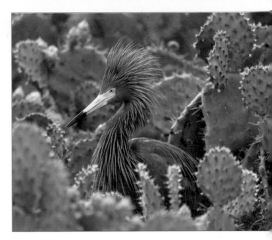

Reddish egret, Aransas National Wildlife Refuge.

BEST STATE AND NATIONAL PARKS

Big Bend National Park. This remote desert park in far West Texas showcases towering mountains, deep canyons, wild rivers, and the Chihuahuan Desert. See page 253.

Lost Maples State Natural Area. A Hill Country treasure, this park has rare outcroppings of bigtooth maples and Texas madrones, which provide some of the state's most beautiful fall colors. See pages 286.

Palo Duro Canyon State Park. A dramatic slash in the Panhandle, Palo Duro Canyon has a long natural and cultural history that inspired the painter Georgia O'Keeffe. See page 289.

Franklin Mountains State Park. Skyline drives reveal dramatic views of El Paso and neighboring Juárez, Mexico, from the nation's largest city park. See page 237.

Aransas National Wildlife Refuge. A birdwatchers' paradise along the middle of the Texas Coast, and home to the largest migrating colony of endangered whooping cranes. See pages 287.

San Antonio Missions National Historical Park. Spain's legacy in Texas had its origins in this ruggedly beautiful chain of churches along the San Antonio River (of which the Alamo is but one) in the San Antonio metropolitan area. See page 167.

Caddo Lake State Park. Texas's only natural lake (the others are man-made reservoirs) is a watery wilderness of cypress-shadowed sloughs and channels for canoers, kayakers, and fishermen to explore to their hearts' content. See page 283.

Barbecue pit at the Salt Lick, Austin.

BEST TASTES OF TEXAS

Here is but a small selection of the many restaurants serving the best of Texas cooking around the state.

Barbecue. The Salt Lick (Austin).

Chicken-Fried Steak. Mary's Café (Strawn).

Tex-Mex. Molina's (Houston).

Gulf Coast Seafood. Gaido's Seafood Restaurant (Galveston).

Southern Comfort Food and Soul Food. Threadgills's (Austin).

High End Texas/Southwestern. Hugo's (Houston).

The Texas Longhorn band performs at the Alamodome, San Antonio.

Big Bend National Park.

WHERE BIG IS BEAUTIFUL

The myths are magnificent, but so is the reality. What appeals most about Texas – and Texans – is the huge diversity.

Texas Longhorn.

For many people, Texas is America – the one place where the American dream is still alive, where the values and traditions that helped build the nation are still a viable part of the culture. Think of all the American icons that come from Texas: the cowboy, the sheriff, the six-shooter, the 10-gallon hat, the maverick, the oil baron, the longhorn, and the open range, just to name a few. And how many times have you seen the big-hearted, drawling Texan used to represent Americans as a whole, slapping the world on the back and inviting it over for a barbecue? Distortions they may be, but they evoke an image of an America recognized around the world.

But to really get to know Texas, forget entirely about the "Big Texas" of legend and concentrate on something smaller. Texas has seven distinct regions (surprisingly few of which feature empty desert) and a plethora of cultural influences (as you'd expect from a state that boasts of having been governed by "Six Flags"). Sure, you'll encounter lonesome cowboys, wealthy oilmen, and Hispanics – although remarkably few American Indians – but expect the unexpected: a Vietnamese fishing community along the Gulf Coast, a Czech farming town out on the plains, Cajun enclaves in the piney woods bordering Louisiana, a ghost town that comes alive for country music in the Hill Country, and a community

Texas State Fair, Dallas.

of contemporary New York artists in a dusty border town. Conservative Texas is even growing its own hipster culture in burgeoning Austin these days, as moneyed Silicon Valley types, students, natural foods purveyors, and musicians rub shoulders with politicians in what was once a small, out-of-the-way state capital.

Texas – it's a little bit country, a little bit rock and roll, and all heart. So gas up the iron horse – you'll certainly need to do a lot of driving – and hit the open road for adventures that will stoke your imagination for years to come.

The Texas State Capitol, Austin.

THE LONE STAR STATE

Cultural traditions, economic realities, and the sheer distances involved mean that Texas could actually be five different states under its Lone Star.

Texas is truly a country within a country, befitting a state that was once its own republic. For starters, there's its size. At 267,000 sq miles (692,000 sq km), Texas is larger than many nations, including every country in Europe. It takes two days just to drive from one side of the state to the other, passing through landscapes that shift from southern swamps and dripping forests to high plains and hilly ranch country to vast western desert, where the West really seems to start.

The variety of landscapes and the sheer size and space make for a chili gumbo of experiences, from small town to megacity, canyon country to gulf beaches, borderlands to heartlands, 21st-century skyscrapers and malls to historic missions and forts and villages that hark back to 19th-century Europe. There is a sense of room to stretch out and grow, even though in reality, most Texans live urban lives, and that has had a definite effect on how Texas sees itself, and others, in turn, see it.

> Numerous playwrights have lived and worked in North Texas. Preston Jones wrote A Texas Trilogy and Don Coburn wrote The Gin Game, a Pulitzer Prize-winner. Larry L. King's musical Best Little Whorehouse in Texas was a hit in the 1970s and 80s.

Texans are inordinately proud of their state, and see themselves as Texans first, Americans second. There's a Texas way of doing things, but that takes on a different flavor depending on where you live in Texas, and that, for most visitors, is exactly why a visit here is so enjoyable.

Kicking back at the end of the day, Alpine, Texas.

Distance and difference

Traveling the entire state really does take a good deal of time. There are 940 highway miles (1,500km), for example, between Texline on the northern border of the Texas Panhandle, and Brownsville at the mouth of the Rio Grande across from Mexico. From Texarkana in the northeast corner, beside the Arkansas border, to El Paso at the state's extreme western tip is 810 miles (1,300km).

As you cross this vast surface, everything changes: the configuration of the earth, the economy, time zones, and even the seasons. It is feasible to be snowbound in Amarillo one day and the next day to be sunbathing on the beaches of South Padre Island. Out west, in the mountainous areas of Big Bend and Fort Davis, or the Guadalupe Mountains adjoining New Mexico, the state's tallest peaks, the torrid summer endured in most of the state is pleasantly tempered by altitude. It takes only a little traveling around to understand why Texans never think of their province as one place, one thing, or one society.

Cattle and oil

Cattle, then oil, originally fueled the state's economy and made it what it is, and both can be found, or have thrived, in almost every part of

Shale deposits in South Texas and the potential for drilling in the newly discovered Barnett Shale in North Texas, it's back and it's booming again, driving a thriving economy that attracts new residents lured by jobs, lack of state tax, an inexpensive cost of living, and generous benefits for new business.

Though a sense of the past comes from human works – the buildings, roads, and other monuments resulting from centuries of creative efforts – what is under the land has often been more important in Texas than what is on top. Beginning 250 million years ago, during the

Big Bend National Park.

the state. In the early days, land and cattle were pretty much the only assets of the fledgling republic, which wasted no time in converting them into money, selling land to the federal government and longhorn steers by the millions to buyers in the American North and West.

Oil and gas, of course, are almost everywhere in the state, with only a handful of Texas's 254 counties not having found oil or natural gas within their boundaries. Texas is the largest petroleum-producing state in the US, and it has been estimated by economists that, if Texas were an independent nation, it would rank as the world's fifth-largest petroleum-producing country. Oil production took a hit during the recession, but thanks to oil- and gas-rich Eagle

Permian era, faults, folds, intrusions, and other geological movements formed the hidden reservoirs and basins that contain the great supplies of petroleum, natural gas, coal, salt, sulfur, and other minerals. Drilling has uncovered oil and gas in even older formations such as the Mississippian in North Texas and much younger Cretaceous era deposits in South Texas. It's clear that for Texas, its geology has been its destiny.

Not only has Texas increased in wealth and importance as a result of its subsurface minerals but also, in its most important agricultural region, the High Plains, water pumped to the surface from aquifers has transformed a desert into one of the world's great cotton- and food-producing areas.

Five states

When the old Republic of Texas became part of the United States in 1845, it retained the right to divide itself into as many as five states, should it so decide. Although Texas has so far not taken up this option, it still lurks at the back of some minds (along with notions of secession, a fantasy of some of the more fanatical Tea Party elements headquartered in the state, who have seized headlines on a national stage). Certainly breaking up the state would make this huge behemoth more manageable. As it is, in practice, the so-called "Five States of

its subregions, which are also recognizable to most Texans, including the Gulf Coast, the Rio Grande Valley, the Hill Country, the Texas Panhandle, and the High Plains, although these subregions have not acquired their own unique cultural patterns in the ways the larger geographic regions of Texas have.

West Texas gambles

West Texans are considered highly individualistic, quick to react, but free with their purse and time. In West Texas one is seldom told, "I don't have time to see you now." Because so many

View from South Padre Island.

Texas" are mostly recognizable by the manner in which the inhabitants earn their living, the crops they farm, and their attitude toward their own and other people's customs, religions, and traditions.

Boundaries

The exact boundaries of North, South, West, East, and Central Texas may vary, but the inhabitants of each region seem to accept the fairly general definitions. For example, when a Texan mentions West Texas, it is not just the geographical portion of the state that is being described; it is also a collection of traditions associated with that part of Texas and attached to its residents. And each major region contains

of the region's leaders have associated themselves with ranching and the oil business, West Texans are seen as people willing to gamble – forced to gamble, in fact, by the nature of their enterprises. Ranching, whether cattle or sheep and goats, is a cyclical undertaking, dependent on the fluctuations of both the weather and the market.

Oil is famous for not always being where the prospector drills, but it can also reward its finder, and the landowner, with instant wealth. Most West Texas ranches today depend on oil and gas from their vast acres for economic survival. But all over Texas, the sight of the "horsehead" pump is common, some towering as high as a three-story building, pulling oil from those ancient Permian reefs and sea-beds many meters below the surface. You'll see more pump jacks than cowboys, even in West Texas, which was once informally known as "Big Ranch Country."

These days, you're also likely to see a great many wind turbines in the state: over 40 projects produce the largest amount of wind power in the nation. Wilderado Wind Ranch, off I-40 near Amarillo, is the largest in the state, with 161 turbines.

The stark flatness of the area, the open spaces that seem to go on forever, and the huge sky are of earthy humor and wisdom. Or, as one may still hear in certain parts of East Texas, they're "coonier" – not an offensive term but, in fact, a tribute to the clever tactics of the raccoon, an animal quite prevalent in the region.

This is the part of Texas most like the Old South back in the time of its agricultural dominance, with former cotton plantations and slow, unhurried ways. Here, you'll find a more humid climate, dense forests, swamps, and wide, slow-moving rivers, while, at its western edges, some 500 miles (800km) away, lie arid deserts, barren mountains, and streams that,

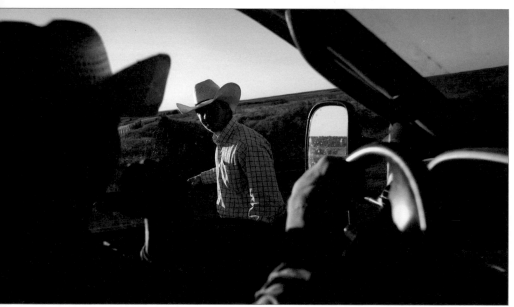

Workers on the 6666 ranch, Guthrie.

often startling to newcomers, who will immediately understand the meaning of the term "high lonesome." Texans make a distinction between the part of West Texas that stretches from the western edge of Hill Country, southwest of Austin, to El Paso, in the state's southwestern corner, bordering Mexico and New Mexico, and the northwestern Panhandle, which includes the cities of Lubbock and Amarillo, along old Route 66 (now I-40), and into New Mexico.

Southern folk

East Texas natives, especially old timers, are held by the rest of Texas to be shrewder, more southern-rural, and often gifted with a special kind although they turn into "gullywashers" when full, are often dry.

Even today, East Texas is a region of mostly smaller towns and many rural communities of the crossroads variety, consisting of a general store, a service station, a couple of churches (usually Protestant), and maybe a schoolhouse, left empty when the country schools were consolidated years ago. East Texas, incidentally, has produced some of Texas's better-known writers and other artists, many of them working from the strong sense of tradition that seems to come with the land. The late William Goyen's writings were filled with East Texas imagery. Alvin Ailey, the renowned choreographer, was born in East Texas. And sculptor James Surls is based in

East Texas and uses woods found in the area as his main medium.

Down to the border

South Texas starts (in the Texas mind) at San Antonio and continues southward to the Rio Grande, which forms the natural and official US–Mexico border, or as it is known, *La Frontera*. Along its edges, it supports two separate cultures: the long, well-populated curve of the Gulf Coast and that other world of mostly Hispanic Texans along *La Frontera*. South Texas was the birthplace of the Texas cowboy, who began

political leaders. The lower Rio Grande Valley, called simply "The Valley" by Texans, furnishes a significant percentage of the citrus fruit and vegetables for sale in the US.

One of two major new oil deposits in Texas has recently been discovered in South Texas in the younger Cretaceous-era Eagle Ford Shale underlying most of this region. While the shale reaches the surface in North Texas, the oil-bearing portions are deeper down and occur entirely in South Texas, where most drilling is taking place. It is now one of the leading oil drilling regions in the country.

Wall mural near Mission Concepción.

as a Mexican *vaquero* (the Western term "buckaroo" is a corruption of the Spanish word), and of the 19th-century cattle drives made famous in story, film, and song. It remains a spread-out, sparse land, containing several of the state's major ranches, including the famous historic 825,000-acre (334,000-hectare) King Ranch on the far southwestern border.

Several huge Hispanic land grants in South Texas, granted by the king of Spain to the ancestors of current holders for services rendered centuries ago, remain today. That kind of centuries-old tradition strongly influences the attitudes of South Texans, who have the reputation of being easy-going yet fiercely loyal when it comes to *"familia y fe"* (family and faith) and

Selling the goods

North Texans share fewer traditional traits, probably because of the region's long-time role as merchant to the rest of Texas and the Southwest. North Texas is famous for its mega shopping, including the flagship Neiman Marcus department store in Dallas, and sells everything from clothing to electronics. Because the metroplex of Dallas–Fort Worth is so huge and wealthy, North Texans see themselves as more sophisticated than other parts of Texas, although the statement meets fierce and determined resentment if repeated too often: citizens of Austin in Central Texas and Houston in East Texas are not known for their high opinion of Dallas, though almost everyone praises Fort Worth for its old-fashioned charm and ranching traditions.

The local economy may be transformed by the recent discovery of the Mississippian-era Barnett Shale, much older than the Permian era deposits found in West Texas. The Barnett formation is rich in natural gas, as well as having oil in significant quantities. Extraction may, however, be an issue, as most of the formation lies under Dallas–Fort Worth within extremely hard shale.

In the middle

In the past, Central Texas has not been as well defined geographically as other parts of

Friday night football is popular across Texas. Buzz Bissinger's book Friday Night Lights tells the true story of a high school football team that boosted morale in the depressed town of Odessa. The book spawned a cult film and TV series.

neatly summed up by the "Keep Austin Weird" slogan adopted by the city's many small businesses, is in marked contrast to the conservative nature of the rest of the state.

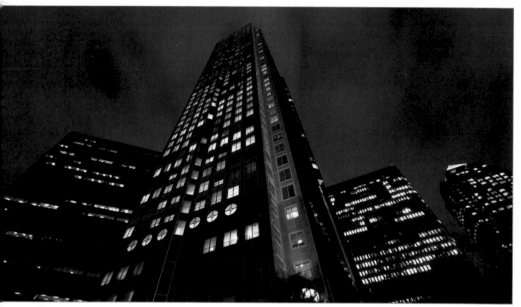

Dallas skyscrapers.

the state. That's certainly not the case now. Its lovely, rolling, wildflower hills, freshwater lakes, viticulture scene, traditional German- and Czech-influenced small towns, and scenic backroads have become a major Texas destination for cultural travelers – and those who just enjoy a more relaxed and human-scale way of life.

Hill Country, as it's known, is within a stone's throw of the state capital of Austin, famed for its own (taller) version of the US capitol, a growing high-tech sector, and the University of Texas, whose students have helped foster an exciting live music scene, natural and gourmet foods (this is home base for Whole Foods), and a fun and funky attitude to everything, from outdoor pursuits to culture. Its alternative vibe,

Central Texas has contributed a large proportion of political figures to the lore of the Lone Star State. Foremost among them, of course, is Lyndon Baines Johnson (LBJ), US Vice President under John F. Kennedy, who ascended to the presidency under tragic circumstances in 1963, won election on his own terms, and presided until 1969, passing a remarkable amount of important legislation, including Civil Rights. LBJ was born in Hill Country and taught school there. He never attempted to pull up those roots during his journey to the White House, and visiting his ranch (as well as the Lady Bird Johnson Wildflower Center in Austin founded by the first lady in Austin) is one of the most enjoyable destinations as you tour the region.

Country road, West Texas.

DECISIVE DATES

1519
Spain lays claim to the region comprising the present state of Texas.

1685
La Salle lands in Matagorda Bay and sets up a short-lived French colony.

1718
The presidio (president) San Antonio de Bexar and the mission San Antonio de Valero (the Alamo) are established on the San Antonio River.

1754
Construction begins on the present Alamo chapel.

1793
San Antonio de Valero mission is closed and its lands are divided up among Indian families.

1801
A Spanish cavalry unit from San Carlos del Alamo de Parras occupies the mission as a garrison.

The storming of the Alamo.

1823
Stephen F. Austin brings the first 300 families to help Mexico settle Texas.

1824
Mexican constitution promises Texas statehood.

1830
Law of April 6 toughens restrictions on immigration from the US into Texas, heightening tensions between Anglo settlers and Mexico.

1834
Santa Anna is elected president and starts to centralize the Mexican government.

Revolution

1835
Texas revolt begins; San Antonio is occupied. The Texas Rangers are officially instituted.

1836
Santa Anna invades. Texas declares independence.

Siege and battle of the Alamo. All defenders of the mission are killed. Santa Anna is later defeated at San Jacinto. Texas becomes an independent republic.

1839
Austin, formerly the village of Waterloo, is established as the new nation's capital.

1841
Republic of Texas' President Mirabeau Lamar sends a small armed force to New Mexico in a vain attempt to seize territory from Mexico.

1842
Santa Anna retaliates by twice seizing San Antonio, leading to an expedition by mutinous Texas volunteers that ends in disaster at Mier.

1844
US Senate rejects annexation treaty with the Republic of Texas, dashing hopes until the election of US President James K. Polk, who revives the annexation effort; it passes the following year.

1846
Ending almost a decade of independence, Texas joins the US. War breaks out between Mexico and the US.

1848
War ends. The Rio Grande becomes a permanent international boundary in the Treaty of Guadalupe Hidalgo.

1850
US Army repairs the Alamo.

Battle of Resaca de la Palma, 1848 (Mexican–American War).

1853
The Buffalo Bayou Brazos and Colorado – the first railroad chartered by Texas – begins operating.

1854
The state establishes two Indian reservations.

1858
The army imports camels for use in the arid western part of the state.

1861
Texas secedes from the Union in favor of the Confederacy. The Alamo is used by the Confederate Army during the war between the states.

1865
Final battle of the Civil War fought near Brownsville, Texas, after the war's official end. Announcement at Galveston that slavery has been abolished.

1866
Large-scale cattle drives to the north begin.

1870
Texas is readmitted to the Union.

1873
Record annual rainfall (109ins/279cm) at Clarksville.

1875
Comanche Chief Quanah Parker loses his last fight and is forced onto a reservation, effectively ending Indian wars in Texas.

1876
Charles Goodnight founds the J.A. Ranch at Palo Duro

Spindletop oil field, 1915.

Canyon, the first cattle ranch in northwest Texas.

1884
Fence cutting wars; new laws ban the practice.

1888
The Alamo chapel, having been used as a warehouse, is sold by the Catholic Church to the state.

1894
Oil is discovered at Corsicana.

Early 20th century

1900
Hurricane destroys half of Galveston and kills 6,000 people.

1901
Mining engineer Captain A.F. Lucas discovers the Spindletop gusher near Beaumont.

1905
State of Texas grants custodianship of the Alamo to the Daughters of the Republic of Texas.

1907
Neiman Marcus department store opens in downtown Dallas.

1910
First military flight in a Wright Brothers plane at Fort Sam Houston.

1916
Pancho Villa and his men cross the border to raid Texas communities.

1917
Race riots occur in Houston. Texas legislature votes to impeach Governor Jim Ferguson for mismanagement of state funds.

1920
Texas–Mexico border skirmishes come to an end.

1925
Miriam "Ma" Ferguson, wife of impeached Governor Jim Ferguson, becomes the first female Governor of Texas. She is re-elected for a second term in 1933.

1930
Oil strike by C.M. "Dad" Joiner 100 miles (160km) east of Dallas becomes the East Texas Oil Field, the largest petroleum deposit on earth at that time.

1932
Texan Babe Didrikson Zaharias wins three Olympic gold medals.

Pancho Villa and his men.

1933
Texan Wiley Post makes first solo flight around the world.

1934
Career of Depression-era bank robbers Bonnie Parker and Clyde Barrow ends in a hail of bullets, after a 102-day manhunt led by Texas Ranger Frank Hamer.

Post-depression Texas

1947
Fiery chain explosions demolish much of the coastal refinery town of Texas City, killing almost 600 and injuring almost 4,000.

1953
Dwight D. Eisenhower becomes the first Texas-born President of the US.

1956
George Stevens' movie of Edna Ferber's novel *Giant* is released to wide popularity, forever fixing the myth of tough Texas oilmen in American folklore.

1958
Texas Instruments' Jack Kilby ushers in the electronics age with his revolutionary development of the silicon chip.

Dwight D. Eisenhower.

1959
Lubbock-born rock 'n' roll singer Buddy Holly dies in an airplane crash.

1962
NASA opens Manned Spacecraft Center at Houston.

1963
President John F. Kennedy is assassinated while touring Dallas in a motorcade with Texas Governor John Connally. Kennedy's Texan-born Vice-President, Lyndon B. Johnson, is elevated to presidency.

1964
Lyndon B. Johnson wins election for the presidency in the largest landslide in US history.

1969
Apollo 11 commander Neil Armstrong calls Houston from the moon.

1976
Houston Democrat Barbara Jordan becomes the first African-American woman to deliver a keynote address at a party conference.

1978
Dallas TV drama series begins and is soon screened all over the world.

1985
Larry McMurtry's novel *Lonesome Dove*, about a Texas cattle drive, is published to immense popular and critical acclaim; TV adaptation follows.

1988
Sometime Houstonian George H.W. Bush is elected US President.

1993
Federal agents storm the compound of the Branch Davidians sect near Waco, resulting in more than 80 deaths. El Paso author Cormac McCarthy wins the National Book Award for *All the Pretty Horses*.

1998
Murderess Karla Faye Tucker becomes the first woman to be executed in Texas since 1863.

2001
Texas Governor George W. Bush, Jr, son of George H.W. Bush, is sworn in as the 43rd President of the US. Tropical Storm Allison claims 23 lives. Thousands lose their jobs as Houston-based energy company, Enron, collapses.

2005
When Hurricane Katrina devastates the city of New Orleans in neighboring state Louisiana, East Texas takes some 200,000 refugees, most settling in Houston. The majority are still living there.

2006
The Dallas Cowboys start construction on a new

Former president George W. Bush.

stadium, moving the team from the suburb of Irving to the suburb of Arlington.

2007
Former First Lady Texan and conservationist, Lady Bird Johnson, dies at age 94.

2008
Hurricane Ike hits the Gulf Coast island of Galveston, causing destruction and power outages in Galveston and parts of nearby Houston for 21 days. The adjoining Bolivar Peninsular, a popular birding and vacation spot, is hard hit.

2009
The Texas Board of Education approves a science curriculum that opened the door for teachers and textbooks to raise doubts about evolution.

2010
Charlie Wilson (b.1933), former Texas congressman (1973–96), dies. His deal-making funneled millions of dollars in weapons to Afghanistan to back rebels fighting the Soviet Army. Tom Hanks starred as Charlie Wilson in the 2007 film *Charlie*

Wilson's War, based on the 2003 book by George Crile.

2011
The underdog Dallas Mavericks defeat the Miami Heat four games to two, to capture their first ever NBA championship.

2012
Texas governor Rick Perry ends his presidential campaign and endorses Newt Gingrich's candidacy for the 2012 Republican presidential nomination.

2013
A fiery explosion rips through the West Fertilizer Co. in West (pop. 2,700), north of Waco, injuring more than 200 people and causing $100 million in damage. The Czech government later donates $200,000 in aid to assist West, in solidarity with the many people there with Czech roots.

2014
TransCanada begins delivering oil from Cushing, Oklahoma, to customers in Nederland, Texas, through the southern portion of the controversial proposed Keystone XL pipeline.

The famous six flags of Texas.

SIX FLAGS OVER TEXAS

Control of Texas has been handed from one external power to another, but independence and self-determination remain the watchwords of its people.

Pass through a few Texas towns large enough to have an independent school system, and the names on the schools begin to take on a familiar sound: Austin, Crockett, Fannin, Bonham, Lamar, Travis, Houston. Every town will have buildings or streets carrying one or more of those names, too.

Schoolchildren, taught Texas history by legislative decree, grow up on stories about its legendary heroes. Today, with thousands of Hispanic and black students, schools are beginning to be called by the names of ethnic heroes such as Benito Juárez, Emiliano Zapáta, or Martin Luther King. Historical mythology is strong in all ethnic groups.

Unlike New England or the Atlantic seaboard states, Texas had no single source of settlement. White men came quite early to some parts of the state and arrived 350 years later to the others. The famous "Six Flags Over Texas" theme is rooted in historical fact. Each flag – those of Spain, Mexico, France, the Republic of Texas, the Confederacy, and the United States – represented a separate, if brief, period of the state's history.

The Texan coast may have been sighted by Amerigo Vespucci as early as 1497, but there is evidence of much earlier inhabitants – some possibly as far back as 37,000 years. Archeological studies have revealed no grand past civilizations in Texas such as were found in Mexico and Central and South America, but there were cliff dwellers in the Texas Panhandle, and cave dwellers left traces of their fascinating paintings for us to ponder throughout West Texas. The Caddo confederations encountered in East Texas by the first Europeans were an agricultural people.

Stephen Fuller Austin rallies colonists against the Karankawas, c.1824.

Colonization

Along the Gulf Coast, from Galveston Bay southwestward to Corpus Christi Bay, lived the nomadic Karankawas. Practitioners of ceremonial cannibalism, and always incredibly fierce, they had been wiped out by the white man's diseases and bullets by the 1850s. The American Indians that the Texas settlers battled against were Plains tribes who rode in from the north on horses descended from those brought to the New World by early Spanish explorers.

One of these Spanish explorers, Alvar Núñez Cabeza de Vaca, was cast ashore on what is believed to have been Galveston Island, working his way across Texas for eight years before finally reaching Spanish Mexico in 1536. He and three other shipwrecked survivors of the Narvaez expedition, including his Moorish servant Esteban, thought to have been the first black man in the New World, were enslaved by the Karankawas. But after escaping, they gained such reputations as medicine men that, when they approached a strange tribe, everyone turned out to welcome them.

When Cabeza de Vaca and Esteban returned to civilization with tales of cities of gold and pearl in El Norte, the myth of the Seven Cities of Cibola became the motive for several Spanish

> *The Caddo Indian cry "tejas" ("friend"), from which the state derived its name, has been translated over the years into the Texas state motto: "friendship."*

expeditions to Arizona, New Mexico, and Texas. The search for these golden cities, and the equally mythical Gran Quivira, led to Spanish colonization of the Southwest.

It was France laying claim to the area around Matagorda Bay that caused the Spanish to begin settling Texas. In 1685, French explorer René Robert Cavelier, Sieur de La Salle, had landed on the Texas coast and built a fort. By the time Spanish authorities in Mexico heard of the French intrusion, La Salle had been killed by his own men and the colony wiped out by American Indians. Nevertheless, the nervous Spanish began to build missions on the border between French Louisiana and Spanish Texas.

In East Texas they met Caddo Indians, who greeted them with the cry "Tejas!" Thinking this was the name of a large tribe, the Spanish explorers called the area *Tejas*, or Texas. Later, settlers realized the word was a widely used greeting meaning "friend."

Spanish heritage

Despite owning Texas for nearly three centuries, the Spanish settled it only for protection, in narrow strips along the coast and the rivers. Even San Antonio, the major Spanish settlement, was more important militarily and as a mission than as a commercial center.

Sam Houston, Governor both Tennessee and Texas.

THE ALAMO

The Alamo's defenders were recent arrivals from England, Ireland, Scotland, and Denmark, as well as the United States. Their 26-year-old commander, William B. Travis from South Carolina, wrote three days before he died that "the citizens of this municipality are our enemies." His associates included Jim Bowie, remembered for his namesake knife, and the legendary Davy Crockett, a three-term congressman from Kentucky who sought his fortune in the West after his presidential ambitions evaporated. The independent Texas for which they fought and died survived just nine years before being subsumed by the United States.

Spain's mark, however, is still strong in Texas, with many of the outstanding geographical features and major rivers bearing Spanish names. Numerous Spanish missions still stand, at least partly restored, and various Spanish legal terms and property laws survive as Texas statutes.

Perhaps the most important Spanish inheritance was passed to cattle ranching. Almost every practice and piece of equipment used by ranchers has a Spanish name and origin. These range from *chicote* (a rawhide whip) to *tumbador* (someone who throws calves ready for branding).

The older regions of greatest Spanish colonization, from San Antonio and Laredo south, especially those along the Rio Grande, still show evidence of this influence in their architecture, language, religion, and everyday customs.

Between 1811 and 1821, Spain found itself continually putting down rebellions in Texas. In 1811, the young Santa Anna, later to be the scourge of the Alamo but then still a junior officer, was in one of these disciplinary forces. At the same time, the Spanish authorities recognized that the sparsely occupied parts of Texas were always under threat unless developed, so they encouraged immigration. Moses Austin was among the men who applied for an *empresario* grant but, when he died just after receiving it, his son, Stephen Fuller Austin (today known as the "Father of Texas"), renegotiated it in his

to restrict Anglo immigration, the Anglo-American majority in Texas led a rebellion against what were considered despotic governmental practices in 1835. In reality, the despotism was mainly created by Mexican dictator Santa Anna.

The Texas Revolution lasted only eight months, but it gave Texas the myth and image that Texans are exhorted to live up to. It was this short but successful period of rebellion that created the Texas Valhalla, with such heroes as Ben Milam, James Fannin, Jim Bowie, William B. Travis, James Bonham, Davy Crockett with his fellow Tennesseeans, and General Sam Houston.

Texas battle flag in Austin's State Capitol.

own name and brought in 300 settlers.

Those first colonists are to Anglo-Texas what the passengers of the *Mayflower* are to Massachusetts: the proudest bloodlines go back to "The Old 300." In 1821, Mexico gained its independence from Spain and, within the next decade, 41 *empresario* contracts were signed, permitting the arrival of nearly 14,000 Anglo-Americans to supplement the original Spanish population. Eventually, hundreds more settlers joined the Austin colonists.

The Texas nation

"Texians" (as they were then called) never learned to get along well with the Latin laws, religion, and political practices of Mexico. Aggravated by the unpopular Law of April 6 1830, which aimed

From the Texas Revolution came the stories of the Alamo (still largely a matter of conjecture), those 13 fateful days in 1836 when 189 patriots held out against the fierce onslaught of 4,000 Mexicans, who eventually overran the fort, killing all its defenders, save for a few women, children, and slaves.

Minimizing his losses, Santa Anna said: "It was but a small affair," and ordered that the bodies of the heroes be burned. His aide, noting that he took many casualties, losing many of his best men, muttered: "Another such victory and we are ruined." Forty-six days later, the Texans got their revenge. Along with a group of American volunteers, and led by General Sam Houston, they avenged their fallen at San Jacinto.

Taking Santa Anna and his 1,500 men by surprise, Houston's force, though greatly outnumbered, routed the Mexicans within minutes. "Remember the Alamo," they shouted to each other as they charged, and it has never been forgotten. Santa Anna was captured, 600 of his troops were killed, and Texas was free. A new republic was born.

The period that followed sowed the seeds of the feelings of loyalty for which Texans are so famous. And no matter how diverse their lives, or how far from Texas they may wander, all Texans hold the Alamo in common ownership.

The dome of the Texas Capitol building, Austin.

For less than a decade, from 1836 to 1845, the Republic of Texas was an independent nation with its own flag, its own ambassadors, its own president and congress, and, after some moving around, its own specifically designed national capital at Austin. It is true that millions of Texans today may recall the republic only occasionally, but they have never entirely forgotten it.

Their self-reliance and fierce loyalty (which has not always endeared Texans to their fellow American citizens) come from that decade of independence. The state seal and the Lone Star flag, which is still displayed as frequently as the national banner, remain from that independent government.

First president

Commander of the army Sam Houston was elected as first president of the new Republic of Texas, his 5,119 votes far outnumbering the total votes of his rivals (Henry Smith, 743; Stephen F. Austin, 587).

The Mexicans caused further trouble when, in 1842, they briefly captured San Antonio. And there was also the American Indian problem. Sam Houston had lived among the Cherokee, and understood their mentality more than most. He proposed a guarantee of tribal rights through legal title to their lands. But he found that he was unable to keep the promises he made to the Cherokee. When Houston's term expired, the new president, Mirabeau Lamar, proposed that all American Indians be expelled from East Texas: "Nothing short of this will bring us peace and safety," Lamar thundered, "the white man and the red man cannot live in harmony together… Nature forbids it…"

SAM HOUSTON

Sam Houston's victory at the Battle of Jacinto over Mexican General Santa Anna, in April 1836, secured Texas's independence from Mexico and, using the rallying cry "Remember the Alamo," avenged the deaths of the ragtag band of martyred revolutionaries at the Alamo two months earlier. Houston was the only American to be elected governor of two different states – Tennessee (1827–9) and Texas (1859–61) – and the only Southern governor to oppose secession and refuse to swear an oath of allegiance to the Confederacy when Texas seceded from the Union in 1861, following the outbreak of the Civil War.

Houston was a complex character. He was born in Virginia and moved to Tennessee, where he lived among the Cherokee, married into the tribe, and was later adopted as a citizen. He resigned the governorship of Tennessee and moved to Arkansas, only to become embroiled in politics again, which led to his migration to Texas. Following his removal from office as Texas governor, he moved to Huntsville, where he died in 1863. Houston was honored after his death with a memorial museum, four US warships named USS *Houston* a US Army base, a national forest, a historical park, a university, and a prominent roadside statue outside Huntsville. Best known, of course, is the city in East Texas to which he gave his name – the fourth largest city in the US.

The republic expanded rapidly, tripling its population, but the influx of slaves – brought by southerners settling on the Gulf Coast to develop the cotton crop – led to disputes when Texans voted to join the Union in 1845.

As part of the annexation arrangement, the US Congress assumed the Texas Republic's $5 million in debts and allowed Texas to retain possession of all undistributed land (although, in the 1840s and 1850s, much of it was still in the possession of the Comanche). There were no federal taxes in effect, but Texas had no wealth, only land. It sold to the US its rights to

broke out, Houston was forced to resign after he refused to swear allegiance to the Confederacy. Houston died in 1863. Three months after his burial, the Confederate legislature of Texas passed a resolution: "His public services through a long and eventful life, his unblemished patriotism, his great private and moral worth, and his untiring, devoted and zealous regard for the interests of the state of Texas command our highest admiration, and should be held in perpetual remembrance by the people of this state."

During the period of revolution, resettlement, and republic, thousands of people came

Map of Austin, 1840.

New Mexico and Colorado, and Sam Houston and other conservatives supported the Boundary Act on the grounds that the state had more desert land than it could use.

Pressing for funds for frontier defense, Texas persuaded Congress to give it an extra $7.75 million in 1855. With the money, the state launched a major building program of state structures, courthouses, schools, transportation systems – all of which was achieved without imposing taxes. This then conditioned Texas to look for sources other than taxes to finance its activities, a situation that continues today.

By 1860, when Sam Houston was elected governor for a second term, Texas was again in debt. The following year, when the Civil War

to Texas to get away from whatever their life had been "back home." They weren't always fleeing from the law. More often, the new Texans came west to escape failure or some sort of unhappiness that could be left behind. This is very much a continuing tradition as, even today, Texas becomes home for thousands who leave other parts of the nation every month to seek new opportunities in the Lone Star State. A high percentage of the dead at the Alamo, and a majority of the unfortunates who were slaughtered earlier at Goliad, were recent arrivals in Texas; even Davy Crockett, the superhero of the Alamo, had only been in Texas for a few weeks. The tradition of the newcomer hero has a long history.

Unusually, Texas still owns all its public lands. If the federal government wishes to create a park, or cut a stand of timber, it has to ask the state's permission.

At the time of the Civil War, most Texas settlers were from the agricultural South. A plantation economy, with its accompanying slavery, controlled East Texas and the Coastal Plains, where cotton was a profitable crop. Thus, Texas was overwhelmingly drawn into the Civil War on the side of the Confederacy. It was never torn by any major battles, and, after the war, sectional wounds healed quicker in Texas than in any other southern state. Within a decade, newcomers from northern states were not only arriving in great numbers but were assuming positions of business and economic leadership.

Opportunity frontier

When the Union blockaded the Gulf Coast during the Civil War, Texas managed to smuggle some cotton across the Rio Grande for shipment to world markets, but the blockade was serving another purpose then unknown. Unable to export its cattle even to the Confederate Army, Texas's herds built up to more than 3 million during the Civil War. Once the war was over, there was tremendous demand for this beef in northern and western states.

Texas went through relatively little of the sorrow and desperation of the Reconstruction period. And because it was the only ex-Confederate state that offered its southern sister states hope of a new beginning, southerners flocked there. The 15 years that followed Appomattox saw Texas emerge as the opportunity frontier of the whole nation, north and south alike. It has retained that position, and has continued to uphold that reputation.

Families from every social level picked up and moved to Texas, pushing forward the old frontier boundaries until, like a flooding river, newcomers swept out onto the prairies and battled American Indians for the wealth of grass and soil that was once thought to be the "Great American Desert." This movement to the frontier created two new Texas myths: one was the frontiersman and his sturdy pioneer wife, and the other was the cowboy.

The end of the open range

Texas was readmitted to the Union in 1870 and, with the 1875 surrender of Comanche chief Quanah Parker at Fort Sill, Oklahoma, the far western portion of the state was finally ready for ranching on a large scale. Barely a decade later, though, the wide open spaces were being fenced and confined as settlers and sheep farmers fought to contain the open range. In 1894, oil was discovered at Corsicana by workers drilling for water. With the discovery of the major gusher at Spindletop in 1901, Texas entered the new century with an economic boom.

Bird's eye view of Houston, 1873.

BARBED WIRE

By the 1880s, would-be ranchers from all over the world were flocking to Texas, but overstocking, followed by a severe drought, led to the inevitable bust. People believed that stock had to be conserved and contained. Until then, fencing had been constructed primarily from the osage tree, but this changed in 1874 when an Illinois man, Joseph F. Glidden, was granted a patent for new fencing material that consisted of barbs wrapped around a single strand of wire. Out of hundreds of competing designs, Glidden's was the one that eventually won out. The Devil's Rope Museum in McLean, Texas charts the history of this and similar fencing tools.

The Great Cattle Drives

With hardy livestock and even hardier cowboys, life on the great cattle trails of the 19th century was no picnic but remains one of the iconic images most associated with Texas.

The first cattle known to have entered Texas were 500 cows that had been brought in by Spanish conquistador Coronado in 1541. Subsequent explorers also brought cattle, which gradually wandered into the wilderness. By 1757, Reynosa (pop. 269) had 18,000 head of cattle. A fat cow was worth four pesos in 1779, with hides and tallow more valuable than beef. Mission Espiritu Santo, on the banks of the winding Guadalupe River, between present-day Victoria and Mission Valley, was the first great cattle ranch in Texas. Around 1770, it claimed 40,000 head of cattle.

The definitive Texas cow was the longhorn – a hybrid breed from Spanish *retinto* (criollo) stock and English Hereford and Bakewell cattle that were brought in from Ohio, Kentucky, and other southern and midwestern states in the 1820s and '30s. Their long horns had a spread of 5–6ft (1.5–2 meters), with some spanning a full 8ft (2.5 meters) from tip to tip. They were apparently "tough to eat and tougher to handle" but, with their long legs and hard hooves, were ideal trail cattle that gained weight even on the way to market.

By the mid-19th century, great hordes of Texas longhorns that had been roaming freely, and shaped by nature and environmental conditions, were being gathered into herds for the trail drive north. Cattleman Edward Piper made what may have been the first northern drive in 1846, moving a herd from Texas to Ohio. He was followed almost immediately by many other contractors, especially after the end of the Civil War.

Trail bosses and crews

The drive cost the herd's owner about $500 per month, worked out on the basis of about 75¢ per head of cattle for three months. Eight to 20 hands were needed to trail a herd of 2,000–3,000 cattle, about one man per 250–350 animals, with crews including a trail boss and cook plus a horse wrangler (usually a young boy), to handle the six or eight mounts needed for each man. The all-important trail boss had "as many duties as the captain of a

steamboat." He arose early to wake and assign the men, ensured there were always enough provisions, settled all disputes, kept counting the cattle to see none had been lost, and rode ahead to check on water supplies. Exploring ahead, the boss would ride part way back and, from some hilltop, wave his hat to indicate which direction the herd should take.

The herd itself was usually a mix of beeves – mature steers – and cows (which walked with a less steady stride). It had a head (point) and feet (drag), with swingmen watching the "shoulders" and flank men watching the "hips." Riders bringing up the drag, sometimes physically pushing the laggards

Cattle herd fording a river, c.1860.

ahead, were enveloped in dust, especially on the alkali flats, and kept a "wipe" (bandanna) across their faces. The best place to learn cuss words, recalled one veteran, was always on the drag.

Cattle drives began in early spring when new grass was emerging but before the rivers were swollen with heavy run-offs. In the north, drives had to be completed before the autumn snowfalls. Once under way, the trail drive would cover up to 16 miles (26km) per day, although a herd making only 10–12 miles (16–19km) could take a leisurely lunch by grazing and thus put on some weight en route. The easiest part of each day was the afternoon, when the thirsty cattle were eager to reach water – the basic secret of successful trailing being the grazing and watering: well-fed cattle were less likely to stampede.

MODERN TIMES

After the legacy of the longhorn came the bounty of black gold, and with it an increasingly urban sophistication for the rural state of Texas.

The greatest change in the way Texas lived and viewed itself began in 1901, when the Spindletop oil field near Beaumont, in the far southeastern corner of the state, blew in with billions of barrels of oil each year. Spindletop was where the world's modern petroleum industry was born. No field like it had been dreamed of before and, with the later development of the East Texas oilfield in Rusk County, it ensured that Texas, and the world, would never be the same again.

With the Spindletop discovery, the state had jumped from an agricultural economy to a financial-industrial economy. At first, Texans were slow to recognize change, and many still haven't fully accepted it. To this day, the struggle between rural and urban values continues to divide the state. In the 1960s, the trend toward suburbanization increased, as more and more farmers preferred to live in town and visit their fields by car. Indeed, 80 percent of Texans now live in urban areas, a fact not always apparent from the many movies and novels about the state that turn on the romance of the past.

Since Spindletop, Texas has rarely failed to lead the US in petroleum production. In the early days, it was the global leader. This has added to the state's tendency to measure itself not against sister states but against the world.

Oil and politics

The 1960s produced a series of events bigger even than the state itself. The traumatic assassination of President John F. Kennedy in Dallas in 1963 swiftly led to the swearing in of Kennedy's Vice President, Lyndon B. Johnson – a Texan – as the 36th US President. The year before had seen the opening of NASA's Manned Spacecraft Center at Houston, and, before the decade was

Cowboy boot store, Fort Worth.

over, Apollo 11 astronaut Neil Armstrong was transmitting the first words from the surface of the moon: "Houston, Tranquility Base here. The Eagle has landed." Somehow, it seemed appropriately Texan in style.

In the 1970s, while price freezes, gas shortages, and civil rights became as familiar concepts to Texans as to the rest of the country, the state continued to grow. In 1973, it became the fourth most populous state in the Union. The Arab oil embargo increased domestic production in Texas oilfields. Towns such as Lubbock, Abilene, and Odessa doubled in size.

After a slump in prices and a major global recession, things have been looking up in oil and gas. In 2008, the first extractions began from the Eagle Ford Shale, which extends from the US border with Mexico into East Texas. Some 3 billion barrels of oil are projected to be found in the Eagle Ford formation, and the average well is thought to contain some 2.36 billion cubic feet of gas. By the end of 2013, production had skyrocketed to over 1 million BOE (barrel of oil equivalent) per day and now extends into 24 counties in Texas, making it the most productive oil and gas field in the US.

In addition, substantial oil and gas deposits have been located in the ancient Mississippian Barnett Shale formation beneath the Dallas–

Texas elected its first female US senator, Kay Bailey Hutchison. In fact, strong, practical women are a feature of the Lone Star state; they form the backbone of many a venture, as was evident in the TV series *Dallas*. The late political commentator and humorist Molly Ivins is a case in point: like Ann Richards, she could go toe to toe with any Texas good ol' boy and put them in their place. Texas even had one of the country's first women's museums, a Smithsonian Institution affiliate located in Fair Park, Dallas, until 2011. So if you imagined all Texan women with big hair,

Senator Kay Bailey Hutchison.

Fort Worth area of North Texas, although drilling here may prove trickier as the shale is very hard and it lies beneath the metroplex.

Texas is well known for its brash politics and larger-than-life politicians – not so surprising given the outsize personality of the state. Texas has been either the birthplace or adopted home of four US presidents – Dwight D. Eisenhower, Lyndon B. Johnson, George H.W. Bush, and George W. Bush, not to mention presidential candidates, including most recently Governor Rick Perry, who threw his hat into the ring in 2012, and may well do so again in 2016.

Texas has had two female governors – Miriam Amanda Wallace "Ma" Ferguson in the 1920s and Ann Richards 1991–94; in 1993,

Wranglers, walking two paces behind their man, and staying home while the boys go drinking, think again.

Superlative Texas

Texas facts and figures are seldom expressed in other than superlative terms: *The* biggest; *The* best. And Texas planners tend to think along the same lines. That's one of the reasons why such a high percentage of recent US building and real estate development has taken place in cities like Dallas, Houston, and Austin. There has been uncontrolled growth in some areas, but this has not discouraged Texas developers.

Today, in the wake of the Iraq War and volatile prices, oil is of critical importance. Aside from that, though, it is an element of Texas's identity. Even in nonproducing counties, the commodity plays a vital part in local business because of the jobs and buying power it creates. Dallas is a perfect example: it is a city legendary the world over for its involvement in the oil business, but it is located in a section of Texas that has never produced any, although that may change now that the Barnett Shale formation looks to be worth drilling.

Texas's rich oil and gas resources have traditionally been a double-edged sword. On the one hand, oil has brought immeasurable wealth to the state, especially now that domestic sources of energy are so highly valued, but until the economy began to diversify in recent years, the reliance on oil had made the state vulnerable. The crash in world oil prices caused hardship in Texas in the early 1980s and was followed by the shock of the Savings and Loan crisis of the late 1980s, when over a million Texans lost their homes.

As a result, state leaders have recognized the importance of economic diversification and have gone out of their way to attract high-tech firms. Computer chip fabrication and software

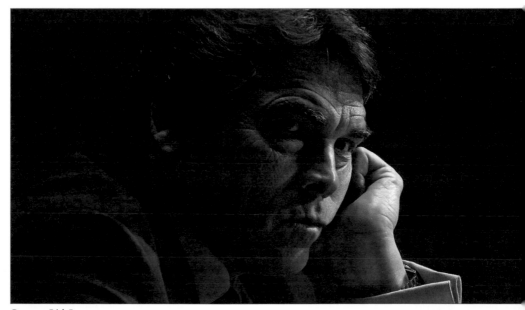

Governor Rick Perry.

BILLIONAIRE POLITICS

While it may seem that big money buys political favors in places like Texas (and beyond), not all billionaires in Texas politics can be considered the "guys in black hats." Ross Perot, an Independent candidate for the US Presidency in 1992 and 1996, brought deep pockets and his own strong agenda on fiscal policy, overseas job losses, and opposition to gun control to the table and won the support of numerous undecided and disaffected voters looking for a different choice.

During the 1992 election, he garnered 18.9 percent of the vote, and 8 percent in his subsequent candidacy, a healthy percentage for a third-party candidate. Perot came out against the North American Free Trade Agreement (NAFTA) in his campaign, citing the loss of US jobs to Mexico, and also focused on education. The state's controversial "No Child Left Behind" campaign requiring extensive mandatory testing in schools was adopted by George W. Bush as governor and then at the national level during his presidency – a policy that has had mixed success.

Perot philanthropy has endowed several institutions in Texas, including the Perot Museum of Nature and Science in the Dallas Arts District, but the man himself has now disappeared from politics. He supported Republican Mitt Romney in the 2012 election.

development have found a receptive home in Austin, and Dallas has become a significant financial market. Consequently, Texas has weathered the Great Recession much better than most places in the US, making it one of the top places creating new jobs (albeit largely in the minimum wage sector), building new infrastructure, and growing in population and demand.

The new economy

Everything – from the fashion industry to movie and television production to a burgeoning art market – is currently taking root in Texas, and

big business in Texas, which has enthusiastically adopted huge wind generating farms through its Central and West sections. Wind power accounted for 8.3 percent of the electricity generated in Texas in 2013.

The state's location in the Sunbelt is also enticing. All kinds of corporations are shifting their headquarters to the Lone Star State, not just for its more favorable climate but also for its access to world markets, its central location, and its eagerness to acquire fiscal and industrial families. Major international corporations, too, have opened branches in Dallas and Houston.

Wind turbines on the Lone Star Wind Farm, Abilene.

all of these new players are challenging the oil industry's long tenure at the head of the state's economic pyramid. The new economy is based on a sounder combination of technology, manufacturing, and finance.

Texas has taken over national leadership in many phases of the chemical industry (not just petrochemicals). It has remained an important aerospace center, and is attracting more technological manufacturing firms. Still a major farm and ranch center, it contains the most farmland of any American state and ranks third among the states in total agricultural income. It is first in the production of cotton, cattle, sheep, goats and, in most years, rice. In addition, alternative energy production from wind power is now

First in jobs, bottom in social services

It doesn't hurt that business taxes are low in Texas, and there is no state income tax – although a high sales tax ensures that those on low incomes, generally making one of the country's lowest minimum wages, end up paying a disproportionately higher amount of their income in taxes than corporations and the wealthy.

This, indeed, is one of the ironies of the Texas Miracle that has gripped the country during the Recession years: companies and job seekers are flooding there, swelling the demand for goods and services, but the apparent success is tempered by other forms of taxation that make living in the state more expensive than at first appears.

Texas is also bottom of the league in social services, particularly health care, since this is one of the states that refused to expand Medicaid for its lowest income residents under the Affordable Care Act, otherwise known as Obamacare. Those at the bottom of the social scale struggle more in Texas than in many other states, even though the state's ability to attract business and grow jobs has helped its economy greatly overall.

Tea Party politics

The widening gulf between rich and poor in Texas – and the country as a whole – is not news for

powerful minority. Texans are largely urban nowadays, and its cities – the largest and most rapidly growing in the US – are overwhelmingly liberal and vote Democrat. Rural areas with large numbers of Hispanics, such as South Texas, along the US border with Mexico, also are Democrat, but tend not to vote – an issue now on the radar of both Republicans and Democrats – and Texas demographics influence the outcome.

The fast-growing Hispanic and urban liberal populations are, in fact, changing Texas political demographics, as has already happened in other western states that have traditionally voted

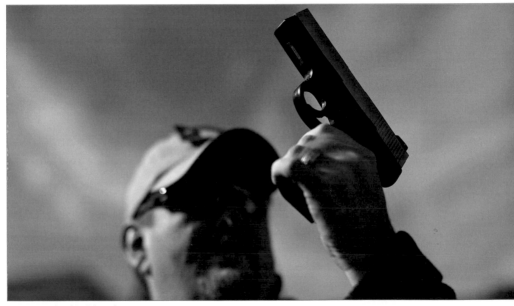

A man exercises his right to bear arms.

anyone who has been following the split along Republican and Democratic lines in US politics in recent years. Much of it can be put down to the rise of a small number of older, conservative voters in the Republican Party's minority Tea Party faction. Texas politicians Governor Rick Perry, US Senator Ted Cruz, and former House Majority Leader and Congressman Tom Delay have been driving forces in this new factional politics. All have brought their hard-line, religious-based agendas to the national stage as they have risen through the ranks and been elected, driving a wedge into the old school Republican party, which in turn has fractured the US political discourse.

That's not to say that all of Texas is Republican and ultraconservative, just a very vocal and

A TEXAS PRESIDENT

Lyndon Baines Johnson (1908–73) was born into a Texas Hill Country farming family. Ruthlessly ambitious, he became a senator in 1948 and John F. Kennedy's Vice-President in 1960. Three years later, aboard Air Force One, he was sworn in as US President, just 99 minutes after Kennedy's assassination in Dallas. Johnson had a landslide victory in the 1964 election, but his years at the White House, dedicated to creating "the Great Society," were darkened by the shadow of the Vietnam War. Vociferous domestic opposition to the conflict led "LBJ" to step down in 1968, and he retired, with his wife, Lady Bird, to their Texas ranch.

Republican, such as Colorado. In San Antonio, this has already come to pass, with the city's talented young Democratic mayor Julian Castro tapped by President Obama to head the Housing and Urban Development division in Washington, and Julian's identical twin brother, Joaquín, elected as Democratic congressman for Texas's 20th congressional district, including San Antonio, in 2012.

Sporting artists

These days, art districts are part of every major city in Texas, offering a huge variety of traditional

Dallas Cowboys game.

and modern art. That's true even in far-flung places such as West Texas, where Marfa, a little ranch town in Big Bend Country, has been taken over by contemporary artists, and in Amarillo, home to the famous Cadillac Ranch art installation in a field west of town.

Oil and developer money supports many artistic endeavors in Texas, and some of the best art collections and well-endowed museums in the country, if not the world, can be found in Dallas and Houston and other cities funded by the likes of Trammell Crow and the Menils.

Texans work hard and play hard. Most are mad about sports, particularly baseball and football. Soccer is increasingly popular with younger Texans, more of whom are playing the game. The state has a professional soccer team, and Texans came out in healthy numbers to support the US in the 2014 World Cup in Brazil.

Texas athletes of both sexes have established themselves as stars and record-holders in track and field, swimming, gymnastics, golf, baseball, basketball, tennis, motor and horse racing, bicycling, sailing, and polo. There is scarcely a Texas town that cannot volunteer the name of some native son or daughter who has gone on to receive national or international sporting acclaim. And visitors who participate in such activities as golf or tennis will find doors opened to them.

Increasingly urban

Although in the eyes of the United States, as well as the rest of the world, the prevailing image of Texas remains rural, its 26.5 million residents are overwhelmingly urban. Life today in the larger Texas cities has scant connection with the Texas of history and romance. Nevertheless, urbanites were fascinated, along with everybody else, by the TV drama *Dallas*, which – despite the cast working in high-rise offices – pictured the ranch as the center of Texas family life, even if the Ewings were not exactly an average family. The series was revived in 2012 but unfortunately its principal star, Larry Hagman, passed away during filming.

Dallas ranks as one of the largest fashion marketing centers in the country. Home to the flagship Neiman Marcus store, famed for its selection and customer service, Dallas has some of the best shopping in the US, and has long attracted celebrities to its upscale malls and glittering boutiques. Small towns in the metro area are also benefiting, including places like Denton, north of Dallas, a university town with a popular live music and arts scene and funky stores, much like Austin.

A mini-US

As Texas has grown, it has acquired the vices and problems it long scorned as "big city" or "foreign." It now has three of the largest US cities, so slums, pollution, and traffic are a part of the urban scene.

Texas is said to be modern America in microcosm, bowing to changes while proclaiming a rugged individualism, celebrating past glories but with one foot firmly in the future and pragmatic about what it takes to thrive in the 21st century. Perhaps this is the best way for personal independence in the US to survive – honoring traditions while, at the same time, regarding them with a flexible state of mind.

Cowboys at daybreak.

Metal-art vendor at the San Antonio Stock Show and Rodeo.

TEXANS

Peoples from all over the world have made Texas – the land of opportunity – their home, bringing with them their own individual cultures and traditions.

Anglo immigrants established the overall trends of the state's cultural development, when they wrested the area from Mexico in the 19th century. But there have been other cultural influences: Texas is crosshatched with a complicated pattern of regional and ethnic divisions. The state welcomes people from many countries, and as a result it has one of the top rates of foreign immigration in the US.

"Anglos" – American citizens – who settled in Texas before annexation, were mainly from the South, although, even within this group, there were major cultural differences. Immigrants from the Deep South, where slavery was deeply rooted, tended to settle east of San Antonio, in the wetter agrarian sections of East Texas. Those from the mid-Atlantic states, where slavery was less pervasive, tended to settle north and west of the Colorado River in North and West Texas.

Like southerners today, these settlers held a wide range of political, religious, and moral views, some of them in direct opposition to each other, and to those of foreign Anglo emigrants from the British Isles and central and eastern Europe.

American cowboy image

For a long time, the homesteading, agrarian Anglos east of San Antonio set the tone for the whole state. East Texas was not just southern – it was an extension of the Deep South. In the early 20th century, thanks to the ubiquitous presence of the cowboy in the societal media of the day, this southern influence in the popular imagination waned, replaced by that of the West, with its powerful icons. Denim overalls and cotton growing gave way to cowboy boots and cattle raising as essential elements in the

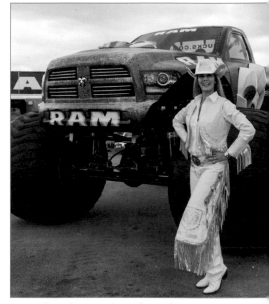

A cowgirl poses by a supersize truck at Rodeo Austin.

international image of Texas – at least until the wildcatter and the oil baron joined the cowboy in the Lone Star pantheon. Non-Southern dishes like chicken-fried steak, tortillas, and chili have by and large replaced the traditional offerings of grits, greens, and cornbread on the Anglo table in Texas.

Recent immigrants seem to prefer the state's cowboy image to its connection with the Confederacy. Although for the most part cowboys are a thing of the past, the cowboy image seems more in keeping with the state's vitality than the cultivation of southern memories. And, because being a cowboy was never an exclusively Anglo experience, it tends to run right across Texas's many ethnic boundaries.

Anglo-Southerners are not just being westernized; they are disappearing. Whites of Old South descent make up less than half the population, especially after heavy immigration from California, the Midwest, and the Northeast during the mid-1990s boom years. And, due to the large number of Mexican-Americans in Texas, white non-Hispanics form a smaller percentage of the population here than in the country as a whole.

The composition usually called "Anglo" is likely to consist of several European and possibly some non-European elements. Texas was

Visitors at the Zapata Fair.

the location of the earliest Polish community in the United States and some of the first Irish ones. The largest group of immigrants to come directly from Europe was German.

Hispanic ascendance

In his book of essays, *In a Narrow Grave*, Larry McMurtry put forward the view that Texas cities are always improved when the Hispanic culture influences the Anglo. If this is true, Texas cities must be improving: their Hispanic populations are increasing steadily. San Antonio, Houston and El Paso are among the top US metropolitan areas in total Hispanic population, and Texas follows only California in the number of Hispanics: people with Spanish surnames make up

37 percent of its population. And that is just legal residents: Texas leads the country in its number of illegal immigrants, most from south of the border (around 1.65 million, according to the Pew Charitable Trust). Border immigration issues remain some of the most emotional and contentious politically in the US, made all the more so by the explosion in numbers of unaccompanied young children crossing the border, only to be rounded up and placed in detainment centers.

In big cities like Dallas and Houston, where blacks used to be the largest minority, Hispanics are surpassing them. In the state as a whole, Hispanics overtook blacks as the dominant minority group in the late 1940s. Texas has fastest growing birthrate in the country, with two-thirds of that coming from Hispanic births. By 2024, it's expected that young Hispanics will outnumber the aging Anglo population in the state.

It's clear that Spanish-speaking peoples are gradually re-Hispanicizing the state, following much the same immigration patterns as Anglos. Hispanics are no longer confined behind the imaginary boundary that once kept them west and south of the San Antonio River. Today there are *barrios* in Dallas and Fort Worth, Corpus Christi, El Paso, and even in the Texas Panhandle, bringing Mexican and Central and South American customs, traditions, and color the length and breadth of the state. Hispanics are integrated into every element of public and private life in the state. Cinco de Mayo and Diez y Seis, two holidays celebrating Mexican independence, are widely celebrated outside of Hispanic communities as well.

Hispanic influence is strongly felt throughout the state in every aspect of daily life, and increasingly in politics; Republican senator Ted Cruz is the first Latino in that office in Texas, and the first Cuban-American. Hispanics traditionally lean Democrat, and their increasing numbers and clout have shifted American politics in western states like California and Colorado. Until now, though, voter turnout among Texan Hispanics has been low – 35 percent in the 2012 presidential election – but that's changing, as both major parties accept the realities of changing demographics and lobby for the Hispanic vote. What is clear is that the influx of liberal urban residents from

California to booming cities like Houston, Austin, and San Antonio, along with growing numbers of more politically active Hispanics, is likely to shift state politics yet again.

More than any other minority group, Spanish-speaking Texans have made their cuisine part of the mainstream of Texas life and, increasingly, that of the rest of the nation. Tacos, enchiladas, fajitas, and all the rest of the Tex-Mex menu (a culinary style derived from the cross-cultural influences of the border regions of both countries) are found as often on the Texas table as chuck roast and iced tea.

African-American heritage

The state's other major minority group, African-Americans, have lived in Texas since it was ruled by Spain. When Cabeza de Vaca was shipwrecked on the Gulf Coast in 1528, an African slave named Esteban was with him. Blacks, enslaved or free, were found in subsequent Spanish settlements, and intermarriage resulted in a significant *mulatto* population in Spanish Texas.

The first large infusion of blacks came after the Republic of Texas was established. The Mexican stand against slavery had made owners reluctant to import their human chattels, and the absence of slavery had created a haven for free blacks. But, after independence, slavery became legal, and former Deep Southerners began to bring in slaves. Slavery tended to be concentrated east of the Texarkana–San Antonio line, where the Anglo masters were settled, and where the agrarian economy was more conducive to farms and plantations.

Following Emancipation (which Texas slaves learned about on June 19, 1865 – two and a half years after its issue, giving rise to the state holiday of Juneteenth), and into the 20th century, blacks often lived a rural life on scattered farms or in small black "freedman" communities. Today, as they move to cities within Texas and elsewhere, the rural communities that preserved black culture are dying out or, as in the case of Austin's historic Clarksville neighborhood, becoming gentrified by an influx of affluent white homeowners.

The popularly accepted idea that blacks were not an important part of western frontier life ignores some significant black history. Many runaway slaves and free blacks joined American Indians and lived among them, not just on the frontier but beyond it.

The black soldiers of the ninth and 10th Cavalry and the 24th and 25th Infantries who fought American Indians were called "Buffalo Soldiers" by the tribes (owing to the coarse, kinky quality of the troopers' hair). After they mustered out of the service, many of these soldiers stayed out West to ranch, raise crops on dryland farms, or work as cowboys. Despite this role played by black soldiers in the Indian Wars and the settling of West Texas, most Texans continue to associate blacks only with the southern strands of Texas's history. The Spanish-ruled Mexicans were the first non-Native

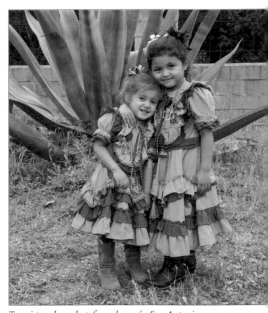

Two sisters dressed up for a charrería, San Antonio.

American Texans, or *Tejanos*, and descendants of these original settlers form a small, stable, and often wealthy core of the Spanish-speaking population of Texas. Sometimes intermarrying with wealthy Anglos, these *Tejanos* have succeeded in preserving a culture distinct even from the rest of the Spanish-speakers.

Black communities are more often urban in modern times, so their political and cultural influence is most strongly felt in the cities. Southern Dallas, eastern Fort Worth, and southern Houston have African-American majorities, and Texas's most famous African-American politician, the late US Senator Barbara Jordan, came from the heart of Houston's inner city black wards. Following the devastation of

Hurricane Katrina in 2005, nearly 200,000 refugees from New Orleans were taken in by the city of Houston, most of them African-American. The vast majority settled in the city permanently, and the city is now 24 percent black. As of 2014, Texas has the third largest black population in the country, after New York State and Florida.

American Indian population

American Indians lived in what would become Texas for centuries before Europeans arrived. A paleohunter burial in the Permian Basin, dated

Unusual place names in Texas are a clue to its rich American Indian history – places like Nacogdoches, Waxahachie, Anahuac, and Comanche Lake. Some 50 tribes once lived in present-day Texas, including the Alabama, Apache, Atakapan, Bidai, Caddo, Cherokee, Chickasaw, Choctaw, Comanche, Coushatta, Hueco, the Karankawa of Galveston, Kiowa, Lipan Apache, Muscogee, Natchez, Quapaw, Seminole, Tonkawa, and Wichita.

It is a heartbreaking fact of European settlement that the country's diverse First Peoples, who had lived for centuries on their lands, were

Members of the Pacuache-Tilijaya Coahuilteca tribe perform a traditional dance.

to the Folsom culture, 12,000 years ago, was discovered in 1953 and the remains labeled "Midland Minnie"; Lubbock Lake Landmark is on another Folsom site.

Texans tend to think their American Indian population simply dispersed to other states, when, in fact, many Texas tribes were destroyed. Among them were the Hasinai Caddo of East Texas, the southwesternmost branch of the powerful Mississippian Mound Builder culture, part of the powerful Mississippi Valley trading empire 1,200 years ago. The Caddo word for friendship (*tejas*) gave the state its name. Caddo Mounds State Historic Site near Nacogdoches interprets the Caddo culture today and preserves several mounds.

either wiped out by disease or war or subdued and removed to reservations. Today, however, American Indian populations are rebounding somewhat in Texas, compared with a century ago, and can be found in pockets throughout the state and on three federally recognized reservations.

The Alabama and Coushatta, two southern tribes, migrated to East Texas and now live as one tribe. In West Texas, Ysleta Del Sur Pueblo in El Paso is home to a group of Pueblo Indians, the Tigua, who fled over the border from New Mexico along with Spanish missionaries during the 1680 Pueblo Revolt and did not return. In the Rio Grande Valley, the Kickapoo migrate annually from Mexico across the Rio Grande to Eagle Pass.

Dallas and Houston also attract numbers of American Indians, especially from the Cherokee and Navajo nations of neighboring Oklahoma and New Mexico.

Spanish and Irish arrivals

The Irish were among the first Europeans in Texas. In fact, Hugo O'Conór was a governor of Spanish Texas in the late 18th century. Where O'Conór came from and how he ended up in the employ of the Spanish are questions to which the answers are lost. More Irish arrived in Texas in the 1820s and '30s, when the Spaniards granted what are now the counties of Refugio and San Patricio (St Patrick) to Irish settlers. The Mexican government evidently wanted an Irish Catholic buffer between the areas of Protestant-born Anglo settlements and the Spanish-speaking Catholics.

After the Republic of Texas was declared in 1836, Europeans viewed the area as more stable politically than when it was part of Mexico. Leaders of the Republic encouraged immigration more actively than had the Mexican government. Whether Texas would be annexed by the United States was then unknown, but these factors combined to open Texas up to a flood of Europeans whose imagination had been captured by the Texas Revolution. From the beginning, the Texas government saw to it that new settlers received land, and immigrant aid groups, like the Adelsverein, who settled New Braunfels and Fredericksburg, organized migration to Texas. However, the group was not well administered and ran short of badly needed relief funds.

German farmers

The largest European group in Texas, the Germans' first permanent settlement was Industry, in Austin County, west of Houston, so-called for its cigar factory. Many Germans settled in the port cities of Galveston and Indianola. Typically, they wrote home an "America letter" that described – often with exaggerated, if not downright false, hopefulness – the human happiness, fertility, and wonderful climate of Texas. Their letters were shared among a village or other group of acquaintants from which more brave Germans, despite the danger, would set out. German immigrants tried to bring along an entire support group, motivated in varying degrees by wanderlust, political idealism, and the desire for social and economic improvement. Some stayed in the relatively urban ports, while others settled for a

while in the interior where there were friends and relatives. After they had found their bearings, they proceeded to establish daughter communities. Constrained by the settlement patterns of previous groups and the threat of Comanche raids farther west, most Germans made their homes in a 10-county strip north of San Antonio, designated as the "German Belt," which became the center of German influence in the state.

German immigrants came from all walks of life. Some were peasant farmers, while others were well educated. Some brought with them libraries that were extensive for the time and

A cowboy heats rosin on his gloves in preparation for a rodeo.

place, and they belonged to learned organizations such as the Goethe Society. Some formed orderly farming communities, while others organized into utopian-style communes, such as Bettina, now disappeared, and Tusculum, now known as Boerne.

In *Journey Through Texas*, famed landscape architect Frederick Law Olmsted, who traveled throughout the South from 1856–7, wrote with surprise and admiration about the intellectual attainments of the German colonists in Texas. He described their primitive but neat log cabins, plastered and stuccoed, and their books, musical instruments and paintings. Olmsted hoped their liberal influence would move Texas out of the Old South sisterhood of slave states.

Olmsted recorded: "One of the party said to me: 'I think if one or two of the German tyrants I could mention could look in upon us now, they would display some chagrin at our enjoyment...' I have been assured, I doubt not, with sincerity, by several of them, that never in Europe had they had so much satisfaction – so much intellectual enjoyment of life, as here."

Most of the Germans disliked slavery. In fact, at least 19 German-born Union sympathizers were killed by Confederate troops near the town of Comfort in 1862. Nor did they wish to annihilate American Indians, who considered Germans a distinct tribe, superior to the loathsome Spaniards, Mexicans, and Anglo-Americans. German influence can still be felt today in the music (polkas and conjuntos), the bock and lager-style native-Texas beers, and the architecture (the churches, courthouses, and "Sunday Houses") of Central Texas and the Hill Country.

Latin-speaking Communities

In the German agricultural villages of Sisterdale, Bettina, and Comfort, Latin was spoken in everyday life; the communities are remembered as "Latin colonies," and, understandably, they

A Texas polka band.

TEXAS BARBECUE

Barbecue is a big deal in Texas – each region has its own favored style of preparing beef and those associated with East and Central Texas have fanatical followings. In East Texas, beef is marinated in a sweet, tomato-based sauce and slow-cooked over hickory wood until it falls off the bone, southern style; the South Texas variant features molasses-style sauces to keep the meat moist. Central Texas, meanwhile, is all about dry barbecue, western-style, where meat is rubbed with spices and cooked over pecan or oak wood; in West Texas, they cook their barbecue over mesquite instead, giving it a distinctive smoky taste. Lastly, *barbacoa*, Mexican-style

barbecue, features a variety of meats from hogs to goats, which are barbecued in a pit in the ground covered with marguey leaves.

German settlers in Central Texas were instrumental in boosting the popularity of sausage and barbecue. They often gathered on market days and holidays to sell their produce or celebrate, and whether revisiting a large market city such as San Antonio or just celebrating at one of their villages, they roasted a calf, sheep, or goat. Some people believe that another unique Texas preparation, chicken-fried steak, is of German derivation, citing its obvious similarities with schnitzels, breaded and pan-fried cuts of meat.

mystified their Anglo neighbors at the time. It is just as well that the neighbors understood little of what the Germans had to say, for their beliefs were on the whole very different from those of Anglo-Southerners. Not only were many of them opposed to slavery, as Olmsted noted, but several communities – Sisterdale and its daughter village of Comfort, in particular – were the centers of free thought and agnosticism. Many of the German settlers were Lutheran, and a few Catholic, but their free-thinking may have been unique on the frontier.

Broad German influence continues to this

they were probably a custom brought from southern Germany which can be traced to pagan roots. The *Wurstfest* in New Braunfels usually comes in fall, at more or less the same time as the German *Oktoberfest*. Sausage and beer consumption, and a *gemütlich* sociability, link this New World celebration to the boisterous beer halls and *kellers* of Munich.

Slavs in Central

The Texas State Historical Marker at Serbin, Texas, makes interesting reading: "Trilingual (Wendish-German-English) community

Young cowgirls at the Rodeo Austin Stock Show.

day in certain parts of Texas. Until the 1950s, the Tex-Deutsch dialect, an amalgam of English and German, was spoken in many settlements of San Antonio, such as the King William District. Today it has almost disappeared, and the Germans of the Texas Hill Country are becoming more like the Anglo majority and less like a true minority group.

Deliberate attempts to preserve German festivals have resulted in the regular celebration of the Fredericksburg Easter Fires and the *Wurstfest* in New Braunfels. The Easter Fires are lighted on the hills surrounding Fredericksburg on the Saturday before Easter. While local legend holds these fires were originally set by Comanche Indians, scholars have demonstrated that

founded in 1854 by 588 Wends under the leadership of the Rev. John Kilian. The Rev. Kilian (Evangelical Lutheran) named the place Serbin because the Wends were descendants of Lusatian Serbs (or "Sorbs"). A thriving town 1865–1890; had grocery, dry goods, jewelry, drug and music stores, shops of wagon maker, blacksmith, saddler, post office, three doctors, two dentists. On Smithville–Houston Oxcart Road – sending out cotton, other produce, and hauling in staples. Decline began about 1890 as railroads bypassed settlement by several miles."

While German communities have adapted more and more to the dominant Anglo culture, other small groups, have been similarly absorbed. A group of Polish Catholics followed their priest southeast of San Antonio in 1854 to set up the first Polish colony in the US, Panna Maria. Later, several more Polish towns were established in Texas.

Two other major Slavic groups in the state are Wends and Czechs. Czechoslovakia was dissolved in 1993, but the groups here retain a strong affiliation with the Czech Republic, as was clear when that country stepped in and donated funds to assist with rebuilding after 2013's explosion at the refinery in West, home to many Czechs. Together, several central and eastern counties still have the largest rural populations of Czechs in the US. Czech settlements are generally agricultural, and most Texas Czechs have made their names and fortunes as farmers. Not as numerous as the Germans, the Czechs have nevertheless preserved many of their culinary traditions, including baking kolaches, a delicious pastry, for which many people make a pilgrimage to Hill Country.

Several Czech communities hold celebrations to honor their heritage. Annual festivals in West, Taylor, and Ennis draw city-dwellers to eat sausage and sauerkraut and dance the polka.

Wends are a German-speaking group who

Contestants at the annual World's Largest Rattlesnake Roundup.

OTHER ANGLO RESIDENTS

Other smaller groups have blended into the Anglo culture. A substantial Scandinavian population immigrated to Texas; Greeks settled along the coast, particularly around Galveston; and a small Italian contingent lived in the larger cities but also had agricultural settlements in the Brazos Valley. The Jews' principal migration took place in the 19th century, when German and eastern European Jews came to Texas. Today, Jews are an urban group, but synagogues in towns like Brenham and Corsicana are reminders that they have been in Texas as long as many other European settlers. Jewish merchants founded several thriving Texas mercantile chains.

left their homes in Prussia in the 1840s. Those in Texas settled in two counties east of Austin: Lee and Fayette. The church and farm were the centers of Wendish life. Today, most Wends have left the smaller towns for the city, but their colony in Texas was the only such community in North America.

Cajun immigration

French colonization of Texas was sporadic. While La Salle and other French explorers were among the early visitors to Texas, and Jean Lafitte and his pirate band established an early enclave in Galveston, the French influence seen today has mainly come from a group of French-American settlers who traveled to Texas from Louisiana.

The Cajuns are descendants of Acadians, French settlers who were removed from their Canadian homeland by the British in the 1760s to '80s. After resettling in French-owned Louisiana, they developed their own culture, combining French, Spanish, American Indian, and Creole elements.

At the turn of the 20th century, the discovery of oil in East Texas lured Cajuns to the area. Texas Cajuns retained – (and still retain) – their regional French patois, their string band music, and bayou-bred culinary traditions, and a certain *laissez les bon temps rouler* (let the good times roll) outlook toward life. They lend a distinctive flavor to the East Texas and Gulf Coast areas where they have settled. Jambalaya, gumbo, and crawfish étouffée are eaten throughout the bayou country of East Texas. Cajun music is also enjoying renewed popularity. Usually played on accordions and guitars, and sung in the Cajun French patois, this music enlivens many East Texas dancehalls.

Asian ingenuity

Asians are the most recent group to be added to the Texas mix. They first came to the state on their eastward trek after the California gold rush. Chinese laborers worked on the railroad, but were abandoned by the rail companies when the tracks were finished. Isolated in a strange world, the Chinese were then usually hired as cheap labor to undercut emancipated blacks.

The first wave of Chinese immigrants did not have much lasting impact on Texas, since US immigration laws banned most Chinese women from the country. Some agricultural laborers in Robertson County intermarried with local women, producing the "Black Chinese" of Calvert. More or less permanent Chinatowns were formed in El Paso, and later in San Antonio, but restrictive immigration policies kept the Asian population to a low level in Texas until fairly recent times.

In the early 20th century, Japanese settlers started experimental rice-farming communities along the coast, while Chinese and Japanese merchants set up small businesses in San Antonio and other cities. Until recently, Asian-run groceries served the black community, but a new influx of Southeast Asians has made Asian products more profitable.

The Asian migration of the 1970s, the result of the Vietnam War, included Vietnamese, Cambodians, and others. Many settled on the Texas Gulf Coast, where they fish in areas traditionally harvested by other groups, particularly Anglos.

Misunderstandings and prejudice at first resulted in several killings and other ugly incidents that involved the influence of the Ku Klux Klan. However, the coast is now fairly calm, and

Mardi Gras in Bandera.

Texas seems ready to add another piece to its mosaic of cultures. The most famous assimilation story may be that of Dat Nguyen, the son of Vietnamese "boat people" who grew up to be a star defensive player on "America's Team," the Dallas Cowboys.

While a distinctive Vietnamese culture might seem most likely to thrive in fishing settlements along the coast, not all Vietnamese live in these areas, nor do they all earn a living by fishing. Many of the latest immigrants are technicians and other highly trained people who have settled in Texas's urban areas (the Asian populations of Austin and Houston more than doubled in the 1980s and '90s). Others are found in rural communities as professional workers, farmers, and ranchers.

THE TEXAS RANGERS

Efficient, tough, and uncompromising: the Texas
Rangers are a remarkable band of law enforcers – a
legion of heroes with a reputation second to none.

For most of the first century of Texas history, the Texas Rangers were almost synonymous with that history. No police force in the country had the prestige of the Rangers. The *WPA Guide* noted in 1940: "The man in the tan trousers and shirt, wide-brimmed Western hat, black tie, leather holster and sidearms not only commands respect but admiration."

Today, although Rangers uniform is largely just Western dress, the Rangers badge, carved from 1940s-era silver Mexican five-peso coins, is one of the most famous law enforcement emblems in the world. Texas Rangers were "one of the most colorful, efficient and deadly bands of irregular partisans on the side of law and order the world has ever seen," one historian noted "...called into being by a society that could not afford a regular army." Many of these adventurers were famous before reaching their thirties, men who showed "an utter absence of fear," superb psychologists at understanding not only the enemy but also the men around them.

There is an apocryphal story still told of a 1930s oilfield boomtown in East Texas caught up in the grip of a riot. Frantic with fear, the local sheriff wired the governor in Austin for help in the form of the Texas Rangers. A day later, the train pulled into the boomtown station, from which alighted a single Ranger. "They only sent one?" asked the incredulous sheriff. The Ranger did not bat an eye. "You've only got one riot, don't you?" he replied.

In the 1880s, Texas Ranger Captain Bill McDonald, who was known for his readiness "to charge hell with a bucket of water," confronted three gunmen who had tried to ambush him. He dropped one, and, after taking bullets through his left side and right

Rangers badge.

wrist, was busy cocking his pistol with his teeth when the other two outlaws fled. "No man in the wrong can stand up against a man in the right who keeps on a-coming," was the romantic assessment of this episode by a fellow Texas Ranger.

Origins of the force

"In 1823," wrote journalist Pamela Colloff in the April 2007 issue of *Texas Monthly* magazine, "Stephen F. Austin hired ten men 'to act as rangers for the common defense.' Nearly two centuries later that group – known as the Texas Rangers – is alive and well, having adapted from being frontier lawmen to an elite investigative force, trading their horses and bedrolls for cellphones and laptops." In 1835, the Texas legislature instituted the Texas Rangers as an official body: 56 men in three companies, each with a captain and two lieutenants.

The Head Ranger, a major, was subject to the army's commander-in-chief. Earning the same pay as the army ($1.25 a day), Rangers supplied their own mounts and rations and had to be equipped with "a good horse (and) one hundred rounds of powder and ball" at their own expense. They protected the frontier against raiding Mexicans, and fought against outlaws and Indians.

When Sam Houston was reelected in 1841, he realized that the Rangers were the most effective and economical way of protecting the frontier, when Captain John Coffee "Jack" Hayes and 150 Rangers helped repel an 1842 invasion from Mexico.

A few years later, the 1846 US War with Mexico brought the Rangers worldwide fame. "Armed to the teeth," they successfully guided the US Army to Monterrey and were at home in the remote deserts of northeastern Mexico, where, battling guerrillas, they earned a fearsome reputation as *los diablos Tejanos* (the Texan

19th-century Texas Ranger, Benjamin McCulloch.

Rangers in the Republic

Throughout the years of the Republic of Texas (1836–45), the Rangers worked as scouts and couriers during the first presidency of Sam Houston, who fostered friendship with the Indians. But, from December 1838, under the presidency of Mirabeau B. Lamar, 13 new Ranger companies were commissioned, which "over the next three years... waged all-out war against the Indians," according to The Handbook of Texas.

The army and the Rangers were often at odds, due to conflicting sets of rules and orders; the former sought to police the frontier and keep peace, while the Rangers rode to push back and punish the Indians.

devils). Between 1845 and 1875, Rangers fought in the big and little wars against Indians and Mexicans, as well as tracking down robbers and horse thieves.

Revolver revolution

In 1851, when 21-year-old former sailor Samuel Colt began manufacturing the first .34-caliber six-shooter weapon, nobody seemed particularly interested. Then one of the revolvers found its way into the hands of a veteran Ranger, Captain Samuel Walker, who saw its potential for a man fighting on horseback. At his suggestion, Colt designed a heavier .44-caliber gun (later .47), which became the standard weapon for US cavalrymen.

Although present-day Rangers wear the familiar "star in a wheel" badge, it was adopted officially only in 1962, when enough Mexican five-pesos coins were donated to the DPS to provide badges for all 62 Rangers working at that time.

The first to use Colt's new six-shooter on the Plains Indians was the aforementioned Captain Jack Hayes, a 23-year-old former Tennesseean who had arrived in Texas as a surveyor, before

decline and were little used. One Ranger captain, arriving to help a community fight off the Indians, said that all he was doing afterward was hearing complaints from farmers about Rangers killing their hogs. At the onset of the Civil War (1861), many joined the Confederate forces.

State Democrats, back in power in 1874, declared Texas was "overrun with bad men," and, to counter these, plus Indian attacks on the western frontier and border raids by Mexicans, the Rangers were regenerated. Their Special Force unit gained a fearsome reputation,

The law enforcement team that tracked down notorious outlaws Bonnie and Clyde.

he was appointed by President Lamar to be Chief of Rangers at San Antonio. All the ideal requirements for a Texas Ranger seemed to come together in this handsome, quiet "gentleman of purest character," and, when he ended his service, at 34, he was the model to which all Rangers aspired. One Comanche war chief swore never to confront Hayes, "who has a shot for every finger on his hand." Largely thanks to Hayes and his men, the Rangers learned to embrace the most advanced technology of each era, which has enabled them to stay relevant to their times.

Taking out bad men

After the end of the US War with Mexico (February 2 1848), the Rangers went into a

on one occasion stacking a dozen dead rustlers "like cordwood" in a Brownsville square "as a lethal response to the death of one Ranger." Among the 3,000 desperados they "thinned out" was the multiple killer John Wesley Hardin.

The Rangers endured another lean period at the beginning of the 20th century, when the force was trimmed down to just four 20-man companies.

But the 1910 revolution against Mexico's president Porfirio Diaz created unrest at the border. Then the onset of World War I, with its need to counter German intrigues and protect internal Texas security, was followed by Pancho Villa's raid on Columbus, New Mexico, in

1916, which fueled antagonisms between the two nations.

Executed without trial

In responding to these challenges, sometimes, critics charged, the Texas Rangers' actions were high-handed, and they were not being held accountable. If an ethnic Mexican, be he a Tejano US citizen or Mexican national, was found armed, he was often accused of banditry and killed outright. In 1915, a group of Rangers, having captured a carload of Mexicans suspected of robbing a train

> One early writer once said of the Texas Rangers that they "could ride like Mexicans, shoot like Tennesseeans and fight like the very devil."

the lawless oil boomtowns. The Rangers were often at odds with local lawmen, who preferred to leave gambling casinos and illegal drinking joints alone.

In 1932, the Rangers ill-advisedly backed Governor Ross Sterling in the Democrat pri-

Texas Ranger Hall of Fame and Museum, Crawford.

near Brownsville, took them into the bushes and shot them. The indiscriminate killing of approximately 5,000 Hispanics between 1914 and 1919 (according to *The Handbook of Texas*) became a source of "scandal and embarassment" and, in 1919, prompted a legislative investigation that discredited Ranger tactics. The force was overhauled by recruiting "men of high moral character." Higher salaries – as well as more restraints – were introduced.

The Prohibition years

Prohibition found Rangers patrolling the border against tequila smugglers, protecting Federal tick inspectors, monitoring labor and Ku Klux Klan demonstrations, and taming

mary, and, when his opponent, Miriam "Ma" Ferguson, took office, all 44 Rangers were fired or resigned in protest. Ferguson politicized the force, handing out Ranger badges as political favors to contributors and cronies. Salaries were slashed, and Texas became a haven for the likes of George "Machine Gun" Kelly and Bonnie (Parker) and Clyde (Barrow). Parker and Barrow were eventually hunted down by renowned Ranger Frank Hamer.

New qualifications

In 1935, under Governor James Allred, the Rangers became part of the Texas Department of Public Safety, which included the Texas Highway Patrol. New qualifications were laid down for Rangers, who had to be between 30 and 45 years of age (later extended to 50), 5ft 8 inches (1.74 meters) tall, and "perfectly sound" in mind and body. Each Ranger was required to be "a crack shot" and underwent extensive training in ballistics and investigation techniques.

Rangers were spread throughout the state, becoming plain-clothes officers and sometimes a sort of rural constabulary. When World War II arrived, they were kept busy rounding up enemy aliens and helping protect vulnerable sites. Their attitude toward America's

are attached at the hip to Mexico," says one Ranger.

Today, the Rangers remain an elite force, with over 100 applications for every vacancy, most of which are never advertised. In 2014, the Rangers included 216 men and women who make up a division within the Texas Department of Public Safety. They are supplied with powerful cars, sophisticated weapons, and forensic and communications equipment. Noted *Texas Monthly*: "A typical day [for the Rangers] looks more like CSI than *The Lone Ranger*."

A Texas Ranger patrolling the US–Mexico border.

Mexican neighbors changed as a modern era between the two countries began.

The job of the Rangers widened enormously in the 1960s, when the 8,000 cases they had been dealing with annually almost doubled, due to increasing urbanization. Rangers became involved on both sides of labor and civil rights issues. Rangers sometimes acted as strikebreakers against farmworkers in South Texas, even while they helped guarantee voting rights and civil rights in other areas. Some of the old complaints began to resurface, as the Rangers again began to hear accusations about their attitude toward brown-skinned citizens. Today, however, around a quarter of the Ranger force is of Hispanic heritage. "We

THE LEGEND OF BONNIE & CLYDE

Bonnie Elizabeth Parker and Clyde Chestnut Barrow were Dallas outlaws who led a gang to rob stores and gas stations, and eventually a dozen or so banks, in the Depression era. Pursued relentlessly by the Texas Rangers, they killed at least nine officers and several civilians before being gunned down in a shootout in Louisiana in 1934. The romantic relationship of Parker and Barrow, and photogenic glamor exuded by the 20-somethings – played up in the 1967 movie Bonnie and Clyde starring Warren Beatty and Faye Dunaway – were at odds with the grittier reality of their lives on the run but fueled the legend that endures to this day.

A cowboy and his trusty horse.

DON'T FENCE ME IN

The real Texas cowboys bore little resemblance to the Indian-fighting, songs-around-the-campfire heroes created by Hollywood.

To much of the world, the cowboy is the embodiment of the American character; stoic, self-reliant, loyal, taciturn, hardy, and – sometimes – reckless or violent. His iconic status has outlasted two world wars, the Space Age, rock 'n' roll, the arrival of the internet, and the whole of the 20th century and 150 years after his brief heyday his heroic aura remains undiminished.

He has been celebrated in books such as Owen Wister's *The Virginian*, Teddy Blue Abbott's *We Pointed Them North*, and Larry McMurtry's *Lonesome Dove*; in the paintings and sculptures of Charles Russell and Frederic Remington; in the photographs of Erwin E. Smith and Richard Avedon; in song, from cowboy ballads collected by Texas folklorist John Lomax to the chart-topping hits of Waylon Jennings and George Strait; and on film in John Ford's *The Searchers*, Howard Hawks's *Red River* – both starring John Wayne – and Fred Zinnemann's *High Noon*.

The zenith of the American cowboy was brief, roughly the last 25 years of the 19th century. And, contrary to the tall-in-the-saddle imagery perpetuated by the movies and television, the typical cowboy was a wiry man – be he Anglo, African-American, or Hispanic – of slight stature whose six-shooter was most typically drawn to defend against a rattlesnake or coyote, not a bandit or Indian.

He was a blue-collar working man, a laborer who toiled for seldom more than a dollar a day. But what set him apart from the rest of mankind, in his eyes, was that he was first and foremost a horseman, heir to a centuries-old tradition.

"The cowboy's contempt of the farmer was not unmixed with pity," wrote *Lonesome Dove*

Cowboy buckles with ornate engravings.

author Larry McMurtry. "Cowboys could perform terrible labors and endure bone-grinding hardships and yet consider themselves the chosen of the earth; and the grace that redeemed it all in their own estimation was the fact that they had gone a-horseback."

Though his lineage belongs to history, he has an enduring hold on our imagination, and his descendants still practice his craft today.

The working cowboy

Underneath the storybook and movie glitter, there was always a real working cowboy, and there still is today. Not until the Comanche and Kiowa were largely "subdued" in the mid-1870s by the army and the Texas Rangers could

> *The boot was one of the cowboy's tools: he had no need of the exotic leathers and elaborately stitched tops seen on today's fashionably macho and expensive footwear.*

much of the vast Texas prairie be safely opened to rancher, and so the working cowboy did not fight nearly as many Indians as we see him fighting in the movies.

When he was on the trail, the cowboy lived out under the stars and he had a closeness to

Texas cowboys in traditional costume, c.1890.

nature. He supplied his own strong code of frontier ethics in a land with no established law, and he enforced it with a gun – though the gunfighter was a rare and endangered species in the West, compared to the ubiquitous cowboy.

The history of the working cowboy begins with the introduction of cattle into the New World by Spanish explorers as early as the 16th century. Most of the details of cattle ranching had been worked out by the Spaniards in northern Mexico and southern Texas by the time the first Anglos came into the area in the 1820s.

The Spanish cattle-ranching vocabulary was assimilated by the early Texas cattlemen, along with the rest of Spanish/Mexican cattle culture.

Words like *la reata* (lariat or lasso), *remuda* (string of riding horses), *corral* (holding pen for cattle) and *dally* (from "dar la vuelta," or "take a turn") are still in use today. Words for land forms, such as *mesa* (literally, "table" – a high desert plateau or tableland) and *arroyo* (gully or dry wash), were also adopted.

Cowboy costume

Much of the Texas cowboy's costume came from the *vaquero*, as the Mexican cowboy was called. The angled high-heeled boots helped to keep a cowboy's feet in the stirrups when he was riding his horse. The narrow toes of the boots and the slick, treadless leather sole were designed to slide easily into the stirrup, while the boot tops were 12–16 inches (30–40cm) high and perfectly plain in design. The leather was good quality and durable.

Being generally concerned with the well-being of his animals, the Texan cowboy replaced the sharp, revolving roweled spurs favored by the *vaquero* with larger, blunt wheels, in order to protect his horse's flanks. The jingle of spurs was "saddle music" to the cowboy. While the *vaquero* usually wore spurs only for work, many a Texas cowboy felt naked without them, and only removed them upon entering his house.

For a long time, cowboys wore a very characteristic pair of striped breeches. These gave way in the 1870s to the blue denims manufactured by the Levi-Strauss Company of San Francisco. A cowboy covered his breeches with heavy leather leggings, called chaps, when he rode through brushy country. "Chaps" is a corruption of the Spanish word *chapparal*, meaning heavy brush.

The bandana, an oversized neckerchief, was the Swiss army knife of the West. It was invaluable to cowboy and *vaquero* alike: it kept the sun off the back of his neck and mopped the sweat from his face; it could be a sling for a broken arm or a mask to filter the acrid dust; wrapped around a couple of biscuits, a bandana could serve as a lunchpail.

The tall-crowned, wide-brimmed *sombrero* worn by the *vaquero* was never favored by the Texas cowboy; nor was the fabled 10-gallon hat ever worn by anyone but movie cowboys. There was a wide variety of headwear among real cowboys, from the cavalry-style fedora to the shapeless farmboy's hat, but, by the 1870s, the hats made by John B. Stetson of Philadelphia had become standard western wear.

Cowboys who worked for a dollar a day would pay $10–20 for a good hat and $20–30 for a good pair of boots.

Shirts were widely varied, some no more than homemade flour-sack affairs. As likely as not, they were covered with a vest. The sleeveless vest gave warmth and protection, but did not bind the cowboy's arms while he worked. For cold weather, a cowboy wore a blue denim jacket or a fleece-lined leather shortcoat. An oilcloth slicker kept off the rain. A cowboy rarely carried more than one change of clothes, which he packed into a bedroll.

Trail driving days

The cowboy's life was a hard one. As many a "greenhorn" quickly learned, a cowboy had to have common sense and a head for survival.

The heyday of Texas cowboying was the trail-drive years from the mid-1860s through the 1880s. Prior to this time, the cattle business in Texas was rather low key. It centered on Spanish-style ranches that were loosely run and generally unfenced – prime conditions for creating "mavericks" in the rich South Texas grasslands where the hardy longhorn cattle could easily survive on their own.

After the Civil War, a flood of immigrants from the South entered Texas, many of them young single men looking for a new life. They found it as cowboys.

The price of cattle in the industrial cities of the North was as much as $40 a head, whereas, in South Texas, longhorns could be bought for $4 apiece. Thus, there was plenty of work for cowboys, driving cattle from Texas to the railheads in Kansas, from where beef was shipped to city markets. The great cattle trails of the era – the Chisholm Trail, the Goodnight-Loving Trail, the Western Trail, and others – came into being to transport cattle across the unfenced plains to railheads or army posts in New Mexico, Kansas, Missouri, or even Wyoming and Montana.

A cowboy's work began in spring with the cattle roundups or "cow hunts." Nursing calves followed their mothers as the cattle were herded into holding pens. There the animals were separated by their brands and claimed by their owners. Young calves were marked with the same brand as their mothers. They came to be known on the trail as "dogies," from the

short rope that tethered the newborn calf to its mother. As herds became larger and cattle thieves began to alter brands, some ranchers took to cutting notches in the ears of their cattle as a secondary form of identification.

Trail ballads

After all the rounding up and branding, the trail drive began. Many a cowboy ballad was composed on the open trail, as the cowboys sang to comfort their cattle and keep them from stampeding. Cowboy ballads were usually laments about loneliness, lost love, and the hard life on

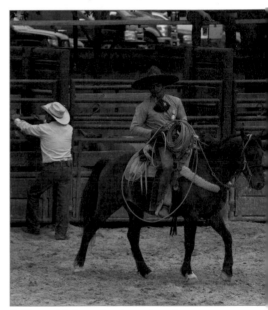

A rider at a Mexican-style rodeo, or charrería.

the trail. Many, such as *Streets of Laredo*, derived from English or Celtic ballads. "The chief contribution made by white men of America to the folksongs of the world," observed Texas folklorist J. Frank Dobie, are "the cowboy songs of Texas and the West… rhymed to the walk, the trot, and the gallop of horses."

Hollywood Western stars like the late Gene Autry and Roy Rogers capitalized on this aspect of cattle trail life, making their careers as "singing cowboys." But historians point out that a hard day's drive more usually ended with conversation around the fire, or perhaps a game of poker. Few cowboys would have had room in their saddlebags for musical instruments any larger than a harmonica or a concertina.

Beginning the drive

To start a drive, small herds of cattle rounded up in South Texas by four or five cowboys would be driven toward a pre-arranged point, at which point a trail herd was formed. The trail drives then followed well-known routes that were determined by designated passes or river fords. Small operators with only 10 or 12 cowboys went up the same trails used by big outfits with 50 or more cowhands. The biggest drive recorded, in 1869, set out from Texas with 15,000 head of stock. Between 1865 and the mid-1880s, some 10 million animals went

Prize longhorn steer, Zapata County Fair.

up the trails, the largest artificial migrations in history.

With the sale of the cattle in Abilene, Kansas (or Dodge City, Denver, Cheyenne, or Kansas City), the cowboys were paid for the first time on their long ride from Texas. For many of them, all the nights of sleeping on the ground and days of herding cattle over the open plains were erased in wild drinking and carousing in brothels. When the last dust of the trail drive had been washed away, the cowboys mounted up for the long ride home.

Not all cowboys wasted their money in the saloon and the bordello for, as often as not, the wages of the trail drive were used to buy cattle back in South Texas or in Mexico.

A cowboy might also take his pay in cattle when he returned home, driving them north as part of a larger herd the following summer. In this way some working cowboys, such as the legendary Charles Goodnight, became great ranchers. They invested their profits in land and cattle, building up small spreads of their own.

The fenced range

When J.F. Glidden was issued the first patent for barbed wire in 1874, it portended the end of the open range and the great cattle drives. At

> *Charles Goodnight composed this epitaph for his friend in 1929: "Bose Ikard served with me for four years on the Goodnight-Loving Trail, never shirked a duty or disobeyed an order, rode with me in many stampedes, participated in three engagements with the Comanches, splendid behavior."*

the same time, the railroad was expanding. In Texas, Fort Worth became the major railhead. Slaughterhouses and packing companies were built in Fort Worth and San Antonio, making it unnecessary to drive cattle to Kansas. Additionally, the introduction of refrigerated boxcars meant beef could be shipped longer distances. Amarillo and Abilene became active markets in West Texas.

It was not uncommon for a rancher to marry a woman much younger than himself, his own younger years being given to building up a ranch that would support a family. Charles Goodnight, at age 91, married a woman 65 years his junior. This practice left many women widowed and in charge of ranches. Some women took an active part in the management of Texas ranches and still do so today.

Hard work was and is still a major part of life for the ranch cowboy. In addition to the spring roundup and branding, the ranch cowboy had to look after his cattle year-round. Cowboys still practice their riding and roping, but now they work in the corral or inside the fences of the ranch, rather than on the open range. In the fall and winter, cowboys ride the fencelines in order to mend them. Winter is also a time for repairing saddles, bridles, and other pieces of important ranch equipment.

Gigantic spreads

It was in the era of the open range that the great ranches of Texas began to form. The King Ranch in South Texas is the largest in the state. Texans measure the ranch's current size as 1.23 RIs (Rhode Islands), or 823,000 acres (333,000 hectares). It was founded in 1853 by a former Rio Grande steamboat captain, Richard King. Even though the original boundaries of the ranch are no longer the same, the King Ranch is substantially intact and still family owned. There are organized tours, and any highway that goes to Kingsville will cut through some part of it.

The enormous King Ranch in South Texas was modeled so closely on the Spanish rancho that patrón King even led an entire village out of Mexico to work on it.

The celebrated XIT Ranch in the Texas Panhandle was started by midwestern and British land and cattle syndicates and was the largest range in the world under fence. In the 1870s and '80s, the state sold the land to the syndicates to finance the present State Capitol in

Cowhands take a break from branding longhorns at the Lonesome Pine Ranch.

BRANDING

Brands are used to identify cattle from individual ranches. Branding requires skill and experience because, if the branding irons are pressed too hard, the mark will go too deep and leave sores. There are other preliminaries, too: the male calves have to be castrated (the roasted testicles, also known as Rocky Mountain oysters, are a prized snack), and horns have to be trimmed to prevent the animals injuring each other.

Each Texas ranch had its own distinctive brand, which was registered with the Cattleman's Association, and established brands were recognized by their distinctive pattern everywhere on the range.

Before the Civil War, it was not uncommon for a South Texas rancher to start a herd by rounding up unbranded cattle and giving them his brand. "Mavericks," or unbranded cattle, are said to have gotten their name from Samuel Maverick, the Matagorda County entrepreneur of the 1840s.

In historic times, brands were not widely used by Spanish and Mexican ranchers because their ranchos operated on the patrón system. The patrón, in the manner of a feudal lord, owned all the cattle and land within the "fiefdom" of his rancho, so there was very little need to establish his ownership by branding. If the cattle were on his land, they were his.

Black Cowboys

It is a lesser-known fact that some of the best cowboys to come into Texas were black Americans leaving the war-ravaged states of the South.

African-Americans in the West often met the same prejudice they faced elsewhere. Few acquired property or social distinction. But, to a range boss, character and willingness to work trumped skin

A cowboy at the National Black Rodeo Finals.

color. It was estimated that about one-quarter of the cowboys on the northbound trail drives between 1866 and 1895 were black.

Many of the early black cowboys had been born as slaves or sons of slaves and eventually found more freedom on the open ranges than in urban areas. Others were army veterans from the corps of black cavalrymen called "Buffalo Soldiers." After the Civil War, some 5 million head of loose stock roamed the Texas plains and cowboys of all skin colors were in high demand. Some ranches east of the Trinity River had all-black crews, and many became horsebreakers, but very few achieved the elevated status of foremen or managers. A handful became federal peace officers or took up careers as rodeo performers. One

Texas-born African-American cowboy, Bill Pickett, achieved enormous fame by inventing the rodeo sport of bulldogging (or steer wrestling). A life-size bronze statue of Pickett subduing a steer stands today in the historic Stockyards District in Fort Worth.

Bose Ikard

Bose Ikard, a slave born in Mississippi in 1843, was brought to Texas by his master in 1852 and learned the cowboy trade on a ranch near Weatherford. Freed as a result of the Civil War, he went to work for the famed western rancher Charles Goodnight, eventually becoming the cattle baron's right-hand man. Goodnight said he trusted Ikard "farther than any living man." Ikard's story was among those told in fictional fashion in the novel and TV mini-series by Texas author Larry McMurtry, *Lonesome Dove*.

Another former slave, Isom Dart – who was born Ned Huddleston in Arkansas in 1849 – had an early career stealing horses in Mexico and swimming them across the Rio Grande to sell in Texas. Later, his gambling and fighting in northwest Colorado entangled him with the law. After that, he changed his name to Isom Dart, bought a ranch, and tried to go straight but was tracked down and killed, at the age of 51 by bounty hunter Tom Horn.

The 1993 made-for-television movie *Return to Lonesome Dove* featured a fictional character named Isom Pickett, who was a composite of the real life Dart and Bill Pickett.

A cowboy and broncbuster named Nat (or Nate) Love was one of many who claimed to have been the original model for Deadwood Dick, saying he had acquired the nickname by winning a roping contest in Deadwood, South Dakota in 1876.

Today's black cowboys can showcase their skills through a series of African-American rodeos, sponsored by the Cowboys of Color, the Bill Pickett Invitational Rodeo, and other organizations.

In recent years, black cowboys have begun to assume their rightful roles in the cinematic history of the West via such actors as Woody Strode (*Sergeant Rutledge, The Man Who Shot Liberty Valance*), Morgan Freeman (*Unforgiven*), Danny Glover (*Lonesome Dove, Silverado, Buffalo Soldiers*), Louis Gossett, Jr. (*Return To Lonesome Dove*), and Jamie Foxx (*Django Unchained*). Mel Brooks famously used his 1974 parody Western, *Blazing Saddles*, to send up modern racial attitudes.

African-Americans made their way to the frontier after the Civil War, and many signed on as admired, hard-working cowboys for famous outfits in Texas.

Austin. Originally a monstrous 4.54 RIs (more than 3 million acres/1.25 million hectares), the XIT was split up in later years as the out-of-state investors went their separate ways. At its peak, the ranch was bounded by more than 1,500 miles (2,413km) of fencing.

Texas ranches have become more mechanized and modernized. The only contemporary ranch of any size doing business in the 19th-century way is the Kokernot 06, between Fort Davis and Balmorhea in Davis County.

However, large modern-day Texas ranches such as the Green, the Matador, the 6666, the Waggoner, the Y.O, and, of course, the mighty King Ranch still endure and thrive, though some have had to incorporate oil exploration and tourism into their traditional livestock vocations.

Rodeo is the sport of cowboys, developing naturally out of their skills and tasks as they

Over the fence at a Texas rodeo.

SAVING THE LONGHORN

With the introduction of barbed wire fencing and the end of unlimited free range grass in the 19th century, it became more economical to raise cattle that developed faster than longhorns, which, by the 1920s, had been almost bred out of existence. Shorthorns and Herefords predominated.

Longhorns were saved from probable extinction by Will C. Barnes and other Forest Service men, who collected a small herd of breeding stock for Oklahoma's Wichita Mountains Wildlife Refuge. A few years later, oilman Sid Richardson financed the acquisition of small herds for Texas state parks. Eventually, cattlemen rediscovered the longhorn's longevity, its

resistance to disease, fertility, ease of calving, ability to thrive on marginal pastures, and also the fact that its leaner beef was in tune with the times.

One result of the cattle drives was that ranches were established not only in the uninhabited parts of Texas but also on the hitherto remote plains of the Middle West and in the Indian Territory that is now the state of Oklahoma. As the tribes were pushed farther and farther back, even the mountains and desert plains in the far western parts of the state, beyond the Pecos River, became valuable property. These are the major cattleman's strongholds today, and they contain some of the largest ranches in the state.

worked with livestock. Early rodeos were just informal gatherings of locals who all pitched in to provide the livestock, riders, and entertainment. Pecos, in the Big Bend Country of West Texas, claims to have held the first rodeo in 1883 (strongly disputed by Prescott, Arizona, which claims to have hosted a rodeo since 1888). Rodeo is now controlled by the Professional Rodeo Cowboys Association (PRCA), which sanctions more than 650 rodeos each year all over the United States – even in places such as New York City. There are national finals held annually in mid-December in Las Vegas,

Nevada, and the top rodeo cowboys make six-digit salaries competing in as many as 125 competitions a year.

The traditional rodeo events are bull riding, bareback bronc riding, calf roping, steer wrestling, saddle bronc riding and, for women, barrel racing. In the 1930s and 40s, there was an extensive women's rodeo circuit. Women competed in the same events as men and added gymnastic trick riding, too. However, during World War II, women's rodeo was discontinued and never regained popularity. There is still today a thriving circuit of African-American rodeos officiated by several organizations.

Rodeo contests can be held indoors or out, but the basic requirement is a large, dirt-floored corral or arena, with chutes along one side and escape gates for the livestock opposite them. The arena is surrounded by stands, and behind the stands are barns and holding pens. Bull and bronc riders mount up in small pens that open directly into the arena.

When the gate swings open, a rider tries to stay on the animal for eight seconds. Half of the points scored in a ride come from the total time the rider stays mounted; the other half are awarded for the competitor's style and daring.

Rodeo can be dangerous: the animals are wild, and often try to trample or gore dismounted riders. The rodeo cowboy's best friend is the clown, who runs into the arena to distract the mount while the rider is on the ground. Elaborately inscribed belt buckles, displaying the cowboy's name and the event, are presented as trophies.

Rancher and renowned chuck wagon cook, Cliff Teinert.

SAMUEL MAVERICK

Samuel Maverick moved to Texas in 1835, where he became a land speculator, buying land at 15¢ per acre, and by 1842, was said to be the biggest landholder in the state. Later that year, Maverick was caught during the invasion of San Antonio and imprisoned in Mexico for seven months. On his return, he reluctantly accepted 400 cattle from a neighbor in lieu of a debt, thus becoming a rancher. Without much interest, Maverick placed the cattle on his Gulf ranch under the care of his black slaves, who reported that their boss was unenthusiastic about applying a burning iron to flesh. The slaves branded about one-third of the growing herd and the others often strayed to the mainland, where they

were seized by less scrupulous ranchers, "maverickers," who stamped them with their own brand.

Some ranchers hired "maverickers" to brand as many as 18 "mavericks" per day, at 50 cents to a dollar apiece. Eventually, in 1854, Samuel Maverick sent a party of vaqueros to round up his herd, which numbered several hundred, and move it to Rancho Conquista, a spread he'd acquired on the San Antonio River, 50 miles (80km) from the city.

Disenchanted with the cattle business, Maverick sold his herd, but the use of his name to describe stray cattle lives on today to signify people who make their own way in life, independent of the crowd.

Cowboy heritage

The world of the cowboy and the Wild West has been preserved in several modern museums dedicated to its memory. One of the finest collections can be found in the Panhandle-Plains Historical Museum in Canyon, Texas. The T-Anchor Ranch Headquarters, built in 1877, is on the museum grounds. Another fine collection is in the Longhorn Museum in Pleasanton, which claims to be "the birthplace of the American cowboy." Exhibits in this museum document the cowboy and his American Indian and Hispanic antecedents. San Antonio

In 1884, the cattle-driving Pryor brothers were contracted to deliver 45,000 head in 15 separate lots, earning themselves a handy net profit of around $20,000.

has The Trail Drivers Association and the Institute of Texan Cultures, both displaying collections of cowboy – and cowgirl – memorabilia. Austin's modern Bullock Texas State History Museum details the Lone Star State's frontier past. The XIT Museum in Dalhart chronicles the history of that famous old ranch, while the National Cowgirl Museum and Hall of Fame in Fort Worth has a collection celebrating women in the West. Also in Fort Worth, the Amon Carter Museum (in that city's Cultural District) and the smaller downtown Sid Richardson Museum feature large quantities of Western art and photographs, including masterpieces by Charles Russell and Frederic Remington.

The National Ranching Heritage Center on the campus of Texas Tech University in Lubbock is the home of 20 buildings representing ranch housing from the Spanish days to the large family ranch houses of 1890s cattle barons. Almost any county historical museum in any town in cattle country preserves some artifacts from the trail driving and cowboy era.

Lost skills

The visitor looking for working cowboys today is at something of a loss. Modern equipment has made many of the cowboy's traditional jobs obsolete. Consequently, contemporary cowboys and ranchers have learned to combine traditional roping and riding skills with modern tools, from DNA breeding research to

computers and "green" technology. A modern cowboy might ride the range on an all-terrain vehicle, with a cellphone in the pocket of his Levis. The best ranch to visit is the Y.O. Ranch near Kerrville. The King Ranch offers tours, as do some of the surviving West Texas spreads. Dude ranches in the Bandera area also offer a taste of ranch life. But, a rodeo is the most accessible form of cowboy life available today.

Beware of imposters

Not all the folks you see strolling around in boots and jeans are cowboys. People who look

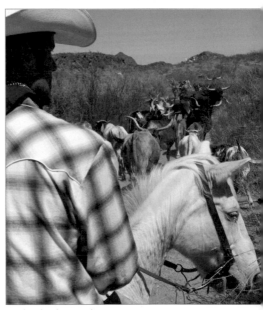

Herding longhorn cattle.

like cowboys may never have been astride a horse. Cowboy hats, Western-cut shirts with pearl snaps, big buckles on tooled leather belts and leather boots are standard fashion for many modern Texans. By contrast, some of today's younger working cowboys wear "gimme" caps and T-shirts emblazoned with the names of rock 'n' roll bands. Find a fellow who takes things too far by adding a swagger and some big talk to this costume and you have what's popularly referred to as a "drugstore cowboy." He's the cowboy who spends more time at the drugstore lunch counter than he ever does astride a horse. A real cowboy is apt to say of such a fellow, "He's all hat and no cattle."

Luckenbach musician David Harris.

MUSICAL TRADITIONS

From country, blues, and folk to conjunto,
western swing, and good ol' rock 'n' roll –
musically, Texas has it all.

The enduring glory of the music from the Lone Star State is rooted in its free-form eclecticism, its gumbo of cultural influences, and a cheerful disregard for the artificial boundaries erected between musical genres in other parts of the country. Texas has always been a crossroads, and over the past 300 years Texas music has been informed and enriched by Anglo-Celtic ballads, Mexican norteño, Appalachian mountain folksongs, African/ Caribbean blues, Cajun and zydeco music from the wilds of Louisiana, Bohemian oompah polka bands, and British Invasion pop, not to mention the various practition-ers of punk, rap, reggae, jazz, techno, funk, and rock who have managed to find a home within the joyfully elastic boundaries of the state's musical community. The constant cross-fertilization of distinct ethnic sources accounts for both the diversity and the simi-larity of traditional Texas music.

Country music legend Willie Nelson.

Home of country

The tendency to think of Texas as the home of country and western and cowboy music is understandable (no matter what those folks in Nashville say). Texans have made some of the most important contributions to the develop-ment of country music. Texan Vernon Dalhart's 1924 recording of "The Wreck of the Old 97" was the first million-selling country album; Bob Wills and his Texas Playboys took western swing to the world; Ray Price and Ernest Tubb formulated the hard-edged honky-tonk sound, which dominated country music in the post-war era; the Dixie Chicks, from Dallas, became the best-selling female group of all time.

When they came to the South, the early Anglo-Irish settlers brought with them a vigorous heritage of folk songs, ballads, and fiddle music. In Texas and the surrounding region, unique southwestern forms soon developed, such as the cowboy songs that were documented extensively in the early 20th century by the Texan John A. Lomax, one of America's earliest and most pro-digious folk-song collectors.

Texans also developed distinctive instrumen-tal styles, such as the swinging, fluid Texas fiddle style that can be heard at the many annual fiddle and bluegrass contests across the nation. One of the Texas fiddle style's earliest practitioners, the legendary A.C. Eck Robertson, was also one of, if not the, first country musicians to record com-mercially. In the early 1920s, he waxed such clas-sics as "Sally Gooden" and "Brilliancy."

The continued vitality of country music in Texas is seen in the ongoing popularity of small dance halls that are dotted throughout the state, such as Austin's Broken Spoke and Gruene Hall in the Hill Country near New Braunfels, the oldest dance hall in the state. And of course, there's also a revolving cast of larger nightclubs in the major cities, including Billy Bob's Texas in Fort Worth, which bills itself as the "world's largest honky-tonk."

One nightclub, the late-lamented Armadillo in Austin, became the launch pad for famous musicians like Janis Joplin and Willie Nelson and the Canadian Ragweed are appealing to the children of the Waylon 'n' Willie audience.

Austin City Limits

Austin rivals Nashville as the country music capital of the United States. When it comes to popularity, nothing beats the annual live videotapings of the popular PBS television show Austin City Limits, celebrating its 40th season in 2014 and now the longest running music series on television. Taped over 13 weeks each season, the award-winning show has featured nearly 1,000 musicians on its outdoor concert

Musicians in Terlingua.

beginning of Austin's fame as the live music capital of the US. Its heyday in the 1970s (it closed in 1980) saw the emergence of Texas's "outlaw country" music scene, led by native Texan "outlaws" Willie Nelson and Waylon Jennings and others, including Michael Murphey, Guy Clark, Townes Van Zandt, and Jerry Jeff Walker. Outlaw country flew in the face of Nashville conformity by blending rock, country and blues, and appealing to younger rock audiences. The fact that its name alluded to the slightly dangerous lifestyles of its leading exponents also added to the allure.

Today, a new "Texas Music" country rock movement mixes regional pride and an edgy vibe with a high-octane rock urgency. Younger performers such as Pat Green, Cory Morrow, and Cross

Pioneer of western swing, Bob Wills was one of Texas's most durable musicians. His career stretched from the 1920s all the way into the 1970s.

stage on the campus of UT in downtown Austin, with the state capitol picturesquely lit up behind the performers.

In recent years, ACL, as it is known, has reached out to embrace alternative rock, rhythm and blues, and singer-songwriters. The show and old UT theater where it was originally taped were inducted into the Rock and Roll Hall of Fame in 2010. In 2011, ACL moved to the purpose-built

Moody Theater and Studio downtown, a venue with a larger seating capacity. ACL itself retains a taping audience of 800 (the original capacity), however; the rest of the seating is used for the ALC Live concert series.

Willie Nelson, who was the very first musician to take the stage at ACL, when he was a relative unknown, achieved the status of American institution many years ago. Nowadays, his weathered visage has become iconic, and his laconic vocal style and fluid guitar playing still refreshing and instantly recognizable. Nelson is honorary godfather to a generation of storytelling Texas singer-songwriters, including Billy Joe Shaver, Rodney Crowell, Steve Earle, Lyle Lovett, and Robert Earl Keen.

Unconventional

While Texas continually generates conventional country stars who succeed in logging big chart hits – including George Jones, Ernest Tubb, and Ray Price over three decades ago, and more recently George Strait and the Dixie Chicks – it is the iconoclasts who make the most compelling music. Grandfathered by Buddy Holly, they make Texas music that belongs to no one genre. Joe Ely, Jimmie Dale Gilmore, and Butch Hancock, from Lubbock, mix folk, country, and rock in their performances and collectively as The Flatlanders. They and other West Texas musicians like Waylon Jennings and Roy Orbison (and, before them, Bob Wills) take perverse pride in bending musical rules and leapfrogging stylistic boundaries. The same can be said for genre-hopping Brave Combo, based in Denton, a small university town north of Dallas known for live music offerings that rival those of Austin.

Western swing

Texas's most original contribution to country music may be western swing. It grew out of jazz and was developed in the early 1930s by two Fort Worth bands, Milton Brown and his Musical Brownies and the Light Crust Doughboys. The latter was co-founded by Bob Wills, who perfected the genre in his band Bob Wills and His Texas Playboys. Wills turned traditional string band dance music on its head by introducing elements of hot jazz, blues, pop, and Tex-Mex ranchera strains. Soloing and improvisation were encouraged, and Wills' twin-fiddle attack, augmented by a keening steel guitar and the soulful vocals of Tommy Duncan made for

one of the swingingest sounds in any genre. Wills sometimes even included brass in his line-up. The western swing torch is carried today by performers such as the Hot Club of Cowtown and Asleep At the Wheel.

The blues, R&B, and hip-hop

"Blues came to Texas, lopin' like a mule," sang the famous Texas bluesman Blind Lemon Jefferson. Texans were certainly indispensable to the style's development. After the Civil War, freed slaves and free migrant black people followed the harvests and worked in the sugar plantations and lumber

Houston-born global superstar Beyoncé.

camps of East Texas. Their field hollers and acoustic "country blues" informed the music of Texas bluesmen like Mance Lipscomb, Huddie "Leadbelly" Ledbetter, and Sam "Lightnin'" Hopkins.

In the 1930s, Dallas' Aaron "T-Bone" Walker was one of the first electric blues guitarists to coin an original style: the single-string solo. A master showman (he did splits while playing the guitar behind his head), Walker was a pivotal influence on B.B. King, Eric Clapton, and others. Walker's contemporary, the late Clarence "Gatemouth" Brown, bristled at being called "just" a bluesman, when he played country, jazz, and Cajun music as the spirit moved him.

After World War II, Houston and Dallas/Fort Worth became the state's hotbeds of electric, urban blues, and rhythm and blues. The Duke and Peacock record labels in Houston waxed hits by Bobby "Blue" Bland, Junior Parker and "Big Mama" Thornton, while the "Texas Tenors" – a group of hard-charging saxophonists led by King Curtis, Illinois Jacquet, and David "Fathead" Newman – set the standard for sax players in R&B, soul, and jazz bands. Other great jazzmen who hail from Texas include the avant-garde master Ornette Coleman, ragtime king Scott Joplin, and keyboardist Teddy Wilson. Today, Houston's R&B heritage is carried on by the breakout superstar frontwoman of Destiny's Child, Beyoncé.

Falco Jiménez, pioneer of conjunto.

Houston, along with New Orleans and Atlanta, has become headquarters for rap and hip-hop in the South. After the success of the Geto Boys in the 1990s, Houston hip-hop (characterized by its slowed-down, hypnotic, "screwed" grooves) is dominated by the influence of the late D.J. Screw, and current performers Mike Jones, Slim Thug, and Bun B.

From blues to rock

Texas has also had younger white artists who draw their inspiration from the blues, a trend that stretches from Port Arthur's Janis Joplin – who was part of Austin's folk revival scene in the 1960s before moving to California, where her rapid rise to stardom ended in a tragic death – through vocalists like Fort Worth's Delbert McClinton and late guitarist Stevie Ray Vaughan. The Vaughan brothers, Jimmie and Stevie Ray, amassed an international reputation as electric blues guitarists of the first order – Jimmie with the Fabulous Thunderbirds and Stevie Ray with his band Double Trouble.

ZZ Top, from Houston, also emerged from the blues rock scene of the 1970s and notched huge hits by combining John Lee Hooker–style boogie with Texas braggadocio. Texas rock is a wellspring of raucous, often bizarre music, stretching from the 1960s-era psychedelic anthems of the 13th Floor Elevators to the avant-punk noise of the Butthole Surfers in the 1980s and 1990s, and today's 20-member rock choir, Polyphonic Spree.

Conjunto and Tejano

Like their Anglo-American counterparts, Mexican immigrants and Tejanos (Texans of Hispanic heritage) brought a vast store of folk songs and ballads, many in the styles of norteño, mariachi, or corridos. Tejanos were innovators and helped develop a distinctive Tex-Mex dance music called conjunto. While the distinguishing instrument of conjunto, the accordion, was introduced to Mexicans by the Germans in the 1840s, by the late 19th century they had developed their own accordion style, while retaining the polka and waltz melodies of their European antecedents. Conjunto was not insulated from other ethnic traditions. The early performer Narcisco Martinez, who is sometimes called "the Father of Conjunto Music," even recorded a version of the Bob Wills standard "San Antonio Rose." Corridos, the storytelling songs of the border country, have kept pace; recently a new strain has arisen, the narcocorrido, chronicling the exploits of drug smugglers and outlaws. Conjunto has had an interesting influence on Texas rock 'n' roll, which could be heard in the early 1960s in the Tex-Mex rock 'n' roll hits ("She's About a Mover", "Mendocino") of the Sir Douglas Quintet. Doug Sahm, and Augie Meyers, two of the SDQ founders, went on to form another Tex-Mex group in the 1990s, the Texas Tornados, which featured conjunto master accordionist Flaco Jiménez and vocalist Freddie Fender.

Tejano, an amped-up, electrified rock 'n' roll cousin of conjunto, received national attention when its brightest young star, Selena Quintanilla Perez, was killed by an employee in 1996. While a clear successor to Selena has yet to emerge, tejano's popularity has continued to simmer in the dance halls and music festivals of the Rio Grande Valley, Corpus Christi, and South Texas.

Cajun and zydeco

Before and after World War II, immigrants from Louisiana flowed west in search of work in the oil refineries of Houston and the East Texas cities of Beaumont, Orange, and Port Arthur bordering Louisiana. The two musical forms they brought with them, Cajun and zydeco, are roughly analogous to country music and the blues. White Cajun musicians tended to adhere to the traditional sounds of the button accordion, the triangle, the fiddle, and the guitar. The peppery, volatile dance music called zydeco is powered by the keyboard accordion and a heavy rhythm section. It was introduced to Texas by black Creoles from the Lafayette, Louisiana area (principally Clifton Chenier, the late "King of Zydeco").

Clubs and festivals

The club scene is capricious, with venues opening and closing, or changing ownership or location, continuously. One Austin club, Antone's, is a good example. In 1997, it opened in its fourth

South By Southwest festival.

WHERE TO FIND TEXAS MUSIC

Good online sources of information on Texas and Americana artists include www.nodepression.com, the community website for the now defunct magazine of the same name, and www.lonestarmusic.com, which also publishes a bi-monthly magazine. Free newspapers such as the *Austin Chronicle* and *Dallas Observer* contain listings. One of the best independent record stores in the country, with an exhaustive selection of Texas music, is Waterloo Records in Austin. The Arhoolie record label is particularly rich in archival recordings of old-time Cajun, folk, blues, country, zydeco, and conjunto artists.

location in 30 years and in 2013 was sold to a consortium who plan to relocate it once again. Texas also has numerous music festivals. The Texas Folklife Festival in June offers a fairly comprehensive sampling of authentic traditional Texas music, as well as revival forms. For folk music fans, the Kerrville Folk Festival in May is mandatory, and every kind of global and regional pop music can be found at Austin's gigantic South By Southwest festival, which overwhelms the capital city every March. Over the past five years, the three-day Austin City Limits Music Festival, in the heart of the city, has earned a permanent spot on the music fan's calendar every September. And Willie Nelson's 4th of July Picnic is a holiday event as revered as parades and fireworks.

TEXAN ARCHITECTURE

From adobe huts and primitive log cabins to glistening glass towers, the state's architecture is a fascinating mix of the functional and the inspired.

In Texas today, the words "Remember the Alamo" also have a special relevance to Texas architecture. For most of the 20th century, and especially in recent years, a battle has been waged between people who want new Texas architecture to reflect native values and styles and those who want to move beyond regionalism to the very cutting edge of international design.

It's an issue that is not likely to be resolved soon, because, at a deeper level, it is a struggle over the image of Texas itself. The conflict between regional design and international design isn't just about architecture; it's part of an ongoing struggle between rural and urban Texas, between native architects and outsiders, and between the mythical Lone Star State and the real, contradictory, contemporary Texas.

Beginning with adobe

To remember the Alamo in San Antonio is, of course, to remember the Spaniards, Texas's first European settlers. The Spaniards gave architectural life to the creamy white limestone of Central Texas, and introduced skill and efficiency to the simple adobe technique of American Indians of the Southwest. Although the late 19th-century Spanish architect, Antonio Gaudí, would have approved of the native method of globbing one handful of mud on top of another to make a wall, the 18th-century Spanish friars taught them how to mold heavy, regular adobe bricks in wooden frames.

Adobe, together with wood and stone, was used by native people, and later Spaniards, all along the lower Rio Grande. It was easier to make adobe bricks than to quarry stone, and an adobe wall protected the interior of a house or church from the heat just as well as stone. Adobe is sturdy and, with its insulation

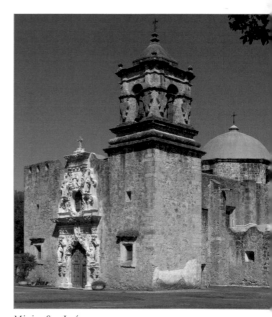

Mission San José.

properties – warm in winter and cool in summer – well suited to the hot, dry southwestern climate, as long it is maintained and water is not allowed to seep in and undermine the walls.

Adobe is an aesthetically pleasing and tactile material, which by its very nature offers many stylistic uses inside and out. For instance, because traditional adobe walls are laid thick – usually around 2ft (0.6 meters) – windows are deeply recessed and may serve as window seats or built-in shelves; plastered adobe can also be used to make built-in seating (*bancos*), display nooks (*nichos*), half-dividing walls, bed platforms, and steps, giving interiors a smooth, sculpted, all-of-a-piece quality that is organic, artistic and endlessly versatile.

The Missions

The Spanish missionaries in Texas, used to the Renaissance churches of their homeland, took pains to create an architecture that went beyond function. They wanted their buildings to express beauty in the wilderness. The Alamo mission is remembered as the bloody place where early Texans sacrificed their lives for freedom, but the building itself, in the heart of downtown San Antonio, is the image of quiet repose. The stone arches and carved niches suggest that the Alamo deserved a different kind of fame. The bell tower and "rose window" of San Antonio's San José

were, if not beautiful, still comfortable in the landscape. The deep porch offered protection against the sun, the dog or possum "trot" (an open breezeway between two essential rooms or cabins) was used for such things as curing meat and for sleeping outdoors, and the steeply pitched gable roof protected the house from the pounding rain. These features not only eased the hardships of frontier life, they created a simple, graceful, appealing style.

Even the Germans who emigrated to Texas from the 1840s onward modified their age-old method of building stone and wood (*Fachwerk*)

A breezeway at Quinta Mazatlan, a historic adobe mansion in McAllen.

Mission are proof that the Spaniards intended not just to survive, but to glorify, too.

Farmhouse style

Such a claim can hardly be made for the early Anglo-American settlers of the 1820s and 1830s. When farmers from Tennessee, Kentucky, Mississippi, and Alabama rolled into Texas, they brought with them the only architecture they knew – the plain log house and its cousin, the functional frame house of roughly hewn boards. There was nothing extra in these houses, nothing to make life on the Texas frontier a little sweeter or softer.

And yet, as is often the case with architecture, function led people to design structures that

houses in order to incorporate elements of the Anglo farmhouse. Their hewn frameworks were joined with mortise-and-tenon joints secured by wooden pegs. In the 1850s, famed American architect Frederick Law Olmsted, traveling to San Antonio, slept in New Braunfels in a "small cottage of a single story, having the roof extended so as to form a verandah, with a sign hanging before it, *Guadalupe Hotel, J. Schmitz*."

Formality and grace

Before the Civil War, most people in Texas did not live in houses as snug and pleasant as those of the Germans in Central Texas. They were only too glad to leave behind their relatively crude houses when life grew easier, and when the classic Greek Revival and later Victorian styles were brought into the eastern, central, and southern parts of the state.

The Greek Revival put classical columns on the porches of even the simplest log houses, and gave a touch of southern formality and grace to larger buildings. Greek Revival is found in Austin (for instance, in the Governor's Mansion), but it flowered in East Texas. Crockett, Jefferson, Marshall, Tyler, and Houston all have charming and varied examples of the Greek Revival style, which remained popular into the 1870s when Victoriana became all the rage. The Victorian buildings

> *One of the most elegant Victorian buildings in Texas, Austin's Driskill Hotel, designed by Frederick E. Ruffini, is still open for business.*

During the Great Depression, courthouses and other public buildings were built by government labor. Their blocky, repetitive shapes and flat reliefs in the Art Moderne style make it easy to date such monumental buildings as the Fort Worth City Hall and the distinctive courthouses of Travis, Brazoria, and Eastland

The Greek Revival Bayou Bend, Houston.

of Nicholas Clayton of Galveston, and the Richardson Romanesque courthouses of James Riley Gordon in many of the county seats (look for his buildings in such places as San Antonio, Waxahachie, La Grange, Stephenville, Sulphur Springs, Giddings, and New Braunfels) are evidence of the growing influence of gentility. When Texans began to concern themselves with porticoes and turrets, high culture had clearly arrived.

Modern Texas

Beaux-arts eclecticism held sway in Texas briefly, just long enough to influence some public and university buildings. The trickledown popularity of the Arts and Crafts Movement in Britain found expression in thousands of Texas bungalows.

Counties to this period.

Not many skyscrapers were built in Texas in the 1920s and '30s. The few that did go up, such as Houston's Esperson Building, were in the then-popular eclectic style.

Within a period of about 50 years, roughly between 1870 and 1920, domestic architecture in the state began to mature. Indeed, wealthy Texans systematically demonstrated that what was fashionable in Paris or London was fashionable in Houston, or even on the ranch. The set for the 1956 film *Giant* (about a Texas rancher and oilman) captured this spirit of brashness, while the movie's Second Empire mansion, silhouetted against endless West Texas ranchland, carried it to absurd limits.

In search of a style

Central Houston's famed River Oaks residential section, established by the Hogg brothers in the 1920s around River Oaks Country Club, and next to the Galleria, is one of the wealthiest and most exclusive communities in the country. With its carefully manicured lawns and gardens, oak-shaded streets, and elegant homes, it has long been a model for planned communities throughout the US.

It could be said that some of the grand homes here, variants on the English Tudor and American Colonial style specified by the planners, reflect a

communities in the nation, with homes worth an average $1.5 million and a top draw for famous residents since it opened.

Exterior influences

In the 1920s and '30s, small groups of architects – in California, New York, and Spring Green, Wisconsin (at Frank Lloyd Wright's Taliesin compound) – formulated new ideas about Modern architecture that would eventually make it acceptable for Texans to look upon their architectural heritage without shame. Their new ideas ranged from the "organic naturalism" of

Gresham Castle, Galveston.

self-consciousness often associated with the nouveau riche tasked with building a home for the first time. Even when the stylistic adaptations are imaginatively and tastefully handled, and local stone such as pink granite has been used, at times it's possible to detect a feeling of uncertainty in some of the design choices. It may be that some newly rich Texans feel the need to rise above their architectural roots – sullied as they were by poverty, struggle, and, not infrequently, illiteracy – and do so by co-opting a pastiche of styles as they gradually work out their own.

In this, however, Texans are by no means unusual – just more obvious, perhaps, given the numbers of super wealthy residents in the state. River Oaks is one of the top 10 planned

DON'T FORGET THE KIMBELL

Fort Worth's much-admired Kimbell Art Museum draws from the past in subtle ways. Its barrel vaults, which allow light to stream down along interior walls, may recall the silos that architect Louis Kahn admired in the Texas landscape, but this is, at best, conjecture. What makes the Kimbell appropriate to Texas is its strength, tranquility, and aura of permanence. It looks back to the years before Texas dressed its buildings up in the styles of the East, beyond the Victorian and Greek Revival periods to the simple, functional early Texas buildings. It is regional in the finest sense of the word. Remember the Alamo, but don't forget the Kimbell.

Wright's "Prairie Style" to the "machines for living" of the Frenchman Le Corbusier, but all of them respected what was functional in architecture – and opposed what was merely applied and decorative. In this light, the functional and formal aspects of missions and ranch houses were reevaluated. If early Texans had allowed "form to follow function" out of necessity, a later generation of Texans made a conscious choice to do so. The result was the flowering of Texas architecture in the mid-20th century.

It was at this time that Texas buildings began to show not contempt but deference to their building techniques. Throughout his life (he died in 1982), Ford had great influence on Texas architects. His teachings still form the basis of the regionalist school of thought.

Boxy towers

Ironically, the Modern emphasis on function, which prepared the way for a new appreciation of Texas's early buildings, was also responsible for giving birth to the attitude that the architecture of the past did not stack up well against the box. When the German Bauhaus architects sold Americans on their philosophy in the 1940s, cit-

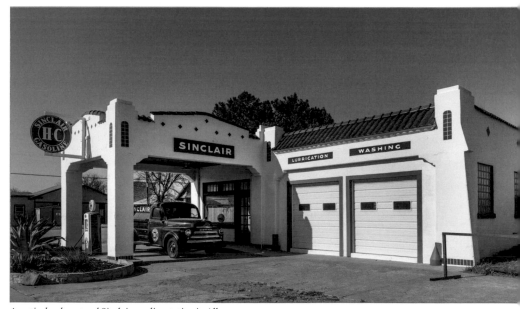

A meticulously restored Sinclair gasoline station in Albany.

older neighbors. San Antonio architect O'Neil Ford, who, along with others, became interested in the accurate restoration of Spanish Colonial architecture, taught Texans to respect the scale and character of indigenous buildings, and to appreciate the native materials used in them. Ford's own Trinity University campus in San Antonio (begun in 1949), a group of brick buildings that beg comparison with Italian hillside villages, is faithful to the nature of the hilly Texas landscape. His Johnson City Post Office (1970) is a modified ranch house of limestone blocks with a wide front porch and a sloping roof. His Cowboy Artists of America Museum in Kerrville (1983) is both a fortress built of creamy limestone and a gallery of near-forgotten

Chinese-born architect I(eoh) M(ing) Pei, responsible for some of the most distinctive Modern architecture in Texas, is also famous for the Louvre's glass pyramid in Paris.

ies like New York and San Francisco began to build boxy skyscrapers.

Texas cities were still young at that time, and possessed a few fine old buildings and almost no tradition of urban architecture. Thus, when cities like Houston and Dallas began to expand, much of their growth took the logical form of the Modern glass box. Their new urban buildings delivered a message as honest as that conveyed by the early settlers' houses: unadorned simplicity was still at home in Texas. Later, the boxes were criticized for their brutality.

Early Texas structures were admired for their utility and for their rural beauty, but they certainly didn't influence high-rise architecture in the heyday of the box. A golden sunset reflected by the limestone facades of Central Texas could evoke the memory of Coronado and his search for the Seven Golden Cities; or a lonely wind whistling through a broken windmill near an isolated ranch house could conjure up romantic images of the hard frontier life. But what, after all, did rough-cut

Texas architecture. The state that was famous for its rugged individualism at last had a Modern architecture that expressed it.

Even the more conservative Dallas received oddly shaped, shimmering, reflective glass buildings and a city hall (dedicated 1978) that broke out of the box completely. I.M. Pei's design, which took the form of an immense triangle balancing on one edge, sent cantilevered floors of offices precariously (it seemed) out over a plaza. O'Neil Ford was outspokenly annoyed by the Dallas City Hall, believing its effectiveness depended on playing tricks with the viewer's

The Kimbell Art Museum, Fort Worth.

limestone blocks or pitched roofs have to do with multistory, steel-framed buildings?

During the years dominated by the glass box, Houston architecture came into its own. The Tenneco skyscraper (1963), with its exposed steel frame, and One Shell Plaza (1965), with its clean white facades, were as sophisticated and current as any new buildings anywhere.

Famed architect Philip Johnson set the stage for his Houston breakthroughs with his Amon Carter Museum in Fort Worth (1960), which has the stately order of a Greek temple. Later, by breaking up the rigidity of the Bauhaus box with the trapezoidal towers of his Pennzoil Place and his round-cornered Post Oak Central buildings (both 1976), Johnson drew international eyes to

expectations. It was intentionally unnerving. Ford and his opinions are relevant to the shift in taste in skyscraper design in the early 1980s.

Once again, with his Houston skyscrapers, Philip Johnson led the way for developer Gerald Hines, but this time he did more than break out of the box. His designs now referred openly to the architectural styles of the past. His lighthouse-like Williams Tower, with Art Deco setbacks, and his Gothic Republic Bank tower were the world's first Postmodern skyscrapers.

In search of regionalism

Regionalist architecture is still practiced by Texas architects on a small scale in rural areas, but many large urban commissions still go to outsiders. In recent years, for instance, the green glass Wells Fargo Bank Plaza, by Skidmore, Owings and Merrill; the steel and glass Four Leaf Towers, by Cesar Pelli; and the silvery granite needle of I.M. Pei's JPMorgan Chase Tower were added to Houston's skyline.

Dallas, meanwhile, is becoming more daring. The designs for new office towers have not been innovative – most go no farther than the now-clichéd sawtooth edge – but things are changing. I.M. Pei designed two 60-story rockets of glass docked in a water garden downtown. Philip Johnson's last project, the Cathedral of Hope's

National Bank Building on the River Walk, restored and converted to a flagship historic hotel by Drury Hotels.

The place to find exciting contemporary architecture, though, is the vibrant state capital of Austin, previously known for its many Victorian buildings – most famously, the Driskill Hotel, built as a showstopper by a cattle baron with deep pockets. Austin is experiencing a huge construction boom, and the local joke goes that the new state bird is the crane. Among the many significant contemporary residential and commercial buildings are the Long Center for the

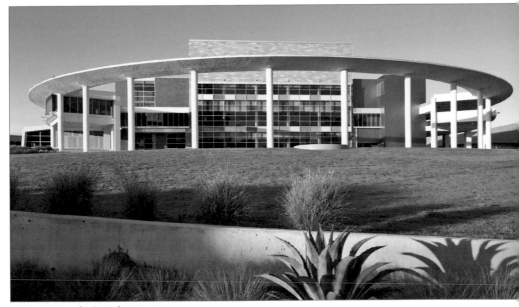

The Long Center for the Performing Arts.

Interfaith Peace Chapel, was completed in 2011, six years after the architect died. With its soaring, smooth white sculptural forms, Johnson considered the building his memorial, the capstone of his career. In 2012, the Perot Museum of Nature and Science, designed by award-winning Thom Mayne of Morphosis, opened in Victory Park. The large building looks like a huge floating cube on a landscaped plinth. The sustainable building has received the highest green rating.

Austin's cranes

As Texas grows, its architecture continues to change. San Antonio has a controversial new library as well as sensitively repurposed historic buildings such as the 1929 Art Deco-style Alamo

Performing Arts; the Kimber Modern Boutique Hotel; Mueller Central, a planned redevelopment of the old Austin airport; and Soaring Wings, a home located in Westlake Hills outside Austin.

While much of Austin's new architecture is spare and elegant, with use of soaring structures, open space, and glass, other buildings reference the old: One of the new office buildings on Congress Avenue, which leads to the Capitol, is made of pink granite from the same quarry as that building and has a gable roof. Organic architecture is much in evidence in this woodsy environment, too, like the Lost Pines Chapel in the woods. The challenge for architects is to keep buildings honest and original – learning from the past, but anticipating a new Texas.

Texas bluebonnets on a railroad track.

Cypress trees, Caddo Lake.

Houston skyline.

INTRODUCTION

**A detailed guide to the entire state, with principal
sites clearly cross-referenced by number to the maps.**

*El Capitán, Guadalupe
Mountains National Park.*

Texas has it all: sophisticated cities, beautiful beaches, colorful deserts, sleepy border towns, wide open plains, and dramatic mountains. In both geography and culture, it is a microcosm of the entire country. You'll find wild rodeos and honky-tonks, but also fine museums and elegant restaurants; towering glass skyscrapers and bustling sidewalks, but also quaint Victorian homes and old-time country fairs. You'll notice the influence of the Old South in East Texas, and the vibrant mix of Mexican and American cultures along the Rio Grande in southern Texas. You'll find that Texans are still struggling with the conflict between rural and urban values, and that there are more "cowboys" walking the streets of Houston or Dallas than there are on the range.

Tours of Texas generally start in the north, in the Dallas–Fort Worth Metroplex, two cities that have grown into a single bustling metropolitan area. The Metroplex has been a major business center for years, but recently the cities have made strides in the cultural arena as well. Fort Worth's museum district houses some of the finest collections in the state and the new Dallas Arts District is fast becoming a hub of culture and entertainment.

Four hours south of the Metroplex in Central Texas lies Austin, the state capital, famous for its live music and liberal attitudes. Houston in East Texas is the state's largest city, however – and with its rich ethnic mix, great wealth, exciting architecture, and thriving arts community, it is also one of the liveliest. People don't often think of Texas as a coastal state, but

*Pumpjack and cottonwood tree,
West Texas.*

Texans have been enjoying the warm breezes, glorious sunshine, and brilliant blue waters of the Gulf of Mexico since the early 20th century. America's "Third Coast" has over 300 miles (500km) of white, powdery beaches, quaint Victorian villages, modern resorts, bustling fishing towns, and major ports.

As you head south and west to the Rio Grande, in South Texas, Texas's Hispanic roots become apparent. San Antonio is the urban capital of Hispanic politics and culture in Texas – as well as the home of the Alamo – but it is in the small towns along the Rio Grande that the Tex-Mex blend of *la frontera* is most distinct. The scene changes dramatically as you travel west of Dallas. In Central Texas, in the Hill Country, the land begins to open up and the towns grow farther apart. In the state's westernmost corner, West Texas, the plains give way to desert. El Paso, this region's largest city, has more in common with its New Mexican neighbors than it does with its sister cities to the east.

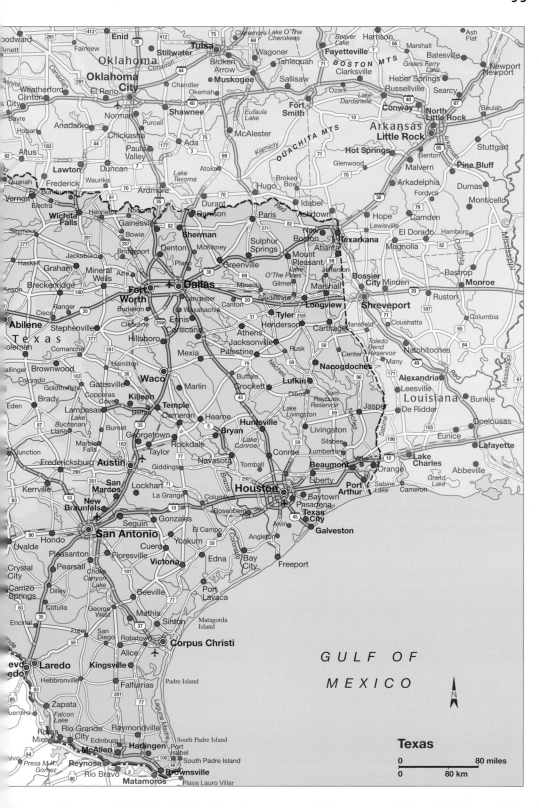

Texas

0		80 miles
0		80 km

GULF OF

MEXICO

The Hunt Oil building.

DALLAS

Swanky Dallas is beginning to outlive its tragic history, and today is home to cutting-edge architecture, the country's largest arts district, and the world's best shopping.

Known for its glitz and glam and financial sector, the tragedy of President Kennedy's assassination here in 1963, and a certain popular TV program from the 1970s selling excess, the gleaming city of Dallas has risen above its infamy in recent years and is showing promising signs of becoming an exciting place to live and visit.

Dallas has always had boatloads of money, but now it is showing that it can corral its excesses and focus its energy and can-do attitude into a coherent whole. As a result, it is fast becoming a diverse city of planned neighborhoods linked by well-thought-out green spaces with world-class buildings, museums, and performing arts venues, and vibrant reclaimed arts and historic districts. In its more gentrified areas, it has the kind of edge more commonly seen in places like Austin.

Downtown

Downtown Dallas is quite compact – but only relatively speaking. The easiest way to explore it is to hop on the expanding light rail system, which runs predominantly on the west side of town, where many of the attractions are. This rail system (DART) shares Union Station with Amtrak and here, beside the Stemmons Freeway (I-35) in the southwest corner of town, is a good place to begin.

Four stepped, perpendicular glass boxes house the **Hyatt Regency Hotel**, connected to which is the 560ft (172-meter) **Reunion Tower** ❶ (300 Reunion Boulevard E; tel: 214-712-7040; www.reuniontower.com; Sun–Thu 11am–8pm, Fri–Sat until 10pm). Topped by a geodesic dome with 260 lights, the tower adds a dramatic nighttime star to the city's skyline. An observation deck and revolving restaurant and lounge are accessible via fast elevators and the views, understandably, are the best in Dallas.

Main Attractions

Reunion Tower
Sixth Floor Museum
Perot Museum of Nature and Science
Dallas Arts District
Fair Park
Southfork Ranch

The bronze longhorns in Pioneer Plaza.

The sixth floor of the Texas School Book Depository building, from where Lee Harvey Oswald shot President Kennedy.

Reunion Arena, just to the south, was the home of the Dallas Mavericks basketball team and the Dallas Stars hockey team until they moved to the American Airlines Center in 2001. Reunion Arena is now mostly used for rock concerts.

The city began in this area, in the **Cabin of John Neely Bryan ②** beside the nearby Trinity River, which Bryan mistakenly believed to be navigable for trade all the way to the Gulf of Mexico. An earlier colony, La Réunion, founded by French settlers, had failed, largely because the colonists had been artisans in Europe, not farmers. Bryan, however, survived and lived long enough to welcome, in 1872, the first passengers arriving on the Houston and Texas Central Railroad. This

was the beginning of the city's major expansion.

Between 1880 and 1890 Dallas' population tripled to 38,000, the mule cars that transported passengers around town were replaced by electric trams, *The Dallas Morning News* began publication, and the forerunner of the annual State Fair of Texas took place. Bryan's reconstructed cabin now sits on a grassy sward across from the Old Red Courthouse on Houston Street.

Just east of the Reunion Tower is the city's huge **Convention Center ③**, flanking a grassy hillside that is home to *A Herd of Longhorns*. This exhibit, which shares **Pioneer Plaza ④** with an ancient cemetery, is collectively the world's biggest bronze monument. Created by Texan sculptor

Downtown Dallas

Robert Summers, it depicts dozens of longhorns and three cowboys and sprawls down a realistic cattle trail in a setting enhanced by native plants and a stream that cascades over a miniature limestone cliff. Beyond the Plaza, facing the public library, the futuristically stepped-back **City Hall** ❺ is the work of Chinese-American architect I.M. Pei.

From the Reunion Tower's observation deck, it is easy to be impressed by Dallas's architecture. This tangible display of big-money investment began way back in 1908, when Texas law demanded that every insurance company doing business in the state should keep a substantial part of its assets in Texas.

Insurance remains essential to the city's economy, along with banking, merchandising, and, most recently, high technology. For many years, Dallas was the world's largest inland cotton market and all the farmers of North Texas did their banking here. Following World War II, the city began its accelerated growth. Two large aircraft factories were built in the suburbs, and, for a time in the 1950s, oil companies swarmed to Dallas, where banks were eager to finance them. Eighteen Fortune 500 companies, including Exxon, J.C. Penney, and Kimberly-Clark, currently have their headquarters in the Dallas area.

Northeast, on Main Street, is the **Bank of America Plaza**, a 72-story giant outlined with 2 miles (3km) of green neon, while the sharp angles of I.M. Pei's 60-story **Wells Fargo Building** ❻ (Field Street and Ross Avenue) near Fountain Place catch the eye from everywhere in the city. Also distinctive are the octagonal Thanksgiving Tower (Elm and Ervay) and the J.P. Morgan Chase Tower (Pearl and San Jacinto), whose slit tower had to be modified to cut down its wind tunnel effect.

Almost hidden by the huge behemoths surrounding it is Pegasus, the neon flying red horse trademark (first placed here in 1934 and reconstructed in 1999) atop the **Magnolia Hotel** ❼ (1401 Commerce Street). Formerly the

Magnolia Petroleum Building, this was the tallest building in the South when it went up in 1922. Behind it, at Main and Ervay, is the flagship department store of **Neiman Marcus** ❽ and, two blocks north, close to the light-rail line, is **Thanksgiving Square** ❾ a tranquil oasis designed by architects Philip Johnson and John Burgee.

JFK Memorial

Just north of Reunion Tower is the **West End**. With many of the city's oldest buildings restored as shops and cafés, the area is filled with arts and crafts, pushcart traders, clubs, and boutiques. If walking is too much trouble, visitors can take horse-drawn carriage rides around the area.

Head up Houston Street, past the unmistakable Old Red Courthouse (behind which, at Main and Market, is the simple **John F. Kennedy Memorial**, a cenotaph designed by Philip Johnson), and ahead on the left is the most visited site in Dallas: the former Texas School Book Depository building, from which Lee Harvey Oswald shot President Kennedy.

The Texas School Book Depository building.

Neiman Marcus

Purveyors to the wealthy,
Neiman Marcus has endured for
over a century as America's most
trusted department store because
it goes the extra mile for its
customers.

The Dallas-based Neiman Marcus department store, world-renowned for its Christmas Book offering such "His and Her" gift suggestions as $1,600 mummy cases or pairs of matched camels ($16,000), prides itself on unstinting service. At the request of one customer, for example, the store discreetly investigated Queen Elizabeth's stocking size so that she could be sent a pair of nylons.

Customers were made and kept, Stanley Marcus once explained, "by [the] ability to remember small details, such as anniversary dates... a promise to get a certain evening bag for a specific social occasion... a promise that the dress bought for a girlfriend would be billed to the Mr and not the Mrs account." This was not trivia: "... it's what specialty store retailing is all about."

The world-famous Neiman Marcus department store.

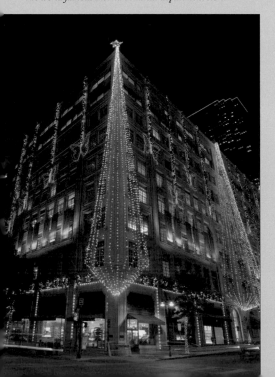

Stanley, one of the sons of co-founder Carrie Marcus, has been probably the person most responsible for developing the store's modern image, but Neiman Marcus – now a chain with outlets in 41 US locations – was a success from the its start in 1907. Soon after that, Nebraska-born Al Neiman teamed up with (and married) Kentucky-born Carrie Marcus who, aged 21, had already proved herself to be the most successful saleswoman at the Dallas department store A. Harris & Co.

Early success
Together with Carrie's brother, Herbert, the trio set up a sales promotion business in Atlanta that was so successful they found themselves looking for further investment opportunities. They considered investing in a new bottled drinks company, Coca-Cola, but decided to set up a retail business instead. It became a family joke down through the years that Neiman Marcus was founded on a bad business judgment.

They soon set up their Neiman Marcus store in central Dallas. Neiman, the flamboyant and egotistical buyer, traveled regularly between Dallas and New York City, acquiring clothes and constantly clashing with his partners over style and design. In the 1920s, Herbert bought him out for $250,000 and the Neiman marriage broke up at the same time.

At first, the store's wealthier clientele was, to a large extent, the state's cotton aristocracy but, just after the Great Depression began (as the store was completing a major expansion), oil was discovered in East Texas. This produced a new group of millionaires who soon became Neiman Marcus customers.

How to spend a million dollars
In a history of American department stores, published in 1979, author Robert Hendrickson wrote that Neiman Marcus operated on the premise that "if we can please the 5 percent of our customers who are the most discriminating we will never have any difficulty in satisfying the other 95 percent who are less critical."

Certainly millions of recipients of the store's Christmas Book seem satisfied. Eight customers, for example, splashed out on the $11,200 Chinese junks offered one year. One page of the catalog is devoted to "How to Spend a Million Dollars at Neiman-Marcus," although other pages offer gifts for $25 and under.

The **Sixth Floor Museum** ❿ (411 Elm Street; tel: 214-747-6660; www. jfk.org; Tue–Sun 10am–6pm, Mon noon–6pm; timed entry, tickets may be purchased online up to two hours in advance) overlooks Dealey Plaza, through which President Kennedy was riding in a motorcade on November 22, 1963, when he was assassinated. Oswald – later arrested and murdered on live television while in police custody – fired the fatal shots from a corner window on the building's sixth floor, a site roped off in the museum. Dealey Plaza was updated in 2013 for the 50th anniversary of the shooting.

The museum, which gets an average of 1,000 visitors each day, houses exhibits about JFK's campaign; his social and economic programs; the space race; and the "Red Threat." Reproductions of newspaper stories from around the world are on show, including the full-page advert in *The Dallas Morning News* on the day of his visit to the city, in which his right-wing enemies accused him of communist sympathies. Cameras used by spectators watching the motorcade can be seen, as can the famous Zapruder camera and some of the footage it recorded of the assassination. A videotape of the dramatic events of that day includes a tearful Walter Cronkite announcing the President's death. A cellphone tour of the museum and Dealey Plaza is available.

Don't underestimate the time needed to see the museum: it is immensely interesting (and moving) and, to the uninitiated, serves as a quick course about a significant era in US history. Among the messages in the visitors book is one from a child who wrote that the assassination was the first time he had seen his father cry.

Victory Park

The West End continues north of the DART rail line, whose station at Pacific and Lamar (shared with a bus transfer station) is almost surrounded by parking lots. Here bars, saloons, restaurants, and cafés keep pedestrian traffic on the move.

Anchoring the popular 72-acre (29-hectare) Victory Park development in the West End is the striking **American Airlines Center** ⓫ (2500 Victory; tel: 214-222-3687), a state-of-the-art sports stadium, opened in 2001, that superceded Reunion Arena as the home of the major sports franchises. It is surrounded by hip restaurants, shops, and hotels, including the gleaming 33-story W Hotel. Designed by architect David Schwarz in retro style, with Art Deco touches, it was built at a cost of $420 million on land that was once home to an old city dump, a meat packing plant, and an old power plant. New transportation links all around have revitalized the area.

Victory Park is the largest Environmental Protection Agency brownfield project in the United States. Its latest attraction is the **Perot Museum of Nature and Science** ⓬ (2201 N. Field Street; tel: 214-428-5555; www. perotmuseum.org; Mon–Sat 10am–6pm, Sun noon–6pm), which was gifted to the city by the Perot family. Designed

A friendly manatee at the Dallas World Aquarium.

by award-winning architect Thom Mayne of Morphosis Architects, the building sits on a large plinth above a landscaped park of native Texas plants. Inside, six floors of hands-on exhibits are a draw for kids and imaginative adults alike. **Dallas World Aquarium** (1801 N. Griffin Street; tel: 214-720-1801; www.dwazoo.com; daily 9am–5pm) is another popular attraction in the West End, housed in two former warehouses. Inside you'll find the world's largest freshwater aquarium, containing manatees, turtles, giant catfish, and more, as well as a saltwater aquarium with rays and sea turtles, among others. The other major draw here is a South American rainforest, featuring exotic plants and wildlife, from toucans and sloths to monkeys and crocodiles, along its jungle walkway.

The Dallas Arts District

The crown jewel of Dallas's downtown is its 68-acre (28-hectare) **Arts District**, the largest in the country. Spread over 19 landscaped city blocks, with a growing number of world-class museums housed in spectacular buildings, this is a wonderful place to stroll, enjoy music, theater and other entertainments, and get a bite to eat.

One block northeast of the distinctively shaped Fountain Place (Wells Fargo Building) is **Dallas Museum of Art** (**DMA**) ⑭ (1717 N. Harwood; tel: 214-954-0234; www.dma.org; Tue–Sun 11am–5pm, Thu until 9pm), designed by Edward Larrabee Barnes. Its collection is impressive: it exhibits American artifacts dating from the pre-Columbian and Spanish eras; Greek and Roman antiquities; a model of a boat from the Egyptian Middle Kingdom, *c*.2000 BC; a magnificent Hindu shrine of silver and wood; plus 18th-century Gilbert Stuart and Copley portraits, 19th-century landscapes, and works by Toulouse-Lautrec, Léger, Picasso, Mary Cassatt, Georgia O'Keefe, Giacometti, Edward Hopper, Andrew Wyeth, and the Modernists. One room alone includes millions of dollars' worth of art by Courbet, Boudin, Pissarro, Degas, Cézanne, Monet, Rodin, Van Gogh, and Vuillard. Contemporary artists represented include Pollock, Rothko, Stella, and Warhol.

Exhibits at the Nasher Sculpture Center.

The **Morton H. Meyerson Symphony Center** ⓯ (2301 Flora Street; tel: 214-TIX-4DSO; www.mydso.com) is another Dallas institution that has been financed by Ross Perot and serves as home to the Dallas Symphony Orchestra. Nearby is the **Nasher Sculpture Center** ⓰ (2001 Flora Street; tel: 214-242-5100; www.nashersculpturecenter.org). This $50-million building and outdoor sculpture garden houses the fabulous modern sculpture collection of the late Raymond and Patsy Nasher, including more than 300 works by Calder, de Kooning, di Suvero, Giacometti, Hepworth, Kelly, Matisse, Miró, Moore, Picasso, Rodin, Serra, and others. The museum was designed by world-renowned architect Renzo Piano, in collaboration with landscape architect Peter Walker.

Adjacent stands the **Crow Collection of Asian Art** ⓱ (2010 Flora Street; tel: 214-979-6430; www.crow collection.org; Tue–Thu 10am–9pm, Fri–Sat 10am–6pm, Sun noon–6pm; free) surrounded by a score of valuable sculptures, including Rodin bronzes, and displaying an important collection of Asian art. Note the enormous Ellsworth Kelly painting in the building's east lobby and the 68-ton (62-metric ton) steel sculpture by Eduardo Chillada, which was requested by the building's architect, I.M. Pei. In front of the building, and flanked by the 1898 Cathedral Santuario de Nuestra Guadalupe, is Artists' Square, a venue for craft shows, with a stage for concerts and cultural events.

Also nearby is the **AT&T Performing Arts Center** ⓲ (2403 Flora Street; tel: 214-880-0202; www.attpac.org). Built at a cost of $354 million, this huge center offers performances of opera, musical theater, classic and experimental theater, ballet, and other forms of dance. Three major architectural firms designed portions of the attractive modern center, including British firm Foster and Partners. The architectural jewel of the center is the **Margot and Bill Winspear Opera**

House (tel: 214-443-1043; www.dallas opera.org), home of the Dallas Opera.

Uptown

Linking the Arts District to Uptown, on the other side of the freeway, is **Klyde Warren Park** ⓳, a 5-acre (2-hectare) urban green space between Pearl and St. Paul streets, which opened in 2012. In an inspired piece of urban planning, it's built right over the Woodall Rogers Freeway and is a vibrant gathering space where people do yoga, play chess, attend book signings, listen to concerts, and relax. Food trucks congregate here, so this is a good place to take a breather.

At Olive and Ross, **Belo Mansion** ⓴, a building now housing the Dallas Bar Association, was, in 1932, the funeral home where the body of Clyde Barrow once lay. The 25-year-old bank robber and his companion, 23-year-old Dallas-born Bonnie Parker, were both shot dead driving down a Louisiana country road. Their four-year crime spree had earned them headlines throughout the country. The gas station at 1620 Eagle Ford Road, built

TIP

Note that it is not the custom to hail taxis in Dallas. Cabs should be requested by telephone.

THANKSGIVING SQUARE

Pocket parks offer relief from the busy man-made environments of urban downtowns, and Dallas has several such spots, including Klyde Warren Park on the edge of the Arts District. None are more soul-soothing, though, than Thanksgiving Square, which occupies the triangle between Bryan Street, Pacific Avenue, and Ervay Street. Championed by four local businessmen in 1964, and funded through a nonprofit foundation, the park opened in 1976 as "a place where people can use gratitude as a basis for dialogue, mutual understanding, and healing." This lovely oasis is now a beloved local feature and a popular destination. It was designed by renowned architect Phillip Johnson and includes a meditation garden, waterfalls and grass, a Wall of Praise, a bell tower with three bronze bells designed in the form of the Liberty Bell that ring every hour, a museum of thanksgiving, and a small but striking interdenominational Chapel of Thanksgiving. The whitewashed spiral chapel is inspired by Middle Eastern architecture. Inside is the famous Glory Window, the largest stained-glass window in the world. It was designed by Gabriel Loire of Chartres, France – a city renowned for its cathedral and the stained glass within – and features brighter colors as the spiral reached its apex. The window famously appears in a shot in Terrence Malick's 2011 film *The Tree of Life*.

FACT

The multi-million dollar Morton H. Meyerson Symphony Center is home to the Dallas Symphony Orchestra, rated one of the finest orchestras in the US.

by Clyde's father, has been replaced with a new structure, but the Barrow house behind it still stands.

To head into North Dallas, take one of the venerable 90-year-old streetcars (with velvet seats and stained-glass windows) that start from outside the DMA and run along bustling, brick-tiled **McKinney Avenue**, which is lined with restaurants, boutiques, and galleries.

North Dallas

Visitors come from all over the US to shop in Dallas and, of course, thousands of locals spend countless hours in the malls that continue to spring up, largely in the northern part of the city. The very first was **Highland Park Village**, a pseudo-Colonial complex with outdoor cafés, posh stores such as Hermes, and an old theater now converted into a movie theater. It was designed by William David Cook, who also designed Beverly Hills, and is America's second-oldest shopping center. It is on Mockingbird Lane near the Dallas north Tollway. A couple of miles north, on Northwest Highway abutting US 75, is **North Park Center**,

filled with such prestigious stores as Neiman Marcus, Nordstrom, and Barney's New York.

Nearby, on the other side of US 75, is the shopping area known as **Mockingbird Station**, home to some local craft shops, boutiques, and restaurants, as well as an **Angelika** movie theater, which shows many art films that aren't on general distribution. DART trains can take you to this area from downtown.

One of only three theaters built to a design by Frank Lloyd Wright, Dallas Theater Center's **Kalita Humphreys Theater** is on Turtle Creek Boulevard. Not far away is one of the most expensive institutions of higher learning in Texas, **Southern Methodist University** (**SMU**).

One of SMU's benefactors was the late Algur H. Meadows, an oil magnate who in middle age began using his large fortune to build up a private art collection. He was aggrieved to discover that he was the owner of a number of Spanish School paintings wrongly attributed to masters, and that many of his supposed Braques,

Clyde Warren Park.

Picassos, and Modiglianis were in fact counterfeits by the Hungarian master forger Elmyr de Hory. Meadows righted his collection with the help of an art historian and kindly donated it to the university. The hundred or so Spanish paintings displayed at SMU's **Meadows Museum** (5900 Bishop Boulevard; tel: 214-768-2516; www.meadowsmuseumdallas.org; Tue–Sat 10am–5pm, Sun 1–5pm), by such masters as Murillo, Velázquez, Goya, and Miró, constitute one of the finest collections of Spanish art outside Spain.

Also on the SMU campus is the **George W. Bush Presidential Library and Museum** (2943 SMU Boulevard; tel: 214-346-1650; www.georgewbushlibrary.smu.edu; Mon–Sat 9am–5pm, Sun noon–5pm). This vast facility contains the full archive of the younger Bush's two terms as president (2000–08) and displays clothing and other personal articles. Its Decision Points Theater provides an interesting insight into how President Bush made decisions about important events such as the September 11, 2001 terrorist attack and the Iraq War. President Bush has no connection to SMU; the university simply outbid other locations to host the library.

Opulent hotels and stores

Dallas has some world-famous hotels, among which are the **Mansion on Turtle Creek** and the **Crescent Court** nearby. The latter, which is more "public," is so opulent that even the house cats live in their own designer "mini hotel" on the grounds. The surrounding Turtle Creek area has some of the classiest homes in the city, as does Mockingbird Lane, which heads west from Highland Park to Love Field airport. Farther north is the upscale **Galleria** (LBJ Freeway and Dallas Parkway; tel: 972-702-7100; www.dallasgalleria.com; Mon–Sat 10am–9pm, Sun noon–6pm), modeled after a prototype in Milan and housing a Westin hotel, dozens of restaurants, hundreds of shops, and an ice rink.

Fair Park

East of US 75, and running roughly parallel to it, is Greenville Avenue, whose lower end is jammed with hip bars, dance clubs, and pool halls. It's the area to find ethnic restaurants of all kinds, although **Deep Ellum** ㉑, farther south, offers a more concentrated experience (drive or take a taxi down Elm Street from midtown). Deep Ellum, which comes alive late at night, has been renowned for its blues and jazz clubs since the 1920s. It was here that famous Texan bluesmen like Blind Lemon Jefferson and Huddie "Leadbelly" Leadbetter began their careers, and today it is also the home of artists, unusual shops, and some of the city's best restaurants.

The 12-block area, which housed a community of freed slaves after the Civil War, has always attracted the avant garde and owes its current revival to the "outlaw parties" in renovated warehouses that a group of musicians organized in the 1980s. Clubs began to open up, followed by art galleries, funky shops, and eating spots.

McKinney Avenue trolley.

Deep Ellum Outdoor Market.

The gift shop at Southfork Ranch.

Across I-30 from Deep Ellum is **Fair Park**, site of the 1936 Texas Centennial Exposition, which celebrated the battle at which Texans won their independence from Mexico. For three weeks beginning in late September each year, the largest talking dummy in existence, Big Tex, greets visitors to the State Fair of Texas.

Fair Park is an interesting place to visit, as it contains the largest collection of Art-Deco buildings in the country. Among the attractions are the **Texas Hall of State** Ⓐ (3939 Grand Avenue; tel: 214-421-4500; www.dallas history.org; Tue–Sat 9am–5pm, Sun 1–5pm; free), complete with mammoth murals and statues of heroes; the 68,000-seat **Cotton Bowl Stadium** Ⓑ; the **Children's Aquarium at Fair Park** Ⓒ (tel: 469-554-7430; www.childrensaquariumfairpark.com; daily 9am–4.30pm), with sharks, piranhas, and 5,000 other marine and freshwater creatures; an amusement park dominated by what is one of the country's biggest Ferris wheels; and several theaters. Next to the park's band shell, pleasant gardens and a conservatory

make up the **Texas Discovery Gardens** Ⓓ (daily 10am–5pm; tel: 214-428-7476; www.texasdiscoverygardens.org), which include a collection of plants indigenous to Texas.

Two smaller museums are also worth a visit. The **Perot Museum of Nature and Science at Fair Park** Ⓔ (tel: 214-428-5555; www.perotmuseum. org; Fri–Sun noon–5pm, daily during Texas State Fair in Sept/Oct), the former Museum of Natural History, features exhibits such as Light Play and Mineral Majesty, as well as old-fashioned dioramas. The **African American Museum** Ⓕ (3536 Grand Avenue; tel: 214-565-9026; www.aamdallas.org; Tue–Sat 11am–5pm, Sun 1–5pm; free) has 1,000 exhibits relating to African-American culture in Texas, and one of the nation's best folk art collections.

East of Fair Park is the little community of **Mesquite**, which stages a rodeo every Friday and Saturday evening between April and September. Here, you can eat Texas barbecue and watch champion cowboys compete at roping, steer wrestling, and bareback riding (tel: 972-285-8777; www.mesquite rodeo.com).

Bishop Arts District

One of Dallas's most interesting up-and-coming areas is in the North Oak Cliff area, immediately south of downtown. Developed as warehouses and shops in the 1930s, this area was once a popular tram stop for shoppers but was on the decline in the 1990s, when local entrepreneur Jim Lake began buying up properties and letting them out rent-free in order to bring the area back to life. It seems to be succeeding. The two-block area that is now known as **Bishop Arts District** is becoming a popular place for boutiques, restaurants, and edgy businesses, and a dynamic place to live, work, and visit. Work has continued on the infrastructure to make this a walkable historic district, including the addition of murals, pedestrian areas, and landscaping. The increasingly popular

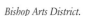

Oak Cliff Film Festival has received national attention, and some of Dallas's most eclectic restaurants are here.

Heading south

Also in the southern part of town is the **Dallas Zoo** (650 SRL Thornton Freeway; tel: 469-554-7500; www.dallas zoo.com; daily 9am–5pm), which offers a 20-minute narrated monorail safari through half a dozen African habitats. Not far away is **Dallas Heritage Village** ㉒ (1515 S. Harwood Street; tel: 214-413-3679; www.dallasheritage village.org; Tue–Sat 10am–4pm, Sun noon–4pm), which has a collection of century-old buildings and a Victorian bandstand on its village green. Nearby is the enormous **Dallas Farmers' Market** ㉓ (1010 S. Pearl Expressway; open daily), one of the largest fresh produce markets in the US.

Out of town

The television series *Dallas*, which ran from 1978 to 1991, and was revived in 2012, probably did more to spread the city's fame than anything else, even if the image of greedy oilmen and dysfunctional families was not what the city fathers might have chosen. It made **Southfork Ranch** (3700 Hogge Road, Parker; tel: 972-442-7800; www. southfork.com; open daily), actually in Parker, half an hour's drive north of downtown via US 75 (take the Parker Road exit), where the Ewing clan supposedly lived, familiar to viewers in around 100 countries. Today, Southfork remains the area's major tourist attraction. The family who lived there was forced to move out by the hordes of tourists, and the ranch has now become a must-see tourist attraction and venue for weddings and special events (there is a hotel nearby). Tram tours start at the visitor center and include JR's Den. When JR Ewing (Larry Hagman) passed away during filming of the new series in 2014, his memorial was held at the ranch.

McKinney (pop. 143,223), a historic county seat 20 miles (32km) northeast of Dallas, is growing so fast that it has now become a suburb of Dallas. Nevertheless, it remains a fine example of a small town, with numerous Victorian houses, that has worked hard at retaining its old-time flavor. Victorian and Greek Revival houses around Chestnut Square, dating back to 1853, are furnished in period style and can be toured (tel: 972-562-8790; www.chestnut square.org; Tue, Thu, and Sat 11am; tours Sept–July). In the sleepy center of town, many old buildings – with their tin ceilings preserved – have been refurbished as shops selling arts and crafts. On Kentucky Street, the Collin County Jail (1880), popular with moviemakers, once housed Frank James of the infamous James gang. The **Heard Natural Science Museum and Wildlife Sanctuary** (1 Nature Place, McKinney; tel: 972-562-5566; www.heardmuseum.org; Tue–Sat 9am–5pm) pays tribute to its founder, Bessie Heard (1884–1988), scion of a venerable local family, meticulously documenting her life. The museum sits in a 287-acre (116-hectare) wildlife sanctuary with trails, a garden, and a picnic area.

Dallas Farmers' Market.

Bishop Arts District.

FORT WORTH

From cowtown to cultural and commercial center, Fort Worth has become a modern, sophisticated city but has never forgotten its dusty, cattle-trading roots.

Fort Worth, which began life as a bastion against rampaging Comanche Indians, spent its first half century as a rough and tumble frontier town, dusty and lawless. The bad guys were quick to take advantage of the situation, and the area became a haven for bandits, outlaws, and military deserters. One neighborhood famous for its notorious residents – including bank robbers Butch Cassidy (George Parker) and the Sundance Kid (Harry Longabaugh) – was known as Hell's Half Acre until its destruction in the early 1900s.

The thing that brought international fame and fortune to what had been just another dusty Western backwater, however, was the longhorn steer. By 1870, large numbers of cowboys had begun to take their rest and pleasure in Fort Worth as they drove great herds of longhorns along the Chisholm Trail from the South Texas ranches to rail-heads in Kansas. In Fort Worth, the trail's last major stop, they bathed, drank, gambled, and whored to forget their arduous, lonely, and monotonous trail driving. After resting and having provisioned themselves, the cowboys went on their way with thousands of cattle, through dust or mud.

With the arrival of the Texas and Pacific Railroad in 1876, hundreds of miles were cut off the cattle drives, and eight lines eventually connected Fort

Worth with northern markets. The cattle were, of course, the worse for wear – and thinner – for every mile they traveled, thus cattle freighted from Fort Worth were in much better condition than they would have been had they struggled all the way to Kansas. Acres of pens were built to receive the herds, which were fattened up before transportation.

Attendant industries such as meat-packing – the Armour and Swift companies became major players – developed here and remained Fort

Main Attractions

Stockyards National
  Historical District
Kimbell Art Museum
Amon G. Carter Museum
National Cowgirl Hall of
  Fame
Six Flags Over Texas

Tarrant County Courthouse.

Fort Worth

Vintage Flying Museum

↑ Denton

NW. 28th Street · NE. 28th Street · NE. 28th Street

TRAIL DRIVER'S PARK

MOUNT OLIVET CEMETERY

0 ___ 500 yds
0 ___ 500 m

RODEO PARK

Stockyards Blvd

Billy Bob's · Stockyards · **A** · Stockyards National Historical District

Cowtown Coliseum · Stockyard Hotel

Exchange Ave.

White Elephant Saloon · Texas Cowboy Hall of Fame

Cliff St.

NW. 26th Street
NW. 25th Street
NW. 24th Street
NW. 23rd Street
NW. 22nd Street
NW. 21st Street
NW. 20th Street

Brennan Avenue

Glendale · Chester · 35W

Goldenrod
Daisy Lane
Honeysuckle Av.
Yucca Av.
Selma
Sylvania Avenue

West Fork Trinity

NE. 21st Street

Dalford
McLemore
Akers

COLD SPRING PARK

GREENWAY PARK

377

Belknap St.

Dallas

Grapevine Vintage Railroad

West Fork Trinity

GREENWOOD MEMORIAL PARK

ROCKWOOD PARK

GREENWOOD MEMORIAL CEMETERY

OAKWOOD CEMETERY

HERITAGE PARK

35W

HARMON FIELD PARK

PADDOCK PARK

Shamrock Avenue

Whitmore Street

Amon Carter Museum · **J** · **I** · Modern Art Museum · **K** · Kimbell Art Museum

West 7th Street

Will Rogers Memorial Center · **H** · **N** · Casa Mañana Theatre

Museum of Science and History · **L**

National Cowgirl Museum & Hall of Fame · **M**

TRINITY PARK

BOTANIC GARDEN · **O**

Thistle Hill · **G**

Austin ↓

Amtrak Station

East Freeway · 30

Arlington, Beltline

287

35W

FOREST PARK

Fort Worth Zoo · **Q**

Log Cabin Village · **P** · Aquarium

Clear Fork Trinity

Texas Christian University Campus

Carter Stadium

Downtown Fort Worth

PADDOCK PARK

0 ___ 200 yds
0 ___ 200 m

Courthouse · E. Belknap St.

Criminal Justice Building

Tarrant County Courthouse · **D**

Sid Richardson Museum · **B**

Sundance Square

Bass Performance Hall · **C**

Central Library

Chamber of Commerce

Greyhound Bus Terminal

Tarrant County Convention Center · **E**

BURNETT PARK

U.S. Courthouse · City Hall

Water Gardens · **F**

Worth's most important source of income through the 1920s. However, just as improvements in transportation had brought the cattle business to Fort Worth, further improvements took part of it away. Larger trucks and better highways made centralized marketing and fattening of cattle unnecessary. Cattlemen could fatten and auction herds locally, for truck delivery.

The Stockyards

Today, Fort Worth's **Stockyards National Historical District Ⓐ**, its streets cobbled and gaslit, looks much as it did a century ago. The cattle pens have been restored and Exchange Street is lined with the shops of artisans hand crafting saddles, chaps, and boots. Even today, in this sleek, modern city, one might still see a Stetson-wearing businessman or a lawman on horseback.

The **Texas Cowboy Hall of Fame** (128 E. Exchange Avenue; tel: 817-626-7131; www.texascowboyhalloffame. org; Mon–Thu 10am–6pm, Fri–Sat until 7pm, Sun 11am–5pm) honors the greats of rodeo and other cowboy pursuits in Texas – 125-plus inductees to date, each of whom has a display with personal memorabilia. Other exhibits include the Sterqueil Wagon Collection, the John Justin Trail of Fame, the Chisholm Trail Exhibit, and the Zingrang Horse Bit Collection.

At the famous **White Elephant Saloon** (106 E. Exchange Avenue; tel: 817-624-8273; www.whiteelephant saloon.com), noted for its bullet-splintered floorboards, there's nightly country and western music, and the notorious 1887 gunfight between owner Luke Short and former marshall Jim Courtright is reenacted on February 8 each year. The **Stockyards Hotel** (where Bonnie and Clyde once stayed) has been decorated in "cattle baron baroque," its saloon bar stools sporting saddles, while the Mission-style **Cowtown Coliseum** (121 E. Exchange Avenue, tel: 817-625-1025), which since 1908 has featured performers as varied as Enrico Caruso and

Elvis Presley, offers weekly rodeos. The world's first indoor rodeo was held here in 1918. Even the 6,000-capacity **Billy Bob's Texas** (tel: 817-624-7117; http://billybobstexas.com), which describes itself as "the world's largest honky-tonk," has live bulls posturing in its indoor ring, inviting visitors to see how long they can stay aboard the pesky critters.

Next to the old hog and sheep pens (now housing art galleries, shops, and eateries), **Grapevine Vintage Railroad** operates steam train trips (705 S. Main Street, Grapevine; tel: 817-625-3185; www.grapevinetexasusa.com/grapevine-vintage-railroad; Mon–Fri 8am–5pm), pulled by its 1896 engine to the little town of Grapevine (see page 119), 21 miles (34km) northeast. Up on the hill, the old Swift meatpacking plant is decorated with early 20th-century antiques and houses an Italian restaurant.

Livestock auctions are still held weekly in Fort Worth and, in keeping with modern technology, entire herds of cattle are bought and sold via the internet. The city has also profited

Live entertainment at Billy Bob's Stockyard.

Sundance Square.

The Sid Richardson Museum is home to a collection of Western art, reflecting both the romance and the reality of the American West.

Fort Worth Water Gardens.

from the West Texas oil boom and serves as a base for many oil companies.

Although the size of sprawling Fort Worth (pop. 653,000) makes it a bit of a problem to negotiate without a car, it has only two other major areas that draw most visitors – the historic downtown area, 2 miles (3km) to the southeast of the Stockyards, and the Cultural District, a mile or two west of that. The three areas make up what is termed a "Western Triangle" and, sensibly, the city runs a shuttle between them.

Downtown

At the heart of downtown, **Sundance Square B**, between 2nd and 5th streets, at Throckmorton, is especially lively at night, with crowded bars and clubs and musicians entertaining the patrons of packed sidewalk cafés. In the old days, when rowdy cattlemen came here to celebrate, they were sometimes entertained by a tightrope walker negotiating a wire between the Plaza Hotel and the Adelphi Theater across the street.

Close by the original 1908 hotel, long ago converted into offices, is

the **Sid Richardson Museum** (201 Main Street; tel: 817-332-6554; www. sidrichardsonmuseum.org; Mon–Thu 9am–5pm, Fri–Sat 9am–8pm, Sun noon–5pm; free), a permanent collection of Western art acquired by the late oilman. At one time, Richardson, who died in 1959 aged 67, owned 125 producing oil wells. His nephew, Perry Bass, and his sons acquired 38 square blocks of downtown after inheriting the Richardson fortune, and the Bass family – unsurprisingly among the nation's wealthiest individuals – have been major local philanthropists.

Surrounded by the collection's 56 paintings, primarily by Frederic Remington and Charles M. Russell, is a magnificent, silver-studded saddle by Ed Bohlin. It was given to Richardson by his close friend publisher Amon G. Carter. Almost everybody who's watched a Western movie has seen some of the art of Ed Bohlin, the Swedish-born farmer who migrated to the US with the dream of becoming a cowboy. He was commissioned by Buffalo Bill Cody to repair leather harnesses used in his traveling show, and then moved to Hollywood to create saddles, holsters, and other leather tack for the studios. Among his customers were Roy Rogers, Tex Ritter, Gary Cooper, the Cisco Kid (Duncan Renaldo), and John Wayne, who habitually donned a Bohlin-made gunbelt and silver hatband. The **Bass Performance Hall** ● (525 Commerce Street; tel: 817-212-4300; www.basshall.com), home of the city's symphony orchestra and ballet and opera companies, is an awesome masterpiece designed by the Washington architect David M. Schwarz and completed in 1998. It is hoped that the 2,056-seat hall will last 300 years – as long as some of its European counterparts: "Great concert halls," Schwarz muses, "are symbols of an age. If they're done well they reflect a great moment in history." Surmounted by Hungarian sculptor Márton Váró's gigantic granite angels, blowing 6ft (2-meter) trumpets, this hall is also noted for such extravagant decorative features as the cloud-filled, 80ft (25-meter) -wide Great Dome, which soars high above the auditorium. This, and the hall's other artwork, was the creation of Scott and Stuart Gentling.

Sundance Square is backdropped by the block-long (and very luxurious) Worthington Renaissance Fort Worth Hotel, which is convenient to everything downtown, including Outlet Square, a vast indoor mall to which it is connected by a mezzanine passageway. This enables guests to bypass the scorching streets. A huge mural flanks the parking lot on 3rd Street: a three-story trompe l'oeil by Richard Haas of cowboys and longhorns on the Chisholm Trail.

Hell's Half Acre

At one end of what was once Hell's Half Acre, not far from the history exhibits in the refurbished Fire Station No. 1 (2nd and Commerce streets; tel: 817-255-9300; open daily; free), is the **Tarrant County Courthouse** ● (100 E. Weatherford Street), dating

from the late 1900s. At the other end is the **Fort Worth–Tarrant County Convention Center** ●, between Houston and Commerce. Opposite are the delightful **Fort Worth Water Gardens** ● at Commerce and 15th streets, created by architect Philip Johnson and his associate, John Burgee, and imitated all over the country. Slabs are tipped at delicate angles to carry, direct, or stop water that is swirling, falling, sprinkling, or lying still. Closed in 2004 after a tragic drowning incident, the gardens later reopened with new safety features and a plaque commemorating the victims. The effects of the pouring, pounding water are not intended to rival nature – rather, they bring to mind leaking dams or streams of industrial coolant in flow to prevent meltdown.

Cultural District

The third region of the city's Western Triangle, the Cultural District, is 1.5 miles (2km) west of downtown. Roughly halfway between the two areas can be found **Thistle Hill** ● (1509 Pennsylvania Avenue; tel:

FACT

One of the most remarkable features of the Kimbell Art Museum is the clever use of natural light, which allows exhibits to be seen to their best advantage.

Kimbell Art Museum.

A trompe l'oeil mural by Richard Haas outside the National Cowgirl Museum and Hall of Fame.

817-336-1212; www.historicfortworth. org; tours Wed–Fri 11am–2pm, Sun 1–3pm), an imposing example of a cattle baron's mansion dating from the turn of the 20th century. Cattleman W.T. Waggoner began building the house at 1509 Pennsylvania Avenue for his daughter in 1903, and another cattleman, Winfield Scott (one-time owner of the Plaza Hotel), completed it in 1910. The landscaped grounds are as interesting as the house restoration, which contains period furnishings and original pieces.

Dominant in the Cultural District is the **Will Rogers Memorial Center** (3401 W. Lancaster Avenue; tel: 817-392-7469), but, apart from the staging of specific events (such as the annual Southwestern Exposition and Livestock Show in January), this is less interesting than the major museums here.

One of these, the **Kimbell Art Museum** (3333 Camp Bowie Boulevard; tel: 817-332-8451; www.kimbellart.org; Tue–Thu and Sat 10am–5pm, Fri and Sun noon–5pm; free), designed by the late Louis Kahn, has long been regarded as one of the top three museums in America. Kahn, revered by many of his fellow architects, also designed La Jolla's Salk Institute, and his work, according to *Contemporary Architects* "had an absolutely monumental impact on the development and redirectioning of progressive design."

Combining concrete, marble, glass, and vegetation with subtle modulations of natural light in a simple, exquisitely detailed whole, the Kimbell is human-sized with a wide collection that is constantly being expanded. There are single objects here that would, on their own, justify a visit: a Duccio, a Giovanni Bellini, Vuillards, a Cézanne, a Rubens, a Rembrandt, and a spectacular Oriental collection. The museum, founded with the art collection of oil tycoon Kay Kimbell on his death in 1964, explains its rationale: "the individual work of outstanding merit and importance is more effective as an educational tool than a large number of representative examples."

Situated nearby is the **Amon Carter Museum** (3501 Camp Bowie Boulevard; tel: 817-738-1933; www.carter museum.org; Tue–Sat 10am–5pm, Sun noon–5pm; free), the work of Philip Johnson, one of the many American architects who were influenced by the work of Louis Kahn. Founded by the publisher of the *Fort Worth Star Telegram* whose name it bears, the museum is best known for collections of paintings and bronzes by Frederic Remington and Charles M. Russell, who specialized in depicting life on the range and along the cattle trails.

In addition to the museum's collection of significant paintings by such revered American artists as John Singer Sargent, Thomas Eakins, Winslow Homer, and Georgia O'Keeffe, there are numerous intriguing paintings by anonymous 19th-century artists and some wonderful sepia prints. These feature gold mining scenes and were taken in an era when advances in photography had reduced the time needed for exposures to a mere 30 seconds. The pioneering "animal movement" photographer Eadweard Muybridge is also represented with an 1887 shot of a horse that shows all of its feet off the ground.

The permanent art collection of the **Modern Art Museum of Fort Worth** Ⓚ (3200 Darnell Street; tel: 817-738-9215; www.themodern.org; Tue–Sun 10am–5pm; free) – ironically the city's oldest – includes works by such post–World War II favorites as Frank Stella, Mark Rothko, Clyfford Still, Morris Louis, Joseph Cornell, and even Pablo Picasso, with contemporary sculpture dotting the adjoining garden. The striking building was designed by Japanese architect Tadao Ando.

Fort Worth Museum of Science and History Ⓛ (1600 Gendy Street; tel: 817-255-9300; www.fwmuseum.org; Mon–Sat 10am–5pm, Sun noon–5pm) employs every inch of space to entertain and educate its visitors, with even its restroom walls adorned with charts explaining aspects of the human body. Notes by the fountains reveal that water covers three-quarters of the earth's surface, with only 3 percent of it fresh. The museum is exceptionally

friendly to kids who can sit in a helicopter or dig for dinosaur bones.

Additional attractions are an Omnimax theater, astronomy programs and daily shows at the Noble Planetarium. Inside the science museum is the **Cattle Raiser's Museum** (www.cattle raisersmuseum.org), where among other things you'll find famous branding irons and a "talking longhorn." One exhibit here explains the importance of the brand inspector in the never-ending fight against rustlers.

For information about the women who worked the ranches on horseback, there's the **National Cowgirl Museum and Hall of Fame** Ⓜ (1720 Gendy Street; tel: 817-336-4475; www. cowgirl.net; Tue–Sat 10am–5pm, Sun noon–5pm), whose 200-plus inductees include Henrietta Chamberlain King, co-founder of the enormous King Ranch; sharpshooter Annie Oakley; world champion bull rider Lynn Jonckowski; and trick rider and calf roper Dixie Reger Moseley.

Casa Mañana Theatre Ⓝ (3101 W. Lancaster; tel: 817-332-2272; www.casamanana.org) is a venue for

Modern Art Museum of Fort Worth.

The Chisholm Trail

The great trail drives of the 19th century passed through Texas towns and characterized an era with their herds of longhorns, cowboys, and long days in the saddle.

From 1867 to 1884, the major route north for cattle was the Chisholm Trail, named for Jesse Chisholm who had established regular trade with northern American Indian camps.

At first the trail went by such names as the Kansas or Abilene Trail, but "Chisholm" soon became the common term for its entire length, from the Rio Grande to Central Kansas. It became the most favored route after fears about Texas tick fever led six states, including Missouri where cattle driving was later outlawed, to close off other trails. (Texan longhorns had built up an immunity to the fever, but it had caused huge losses of cattle in other regions.)

Running from San Antonio through Austin, following what is, roughly speaking, today's I-35, and splitting up at Waco, the Chisholm Trail

A map of the Chisholm Trail.

headed up to Fort Worth and turned eastward at Decatur, to the crossing at Red River Station, which marked the beginning of Indian Territory.

Author Wayne Gard, a former president of the Texas Historical Association, who wrote the definitive book on the Chisholm Trail, observed that it was like a tree, with the roots being the feeder trails from South Texas, the trunk the main route from San Antonio across Indian Territory, and the branches extending to the various railheads in Kansas.

Cattle crossing

In many places, such as Salado, the trail headed right up a town's main street. Only here, and at river crossings, were the cattle squeezed down to a group 50–60ft (15–18 meters) across and confined to a specific trail: they were normally spread out across possibly half a mile (nearly 1km) of prairie, grazing as they continued on their guided drift north.

Individual cattle tended to keep roughly the same position each day, but there was always an ambitious steer or two to take the lead, and usually a trail boss could rely on a favorite steer to give the herd a lead and be the first into the water at a river crossing.

Wayne Gard once told of a stampeding herd of 1,200 on a northbound trek, in the then small town of Dallas. The two steers that had led the drive stayed in place, remaining perfectly still, and eventually the frightened cattle returned to gather peacefully around them.

Range etiquette

The writer J. Frank Dobie stressed the importance of one's companions. Two sayings on the range, he wrote, best expressed the utmost in trustworthiness: "He will do to tie to" and "He will do to ride the river with."

When the railroads eventually penetrated the state and made the Chisholm Trail an anachronism, Texas had more cattle than there had been at the beginning and, although drives continued until the mid-1880s, they were on a reduced basis. In the quarter-century of its existence, the Chisholm Trail saw the passage of more than five million cattle, plus a million mustangs.

Jesse Chisholm himself died in 1838. "No one ever left his home cold or hungry," said the epitaph over his grave. Today's US 81 follows the route of the old Chisholm Trail from Fort Worth right through to Newton, Kansas.

Broadway-style musicals. Its roof is an early example of the geodesic dome invented by R. Buckminster Fuller, and it was one of the city's tributes to the 1936 Texas Centennial Celebration. Based on the triangle, and requiring no internal support, the geodesic dome grows stronger as it grows larger, can withstand hurricanes and, unlike domes in general, has good acoustics. A later example forms the top of the Reunion Tower in Dallas.

Walks on the wild side

Several blocks to the south, near the intersection of I-30 and South University Drive, is the **Fort Worth Botanic Garden** ⓞ (tel: 817-871-7686; www.fwbg.org; open daily; free), a 114-acre (46-hectare) park watered by natural springs and containing more than 50 species of tree, all sorts of roses, and a Japanese Garden.

Farther south still on Colonial Parkway, west of University Drive, is **Log Cabin Village** ⓟ (2100 Log Cabin Village Lane; tel: 817-926-5881; www.logcabinvillage.org; Tue–Fri 9am–4pm, Sat–Sun 1–5pm), featuring seven homes from the 1850s, with costumed pioneers, a grist mill, and spinning wheels.

A short distance away is the **Fort Worth Zoo** ⓠ (1989 Colonial Parkway; tel: 817-759-7555; www.fortworthzoo.org; Mon–Fri 10am–5pm, Sat–Sun until 6pm) in Forest Park. Set among natural habitats along winding paths are 5,000 animals, birds, and reptiles. The zoo's art gallery contains 28 enormous paintings by the German artist Wilhelm Kuhnert, who went to the East African bush for inspiration. Several American buffalo live here on a 3,400-acre (1,375-hectare) range of their own. There is a prairie dog "town," where small burrowing owls may be seen creeping in and out of abandoned prairie dog holes. Trails of many descriptions divide the refuge.

Aviation buffs will enjoy the **Vintage Flying Museum** at Meacham Airport (505 N.W. 38th Street; tel:

817-624-1935; www.vintageflyingmuseum.org; Fri 10am–5pm, Sat 9am–5pm, Sun noon–5pm, also Thu 10am–5pm June–Aug). Some planes in this collection of historic aircraft and World War II memorabilia still fly, and each October the museum hosts a fly-in of rare and vintage aircraft.

Arlington

Though a separate town, **Arlington** (pop. 375,600) has become something of an eastern adjunct to Fort Worth. Its many residents are fans of the Texas Rangers, and thus flock to watch the team play at **Globe Life Park**, a magnificent facility that costs as much as a night in a Las Vegas hotel and offers almost as many attractions. The complex was designed by Washington architect David M. Schwarz, who designed the Bass Performance Hall and the American Airlines Center in Dallas. An entire entertainment complex is rising around the ball park, but already thousands come to enjoy the walking trails, admire the 19ft (6-meter) architectural friezes depicting scenes from Texas history, see

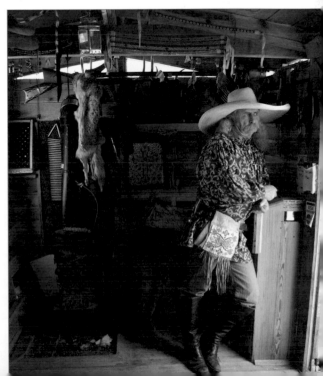

A store on Exchange Street, Stockyards National Historical District.

FACT

In celebration of the local wine industry, Grapevine stages an annual Grapefest every September.

the huge murals of famous baseball heroes, and visit the baseball museum. During games, no fan is ever farther than about 75ft (23 meters) from a bright television monitor – there are 2,000 in the park. In the basement, enormous tanks pump soda to dozens of concession stands.

Visitors who take the 50-minute **Ballpark Tours** (tel: 817-273-5099; http://texas.rangers.mlb.com; see website for details of tours) view the vast, open-air arena with its 49,000 seats, the dugouts, the luxurious player lounge displaying posters of every baseball movie, and the huge press balcony. Then many tourists spend hours in the **Legends of the Game Museum**, where all the heroes – Ty Cobb, Hank Aaron, Lou Gehrig, and Babe Ruth among them – are represented through videos, trophies, jerseys, and other memorabilia. One section is devoted to the little-known women's leagues. Upstairs in the Learning Center, baseball history is taught through interactive video quizzes, and there are various exhibits showing how bats and balls are made. The nearby **AT&T Stadium** is home to

the Dallas Cowboys football team and also hosts bowl games and major concerts. This immense structure has the world's largest column-free interior.

Fun and games

Heading away from Globe Life Park, past Arlington's Convention Center, you reach **Six Flags Over Texas** (2201 Road to Six Flags St E; tel: 817-640-8900; www.sixflags.com/overtexas; open daily), at the junction of I-30 and Highway 360. This is the state's biggest tourist attraction and the original base of what is now a nationwide chain. The 212-acre (86-hectare) theme park devotes an area to each of the nations whose flag has flown over Texas – Spain, Mexico, France, Texas, the Confederacy, and the US – and there are other attractions, too. Next door, **Six Flags Hurricane Harbor** (1800 E. Lamar Boulevard; tel: 817-265-3356; www.sixflags.com; open daily) is the largest water park in the US, and offers a cool respite from the searingly hot temperatures that summer visitors to Texas can always expect.

Grapevine Vintage Railroad steam train.

Louis Tussaud Waxworks and Ripley's Believe It or Not! (601 Palace Parkway; tel: 972-263-2391; www.ripleys.com/grandprairie; open daily) is to the east, in Grand Prairie, along I-30 at Beltline, and offers the usual garish waxwork and emporium fun. Farther afield is the **Johnson Plantation Cemetery** (600 W. Arkansas Lane; tours can be arranged through the Arlington Historical Society, tel: 817-460-4001), a small family cemetery where a major figure in early Arlington history and his African-American slaves are buried. There is an historic log cabin on the site. At the entrance to the River Legacy Parks, near the lake at the west side of town, is the **River Legacy Living Science Center** (703 N.W. Green Oak Boulevard; tel: 817-860-6752; www.riverlegacy.org; Mon–Sat 9am–5pm). Housed in an attractive sustainable 12,000-sq-ft (1,115 sq meter) building, it offers environmental exhibits for all ages.

On the far side of Highway 360, which runs north to south on the eastern edge of Arlington, are shopping opportunities at Six Flags Mall (2911 E. Division), and the enormous Traders Village Flea Market (2602 Mayfield Road), which displays the wares of 1,600 dealers at weekends. The return trip west to Fort Worth on I-20 passes the gargantuan Parks Mall (Cooper at I-20).

Arlington's downtown attractions are clustered within walking distance of each other around Main Street. These include the perennial Johnny High's Country Music Revue at the **Arlington Music Hall** (224 N. Center Street; tel: 817-226-4400; www.arlingtonmusichall.com) and the 200-seat **Theatre Arlington** (305 W. Main Street; tel: 817-275-7661; www.theatrearlington.org). The **Arlington Historical Society Museum** (1616 W. Abram; tel: 817-460-4001; www.arlingtonhistoricalsociety.org; Sat–Sun 1–4pm; voluntary donation) includes a veteran barbershop and general store. The **Arlington Museum of Art** (201 W. Main Street; tel: 817-275-4600; www.arlingtonmuseum.org; Tue–Sat 10am–5pm, Sun 1–5pm; free) concentrates on Texan artists.

Grapevine

More than 30 19th-century buildings have been preserved and restored in the little town of **Grapevine**, which sits at the end of the Grapevine Vintage Railroad line that begins at the Fort Worth Stockyards. Named for the wild mustang grapes prevalent in the area, the town dates back to 1843 when General Sam Houston camped nearby before signing a peace treaty with American Indian tribal leaders. There are numerous wineries in the area, the nearest being the château-style **Delaney Vineyards** (2000 Champagne Boulevard; tel: 817-481-5668; www.delaneyvineyards.com; Mon–Sat noon–5pm).

Grapevine is dotted with historical markers, and much of its Main Street is listed in the *National Register of Historical Places*. The tourist office (636 S. Main Street; tel: 817-410-8136; www.grapevinetexasusa.com) is in the artfully

The Ball-Eddleman-McFarland House is one of the best-preserved examples of Victorian architecture in Fort Worth. Built in 1899, it is located in the Quality Hill area of the city.

The Texas Rangers take on the Houston Astros at Globe Life Park.

TIP

Consider historic Denton as a base for a visit to Dallas or Fort Worth. Not only is it halfway between the two centers, but it also has numerous attractions of its own, including live music venues and a vibrant college scene. The A Train links Denton to Dallas's DART system.

reconstructed Wallis Hotel building, which was filled with traveling salesmen in the early 1900s. *The Sidewalk Judge*, a lifelike sculpture by J. Seward Johnson, sitting on a bench outside, is an irresistible photo opportunity.

Across Main Street, at No. 300, the old **Palace Theater** (tel: 817-410-3100) has been restored as a home for the Grapevine Opry, and in the next block is the former **Grapevine Home Bank**, which was robbed by some of the Bonnie and Clyde gang back in 1932. Many of the buildings on Main Street now sell predominantly tacky souvenirs, but some display genuine arts and crafts. These include **Off the Vine** (324 S. Main Street; tel: 817-421-1091; www.offthevinetexas.com), a wine shop that also sells wine-related art, such as handblown goblets.

What's known as the **Torian Log Cabin**, built in 1845, inhabited until the 1940s and still primitively furnished, sits near the gazebo in Liberty Park at the northern end of the street. The more interesting old homes are behind Main Street at the other end: a group of Victorian houses on College Street. One block west back on Main Street are the Heritage Center and the **Grapevine Depot**, the latter serving as the town's railroad station before being converted into an historical museum.

The St Louis and Southwestern (Cotton Belt) Railroad depot once stood here and today, near the classic 1933 **Aeromotor Windmill**, which at one time pumped water for a nearby farm, is the terminal for the Grapevine Vintage Railroad, which runs daily between here and Fort Worth. At the blacksmith's shop, with its wild mustang grapevine, genial Jim White demonstrates forging brands while posing happily for visitors, and his neighbor, saddlemaker Aubrey Mauldin, presides over a leather shop filled with custom-made boots.

The cowboy boot is something special and the state produces more of them than any other place in the world. There were 600 Texas bootmakers at one time. Now only about one-tenth of that number still painstakingly cut and stitch every inch by hand, from pointed toe (to slip easily

Texas Motor Speedway.

into the stirrup) to elevated arch and heel (to hold the foot firmly in place).

At the far end of the depot is **Grapevine Heritage Garden**, featuring such specimens as the swamp rose, the pink-flowered bouncing bet (once used as a soap substitute), and the crinum lily, all attracting butterflies and hummingbirds and making the garden a visitors' delight.

North of town, 19-mile (30km) long **Grapevine Lake** is a cool recreational oasis offering boating, swimming, fishing, and all kinds of water activities. Beyond the lake, off Highway 26 at 3000 Grapevine Mills Parkway, near the airport, is the huge, brightly lit Grapevine Mills shopping mall, which is not a bad place to while away a couple of hours between flights. A convenient shuttle bus runs to and from the airport.

Denton

Thirty-five miles (56km) northeast of Fort Worth, on US 35, is the attractive college town of **Denton** (pop. 118,700), home to two universities and one of the liveliest (and least known) live music scenes in the US. In fact, it rivals Austin for indie music, and is the hometown of well-known band Brave Combo whose musical style seems to draw from just about everywhere.

Its century-old limestone and granite courthouse dominates a square lined with renovated old buildings that now house eclectic cafés, music shops, funky boutiques, antiques stores, and specialty stores. The **Courthouse-on-the-Square Museum** (110 W. Hickory Street; tel: 940-349 2850; www.dentonmuseums.com/courthouse-on-the-square.php; Mon–Fri 10am–4.30pm, Sat 11am–3pm; free) in the courthouse focuses on the history of the region. The town's pioneer founder, Captain John B. Denton, is buried beneath the lawn.

Numerous movies (including the 1998 film, *Armageddon*) have been shot in Denton, especially among the old homes of the Oak-Hickory Historic District. A free historic walking tour of downtown can be downloaded from Main Street Denton (www.denton mainstreet.org).

Every March, the city hosts 35 Denton (www.35denton.com), a music festival featuring all types of music, from polka to jazz. The A Train connects Denton to Dallas and the DART light rail and bus system. To the south of town, the **Texas Motor Speedway** (3545 Lone Star Circle; tel: 817-215-8500; www.texasmotorspeedway.com) will be of interest to auto-racing enthusiasts, while the **Hangar 10 Flying Museum** (tel: 940-565-1945; www.hangar10.org) at Denton Municipal Airport has vintage aircraft on display and will appeal to flying buffs.

Also in this area is the **Texas Women's University** (TWU), the largest of its kind in the nation, containing the **Daughters of the American Revolution Museum** (tel: 940-898-2000; by appointment only), which displays gowns worn by the First Ladies of Texas. In the vicinity is the **University of North Texas** (tel: 940-565-2000), which has a fashion collection of its own, as well as a famous library.

FACT

The Fort Worth Stock Show and Rodeo (tel: 817-877-2400; www.fwssr.com) takes over Cowtown, as its known, for most of January.

Denton County Courthouse.

CENTRAL TEXAS

Detour from the interstate south of Dallas, between Waxahachie and Austin, and discover quirky towns, artificial lakes, paleontological sites, distinctive architecture, absorbing museums, and Texas A&M.

C entral Texas has long been known as the backyard of Texas – not such a bad thing in a state with so many glamorous frontyards. Too often travelers, unless headed for the lakes or elderly relatives, race from Dallas to Austin without even exiting the freeway. To really understand Texas, leave the interstate between Waxahachie and Austin and "come on around to the backyard."

Waxahachie

Waxahachie ❶ (pop. 31,000), located 35 miles (56km) south of Dallas, is one of the latter's bedroom communities. Take the exit from I-35 East, the Dallas arm of the Fort Worth–Dallas "Y." The town's name derives from an American Indian word for "buffalo creek"; white settlers arrived here in the 1840s.

Much of the honey in Texas supermarkets comes from Waxahachie, a town that has become increasingly industrialized. Nevertheless, it still proudly preserves hundreds of Victorian and early 20th-century houses, many of which can be toured along a "Gingerbread Trail" marked on a free map. This is available from the **Waxahachie Convention and Visitors Bureau** (102 YMCA Drive; tel: 972-937-2390; www.waxahachiecvb.com.)

Photographs and pioneer artifacts in the **Ellis County Museum** (201 S. College Street; tel: 972-937-0681;

Ellis County Courthouse.

www.elliscountymuseum.org; Mon–Sat 10am–5pm, Sun 1–5pm), a former Masonic meeting-house on **Courthouse Square**, are devoted to the history of Waxahachie. The red sandstone and granite 1895 **Ellis County Courthouse** (Mon–Fri; free), a product of Texas courthouse architect James Reily Gordon, is one of the most-photographed buildings in the state. It cost $150,000 to construct – a substantial sum in the 1890s. According to legend, an Italian stonecutter who was working on the building is thought to

Main Attractions
Ellis County Courthouse, Waxahachie
National Polka Festival, Ennis
Armstrong Browning Library, Baylor University, Waco
Texas Ranger Hall of Fame and Museum, Waco
Central Texas Area Museum, Salado
Texas A&M University, College Station

Central Texas

have fallen in love with a Waxahachie telegraph operator, Mabel Frame, whose carved face is a recurring exterior motif.

The museum owns the red-brick Greek Revival **Jenkins Home** (604 W. Main Street; tel: 972-937-0681; open during the Gingerbread Trail Days festival in early June), packed with antique fans, furniture, and Bohemian glass. It was built in 1904, at the height of Waxahachie's prosperity (based on cattle, grain, and cotton), a few years after the 1900 **Chautauqua Auditorium** (www.waxatxchautauqua.org), part of the century-old nationwide Chautauqua educational movement begun in upstate New York and still offering cultural presentations here. Also from the same era is the ornate Roman Revival **Nicholas P. Sims Library** (515 W. Main Street; tel: 972-937-2671; www.simslib.org), with a richly decorated Carrara marble and gold interior.

Waxahachie's proximity to Dallas's already established film industry, its charming small-town feel, and its attractive period architecture have made it popular as a movie location. The 1985 *Peyton Place* remake was filmed here, as were the movies *Tender Mercies* and *Places in the Heart*.

Polka Festival

Many of the state's Czech immigrants settled in Central Texas's fertile cotton-growing belt, and almost all did well as cotton farmers here. Their descendants make up approximately half the population of **Ennis ❷**, on I-45 between Dallas and Houston. Since 1966, Ennis has sponsored the **National Polka Festival** in May, attracting crowds of 30,000. A parade of 14 polka bands rolls down Main Street, which may be the widest in Texas – divided into East and West Main by railroad tracks, it is 340ft (104 meters) across. The town also has a **Railroad and Cultural Heritage Museum** (105 N.E. Main Street; tel: 972-875-1901; www.visitennis.com; Mon–Sat 10am–4pm, Sun 1–4pm), which showcases the Czech influence as well as railroad history.

On the water

Since 1900, more than 200 lakes have been created in Texas. **Lake Bardwell**, or the Bardwell Reservoir, on Waxahachie Creek, 4 miles (7km) outside Ennis, was built by the US Army Corps of Engineers in the early 1960s. Like the other new lakes near Navarro Mills and Mexia, it is a popular recreation area, with pretty lakeside parks and camping. It also acts as the water supply for Ennis, Waxahachie, and Corsicana. Visitors from out of state – especially New Englanders, whose reservoirs are fenced and carefully patrolled – are often surprised to find Texans fishing, water-skiing, and sailing on theirs.

Corsica ❸, the Navarro county seat, is 19 miles (30km) south of Ennis on I-45. It is named for Corsica, home of the parents of the Texas hero José Antonio Navarro of San Antonio, who signed the Texas Declaration of Independence and helped write the first constitution. The first Texas gusher was not drilled at Corsicana as is commonly believed. However, a 12-year oil boom began in 1894 when the city dug

The Ellis County Museum.

Delcious Czech pastries at Caldwell Kolache Festival.

an artesian well and struck oil instead of water. The strike made Corsicana the first oil boomtown in Texas. A current attraction, **Pioneer Village** (912 W. Park Avenue; tel: 903-654-4846; www. cityofcorsicana.com; Mon–Fri 8am–5pm, Sat 9am–5pm, Sun 1–5pm) is made up of reconstructed 19th-century log buildings, including an American Indian trading post and slave quarters.

Corsicana is known for the "Deluxe" fruit cake made by the **Collin Street Bakery** (401 W. 7th Avenue; tel: 800-292-7400; www.collinstreet.com; open daily), featured on Food Network, which has been exported all over the world – 1.6 million fruitcakes per year, to be exact. An essential ingredient is the inimitable Texas pecan, more than a million pounds (just under half a million kilograms) of which are used by the bakery annually. Be warned: American-style fruitcakes are invariably very sweet and not to everyone's taste.

Nameless place

Texas bluebonnets, near Ennis.

Forreston ❹, 10 miles (16km) south of Waxahachie on the interstate, is the oldest town in the area. Another 5 miles (8km) south, near **Italy** ❺, the Confederates operated a hat factory.

Italy was originally called "Houston Creek," because Sam Houston was reported to have camped nearby. Reputedly, the post office would not issue a postmark unless the name of the town was changed and, after six different names had been rejected, settlers wrote back: "Let the post office be nameless, and be damned." The community was Nameless, Texas, from 1880 to 1890, and there is still a Nameless Schoolhouse and Nameless Road. Houston Creek eventually became Italy – a tribute, it is said, to the sunny Central Texas climate. The population of Italy has never exceeded 1,900 souls, but it did receive the first fully endowed public library in Texas – the **Dunlap Library** – from businessman S.M. Dunlap.

Historical towns

Back on I-35, or via State Route 22 from Corsicana, you arrive at **Milford** ❻, a town settled in the 1850s that once adopted the good-humored city motto: "The home of 700 friendly people and three or four old grouches." It is nothing more than human nature to leave the freeway in the hope of catching a glimpse of one of the grouches. The town of **Hillsboro** ❼, just below the point where I-35 West joins I-35 East from Dallas, has been a crossroads since the 1850s, when there was a dirt-floor, elm-pole courthouse here.

Today's limestone Hill County Courthouse was built in 1890, burned down in 1993, and was restored in 1999, with the help of a fund-raiser headlined by Willie Nelson, who grew up in nearby Abbott. At Hill Junior College, the **Harold B. Simpson History Complex** (121 Lamar Drive; tel: 254-582-2555; Mon–Fri) displays paintings, photographs, and documents from the Civil War, around 200 guns and other weaponry from the Civil War to the present, and the uniform worn by Audie Murphy, the most decorated American soldier of World War II.

Northwest of Hillsboro on State Road 144 is **Glen Rose** ❽, where it is rumored John Wilkes Booth once lived – under the name John St Helen – after he assassinated President Lincoln. Glen Rose is sometimes known as the "Petrified City," because petrified wood is a popular building material here. Local history is explained in the tiny hometown **Somervell County Museum** (101 Vernon Street; tel: 254-898-0640; www.historicdowntownglenrose.org; Wed–Sat 11am–4pm; free).

Jurassic Park

Numerous dinosaur tracks can be found in Glen Rose and in the 1,270-acre (514-hectare) **Dinosaur Valley State Park** ❾ (1629 Park Road 59; tel: 254-897-4588; www.tpwd.state.tx.us/state-parks/dinosaur-valley; open daily 8am–10pm), 4 miles (6km) west of the town. The tracks are easy to spot, but there is a steep trail to the river. The Bosque River Valley was once coastal swampland and dinosaurs left their tracks – some of the best-preserved examples in the world – in the limestone riverbed here. There are no "taildrag marks" in the dinosaurs trackway – the water here was deep enough for the dinosaurs' tails to float – but you can see where the mud oozed up between their toes. The park has facilities for camping, picnicking, hiking, biking,

FACT

Texas-born Audie Murphy (1924–71) was able to build on his honorable service record by becoming an actor, starring in a series of war and Western films, most notably the Civil War movie *The Red Badge of Courage* (1951).

Hill County Courthouse.

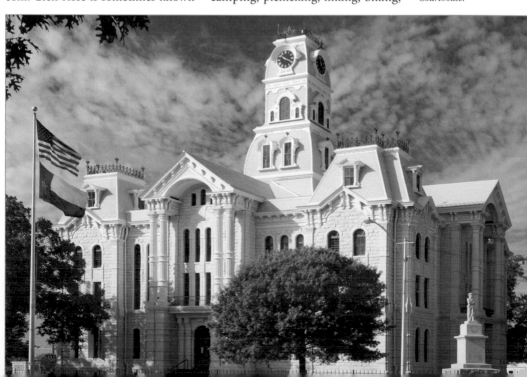

Petrified dinosaur footprints in the Paluxy River, Dinosaur Valley State Park.

and horseback riding, and is one of the state parks in which part of the official state longhorn herd is kept.

West, Texas

The small town of **West** ❿, halfway between Hillsboro and Waco, is sometimes confused with the region "West Texas," so it is often referred to as "West, Comma, Texas." Forty thousand people came here on September 15, 1896, to view the ridiculous, staged spectacular of two locomotives of the Missouri, Kansas and Texas Railroad crash into each other. Their throttles tied back to 50mph (80kmph), the trains exploded on impact, killing two spectators. The agent who dreamed up this reckless stunt was merely fired – and promptly rehired the next day.

More recently, on April 17, 2013, West was hit by tragedy when the West Fertilizer Company exploded, killing 15, injuring more than 160 people, and destroying or damaging more than 150 buildings. West has a large Czech population, like much of Central Texas, and shortly after the explosion, the Czech Republic donated $200,000 to

assist with rebuilding the community.

If you stop in West, be sure to sample kolaches, the traditional individual fruit pies baked in multigeneration family bakeries in Texas's Czech communities. They are a treat that people drive miles to enjoy. You'll see savory versions in Austin's hipper areas, but there's nothing like stopping by the side of a backroad and enjoying a warm, fresh-baked fruit kolache with a cup of coffee.

The Bosque

Twenty miles (32km) west of Hillsboro, across the Brazos River, is the region known as **Bosque County** (Spanish for "woods" and pronounced "boskay"). A number of Norwegians settled here as farmers between 1850 and 1875. They fiercely defended their log houses from attacks by the Kiowa and Comanche Indians. Many relics and household items used by these early Scandinavian settlers have been collected for display in **Bosque Memorial Museum** (301 S. Avenue Q; tel: 254-675-3845; www.bosquemuseum.org; Tue–Sat 10am–5pm) in **Clifton** ⓫ (pop. 3,420). Clifton's Nordic heritage is also celebrated with a smorgasbord each November at **Norse**, near Clifton.

Waco

Until they were driven out, the Waco were a Wichita tribe occupying a site by the 840-mile (1,344km) -long Brazos River in Central Texas. When the whites first settled the area 160 years ago, they took **Waco** ⓬ as the name for their town. First came Fort Fisher, then and now a Texas Ranger outpost, but what really brought attention to the town was the construction, in 1870, of a massive suspension bridge across the river.

"That bridge was very important," explains local historian Roger Conger. "The Brazos was a veritable iron curtain across the center of Texas. After the Civil War, many Southerners were going west. They had to come to Waco to cross the river."

Six bridges span the river within the city today, but the antique suspension

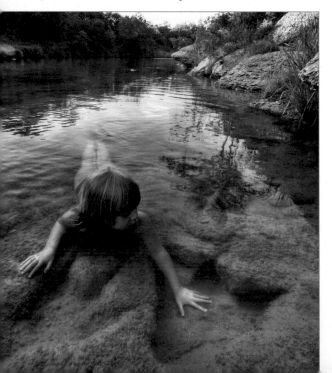

bridge (now pedestrian-only) is still the most significant. When the 475ft (145-meter) bridge supplanted the ferry, it was the longest single-span suspension bridge west of the Mississippi River, and the second longest in the world. Supported by wire cables and 2.7 million Waco bricks, it was built by New York engineer Thomas Griffith from the plans of New York's Thomas Roebling, designer of the Brooklyn Bridge. Longhorns and wagon trains bound for the Chisholm Trail traversed it in its earliest days and, until 1889, a toll was charged: "five cents for each loose animal of the cattle kind."

Earliest site

Start at **Waco Mammoth Site** ⑬ (6220 Steinbeck Bend Drive; tel: 254-750-7946; www.wacomammoth.org; Tue–Fri 11am–5pm; Sat 9am–5pm), where, beginning in 1978, 24 Columbian mammoths were uncovered along the Brazos River, the first and only recorded discovery of a nursery herd of Pleistocene mammoths. The site was excavated and cared for by Baylor University until 2009, when it was opened to the public

as a city park funded by a nonprofit foundation. There is a museum and numerous activities for kids.

Some of the settlers who followed the Texas Rangers to this beautiful valley on the Brazos in the 1840s lived in log cabins on the site of what is now Cameron Park on Rotan Drive. You'll find woods, hiking trails, **Cameron Park Zoo** (1701 N. 4th Street; tel: 254-750-8400; www.cameronparkzoo.com; Mon–Sat 9am–5pm, Sun 11am–5pm), and **Miss Nellie's Pretty Place**, a wildflower preserve donated to the city by a former congressman's mother.

What the earliest settlement probably looked like can be seen in the nine early buildings located next to the riverside Fort Fisher Campground in **The Governor Bill and Vara Daniel Historic Village** (1300 S. University Parks; tel: 254-710-1160; www.baylor.edu/mayborn), on the campus of Baylor University. Inside its Mayborn Museum Complex, Baylor – the largest Baptist university in the world – houses the **Strecker's Cabinet of Curiosities** (tel: 254-710-1110; Mon–Sat 10am–5pm, Sun 1–5pm; free), devoted to natural history. Also

Waco Suspension Bridge.

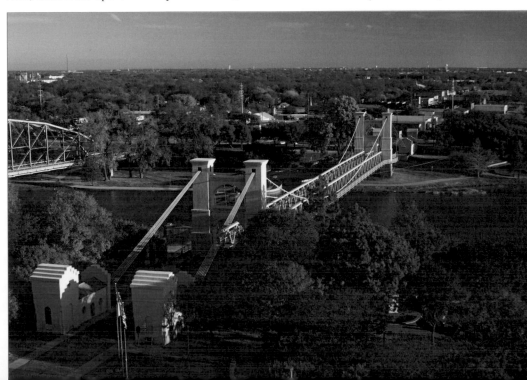

on campus is the fascinating, marble-columned **Armstrong Browning Library** (710 Speight Avenue; tel: 254-710-3566; www.browninglibrary.org; Mon–Fri 9am–5pm, Sat 10am–2pm; free), which exhibits portraits of, and 4,000 letters written by or to, the Victorian poets Robert and Elizabeth Barrett Browning. The library's collection – assembled by Baylor's late Professor A.J. Armstrong – is supplemented by 50 lovely stained glass windows depicting verses by the poetic pair.

Between the Baylor campus and US 81 is the **Tourist Information Center** (106 Texas Ranger Trail; tel: 254-750-8696; www.wacoheartoftexas.com), adjoining the **First Street Cemetery**, which contains Confederate graves. Other attractions are the **Texas Sports Hall of Fame** (1108 University Parks Drive; tel: 254-756-1633; www.tshof.org; Mon–Sat 9am–5pm, Sun noon–5pm), where kids can try on helmets of the Houston Oilers or Dallas Cowboys, and the **Texas Ranger Hall of Fame and Museum** (100 Texas Ranger Trail; tel: 254-750-8631; www.texasranger.org; daily 9am–5pm). Jim Bowie's knife and the rifle he carried at the Alamo are here, as well as a jewel-studded saddle (which cost $5,800 in 1903), novelist James Michener's typewriter, the pistol Pat Garrett used to kill Billy the Kid, and enough of the early Rangers' Colt revolvers to equip an army. If you're interested in Texas history, this is definitely a place you won't want to miss.

Six-shooter junction

In its prime, Waco was a rough cowtown. "Next stop, Waco," the train conductors would yell as the train approached, "Get out your six-shooters." The last legal hanging in Texas occurred here in 1923, witnessed by over 4,000 people, and, in 1955, a Waco television station was the first in the world to broadcast a murder trial. A more genteel era is reflected by the city's group of 19th-century homes, operated from the gingerbread-style Hoffmann House by the **Historic Waco Foundation** (810 S. 4th Street; tel: 254-753-5166; www.historicwaco.org). The foundation also hosts the annual Brazos River Festival in April.

Two of these Victorian homes lie

A pastry chef from the Collin Street Bakery.

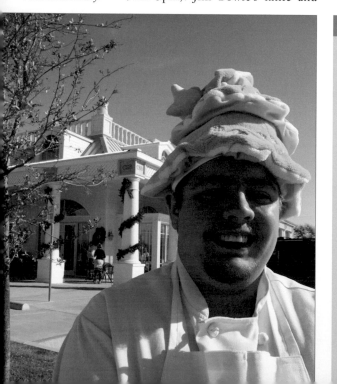

DR PEPPER MUSEUM

The fun Dr Pepper Museum (300 S. 5th Street; tel: 254-757-1025; www.drpeppermuseum.com; Mon–Sat 10am–5pm, Sun noon–4pm) is dedicated to the famous soft drink, which was invented in Waco's Old Corner Drug Store by pharmacist Charles Alderton in 1885. His boss, Dr Morrison, named it Dr Pepper but the reason remains unclear. The museum is housed in a bottling plant opened in 1906. It covers the history of Dr Pepper and the soft drink industry, including Big Red, a drink that was invented a block away. You can sample traditional sodas and sundaes at the museum's soda fountain; there is no entrance fee if you just go in for a drink. The site is on the National Register of Historic Places, but Dr Pepper has not been produced here since the 1920s.

between I-35 and Waco Drive and can be toured on Saturday and Sunday afternoons (except December). They are the Greek Revival **Earle-Napier-Kinnard House** (814 S. 4th Street), completed in 1869, and **Fort House** (503 S. 4th Street), in which Alabama planter William Aldridge Fort lived with dozens of relatives and slaves in the 1870s.

Across the river, at 100 Mill Street, is the Italianate **East Terrace**, shielded by large elm and pecan trees, with walks down to the river. Home of industrialist John Wesley Mann, *c*.1872, it contains original furniture.

Confederate support

At 1901 N. Fifth Street, the **Earle-Harrison House** (tel: 254-753-2032), sitting in 5-acre (2-hectare) gardens, is gloriously furnished. Portraits of General Robert E. Lee abound in some of these old homes, a reminder that Waco's men marched off to support Confederate armies in the Civil War.

A total of six Confederate generals hailed from Waco, which has also been home to former Texas Governor Ann Richards and Madison Alexander Cooper Jr, whose 840,000-word novel, *Sironia, Texas* – on view in the public library – is said to be the longest ever written.

Another among Waco's dozen or more museums is the hometown **Helen Marie Taylor Museum of Waco History** (701 Jefferson; tel: 254-752-4774; Tue–Sat). It sits on the site of one of the Waco tribe's main villages.

In 2001, a downtown park was opened in front of City Hall (3rd and Austin). The walkways and fountains of **Heritage Square** were constructed on the site of an area devastated by a tornado in 1953.

Austin bound

Like most towns south of Waco, **Temple ⓮** and **Belton ⓯** were originally built around loading pens and general stores about a century ago. Today, the area is known primarily for the commanding presence of **Fort Hood**, the largest military base in the US, which is set on no fewer than 217,000 acres (87,800 hectares), near Lake Benton. The base is one of the primary training grounds for US soldiers dispatched to

Baskets of peaches at a farmers' market in Waco.

The Waco Hippodrome on Austin Avenue.

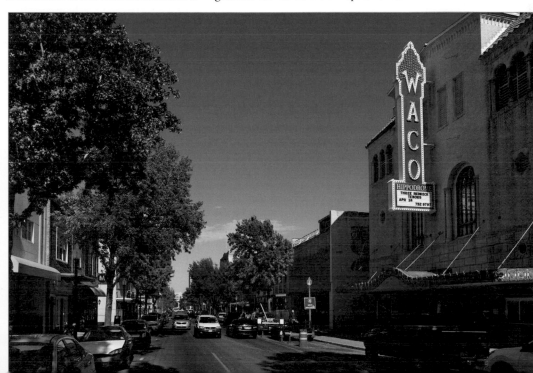

Iraq and other global assignments. The main drag of nearby Harker Heights is lined with car dealerships, eating places, and fairly rowdy nightclubs.

Two historic army divisions maintain museums at Fort Hood: the **1st Cavalry Museum** on Headquarters Avenue and the **2nd Armored Division Museum** on Battalion Avenue (both open daily; free; bring proof of ID). Kids will enjoy sitting atop a tank and learning about soldiers here.

Life and death

There are a number of eateries in the Temple-Killeen area, and, in addition to plenty of hearty Texan specialties, they offer a good opportunity to observe small-town life. In fact, Texan-watching is at its best while sawing a batter-fried corn dog or a chickenfried steak, a cheap cut of hammered beef breaded like fried chicken and served with potatoes and gravy, a country dish invented in Texas.

In towns like Temple, Belton, and **Killeen 16**, there is still much pleasure to be taken in daily life. They have their characters, language tricks, and

Bell Country Courthouse, Belton.

private jokes as anywhere else, possibly more, since the storytelling tradition remains strong in both rural and urban Texas. In this region, times are changing: Temple-Killeen's Standard Metropolitan Statistical Area is one of the 10 fastest-growing in the US.

Local history

I-35 follows the railroad – beside the Chisholm Trail, along which cattle were driven to rail-heads farther north – so busy Temple is a logical place to find the **Temple Railroad and Heritage Museum** (315 W. Avenue B; tel: 254-298-5172; www.rrhm.org; Tue–Sat 10am–4pm) in the 1910 Santa Fe depot at 31st Street and Avenue H. It houses a steam engine and railroad equipment.

The **Czech Heritage Museum and Genealogy Center** (119 W. French Ave; tel: 254-899-2935; www.czechmuseum.org; Tue–Sat 10am–4pm) exhibits an unusual collection related to Czech immigration. Preserved artifacts include a bible dated 1530. The **Bell County Museum** in Belton (201 N. Main Street; tel: 254-933-5243; www.bellcounty museum.org; Tue–Sat noon–5pm; free), is a local history museum occupying a 1905 Carnegie Library building.

Farms and plantations

The pretty little town of **Salado 17**, once a stage stop on Salado Creek, a few miles south of Killeen, is best known for its popular and picturesque historic Stagecoach Inn (1 Main Street; tel: 254-947-5111; www.staystage coach.com), a restaurant with mid-19th-century antecedents and modern motel additions. Across the street is the **Central Texas Area Museum** (423 S. Main Street; tel: 254-947-5232; www.saladoscottishfestival.com), housed in a lovely old rock building where Sam Houston delivered an anti-secession speech from the balcony. In addition to displaying local memorabilia, it hosts the annual Scottish Clan Gathering and Highland Games in November, a three-day Celtic festival.

Texas's first chapter of the Grange,

an important organization of anti-corporate American farmers that flourished during the Progressive era, was founded at Salado in 1873. The related Farmers' Alliance, which had several million members throughout the country in its most successful days, originated at Lampasas, about 50 miles (80km) west of Fort Hood, in 1875. Together they helped elect the famous Populist James Stephen Hogg, who was governor of Texas 1891–95.

Near the I-35 access road at Salado, the antebellum **Robertson Plantation House** is unusually complete, with outbuildings, slave quarters, and a family cemetery. It was built in 1856 by E.S.C. Robertson, son of Sterling Clack Robertson, who settled 600 families in the Brazos River Basin, northwest of Stephen F. Austin's colony.

The steady character, intelligence, and diligence with which Austin won the respect of his fellow "Texans" were also displayed by E.S.C. Robertson. One of the directors of his "Nashville Company" was Sam Houston, who had already been the governor of Tennessee and later became both president of the Texas Republic and governor of the state of Texas.

The complex, ultimately unsuccessful attempt to turn the early settlers into Mexican citizens makes a long and stirring story. The patriarch Moses Austin, father of Stephen, who did not live to see the Anglo-Southerners enter the Promised Land, had wished to give his name to a great port, Austina, which would rival New Orleans. Instead, a new capital in the wilderness was named for the Father and Grandfather of Texas. The now abandoned town of **Nashville**, one of the principal settlements of Robertson's colony, was also considered for the capital. If Nashville had been made capital of Texas instead of Austin, Robertson would be better known today.

College town

Austin, home of the University of Texas (UT), is the state's best-known college town, but the campus of Texas A&M University in the metro area of **Bryan/College Station** ⑱ (pop. 172,463), northeast of Austin, is even larger – some 59,000 students are now enrolled at A&M, while UT currently enrolls 52,000.

A great rivalry exists between A&M and UT. A&M receives a third of the oil revenue from public lands (endowed before the hidden oil was discovered on them), but UT receives the remaining two-thirds. In the budget wars between the Austin campus and the state government, politicians have depicted UT to rural and poor voters as an arrogant, wasteful, privileged school. Part of this has to do with Austin being a bastion of liberal politics, of course, in contrast to the state's general conservatism.

Texans are fond of Aggies (the nickname for students at the university) – trusting, stalwart, and stupid, as portrayed in the innumerable Aggie jokes. Watching an Aggies football game on the huge **Kyle Field** – at 90,000 capacity, one of the largest stadiums in the state – is an unforgettable experience. The roar of the crowd is absolutely

FACT

The settlement of Bryan/College Station is actually two towns, not one. Bryan, founded in 1859, was joined, in 1877, by College Station, developed as a railroad stop and a new site for A&M University.

A sculpture entitled The Day the Wall Came Down outside the George Bush Presidential Library and Museum.

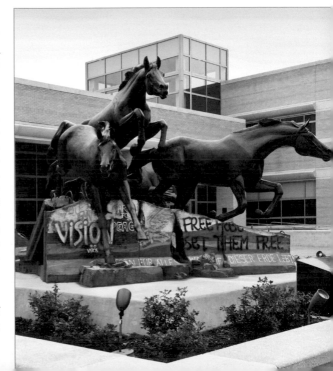

FACT

The armadillo, the State Mammal, is commonly found in rural Central Texas.

deafening. You'll be caught up in the "12th man" tradition, for sure – whereby the entire stadium remains standing for the whole game, a tradition that began in 1922, apparently, during a difficult fixture, when the fans let their team know that they were all ready to serve as the "12th man" to help them out, if need be.

Tours of the enormous A&M campus can be arranged at the **Appelt Aggieland Visitor Center** (tel: 979-845-5851; www.tamu.edu; Mon–Fri 8am–5pm) in the Rudder Tower. Among the attractions on campus are the Sanders-Metzger Gun Collection (free), displaying famous Colt pistols and the George Bush Presidential Library and Museum (1000 George Bush Drive West; tel: 979-691-4000; Mon–Sat 9.30am–5pm, Sun noon–5pm). Bush senior was an A&M student, and the museum houses a record of, and papers from, his presidency.

Independence site

A football game at Kyle Field.

Continuing its journey down to the Gulf of Mexico, the Brazos River reflects significant dates in Texas history at many points along its route. Eighty miles (128km) southeast of Waco, at **Washington-on-the-Brazos** ⑲ in 1836, Texas declared its independence from Mexico. Then the river was the lifeblood of the fledgling republic, as can be seen in the **Star of the Republic Museum** (tel: 936-878-2461; www.starmuseum. org; open daily.)

Inner Space Cavern

At Temple, you can either proceed down I-35 to Austin through **Jarrell** ⑳, an old Czech community with a stagecoach stop, or head south on State Route 95, a picturesque alternative with interesting small towns. (Note: This highway bypasses Austin, so keep an eye out for west-bound US 79 or US 290, to reach the city.)

Inner Space Cavern ㉑ (tel: 512-931-2283; www.innerspace.com; open daily), on I-35 near Georgetown, is one of Texas's most accessible caves. Its large rooms are unusual in this part of the state, and the tour takes visitors into the most beautiful of them.

These caves, the springs, and the change in topography – especially noticeable between Austin and San Antonio – are due to the geological activity that created the Balcones Fault Zone, which runs alongside I-35 from Mexico up to Oklahoma. The ground rose to the west, producing what the Spanish called *los balcones* (balconies), and the springs, around which early settlements grew, gushed up through fissures in the rock. This important geological formation divides East and West Texas.

Round Rock

In **Round Rock** ㉒, 10 miles (16km) south of Georgetown on Brushy Creek, the founding of the county is celebrated with Old Settlers Week. The eroded round rock, for which the city was named, was used to gauge the depth of the water of Bushy Creek, which was crossed by the old Chisholm Trail. Some of the buildings alongside the stage route were built as early as the 1850s.

Sam Bass, the legendary train and stagecoach robber, who claimed never to have killed a man, was ambushed by Texas Rangers in the 100 block of East Main on July 19, 1878. Businesses and condominium blocks are named after the outlaw, who became more famous after he was killed than he had ever been when alive. His grave is in the northwest corner of **Old Round Rock Cemetery** on Sam Bass Road, west of the intersection with Old Chisholm Trail. Covered with wildflowers in spring, the cemetery is easy to find and has an Anglo section, with crooked and cracked Victorian monuments, and a more colorful, smaller Mexican section, with paper and plastic flowers on the graves.

The **Palm House Museum** (208 E. Main Street; tel: 512-255-5805; Mon–Fri; free) doubles as the Round Rock Chamber of Commerce office and adjoins a pharmacy that still has the pressed-tin ceiling once common in small-town stores. Another famous Round Rock son was Vander Clyde, a renowned aerialist, who had great success in Paris in the 1920s. Clyde made his entrance in an evening dress, completely convincing as a woman, and performed to the music of Wagner and Rimsky-Korsakov.

Round Rock is also home to **Dell Diamond**, where the minor league baseball team Round Rock Express (a farm team of the Texas Rangers) plays its games.

Snake sacking

US 79 East is the road to **Taylor** ㉓, famous for its barbecue and annual snake sacking contest. Snake sacking is highly controversial. Have the rattlesnakes been stunned or their mouths sewn up with monofilament? Animal lovers demonstrate outside, while the snake handlers, usually covered with bites, say all that preparation would be too much trouble.

It's something to contemplate as you head to Austin, where the snakepit of politics keeps things lively at the state capitol while the rest of this liberal college town eases on down to the beat of a hundred different bands.

Stalactites at the Inner Space Cavern.

View of Congress Avenue and the State Capitol Building.

AUSTIN

The laid-back Texas state capital – home to the University of Texas, live music, and foodies – attracts lovers of high and low culture, and everything in between.

The Texas state capital of Austin (pop. 843,000) – now one of the nation's fastest growing and most attractive cities – has cemented its popularity by making numerous Top 10 lists in the US in recent years: coolest, best for jobs, best college town, best for doing business, fastest-growing tech center, best to retire, best for women, best for LGBT, best for live music and culture, best barbecue, best to visit… the list goes on. Suffice it to say: Austin is a very happening place these days.

Fueling a boom in downtown redevelopment; a burgeoning jobs market and skilled workforce, particularly in Austin's "Silicon Hills" high-tech sector; and growth on every front is Austin's double act as both state capital and true cultural capital. These strange bedfellows have helped cement Austin's reputation as one of America's top "creative cities," a term coined by sociologist Richard Florida to describe that unique mix of jobs, culture, services, low cost of living, affordable housing, liveability, and general exuberance that makes a city interesting to creative people. This is the home of Whole Foods, hipsters, movie stars, localism to "Keep Austin Weird," University of Texas (UT), and the acknowledged "Live Music Capital of the World" – a bastion of liberal politics and environmentalism

surrounded by a conservative state whose demographics are rapidly changing in Austin's favor. Just about everything is on the table.

Austin gained both its state capitol and UT campus in the early 1880s, but set at the edge of the ranchlands of rural Hill Country it remained a backwater for decades. It began earning its cultural chops during the 1960s, when it was a hippie mecca. It went on to spearhead the "outlaw country" movement of the 1970s, when country singers like Willie Nelson, Waylon

Main Attractions

State Capitol
Bullock Texas State History Museum
Barton Springs Pool in Zilker Park
Driskill Hotel
Lyndon B. Johnson Library and Museum
Lady Bird Johnson Wildflower Center

Tapas bar on Sixth Street.

City skyline.

Jennings, and Jerry Jeff Walker first came to prominence at places like the now-closed Armadillo World Headquarters and other legendary Austin music venues. The music scene has been bolstered for 40 years by the popular PBS television live concert series, *Austin City Limits*, originally recorded in a small studio on the UT campus and now housed in its own purpose-built theater downtown. The TV series led to an annual Austin City Limits Music Festival, and more recently, the immensely popular South By Southwest (SXSW) Festival, which draws acts from all over the world and has spawned a concurrent film and tech festival.

Yet another boom came in the 1990s, with the arrival of high tech companies attracted by a never-ending crop of highly skilled UT grads who wanted to stay put in Austin, a business-friendly environment, low taxes, and that constant – quality of life. In recent years, the film industry has also taken a shine to Austin, which has served as the location for movies by local directors like Richard Linklater

and Terrence Malick. A number of movie stars make their home here, along with various writers, artists, and other creatives who appreciate Austin's easy-going style and attractive mix of Victorian neighborhoods and modern downtown architecture.

Walking downtown

Austin spreads out on either side of Texas's Colorado River, which rises in Lubbock and flows through the state capital. It is dammed in places to form small lakes that offer kayaking, swimming, birding, and a chance to enjoy nature in several riparian nature reserves within sight of downtown. There are lots of places to walk along the river. One of the newest is the **Boardwalk Trail** next to **Lady Bird Lake**, on the southeast side of town, next to I-35. It is popular for its fabulous views of the changing downtown skyline to the north, lit up at night in a blaze of neon.

Although Austin is growing, its downtown is relatively easy to get around. It is dominated by government buildings, notably the distinctive **State Capitol Building** (12th Street and Congress Avenue; tel: 512-463-5494; www.tspb.state.tx.us; free guided tours), which, in typically Texas style, is just a few feet higher than its model in Washington, DC. The local version is made of distinctive pink granite. Its white, classical interior focuses on the great rotunda, commemorating the six governments that reigned over Texas: Spain, France, Mexico, the Confederacy, the Republic of Texas, and the United States. Above, at the apex of the dome, is the lone star that is the state's emblem: independence, self-determination, and singularity. Construction began in 1882, but the building was not completed until 1888. A thorough renovation was completed in 1997, and includes an underground extension, its roof landscaped to fit in with the historic wooded grounds.

The **State Capitol Visitors Center** is in the Old Land Office building (11th Street and San Jacinto Boulevard; tel: 512-305-8400; open daily), a distinctive castle-like building southeast of the capitol. Informative 2-hour walking tours down historic Congress Avenue and along Sixth Street leave the capitol steps at 9am on Thursday, Friday, and Saturday; also Sunday at 2pm (contact the Austin Visitor Center, 602 E. 4th Street; tel: 866-GO-AUSTIN; open daily).

Across from the capitol is the Greek Revival-style **Governor's Mansion** (1010 Colorado Street; tel: 512-463-5516; www.txfgm.org; free tours Mon–Thu). This elegant building was constructed in 1856 by Abner Cook, master builder of many of Austin's most significant 19th-century buildings.

The enjoyable **Bullock Texas State History Museum** (tel: 512-936-8746; www.thestoryoftexas.com; open daily), behind the capitol on the 357-acre (145-hectare) UT campus, is housed in an attractive modern building constructed from the same pink granite as the capitol. Its soaring

Texas-sized atrium contains three floors of well-presented audio-visual exhibits covering the state's American Indian, Spanish, and American history, as well as an IMAX theater. This is the best place in Texas to learn about its history – and there's a lot here for kids to enjoy, too.

Art lovers won't want to miss a visit to the **Blanton Museum of Art** (200 E. Martin Luther King Boulevard; tel: 512-471-5482; www.blantonmuseum.org; Tue–Fri 10am–5pm, Sat 11am–5pm, Sun noon–5pm) across the street from the Bullock Museum. The Blanton houses one of the top university art collections in the US and it is quite wide ranging, with more than 17,000 pieces, including an extensive European art collection and drawings and prints. It's likely to appeal to all tastes.

The UT campus has four excellent museums and takes up a large part of downtown Austin. It has a current enrollment of 52,000 students, somewhat less than Texas A&M, its varsity nemesis. The rivalry between the two schools is on full display during football games in UT's Darrell K. Royal

State Capitol Building.

Visitors to the Bullock Texas State History Museum are greeted by a 35ft (11-metre) -tall bronze sculpture of the Lone Star.

Crowds enjoy a brass band on Sixth Street during the South by Southwest festival.

– Texas Memorial Stadium, home to the college's Texas Longhorns team (who play in orange). Guided tours of the campus's landmark **UT Tower** and observation deck are offered daily (tel: 512-475-6633).

Sixth Street vibes

As the home of the University of Texas (UT), the city melds an air of youthful exuberance with legislative serious- ness, but it is primarily a college town with all that that implies. Only a few blocks from the capitol complex – the heart of state government – renowned **Sixth Street** (www.6street.com) reverber- ates with rock, jazz, blues, country, and reggae until the early hours.

The seven blocks between Congress and I-35, lined with historic buildings that now contain tattoo parlors, clubs, cafés, antiques stores, and art galler- ies, are a bit touristy now, but you can still catch some good music here. Festivals like South by Southwest, the Pecan Street Festival, and other annual events take place here. This is also the venue for some great food, includ- ing Tex-Mex, Cajun, and of course,

the famed "Texas Trinity" of barbecue ribs, sausage, and brisket (whose Holy Grail is **Franklin Barbecue** on 11th Street, east of I-35, voted Best Barbecue in America).

South Congress

Austin's other hip venue is **South Congress**, popularly known as SoCo. Its lively galleries, funky shops, and eclectic cafés come alive during its popular **First Thursday** (www.first thursday.com) event every month, when businesses stay open until 10pm. Many Austinites enjoy the monthly see-and-be-seen block party atmosphere during the stroll between Barton Springs Road and Elizabeth Street. The 1938 **Austin Motel** (1220 S. Congress Avenue; tel: 512-441- 1157; www.austinmotel.com) is in this area, a fun place for budget travelers who yearn for simple retro digs in the heart of the action. There's even a kidney-shaped pool.

Several award-winning Austin hotels can be found in the gentrify- ing **Warehouse District**, bordering downtown and Second Street, along with boutiques, bars, clubs, and restau- rants. The artist-founded **Mexic-Arte Museum** (419 Congress Avenue; tel: 512-480-9373; www.mexic-artemuseum. org; Mon–Thu 10am–6pm, Fri–Sat 10am–5pm, Sun noon–5pm), focus- ing on traditional and contemporary Mexican and other Latin American art and culture, is well worth a visit.

Bat heaven

Surely one of the city's most unusual tourist attractions must be the colony of more than a million Mexican free- tailed bats that congregate under **Ann W. Richards Congress Avenue Bridge** over Town Lake. At dusk, they set off in search of food. Between spring and fall, crowds gather every evening for a spectacle that can be thrilling.

The Austin–San Antonio area was called "bat heaven" by Dr Merlin Tut- tle, the founder and president of Bat

Conservation International. Most of the bats in this part of the country are Brazilian or Mexican free-tails. The largest known bat colony in the world is found in the "nursery cave," Bracken Cave near San Antonio, where experts say there are an estimated 200 baby bats per square foot.

Bats also figure in **The Thinkery E** (1830 Simond Avenue; tel: 512-469-6200; http://thinkeryaustin.org; Tue–Fri 10am–5pm, Wed until 8pm, Sat–Sun 10am–6pm), the new incarnation of the former Austin Children's Museum. It's a fun, hands-on, educational facility in a purpose-designed modern building in Mueller, Austin's important new reclamation project in the northeast-central part of the city. Learning how these mammals fly is just one of the experiences available to all the family, alongside discovering how cities work, learning about health matters, and more. The museum calls it STEAM (science, technology, engineering, art, and math) learning.

Beside Town Lake, on the south side of the bridge, is lovely **Zilker Park**, home of **Barton Springs Pool** (tel: 512-476-9044; open daily), generally regarded as the city's crown jewel. Thirty-two million gallons (121 million liters) of water a day flow from Barton Springs into this idyllic swimming hole, which was reinforced as a pool almost as long as a football field in 1930. The water temperature supposedly hovers around 68°F (20°C), but it feels much colder at first splash.

Elegant museums

Some lovely historic buildings around town have now been converted into museums, and several are worth your time. **The Contemporary Austin** (3809 W. 35th Street; tel: 512-458-8191; www.thecontemporaryaustin.org; Tue–Sat 11am–7pm; Sun noon–5pm) has two locations, one of which is in Laguna Gloria, on the shady banks of Lake Austin. It occupies the 1916 estate of Texas legend Clare Driscoll, who donated the property, and

includes the Driscoll Villa, the Betty and Edward Marcus Sculpture Park, and an art school. The downtown branch, the **Jones Center** (700 Congress Avenue; tel: 512 495 9224), is in an old drugstore building on the site of the first brick building in Austin, built in 1851, and displays a variety of contemporary artworks.

The 1855 Greek Revival–style **Neill-Cochran House F** (2310 San Gabriel Street; tel: 512-478-2335; www.nchmuseum.org; Tue–Thu 1–4pm), a few blocks west of the UT campus, is considered to be one of Austin's three most important buildings and also built by Abner Cook. It is now the Texas home of the grandly titled National Society of the Colonial Dames of America in the State of Texas and archives various historic documents as well as displaying luxurious period furnishings.

The **O. Henry Museum G** (409 E. 5th Street; tel: 512-472-1903; Wed–Sun noon–5pm; free) was the residence of short-story writer William Sydney Porter (who used "O. Henry" as a pen name) from 1893 to 1895 (he also

Bats over Congress Avenue Bridge.

lived in San Antonio). The home displays Porter's desk and writing materials, as well as some period furniture.

Historic sites

The oldest frame building in the city is the **French Legation Museum** 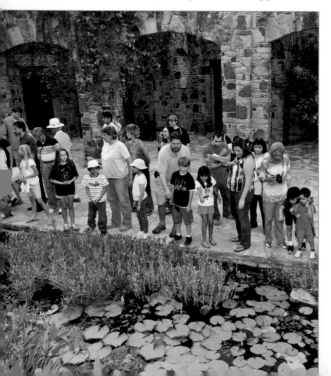 (802 San Marcos Street, east of I-35; tel: 512-472-8180; www.frenchlegation museum.org; Tue–Sun 1–5pm), a Creole-style mansion built in 1840 by Comte Alphonse Dubois de Saligny, French chargé d'affaires, who may never actually have lived in it. Saligny served under Maximilian I, the short-lived French-born emperor of Mexico who was executed in 1867, aged 35. It is a tradition in Normandy, where Saligny bought a château after making himself rich in America, for villagers to "dance on the old count's grave."

In the Maximilian Room of Austin's **Driskill Hotel** ❶ (604 Brazos Street; tel: 800-252-9367; www.driskillhotel. com), you can see mirrors ordered by the tragic Maximilian for his mad Empress Carlotta. The Driskill, whose second owner is said to have won it in a poker game and swapped it five

years later for a California vineyard, is a dramatic building that has stood at the western corner of the historic Sixth Street block since 1886, among other Victorian buildings now doing time as trendy bars and restaurants.

Farther north is the **Elisabet Ney Museum** (304 E. 44th Street; tel: 512-472-8180; Wed–Sat noon–5pm; free), the former home of German sculptor Elisabet Ney, who immigrated to the state in 1870, and whose marble busts and statues grace many European palaces. Three of her statues are in the State Capitol. Her best-known sculpture is considered to be Lady Macbeth; the original is in the Smithsonian in Washington, DC, but you can see a copy here in her studio, along with many other items from her collection. This is one of Austin's oldest museums.

The Elisabet Ney Museum is close to Austin's increasingly busy **Austin-Bergstrom International Airport** (3600 Presidential Boulevard; tel: 512-530-2242; www.ci.austin.tx.us/austinair port), which is currently undergoing expansion to serve the 10 million passengers who pass through it each year.

The wetland pond at the Lady Bird Johnson Wildflower Center.

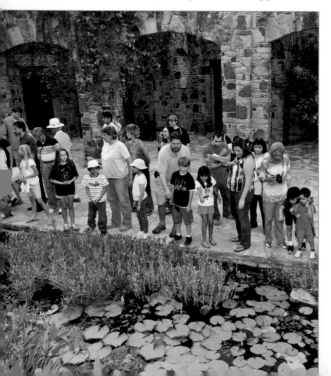

Texan President

The most famous Texas-born US President is memorialized in the grand **Lyndon B. Johnson Library and Museum ❶** (2313 Red River Street; tel: 512-721-0200; open daily; free) on the UT campus. The building was renovated recently to include more audiovisual displays (but thankfully, still has the famous animatronic LBJ greeting visitors with stories, a la Disney's Lincoln).

During his presidency (1963–69), Johnson was the recipient of hundreds of gifts from foreign heads of state, and most of them seem to be here, along with his 1968 Lincoln limousine. There is also an interesting gift shop with authentic political memorabilia. Humanizing his life from boyhood onwards, the exhibitions include a 20-minute multimedia show, as well as a one-hour film about Lady Bird Johnson, who is sometimes regarded with more affection than America's controversial 36th president.

For years, Lady Bird devoted herself to getting the **Lady Bird Johnson Wildflower Center** (4801 La Crosse Avenue; tel: 512-292-4100; www.wildflower.org; Tue–Sat 9am–5pm, Sun noon–5pm), established on 60 acres (24 hectares) along Texas's Colorado River. About 8 miles (13km) southwest of Austin, it is a fine place for picnics among the flowers and a must-see for gardeners. It has a visitor center, a library, and "Ralph, the talking lawnmower." The focus of the center is to conserve Texas's native plants and promote sustainable native landscaping.

Day trips from Austin

Among the best places to see wildflowers, especially Texas bluebonnets, the state flower, blooming in the spring, is in the rolling Hill Country, which begins just west of Austin. LBJ grew up in these lovely ranchlands and taught school there. His ranch and boyhood home is still a popular destination, and a lake is named for him (see page 149).

To the east and southeast of Austin the land is flat and fertile. In **La Grange**, where the "Best Little Whorehouse in Texas" once stood, you'll find the **Texas Quilt Museum** (140 W. Colorado Street; tel: 979-968-3104; www.quiltmuseum.org; Thu–Sat 10am–4pm, Sun noon–4pm), housed in an old mercantile building. The museum grew out of the popular International Quilt Festival in Houston as a permanent venue to display quilts from all over the world, both contemporary and traditional. It has won several awards for the restoration of its building and for its exhibits, and is a must for quilters.

Not far away, **Shiner**, founded by German-Czech farmers in 1909, is home to **Spoetzl Brewery** (603 E. Brewery Street; tel: 361-594-3852; www.shiner.com; gift shop Mon–Fri 9am–5pm, Sat 11am–3pm; tours June–Aug Mon–Fri 10am–2.30pm, Sept–May Mon–Fri 11am–1.30pm; tours and tastings are free), where Texas's famous Shiner Bock beers are brewed.

FACT

The Lyndon B. Johnson Library and Museum contains a replica of the Oval Office in the White House, as it looked when LBJ was president in the 1960s.

The Driskill Hotel.

*A colorful display of Texas
bluebonnets and Indian paintbrush.*

HILL COUNTRY

The Hill Country is a Texas treasure, offering natural beauty, abundant wildlife, an intriguing slice of German culture, and some of the friendliest towns in the state.

One of the most scenic towns in the Hill Country of Central Texas, a gentle area of sheep and cattle raising, is **Bandera ❶** (the name is Spanish for "flag"), which describes itself as "the cowboy capital of the world." Bordered on three sides by the cypress-lined Medina River its origins date to 1854, when a lumber mill was established. However, in the 1870s, it became a staging area for cattle drives through Bandera Pass, where, in the 1840s, the Texas Rangers beat off a Comanche ambush.

Bandera (pop. 857) is reputed to have once had a school operated by John Wilkes Booth under the name William J. Ryan. The old jail, one block north of the County Courthouse, is now the **Frontier Times Museum** (510 13th Street; tel: 830-796-3864; www.frontiertimesmuseum.org; Mon–Sat 10am–4.30pm), which has 30,000 pieces from early Texas cultures and items of technology from the 19th and 20th centuries. Exhibits include a totem pole, a wooden idol from Easter Island, and a 400-year-old pair of stirrups that once belonged to a conquistador. Bandera's Main Street also has two renowned honky-tonk dancehalls. Between May and Labor Day, there are rodeos twice a week, and in front of the Bandera Courthouse stands a bronze monument honoring the many national rodeo champions who lived in the town.

Down on the ranch.

Pretend cowboys

Before the close of the 19th century, Bandera was already a popular vacation area for families from Houston. They would be entertained by hard-riding ranch hands from nearby spreads who would ride in on weekends to show off, and gradually the concept of the "dude," or vacation cowboy, developed.

Today the Bandera area has dozens of dude ranches, with names like Silver Spur (tel: 830-796-3037; www.silverspur-ranch.com); the Dixie (tel: 830-796-7771; www.dixieduderanch.com); Twin Elm

Main Attractions

Enchanted Rock State Natural Area
Fredericksburg
Luckenbach
Lyndon B. Johnson National Historical Park
Gruene Hall

Guest Ranch (tel: 830-796-3628; www. twinelmranch.com); the Flying L (tel: 830-292-5134; www.flyl.com); the West 1077 (tel: 830-796-5675; www.west1077.com); and, on the Medina River, the Mayan (tel: 830-460-3036; www.mayanranch. com), nearly all offering comfortable accommodations, swimming pools, Western cuisine, cowboy-themed entertainment and horseback-riding lessons. Some offer additional attractions such as golf and fishing.

Also of interest is a tour of the **LH7 Ranch** (tel: 830-796-4314; www.lh7 ranch.com), a 1,200-acre (485-hectare) ranch bought in 1982 by Maudeen Marks, whose family is dedicated to preserving the Texas longhorn. At **Mountain Home ②**, near Kerrville, the **Y.O. Ranch** (tel: 877-967-3767; www.yoranchhotel.com) welcomes wildlife lovers, who can expect to see white-tail deer, antelope, and a majestic longhorn or two.

At **Kerrville ③** itself, music plays a big part in everyday life, with a folk festival in the spring, a wine and music festival over the Labor Day weekend, and a traditional folk music festival in the fall

(tel: 877-827-5017; www.kerrvillemusicfest. com). The town's **Museum of Western Art** (1550 Bandera Highway; tel: 830-896-2553; www.museumofwesternart.com) is a treasure house of Western art, most of it executed by artists who have ridden the range, while the **Hill Country Museum** (226 Earl Garrett Street; tel: 830-896-8633; www.txhillcountrytrail.com; Wed–Sat 11.30am–3pm; free), operated by the Hill Country Preservation Society in the restored 1878 Shreiner Mansion, portrays the affluent life of the region's early days. In downtown Kerrville is Old Republic Square, with brick sidewalks, old stone walls, fountains, and cedar-finished buildings shaded by pecan trees.

Wildlife

Near the Guadalupe River, at the Town Creek junction, is the **Riverside Nature Center** (150 Francisco Lemos Street; tel: 830-257-4837; www.riverside naturecenter.org; Mon–Fri 9am–4pm, Sat 10am–3pm, Sun 1–4pm; free), incorporating a wildflower meadow and butterfly garden surrounding a turn-of-the-20th-century house, which has exhibits and displays. It has an arboretum with over 140 species of tree.

The Texas Hill Country is a bird-watcher's paradise, home to such rare species as the golden-cheek warbler, the green kingfisher, and the zone tail hawk. Near Kerrville, at **Ingram**, is the Exotic Wildlife Association (tel: 830-367-7761; www.myewa.org), which has helped introduce to the region such animals as the llama, the greater kudu, the Siberian ibex, the sable antelope, the ostrich, the zebra, and many varieties of deer. Completely out of context, on Farm Road 1340 in **Hunt**, near Ingram, is an inexact but intriguing replica of Stonehenge.

Apple capital

Highway 16 winds for 30 miles (48km) between Kerrville and Medina. This is one of the most scenic roads in the Hill Country, with ancient live oaks and white-flowering yucca plants decorating the roadsides and hairpin bends, while green grasses cling to limestone outcrops. Tiny **Medina** ❹ is known as "the apple capital of Texas," and the Texas International Apple Festival is held here annually, on the last Saturday of July, with displays by bagpipers, balloon blowers, and apple bobbers. You can pick your own apples at **Love Creek Orchards**, on a former ranch that has been given over to apple growing since the 1980s. The big draw here is the Patio Café, located inside a large barn, which is famous for its hamburgers and superb apple desserts, including a killer apple pie. In 2000, the owners donated a large portion of the original ranch to the Texas Nature Conservancy.

The Medina River is a great place to enjoy a peaceful kayak trip. It is shaded by cypress trees, which were harvested from 1853 in a mill staffed by early Polish immigrants. Local wildlife includes deer, antelope, boar, and wild turkey. Medina Lake is a good fishing spot and also the scene every September of the Cajun Festival (held at Lakehills Civic Center in Lakehills), home of the Great Gumbo Cookoff. Cajun music and history are also celebrated.

Camel country

Camp Verde ❺, 60 miles (96km) northwest of San Antonio, is where

Trail ride near Bandera.

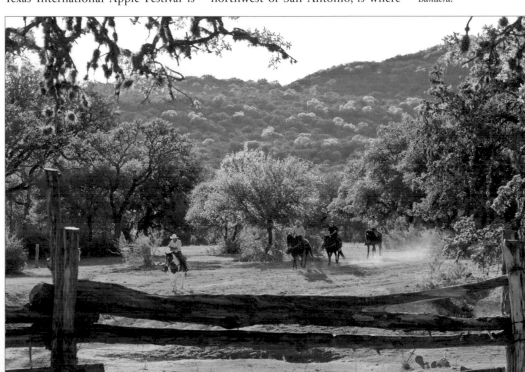

TIP

For a flavor of old Hill
Country, check out the
online Enchanted Rock
Archives (www.texfiles.
com/erarchives), which
reprints the histories of
people – settlers,
adventurers, and outlaws
– who lived in the area
in times past.

Jefferson Davis conceived the idea of training a US Camel Corps to operate in rough desert terrain during the US War with Mexico. Initially, 33 camels were imported, along with experienced handlers from North Africa and, although the sight and scent of the unfamiliar beasts frightened horses and mules, they proved capable of transporting loads up to 500 lbs (227kg) without any trouble. The project ultimately failed, however, and, after the Civil War, the camels were sold to individuals and zoos, although a handful continued to roam the hills for many years.

Enchanted Rock

South of Llano and north of Fredericksburg is **Enchanted Rock State Natural Area** ❻ (tel: 830-685-3636; www.tpwd.state.tx.us), a popular state park centered around a huge pink granite dome rising 425ft (131 meters) above the ground. Tonkawa Indians believed ghost fires flickered at the top and heard weird creakings and groanings, which geologists explain as the noise of the hot rock contracting in the cool of the night. It's a good, stiff vertical hike to the top.

One of Hill Country's most popular destinations is **Fredericksburg** ❼, founded in 1846 by German settlers. The town retains many traces of its ancestry in its architecture and in the German dialect heard on the streets, as well as place names. Main Street, for example, is called "Hauptstrasse" and is lined with pseudo-Teutonic beer gardens, restaurants, and bakeries that offer a wide variety of cuisines. The town is a magnet for shoppers because of its antiques, gifts, ethnic foods, and local wines.

Wineries abound in Hill Country (there were 30 at last count) and wines can be sampled along the highway into town, at numerous German-named farms, such as "Der Peach Garten," which sell wines and liqueurs. If you're passing between June and August, you'll get chance to pick your own peaches in local orchards – a delicious way to while away a summer's day.

Large-scale German immigration continued right up until the Civil War. One notable characteristic is *Fachwerk*

*Shops in
Fredericksburg.*

– a traditional German building technique consisting of heavy framing and diagonal bracing, with an infill of limestone. Early Germanic homes can be explored at the **Pioneer Museum Complex** (325 W. Main Street; tel: 830-990-8441; www.pioneermuseum.net; Mon–Sat 10am–5pm).

Gish's Old West Museum (502 N. Milam Street; tel: 830-997-2794; appointments only) is filled with the saddles, lawmen's badges, guns, and other relics that make up the personal collection of Joe Gish, who will be happy to show them to you.

The **National Museum of the Pacific War** (340 E. Main Street; tel: 830-997-8600; www.pacificwarmuseum.org; open daily), which includes the Admiral Nimitz Museum, is named for the naval officer born in the town and attracts the many visitors with an interest in World War II. Part of it is housed in a "ship-shape" old hostelry and includes a Garden of Peace, donated by the people of Japan.

Nearby **Comfort** ❽, another town settled by German immigrants, has, in addition to numerous century-old stores in the business district, a distinctive 1892 German church.

Tiny **Luckenbach** ❾ (tel: 830-997-3224; www.luckenbachtexas.com; open daily), southeast of Fredericksburg, is a world-famous ghost town. On the banks of South Grape Creek – and easy to miss, so keep your eyes peeled as you wander down this backroad – it was never much more than a store, a post office, and a saloon. But it was bought in its entirety by humorist Hondo Crouch in 1970, and made famous by a No. 1 country-and-western hit, recorded in 1976 by Waylon Jennings and Willie Nelson, that featured the refrain "Let's go to Luckenbach, Texas." After that, people began making pilgrimages here for impromptu Sunday music gatherings, which still take place (often attended by Nelson and other major country-and-western stars). The old bar is a classic spot to stop and listen in on a jam session and buy yourself a famous Frito Pie in the general store.

LBJ Town

Johnson City ❿, at the intersection of US 290 and US 281, stages the

The house of Felix van der Stucken (1823–1912), a Belgian immigrant who ran a steam-powered flour mill in Fredericksburg.

Having a drink at the Luckenbach General Store.

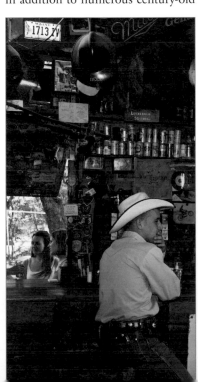

TEXAS BARBECUE TRAIL

No trip to the Hill Country would be complete without a pilgrimage to sample Central Texas's famous "Texan Trinity" – barbecued beef brisket, sausage, and ribs, dry rubbed and slow smoked until the meat is falling off the bone. The Texas Barbecue Trail (www.texasbbqtrails.com), from Taylor through Elgin to Lockhart and ending in Luling, takes in 12 different barbecue joints that are famous for their barbecue and can be driven in about two hours. Many are family-run places, which have been around for years. You'd better come hungry and pace yourself, though, because this is some serious 'cue – and it's served up in mountainous portions. If you're on a budget, never fear. Prices in beef country are rock bottom and you'll be spoiled for choice.

To sample some of the best barbecue in one location make a beeline for the town of Lockhart, proclaimed by the State of Texas as "the Barbecue Capital of Texas." The barnlike Kreuz Market (619 N. Colorado Street; tel: 512-398-2361; www.kreuzmarket.com; daily 10am–8pm) is one of the best known and oldest (since 1900) of the barbecue joints. You can choose from barbecued brisket, sausage, beef shoulder, ribs, or pork chops. All are sold by the pound from the pits and wrapped in paper for carry out, and can be shipped to anywhere in the US.

TIP

Drive carefully when looking for Luckenbach. The little place is not easy to find. After the popularity of the song *Luckenbach, Texas*, so many road signs were stolen that the Texas Highway Department stopped erecting them.

Great Turkey Escape Festival at the end of October each year, when a hundred turkeys are driven through town, mimicking the turkey drives of the early 20th century. The town was named for the ancestors of 1960s President Lyndon B. Johnson, who was raised here. Free tours of his restored **Boyhood Home** are given every half hour. The home is part of **Lyndon B. Johnson National Historical Park** (tel: 830-868-7128; www.nps.gov/lyjo; open daily; free) near Stonewall, between Fredericksburg and Johnson City, which displays buffalo, longhorns, and white-tail deer in enclosures and a restored 1908 house on the site of a working farm. From the park, tours can be taken of the LBJ Ranch.

Another of the Hill Country's little towns that retains some of the quiet style of a bygone era is **Blanco ⑪**. Beside the river of the same name, it promotes its friendly atmosphere and, from Thanksgiving to New Year stages a "Christmas Homecoming" around an immense oak tree on the Courthouse Square.

Lyndon B. Johnson's Boyhood Home.

Untouched by civilization

What was once a 5,400-acre (2,180-hectare) ranch was donated to Texas Parks and Wildlife in 1976, with the stipulation that it "be kept far removed and untouched by modern civilization, where everything is preserved intact, yet put to a useful purpose." Today it is **Hill Country State Natural Area** (tel: 830-796-4413; www.tpwd.state.tx.us/state-parks/hill-country; open daily), 45 miles (72km) northwest of San Antonio, a region of rocky limestone hills, flowing springs, oak groves, grasslands, and canyons.

Five miles (8km) north of Vanderpool, off State Route 187, is **Lost Maples State Natural Area** (tel: 830-966-3413; www.tpwd.state.tx.us/state-parks/lost-maples; open daily), spectacularly colorful in November, but an attractive and very popular park year round. It offers camping and picnicking among rugged limestone canyons and bubbling springs.

Going underground

Over the centuries underground streams have carved out spectacular caverns all through this region. Among the

TEXAS WILDFLOWERS

The spring wildflowers that dot Central Texas hillsides starting in March and continuing to June each year inspire locals and visitors alike to take to the backroads and admire the Hill Country's Impressionistic displays of primary hues. Indian paintbrush, greenthread, Indian blanket, coreopsis, winecup, black-eyed susans, and sunflowers bloom in waves throughout the season – hardy natives well suited to the limestone soil and warm exposures. None is as eagerly awaited as Texas bluebonnets, the state flower, which carpet the swales in early April, particularly plentiful around Burnet. For more information on what is blooming during your visit, contact the state wildflower hotline (tel: 800-452-9292) or Texas Parks and Wildlife (tel: 800-452-9292). Each has travel counselers available 9am–6pm.

best-known are the **Caverns of Sonora** 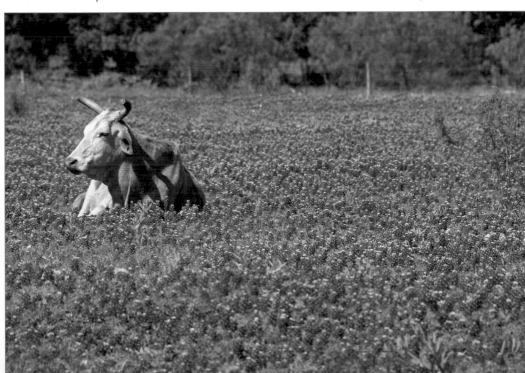 (tel: 325-387-3105; www.cavernsofsonora.com; daily 8am–6pm), at exit 392 of I-10, 8 miles (13km) south of the town of that name. With 8 miles (13km) of passages lined with crystalline stalactites and stalagmites, it is one of Texas's longest caves. The temperature inside the cave is a steady 78°F (25°C) but with high humidity it feels about 86°F (29°C); sweaters are not needed. There is also a picnic area and a campground.

Beginning in **Sonora** ⑬, between 1910 and 1921, a 250ft (76-meter) wide, fenced track called Tillman's Lane ran 100 miles (160km) northeast to Brady. Thousands of cattle were driven to the railroad on this track, which was equipped with holding pens, wells, and windmills.

Natural Bridge Caverns ⑭ (I-35 exit 175; tel: 210-651-6101; www.naturalbridgecaverns.com; daily 9am–6pm, tour days and times vary) offers exotic sights carved over thousands of years out of the area's natural limestone. The tourist brochure describes the colors as resembling "35 flavors of ice cream," with rocks "nearly as translucent as china and rooms nearly as large as football fields." Nearby is **Natural Bridge Wildlife Ranch** (tel: 830-438-7400; www.wildliferanchtexas.com; open daily), a game ranch that is home to zebras, wallabies, camels, baboons, and parrots, among other exotics. Similar to Natural Bridge Caverns are the **Cascade Caverns** ⑮ (on I-10 south of Boerne; tel: 830-755-8080; www.cascadecaverns.com; Mon–Fri 9am–4pm, Sat–Sun 9am–5pm), which include an interior, 100ft (30-meter) waterfall.

One of the oldest commercial caves in Texas is Longhorn Cavern in **Longhorn Cavern State Park** ⑯ (211 Park Road 4, S. Burnet; tel: 877-441-CAVE; www.longhorncaverns.com; open daily), 6 miles (9.6km) outside Burnet. This has seen a number of uses in the past 100 years but was opened as a tourist cave in 1938 by the Civilian Conservation Corporation. Camping is available in nearby Inks Lake State Park (tel: 512-793-2223; www.tpwd.state.tx.us).

Oldest dance hall

In the mid-19th century, several thousand German settlers formed the

A cow rests in a field of Texan bluebonnets.

Watchdog rock formation in Longhorn Cavern.

Independence Day Parade, Wimberley.

farming communities of **Gruene, Boerne**, and **New Braunfels** just northwest of San Antonio, and the German heritage survives here in the form of *fachwerk* houses replete with gingerbread trimmings. Gruene is the most interesting historically and is home to the oldest dancehall in Texas, **Gruene Hall** (1878), where dances are still held.

San Marcos is known for its outlet malls, but it is also home to Southwest Texas State University. The campus is worth a stop to view the large **Witliff Collections** (tel: 512-245-2313; www.thewitliffcollections.tx; Mon–Fri 8am–5pm, Sat 11am–5pm, Sun 2–6pm; free) on the seventh floor of the Alkek Library. The collection is the photography archive of screenwriter and photographer Bill Witliff and includes many images from the TV series *Lonesome Dove*.

Not far from San Marcos, on a side road, is **Wimberley**, an out-of-the-way small town filled with artists. It's a popular weekend day trip for Austinites who come to brows the cute shops and galleries, stay in a quaint B&B, and sample a slice of Wimberley's famous homemade fruit pies and olive oil from one of the few commercial olive groves in the state. The first Saturday of each month, from April to November, is Wimberley Market Days (www.shopmarketdays.com), when local shops, artisans, and galleries set up hundreds of booths on Lion's Field; entertainments include live music and food.

Flying visit

For travelers seeking only a taste of Hill Country, a steam excursion train runs from Cedar Park City Hall, near US 183 and FM 1431, about 15 miles (24km) northwest of Austin. The journey takes travelers through the Hill Country to **Burnet** ⓱, on US 281, once a frontier town from whose quarries marble for the state capitol in Austin was mined. Running on weekends only, the 80-year-old Hill Country Flyer (tel: 512-477-8468; www.austinstreamtrain.org) takes just over two hours each way, traveling through beautiful countryside and allowing a short stopover for shopping, museum browsing, and refreshment.

Texas Wineries

Texas may be dry in places – in every sense of the word – but a flood of wineries in the Hill Country attract millions of visitors.

Many are unaware that Texas is one of the oldest wine-growing regions in the US – older even than California – but wine making began here with the Spanish missions in El Paso in West Texas in the 1650s. Today, the state has eight American Viticultural Areas (AVAs): Mesilla Valley, Texas Davis Mountains, and Escondido Valley, in West Texas; Texas High Plains and Texoma in North Texas; and Bell Mountain, Fredericksburg in the Hill Country, and Texas Hill Country, in Central Texas. Not bad for a state where Prohibition-era dry laws are still on the books in 264 counties.

In all, Texas has 200 wineries producing over 3 million gallons of wine a year, making the Lone Star state fourth in the US for wine production, behind California, New York, and Washington. West Texas is still the number one growing region when it comes to acres in cultivation, courtesy of the University of Texas System, which has 1,000 acres of vines in Fort Stockton. But the majority of wineries can be found in Texas's rolling Hill Country, west of Austin, with 42 wineries clustered in the fruit-growing areas around Fredericksburg, where the limestone hills and warm climate favor Chardonnay and Cabernet Sauvignon grapes. The area attracts more than 5 million wine enthusiasts a year.

Hill Country wine tours

Most wineries welcome visitors and offer tours and tastings. Pick up a copy of the Texas Wine Trail brochure and map (www.texaswinetrail.com) for details and opening times. Many wineries offer special events throughout the year. The long-running Fredericksburg's Food and Wine Fest takes place in late October in downtown Fredericksburg's Marktplatz. Make reservations well in advance for festival tickets and to be sure of a hotel room.

If you'd rather not drive (a wise option, as alcohol and narrow, winding roads do not mix well), you could take a wine tour with one of the specialist companies in Fredericksburg, such as Fredericksburg Limo and Wine Tours (tel: 830-997-8687; www.texas-wine-tours.com) or Hill Country Bike and Wine (tel: 512-887-2154; www.hillcountrybw.com), which offers bicycle tours of three wineries, with lunch overlooking LBJ National Historical Park.

Award-winning wineries

Wineries are coming online regularly in this area, but some to check out are:

Spicewood Vineyards (1418 Burnet CR 409, Spicewood; tel: 830-693-5328; www.spicewoodvineyards.com; Wed–Sat 10am–6pm, Sun noon–5pm, Mon–Tue by appointment). Nine award-winning wines, including a rich 2011 Tempranillo that was a 2013 *Texas Monthly* winner.

Becker Vineyards (Jenscheke Lane; tel: 830-644-2681; www.beckervineyards.com; Mon–Thu 10am–4pm, Fri, Sat 10am–6pm, Sun noon–4pm) Award-winning wines and a lovely stone barn tasting room. The largest wine cellar in the state.

Fall Creek Vineyards (1820 CR 222, near Llano; tel: 915-379-5361; www.fcv.com; Mon–Fri 11am–4pm, Sat 10am–5pm, Sun noon–4pm). On the shores of Lake Buchanan, and known for German Rieslings and Chenin Blanc.

Dry Comal Creek Winery and Vineyard (1741 Herbelin Road, New Braunfels; tel: 830-885-4076; www.drycomalcreek.com; daily noon–5pm). An up-and-coming small winery in a unique setting.

Not to be missed – a wine tasting at a Texan vineyard.

San Antonio's River Walk.

SAN ANTONIO

A cultural crossroads, San Antonio is where the United States and Mexico merge, with a splash of German tradition thrown in for good measure.

San Antonio (pop. 1.4 million), now sprawling over 465 sq miles (1,205 sq km) is the seventh-largest city in the US and one of its fastest growing. It is overwhelmingly Hispanic – with a Latino population that is now the largest of any city in the United States. It is often called Mexico's northernmost city, and the National Autonomous University of Mexico, the oldest institution of higher learning in this hemisphere, has maintained a campus here since 1972.

San Antonio borders both the South Texas Plains – the high desert flatlands sweeping down to Mexico on the other side of the Rio Grande – and the pretty ranchlands of Hill Country, and is the principal city of both regions. Its location close to Mexico has historically placed it on the frontlines of Spanish, Mexican, early Texan, and American ambitions and military might. Today, these historic links remain an integral part of this city's allure, and interest both historians and cultural tourists alike.

There is plenty to do within the attractive and relatively compact historic downtown – from the enchanting River Walk, diverse museums, and colorful Mexican *mercado*-style markets to the photogenic historic Spanish missions strung along the river. The latter include, of course, the

Alamo, the ruins of a small, fortified former mission that looms large in the minds of every Texan – and all who still "remember the Alamo."

A downtown for tourists

Today, much of the early drama that made San Antonio such a prize for newcomers – including its reputation for being a rowdy, multicultural town whose colorful residents liked to shoot up the place – is lost to the mists of time. Ironically, what attracts Texans and tourists alike today is San

Main Attractions
The River Walk
The Alamo
Spanish Governor's Palace
San Fernando Cathedral
Brackenridge Park
San Antonio Missions
    National Historical Park

The Alamo.

A statue of Saint Anthony on the River Walk.

Antonio's relaxed *mañana* attitude and celebratory approach to life.

The city's main attraction is its delightful **River Walk Ⓐ**, where, 20ft (6 meters) below street level, a romantic sidewalk-lined river that has been channeled and landscaped for 2.5 miles (4km) through the heart of downtown, is bordered by shops, restaurants, hotels, bars, and museums. During busy seasons, the sidewalks can become crowded with tourists, but the River Walk, or Paseo Del Rio, is still well worth the trouble. Watch flat-bottomed *chalupa* boats drift by, or board one of **the Rio San Antonio Cruises** (tel: 210-244-5700; www. riosanantonio.com; daily tours) for a 45-minute round-trip boat ride. Tickets are available at the Rivercenter Mall. Private dinner cruises can also be arranged. The River Walk is particularly enchanting at night, when it is all lit up.

Central area

The main river, which runs roughly north to south, makes an almost circular loop between College and Villita streets, with the vast majority of the city's attractions located within those perimeters.

The most convenient starting point for tours of the city is at the **Alamo Ⓑ** (www.thealamo.org; open daily; free), originally known as the Mission San Antonio de Valero. Named after the viceroy at the time, it was built as the first of five missions in 1718, during the Spanish Colonial era, but its worldwide fame was established during 13 days in 1836, when the Alamo was besieged by 5,000 Mexican troops.

Early in the 19th century it had served as a presidio (garrison) for a cavalry unit from Alamo de Parras – hence the name. But, by the time General Santa Anna seized the Mexican presidency, the Anglo settlers in San Antonio (the Texians) were claiming the city for their own. It was in the Alamo that they chose to make a stand when Santa Anna came to reclaim the garrison.

A few volunteers

On February 24, 1836, barricading himself with his small force within the Alamo's thick stone walls, the commander of the Texians, General Travis, sent out a desperate appeal for reinforcements in a stirring letter. Thirty-two Texans from Gonzales, the Lexington of Texas where the first shot of the Texas Revolution was fired, joined Travis. They were supported in their defense by some notable Tennesseeans. These included Colonel James Bowie, who had disobeyed General Sam Houston's order to destroy the fortress, and the now famous Davy Crockett. However, early on the morning of March 6, Santa Anna's men attacked the Alamo, overran the fortress, and killed all 189 of its defenders.

It turned out to be a Pyhrric victory. Forty-six days later, the cry "Remember the Alamo" served as the inspiration for the Texans who surrounded and decisively beat Santa Anna's men at San Jacinto on April 21. (The date is still celebrated by the city of San Antonio with an annual fiesta.) Thus, the Republic of Texas was born, and San Antonio came to be known as the "cradle of Texas liberty."

Preserved forever

In 1883, the State of Texas bought the familiar chapel with its bullet-riddled walls, but the *convento*, the surrounding area where the beautiful Alamo Gardens are planted, belonged to a liquor dealer who was said to be planning to build a hotel.

Two "Saviors of the Alamo," as they have come to be called, stepped forward: Sam Johnson, the father of President Johnson and a state senator in 1905, arranged the purchase of the Alamo convent, and Clara Driscoll – owner of Laguna Gloria, the lakeside mansion in Austin that is now part of The Contemporary Austin art gallery – advanced $75,000 to complete the purchase (the state repaid the loan two years later). From the beginning, the Daughters of the Republic of Texas, who trace their ancestry to the original citizens of the republic, have been involved in lobbying for preservation, then entrusted with managing the Alamo; they remain the day-to-day managers of the shrine, under the auspices of the Texas General Land Office (GLO).

Traditional Mexican paper-cut decorations adorning San Antonio's Market Square.

Musician Phil Collins announces the donation of his private collection of Alamo artifacts to the State of Texas.

VICTORY OR DEATH

In 2013, the Alamo saw the return of a Texas treasure. Through a joint project of the Texas General Land Office, The Alamo, and the Texas State Library and Archives Commission, the original "Victory or Death" letter penned by William B. Travis in 1836 was returned for the 177th anniversary of the siege and battle. Over 24,000 people attended the exhibit. The text of the letter is as follows:

"To the People of Texas and All Americans in the World – Fellow Citizens and Compatriots: I am besieged with a thousand or more of the Mexicans under Santa Anna. I have sustained a continual Bombardment and cannonade for 24 hours and have not lost a man. The enemy has demanded surrender at discretion, otherwise, the garrison is to be put to the sword, if the fort is taken. I have answered the demand with a cannon shot, and our flag still waves proudly from the walls. I shall never surrender or retreat. Then, I call upon you in the name of Liberty, of Patriotism, and everything dear to the American character, to come to our aid with all dispatch. The enemy is receiving reinforcements daily and will no doubt increase to three or four thousand in four or five days. If this call is neglected, I am determined to sustain myself as long as possible and die like a soldier who never forgets what is due his honor and that of his country. VICTORY or DEATH." – William Barret Travis Lt. Col. Comdt.

FACT

Some historians
complain about the
presentation of the
Alamo site today, that too
much emphasis is placed
on the famous battle, and
not enough on the
founding of the mission
itself – effectively the
founding of the city of
San Antonio.

A plaque on the front door of the graffiti-etched **Alamo Shrine**, originally the Chapel, requests "Be quiet friend, here heroes died to blaze a trail for other men." Most visitors focus on taking photos of the famous exterior of the shrine (which is surprising small and underwhelming in real life, almost like a stage set), then head to the lovely garden, shaded by everything from myrtles to a mescal bean tree, then the all-important souvenir shop.

The display cases in the museum at the Alamo hold surprisingly few artifacts – most have spread far and wide and ended up in private collections. So it's heartening to learn that the famous letter penned by Col. Travis pleading for reinforcements prior to the Alamo seige returned to the Alamo in 2013.

Even more significant, in 2014, musician Phil Collins – a knowledgeable Alamo fan and collector – donated his priceless collection of Alamo artifacts to the state for posterity. It includes hundreds of documents, ranging from a letter Stephen F. Austin wrote from a Mexican prison in January 1834 and Sam Houston's original 1835 land grant for property in East Texas to the signed receipt for 30 beeves that William Travis brought into the Alamo on the day the siege began. Other artifacts include uniforms and Brown Bess muskets that belonged to Mexican soldiers, a sword belt believed to have been worn by Travis when he died atop the northern wall, and a shot pouch that Crockett is thought to have given a Mexican soldier just before he was executed.

These donations significantly help the GLO in its aim of bolstering the Alamo's holdings, improving its status, and better portraying the story of the national historic landmark. A longer-range dream is to expand the Alamo, back to its original size. On **Alamo Plaza**, in front of the Alamo, you will find the Alamo Visitors Center (tel: 210-247-0238; www.thealamo.org; open daily), offering advice and discount coupons for San Antonio attractions. A Texas Trolley tour (tel: 210-224-2288) provides an excellent history

Mi Tierra Café and Panadería.

of the city in the shortest amount of time. For $50, a horse-drawn carriage from the Yellow Rose Carriage Company (tel: 210-354-5077) can give you a 30-minute tour. Carriage stands are on either side of the Alamo.

A walking tour

To get away from the crowds, at least for a while, begin your stroll on the quieter stretch of the River Walk – at 4th Street, for example, behind the Municipal Auditorium. The first major landmark on this route is at Travis Street, where the Art Deco **Milam Building** ⦿ has been a landmark since the 1920s, when it housed the offices of early oil companies.

The next bridge – there are 35 within the city limits – is at Houston Street. From here, you can take a trolley to visit colorful **Market Square** ⦿ (514 W. Commerce Street), a few blocks to the west. A network of VIA streetcars continuously circles the most popular attractions and runs until late evening for around 25 cents per ride. There's music in Market Square, as well as many souvenir shops, myriad restaurants, weekend celebrations, and full-scale festivals in summer and fall.

The huge **Mi Tierra Café and Panadería** (800 Dolorosa #24; tel: 210-225-3955; www.mitierracafe.com; open 24 hours) has been a landmark here since 1941, and is also where the mariachi bands gather. They will be happy to perform their music tableside for a gratuity.

Historic homes

Walking back to the river along Dolorosa Street, you'll pass the square, stuccoed limestone **Casa Navarro State Historic Site and Museum** ⦿ (228 S. Laredo Street; tel: 210-226-4801; www.visitcasanavarro.com; Tue–Sat 10am–5pm, Sun noon–5pm), which preserves the home of José Antonio Navarro, one of two Texans who signed the Texas Declaration of Independence. Also here is the beautifully restored **Spanish Governor's Palace** ⦿ (105 Plaza de Armas; tel: 210-224-0601; www.spanishgovernorspalace.com; Tue–Sat 9am–5pm, Sun 10am–5pm). The name is a misnomer, as

Trolley on Houston Street.

no governor ever lived here; instead, the building was occupied by the captains of the Presidio de San Antonio de Bexar, between 1722 and the early 19th century. This is all that remains of the presidio.

Overlooking Main Plaza is the limestone Gothic Revival **San Fernando Cathedral** Ⓖ (tel: 210-227-1297; open daily), North America's oldest sanctuary, founded in 1731 and rebuilt in 1873. A plaque stating that the remains of the Alamo dead are located here may be inaccurate, as Santa Anna probably burned the bodies.

Here, writer Graham Greene was reminded of Victorian albums and valentines by the *mantillas* worn by the Hispanic women. He wondered if the San Antonio River wound itself into a heart shape and, in fact, it very nearly does. In 1938, the pecan "shelleries," as Greene called them, still flourished on the West Side, where impoverished pecan shellers worked for a few cents a day.

The plaza fronting the cathedral is the earliest permanently settled spot (by European immigrants) in the state.

A marching band passes through King William District.

After the Texas Revolution, it became the liveliest place in town, featuring market stalls and feisty, flirtatious "chili queens," who were ordered to remove their chili stands when San Antonio's new City Hall and the red-sandstone-and-granite Bexar County Courthouse, by James R. Gordon, were completed in the 1890s.

The German quarter

Soon after the Republic of Texas was established, a sizeable influx of German immigrants established themselves in the historic **King William District** Ⓗ – named after the Prussian king – between the river and South St Mary's Street. Here, in this 25-block area, many refurbished Victorian homes can be admired on a walking tour conducted by the San Antonio Conservation Society (in the Wulff Building at 107 King William Street; tel: 210-224-6163; www.saconservation. org), which can supply a map of the neighborhood. The Society manages the nearby **Edward Steves Homestead** (509 King William Street; tel: 210-225-5924; daily 10am–3.30pm), an impressive 1876 mansion filled with period antiques and surrounded by an exceptional garden and fountain.

Across the river is the **Blue Star Contemporary Art Museum** (116 Blue Star; tel: 210-227-6960; www.blue starart.org; Thu noon–8pm, Fri–Sun noon–6pm) in the Blue Stars Arts Complex, a restored warehouse district now housing shops, contemporary art galleries, and studios, as well as a brew pub.

The San Antonio Conservation Society, organized in 1924, primarily to preserve and restore many of the Alamo buildings, later turned its attention to saving a trio of the city's Art Deco movie theaters. The facade is all that remains of the Texas (1926), while the Majestic (1929) is now a performing arts center. The third is the **Aztec Theater ❶** (1926), a movie theater on the River Walk whose architect gained his inspiration from studying Mexico's Mayan and Aztec ruins.

The colonnade at Mitla was the model for the foyer, and each column is decorated with a plaster mask of the Aztec moon goddess. A 2-ton (1.8-metric ton) chandelier is a replica of a sacrificial stone. On the fire curtain, the meeting of Cortez and Montezuma is depicted, and over the proscenium Quetzalcoatl, the plumed serpent god of the Aztecs, appears.

Hotels old and new

Behind the Alamo, another loop of the river is flanked by two Marriott Hotels (one of the many points you can board a boat for a sightseeing cruise). Here, too, is the **Rivercenter Mall ❿** (849 E. Commerce Street; tel: 210-225-0000; www.shoprivercenter.com; open daily), with more than 100 shops, and the city's huge Convention Center. The story of the hallowed Alamo is told in appropriately spectacular fashion on the six-story screen of the imax theater (tel: 210-228-0351) in the Rivercenter Mall, between the 1909 Crockett Hotel and the 1859 limestone-and-stucco **Menger Hotel ⓚ** (204 Alamo Plaza; tel: 210-223-4361; www.mengerhotel. com), the city's first deluxe hostelry.

In the 1850s, William Menger opened a brewery on the grounds of the Battle of the Alamo and, soon after,

San Fernando Cathedral.

Colorful sweet treats in a panadería.

he and his wife offered rooms to German farmers from Fredericksburg, Seguin, Comfort, and New Braunfels, who periodically rode into San Antonio in ox carts, bringing their prepared meats and produce to sell.

Old German farmers gave way at the Menger to presidents, generals, and writers, including Oscar Wilde and O. Henry, Jenny Lind, Sarah Bernhardt, and consumptive poet Sidney Lanier, who came to San Antonio for his health. At the Menger, the old lobby (the Rotunda) and patio is a good place to savor the local's favorite cocktail, the margarita.

A few good men

It's said that, just as the Menger had to send all the way to Boston for ice in those days, so Boston sent to Spanish Texas for horses. Accordingly, the horse Paul Revere chose for his famous midnight ride was obtained from a ranch 20 miles (32km) southeast of San Antonio, where the Polish town of Cestohowa is now located.

In a similar vein, in 1898, during the Spanish-American War, Teddy

La Villita.

Roosevelt recruited members of the US Volunteer Cavalry (the "Rough Riders") in the Menger Bar (located at the other side of the hotel). "I need a few good men," he is reputed to have said, "who can ride a horse, shoot a gun, and want to serve their country." This elite corps of cowboys and millionaires from the East generated a great deal of attention before they went on to Cuba.

In contrast, the 21-story **Hilton Palacio del Rio** ❶ (200 S. Alamo Street; tel: 210-222-1400; www.hilton.com), which overlooks the river a few blocks to the south, was built in record time in 1968. It was claimed to have been the world's first hotel put together from pre-constructed rooms produced on an "assembly line." As its honeycomb facade suggests, the rooms, completely furnished and ready to assign to guests, were lifted into place by a crane, and then nudged and straightened with the help of a helicopter.

At the other end of the River Walk, the **Drury Plaza Riverwalk Hotel** (105 S. St Mary's Street; tel:

210-270-7799; www.druryhotels.com) occupies the beautifully restored 1926 Alamo National Bank Building. The hotel's Terrace Rooms overlook a portion of the River Walk that was restored by the family-run hotel chain and donated to the city.

Fun and thrills

For some fun, next to the Visitor Information Center on Alamo Plaza you will find **Louis Tussaud's Plaza Wax Theater**, with 200 waxworks of celebrities, and **Ripley's Believe It or Not** (tel: 210-224-9299; www. ripleys.com/sanantonio), where you'll see all kinds of weird and wonderful items. Two blocks away is the historic (1881) **Buckhorn Saloon and Museum M** (318 E. Houston; tel: 210-247-4000; www.buckhornmuseum. com; daily from 10am, closing times vary), which contains the world's largest collection of horns. The small Texas Ranger Museum here houses hundreds of Texas Ranger artifacts, including revolvers, automatic handguns, sawn-off shotguns, badges, and photographs, along with

a re-creation of San Antonio during its Wild West times.

Panoramic view

Farther down Alamo, past the Convention Center, is **Hemisfair Park N** – site of the 1968 World's Fair – dominated by the 750ft (231-meter) **Tower of the Americas** (open daily), which has glass elevators to take you to an observation deck for a panoramic view of the city. Above the observation deck is a restaurant that rotates once each hour. Here also are the **Institute of Texan Cultures** (801 Cesar E. Chavez Boulevard; tel: 210-458-2300; www.texancultures.com; Mon–Sat 9am–5pm, Sun noon–5pm) and the **National Autonomous University of Mexico's Mexican Cultural Institute** (600 Hemisfair Plaza Way; tel: 210-227-0123; http://icm. sre.gob.mx/culturamexsa; daily 9am–6pm; free), both displaying interesting historical and contemporary exhibits with a multicultural emphasis.

Little Village

Opposite Hemisfair Park is **La Villita O** ("Little Village"), the old town of

TIP

Save a visit to the Rivercenter Mall for a rainy day. As well as plenty of name shops, and the familiar food court, it has the benefit of an IMAX theater, where *The Alamo* movie is just one of a series of daily features.

Buckhorn Saloon and Museum.

FACT

The San Antonio Stock Show and Rodeo (tel: 210-225-5851; www.sa rodeo.com) takes place in February each year.

The San Antonio Museum of Art.

Béjar, now spelled "Bexar" and pronounced "bear," from which Santa Anna's troops set up their cannon line for the Alamo siege in 1836. The previous year, Santa Anna's brother-in-law, General Martin Perfecto de Cos, had stayed in a house here while in command of the Mexican forces sent to calm the Texans.

Despite its name, La Villita was not an exclusively Spanish neighborhood, for Germans and others moved here during the Republic (1836–45). When it was restored, the intention was to honor San Antonio's Spanish, German, Mexican, French, American, and Texan heritage, evidence of which is found in La Villita's architectural styles.

Today, the tiny limestone and adobe buildings contain craft shops, art galleries, restaurants, and boutiques. Head down to the River Walk and you will find the grassy steps of the open-air **Arneson River Theatre** (tel: 210-207-8610; www.arnesonrivertheater. com), which often puts on dance and musical performances in summer and during Fiesta. Bring a blanket or a lawn chair.

To the east of I-37, close to the Alamodome sports and convention hall, is **Sunset Station** ℗ (1174 E. Commerce Street; tel: 210-474-7640; www.sunset-station.com), a distinctive 1902 railroad depot, also known as the "Building of a Thousand Lights," that was refurbished in 1998 and is now part of a 10-acre (4-hectare) historic center and used to host events. Where once the hoots and whistles of steam trains could be heard, today the noise and bustle come from live music and parties.

Hispanics and American Indians

Hispanic politicians from San Antonio have made major inroads into politics at the national level and are proving a dynamic force. The first Hispanic mayor of a major US city, Henry Cisneros, elected in 1981, reelected in 1985, and tapped as President Bill Clinton's Secretary for Housing and Urban Development (HUD), was a groundbreaker. More recently, the dynamic young twins Joaquin and Julian Castro have put San Antonio on the map again – Joaquin, following in Cisneros's footsteps as mayor of San Antonio and, since 2014, President Barack Obama's Secretary for HUD, and Julian as US Congressional representative for the 20th district that includes San Antonio.

San Antonio's early American Indian history, as well as local history and flora and fauna, is explored in the Art Deco **Witte Museum** (3801 Broadway; tel: 210-357-1900; www.wittemuseum.org; Mon–Sat 10am–5pm, Sun noon–5pm) in Brackenridge Park. San Antonio's original inhabitants, the Payaya Indians, were hunters who supplemented their catches with the fruit of pecan and mesquite trees, and prickly pear cactus. The Payayas cooperated readily with the Europeans, but the Apache, who controlled the plains to the north, took more convincing, and the nomadic Comanche were always a threat.

The Witte Museum also includes the four-story H-E-B Body Adventure multimedia exhibit, which offers kids an interactive way to explore their bodies, take virtual adventures, and learn about Texas. Behind the museum is a complex of historic houses, including one owned by Francisco Ruiz, who was the uncle of José Antonio Navarro and the second of the two native-born Texans who signed the Texas Declaration of Independence.

Park life

Brackenridge Park, which adjoins Fort Sam Houston, lies between US 281 and the Austin Highway, northeast of the city. In its 340 acres (138 hectares) can be found the well-stocked **San Antonio Zoo and Aquarium** (3903 N. St Mary's Street; tel: 210-734-7184; www.sazoo-aq.org; daily 9am–5pm), the Japanese Tea Gardens, the Sunken Gardens Amphitheater, Brackenridge Golf Course, riding stables, a sky ride, and a carousel, as well as a miniature train ride.

To the west, in the original 1880s Lone Star Brewery, is the sensational **San Antonio Museum of Art** (200 W. Jones Avenue; tel: 210-978-8100; www.samuseum.org; Tue, Fri, and Sat

The Institute of Texan Cultures.

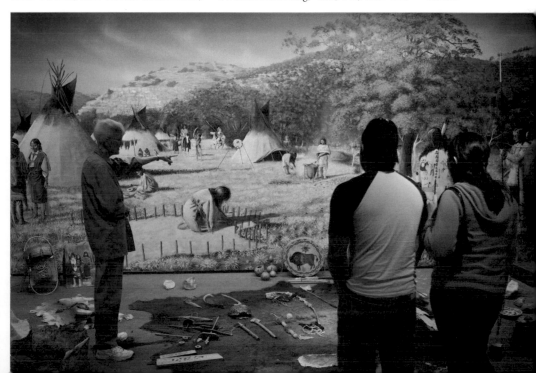

TIP

The Witte Museum is a good place to take children. It depicts the early American Indian history, ecology, and wildlife of Texas through plenty of hands-on exhibits.

10am–9pm, Wed–Thu 10am–5pm, Sun until 6pm). This is a great place to see a wide variety of traditional and modern art from all over the world, but particularly Latin American and Spanish art. The special exhibits here are also a big draw.

Farther north, before the airport, is the **McNay Art Museum** (6000 N. New Braunfels; tel: 210-824-5368; www.mcnayart.org; Tue–Fri 10am–4pm, Thu until 9pm, Sat until 5pm, Sun noon–5pm), housing the collection of an oil heiress, Marion Koogler McNay, who donated it to the state. Artists showcased include Gaugin, Picasso, Matisse, and Cézanne. This is one of the best art collections in the Southwest.

On the trail of the missions

The Witte Museum now stands at the headwaters of the San Antonio River, named by the Spaniards for St Anthony of Padua. It was here that Don Martin de Alcaron and Fra Antonio de San Buenaventura Olivares arrived with settlers, soldiers,

A mariachi band performs A Night in Old San Antonio.

and Franciscans in 1718, and most likely encountered Payaya Indians for the first time.

The missionaries, protected by a presidio (garrison), set about building their missions and took it upon themselves to convert the Payaya, and teach them new building techniques, crafts, ranching, and farming. The missions were large, thriving, self-sustaining enterprises on the frontier, which shipped goods back down the Camino Real trade route to the capital of New Spain in Mexico City and received supplies just once a year. It was a difficult life for all concerned, made even more so for the Payaya by the high expectations of their competing Spanish overlords – priests, military, and private landowners.

Mission San Antonio de Valero (now the Alamo) was originally established on the west bank of the river in 1718, but by 1793, it had been relocated to the east bank and secularized, and Mexican troops were transferred there to protect the pueblo that had grown up on the riverbanks. This converted mission, named the Alamo (meaning cottonwood), was a crucial fortification then and much later, when it played its starring role in Texas history.

Four more missions were founded. Today, all except the Alamo are preserved as part of **San Antonio Missions National Historical Park** (tel: 210-534-8833; www.nps.gov/saan; open daily) and are managed by the National Park Service. The missions stretch over a 6-mile (10km) route to the south, next to the river (see page 168).

Out of town

Heading out of San Antonio along US 90 will bring you to the border at **Del Rio**, around 150 miles (240km) to the west. As you leave San Antonio, there's a parched quality to roadside grasslands that offers a taste of the dessication ahead toward the border and the Rio Grande. At first, however, agriculture maintains a foothold. Historic **Castroville**, 15 miles (24km) along US 90, proclaims itself as "'the Little Alsace of Texas," and has several Alsation restaurants.

Hondo feels like the Great Plains, with huge fields of corn and wheat, while **Knippa** – "Go Ahead and Blink, Knippa is Bigger than you Think" is devoted to stone quarrying.

The Great Depression hit South Texas pretty badly, but the town of **Uvalde** fared better than most because it was the birthplace of President Franklin Roosevelt's vice president John Nance Garner ("Cactus Jack"). Garner took care of his hometown with projects like **Garner State Park**, a riverfront park created in 1941 by the Civilian Conservation Corps, and the **Aviation Museum at Garner Field**, a World War II training base that displays old bombers and other aircraft. The **Briscoe-Garner Memorial Museum** (333 N. Park Street; tel: 830-278-5018; www.cah.utexas.edu/museums/garner.php; Tue–Sat 9am–4pm) is located in the former Garner home and now run by the University of Texas. Its new name honors Garner and former Governor Dolph Briscoe, both Uvalde born, and contains exhibits pertaining to both their lives.

The Japanese Tea Gardens in Brackenridge Park.

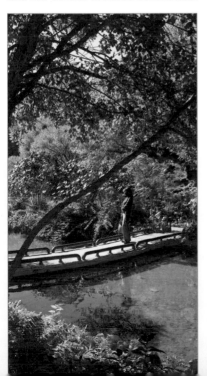

CREATING THE RIVER WALK

For more than a century, the San Antonio River has been the scene of social clubs, carnivals, rodeos, and circuses. It has had private landings and wide lawns, and the entire city has picnicked on its banks, and swum, fished, and been baptized in it. In *A Journey Through Texas*, landscape architect Frederick Law Olmsted noted: "Few cities have such a luxury… the streets are laid out in such a way that a great number of houses have a garden extending to the bank, and to a bathing-house, which is in constant use."

After disastrous floods in 1921 and 1929 left the business district under 8ft (2.5 meters) of water, a three-block-long river cutoff was created, joining the bends of the river where it loops around a 16-block area. It is inconceivable today, but at one time there were plans to fill in the river, or run it underground so it would, in effect, be used as a sewer. Fortunately, the Conservation Society banded together to protect it and nearby landmarks. In 1938, aid was provided by the Works Progress Administration, FDR's New Deal federal works scheme to cut unemployment. The river was dredged. Dams and rock retaining walls, the pleasant cobblestone and flagstone walks, and stairways from bridges were constructed. More than 11,000 trees were planted along the riverbanks and, when it was complete, spotlights were deployed in the bushes. Thirteen bridges now cross the River Walk.

THE CRUCIAL ROLE OF THE SPANISH MISSIONS

Some of North America's oldest buildings survive in Texas, built by Spanish missionaries who sought to educate and "civilize"the local Indians.

Across South Texas lies a chain of early Spanish outposts. Established in the 18th century, these missions are evidence of the early efforts made by Spain to colonize the region, but the missions soon found a role in developing the Catholic faith among the local natives, bringing American Indian communities under the Christian banner.

Missions farther east became threatened by French incursions from Louisiana, and their communities relocated to San Antonio. The city is the mission heartland of Texas today, housing four separate complexes (five if you include the Alamo) within its boundaries. The four lie to the south, at 2-mile (3km) intervals along the San Antonio River. The most beautiful is San José, dubbed "Queen of the Missions." Mission Concepción is noted for its handsome twin towers, while Missions San Juan and Espada have distinctive three-bell towers. All can be explored using the San Antonio Missions Trail, with literature from the tourist office.

Each complex presents a different theme about mission life for the visitor. Concepción deals with the religious role of the mission, San José handles the defense and social functions, San Juan focuses on the economic importance, and Espada looks at the educational angle.

The craftsmanship of the builders working on the missions is demonstrated by the Rose Window at San José Mission, San Antonio.

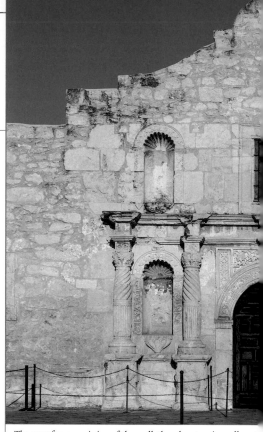

The most famous mission of them all, though not universally known as such, is the bullet-riddled Alamo – or Mission San Antonio de Valero – founded in 1718 and now surrounded by downtown structures.

A shrine to Our Lady of Guadalupe in the San Ysleta Mission, the oldest mission in the state. It was built by the Tigua people who were forced to flee their ancestral home near what is now Albuquerque, New Mexico.

The mission was more than a church: it was the base for a community, housing animals, workshops, granaries, kilns, and sleeping quarters.

AMERICAN INDIAN INFLUENCES

In addition to the one in and around San Antonio, Texas has another mission trail beginning in El Paso. Stretching 9 miles (14km) out to the east of the city, it covers three historic sites: Ysleta Mission, Socorro Mission, and San Elizario Presidio Chapel.

These centers differ from the San Antonio missions in that they were established by the Spanish together with the local Pueblo Indian communities. The Pueblo influence is apparent. The oldest is Ysleta, which stands next to the Tigua Indian Cultural Center; it was rebuilt in 1908. Socorro, like Ysleta, dates originally from the late 17th century, though the current structure was completed in 1840. Its foundation by Piro Indians is reflected in the architecture. San Elizario is the chapel of a former presidio (garrison) and was rebuilt in 1877.

The wooden Mission of San Francisco de los Tejas, the first mission in East Texas, was founded in 1690. It has now been fully rebuilt.

Mission church decor is simple: bare walls and beams, the occasional fresco and a dotting of religious icons.

Socorro Mission, one of the three missions on the El Paso Trail. The original building was destroyed by flooding in 1829.

HOUSTON

Bustling port, financial hub, and home of
Mission Control, Houston is a moneyed
metropolis, with a wealth of cultural
attractions and a laid-back attitude.

Houston is without doubt a city with fascinating contradictions. In just a few decades, it has turned into a sprawling urban behemoth yet possesses one of the country's first historic planned communities in downtown. It has a subtropical climate with almost junglelike vegetation and sticky air within hailing distance of the white sand beaches of the Gulf of Mexico. It's conservative and full of urban cowboys, yet possesses one of the country's largest gay populations and cutting-edge modern art. And even as oilmen have drilled beneath the ground, NASA's celebrated astronauts have soared to the outer edges of space and explored the moon.

There's money and culture aplenty in this city, which channels a little Austin Weird even as it puts on the Ritz – but you'd be hard pressed to find anyone being snobbish. This is much too large and diverse a city to get away with that anymore.

Virtually a small town as recently as the late 1950s, Houston's population of 2.16 million (a staggering 6.22 million if you include the metro area) is incredibly diverse and international, with people from all over the world making their home here – from British immigrants (the United Kingdom has its main consulate in the US

Southwest here) to refugees from the Sudan. Houston's busy international airport serves as an immigration hub for the world.

Houston is now far and away the largest city in Texas and the fourth largest in the US, most of it recently built. The lack of planning has created unchecked urban growth, resulting in a wide-open city overlaid with dizzying intersecting highways and distinct neighborhoods that have a plethora of interesting restaurants, shops, museums, and cultural activities.

Main Attractions

Tranquility Park
Menil Collection
Rothko Chapel
Museum of Fine Arts, Houston
The Galleria
Johnson Space Center

Motorized cupcakes at the annual Houston Art Car Parade.

Surreal scale and proportion result from the lack of zoning: a small boutique may stand next to a 60-story office building, adjoining a house next to a heliport. Houston, more than anywhere else in Texas, operates according to the wildcatter's philosophy: "Dig a little deeper where others have given up, and maybe you'll bring something in."

Risk-taking wildcatters

Its economy is based on black gold, on an oil and gas industry notorious for the eccentrics and risk-takers it spawns. Because of the oil price fluctuation in the 1970s, Houston's fortunes rose more quickly than those of any other Texas city. After the drop in world oil prices and demand for energy supplies, its growth slowed to merely brisk. The boom that had shaped the city for three decades faltered following Enron's spectacular plunge into bankruptcy in 2001. The collapse of the Houston-based energy company left thousands unemployed, accelerating the city's dip into recession.

But Houston's listless economy has rebounded just as spectacularly, following recent big oil discoveries in South Texas and accelerated production. Another legacy of the 1970s is the rich ethnic mix – Hispanics, African-Americans, American Indians, East Indians, Iranians, Chinese, Thais, and Vietnamese. This contributes to Houston's resilience, and is undoubtedly part of the reason that it is so tolerant of individuality.

Near this utterly flat city are low hills and pine forests, salt marshes, swamps and steamy bayous (marshy inlets), some of which are infested with alligators. Far to the west, but no more than a day's drive, are real hills, then cactus and the desert. And it is only an hour's drive to the Gulf of Mexico beaches.

Freeway life

Because of its size, the only logical way to tour Houston is by car, in which many Houstonians spend

more time than at home. The downtown area is enclosed by I-45 on the west and, some way to the east, US 59, with two other much-visited areas – the Museum District and the famed Texas Medical Center – to the southwest. The city yawns between a vast network of busy highways, as a result of which buildings are consciously designed as "freeway architecture." Since there are no changes in elevation, tall buildings function as the only landmarks for the driver.

The I-610 loop that garlands the city also divides it as surely as the Wall once separated Berlin. If there is snobbery here, it's on the part of those who live inside the Loop, where all the desirable neighborhoods and almost all of the tourist attractions are located. Perhaps the best-known downtown structure is Philip Johnson's **Pennzoil Place Ⓐ**, with its two towers that appear to separate and then come together as one drives around the city. One block from Pennzoil Place is I.M. Pei's distinctive **JPMorgan Chase Tower Ⓑ**, formerly the Texas Commerce Bank Tower, a

Statue of General Sam Houston, the Texan hero who gave his name to the city.

Shops in Midtown.

TIP

To get a feel for the
diversity of lifestyles in
the Montrose area, grab
a drink at one of the
sidewalk cafés and
watch a colorful parade
of punks, college kids,
trendy singles, and
transvestites cruise by
on foot and in cars.

cool, gray slab nicknamed "the Texas Tombstone."

Tranquility Park ❻, at Bagby and Walker streets, near Sam Houston Park, and its restored century-old structures, including an 1878 general store, is named for the moon base Tranquility. It is landscaped to look like Tranquility Base, with craters and mounds, fountains, reflecting pools, and copper tubes representing the rockets taking off. Houston Visitors Center (901 Bagby; tel: 1-8004HOU-STON; www.visithoustontexas.com; Mon–Sat 9am–4pm) is near here, on the first floor of City Hall.

The oldest part of the original city is **Market Square** ❼, but more significant is **Allen's Landing Park** ❽, a few blocks north, beside the bayou. Here is where Houston's founders, Augustus and John Allen, first came ashore in 1836.

A 6-mile (10km) system of **underground tunnels** connects 55 buildings with three hotels in Houston's downtown area, making it possible to visit more than 100 shops and some small restaurants without surfacing

into the heat. This subterranean city is open from 6am to 6.30pm weekdays, and maps are available at banks along the route.

Entertainment areas

Downtown Houston is also the upscale entertainment district, home of the **Wortham Theater Center** ❾, (500 Texas Street; tel: 832-487-7000; www.houstonfirsttheaters.com), hosting the Houston Grand Opera and Houston Ballet companies. The Houston Symphony bunks down in **Jones Hall for the Performing Arts** ❿ (615 Louisiana Street; tel: 832-487-7050; www.houstonfirsttheaters.com) along with Houston Society for the Performing Arts. These and other venues operate under the aegis of Houston First Corporation, which has recently joined forces with the Houston Convention and Visitors Bureau to promote arts and culture in Houston. Drama has its main home at the acclaimed **Alley Theatre** ⓫ (615 Texas Avenue; tel: 713-220-5700; www.alleytheatre.org).

Minute Maid Park ⓬ (501 Crawford Street; tel: 713-259-8000; www.

Fashionable Montrose boutique.

houston.astros.mlb.com/hou/ballpark) has a capacity of 41,000 and houses the Houston Astros baseball team. It features a full-size vintage locomotive along one side and has a retractable roof to cater to all aspects of the Texan climate. Tours are available daily.

Hipster Montrose

Heading south on Montrose Boulevard, west of downtown, brings you to the **Montrose** district, established in 1911, a major entertainment area whose center is the intersection of Westheimer and Montrose. This attractive area has been called "the Heart of Houston," and named one of America's great neighborhoods. Driving from downtown along Gray Street takes you through the old Fourth Ward, a tough neighborhood of single-corridor houses. Montrose is the home of the largest gay community in Texas, as well as of artists, designers, museum personnel, and trendy young singles, and, as you might imagine, it has gentrified into an attractive mix of renovated bungalows with wide porches, cute cottages, and updated mansions.

In its back streets, gay bars cater to every taste; on the main drag, Westheimer, entertainment is directed to a broader spectrum and boutiques display vintage clothing, erotic birthday cakes, neon hair ornaments, and punk garb. In the 5,000–6,000 blocks are elegant shops such as Fendi and Barney's New York. East of the intersection is a string of restaurants and bars, characterized by Tex-Mex cuisine, lasers, videos, and neon.

Art and interfaith

As Montrose Boulevard heads south, it becomes more elegant prior to crossing US 59 and heading into the grassy purlieus of the **Museum District**. A few blocks west, in a specially designed building, is the terrific **Menil Collection ①** (1533 Sul Ross Street; tel: 713-525-9400; www.menil.org; Wed–Sun 11am–5pm; free), Houston's premier art museum. The collection is a legacy of the de Menil family, with exhibits ranging from medieval and Byzantine art to contemporary works, including the world's largest private collection of Surrealist art.

Part of Houston's 6-mile (10km) underground tunnel system.

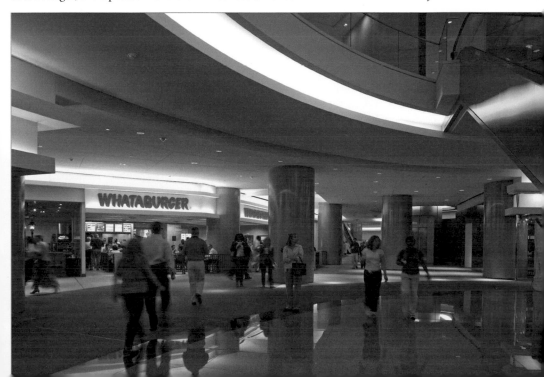

Children's Museum of Houston.

Across the street is a Greek Orthodox church offering a collection of icons for public viewing, and facing it is the celebrated **Rothko Chapel** Ⓚ (3900 Yupon Street; tel: 713-524-9839; www.rothkochapel.org; Mon–Sat 10am–6pm; free), commissioned by John and Dominique de Menil to house 14 paintings by the abstract expressionist Mark Rothko. This interfaith chapel, its entrance flanked by the Broken Obelisk – a memorial to Dr Martin Luther King – is a remarkable space, a hushed temple to art with a meditational aura. Don't miss it.

Near here can be found the **Houston Center for Photography** Ⓛ (1441 W. Alabama; tel: 713-529-4755; www.hcponline.org; Wed, Thu 11am–9pm, Fri 11am–5pm, Sat–Sun 11am–7pm; free), a worthwhile destination if you enjoy photography.

Where Montrose Boulevard crosses Bissonnet Street, heavy culture sets in. The **Museum of Fine Arts, Houston** Ⓜ (1001 Bissonnet; tel: 713-639-7300; www.mfah.org; Tue–Wed 10am–5pm, Thu until 9pm, Fri–Sat until 7pm, Sun 12.15–7pm; free) and

the **Contemporary Arts Museum** Ⓝ (5216 Montrose; tel: 713-284-8250; www.camh.org; Tue, Wed, and Fri 10am–7pm, Thu until 9pm, Sat 10am–6pm, Sun noon–6pm; free) sit across the street from one other. MFAH, whose modern addition was the work of the renowned architect Ludwig Mies Van der Rohe, houses a large permanent collection from all periods, with strong holdings of French Impressionists and 20th-century Americans. Across the street, the museum's Cullen Sculpture Garden, designed by Isamu Noguchi and displaying sculptures by Matisse, Miro, and Giacometti, among others, is open until 10pm. The CAM does not have a permanent collection, but is a stainless-steel kunsthalle staging nine exhibitions each year, featuring the latest wrinkles in new art.

A more somber experience is offered at the **Holocaust Museum Houston** Ⓞ (5401 Caroline Street; tel: 713-942-8000; www.hmh.org; Mon–Fri 9am–5pm, Sat–Sun noon–5pm; free; tours available), an educational facility aimed at eliminating prejudice and

THE ORANGE SHOW

The Orange Show Center for Visionary Art (2402 Munger Street; tel: 713-926-6368; www.orangeshow.org; Wed–Sun 10am–2pm in summer; call for off-season hours) is a remarkable piece of folk art in Houston. It's a labyrinth of passages, murals, antiques, and a tiny museum, otherwise impossible to describe. The life's work of mail carrier Jeff McKissack, who built it over 26 years out of junkyard scraps between 1956 and his death in 1980, it promotes the life-giving qualities of the orange. "Be smart; eat oranges" is spelled out in mosaic tiles. When McKissack died, it was bought by a Houston nonprofit organization of donors, including Texas rockers ZZ Top, then restored and opened to the public.

hatred through poignant permanent and visiting exhibitions.

Science and nature

Four blocks down Binz Street is the **Children's Museum of Houston** ℗ (1500 Binz Street; tel: 713-522-1138; www.cmhouston.org; Mon–Sat 10am–6pm, Sun noon–6pm; free Thu 5–8pm), with hands-on exhibits.

In nearby Hermann Park, you'll find the **Houston Museum of Natural Science** Ⓠ (tel: 713-639-4629; www.hmns.org; daily 9am–5pm; free) home to a Space Age museum and the Burke Baker Planetarium, and one of the top ten attended museums in the US. Part of the complex houses the Cullen Hall of Gems and Minerals, containing more minerals and gemstone varieties than you knew existed, the Wortham IMAX Theater, which projects movies hourly onto a six-story screen (tel: 713-639-4629 for schedule), and the recently donated Gordon W. Smith North American Collection, which displays a stellar 600-piece collection of tribal headdresses and other paraphernalia

acquired from American Indian friends of Smith starting in the 1920s.

As you enter the park, be sure to stop and smell the roses at the Garden Center (open daily; free) and wander through the six-story glass cone that houses the recently renovated and expanded **Cockrell Butterfly Center**, in which thousands of brightly colored lepidoptera flutter around a waterfall in a tropical garden.

Also in the park is the **Houston Zoo** Ⓡ (tel: 713-533-6500; www.houstonzoo.org; daily 9am–7pm) has a Tropical Bird House, which takes the form of an Asian jungle.

More museums

There are more museums and art galleries in Houston than in any other Texas city, and plenty of money to support world-class exhibits. The Museum of Fine Arts Houston, for example, also owns **Bayou Bend Collection and Gardens** Ⓢ (6003 Memorial Drive; tel: 713-639-7750; www.mfah.org/visit/bayou-bend-collection-and-gardens; Tue–Sat 9am–5pm, Sun 1–5pm; free), just before Memorial Park. This stunning

The Houston Gay Pride Parade has been held annually since 1979.

The Museum of Fine Arts.

FACT

The Galleria is home to 400 stores, in three sections and on three levels. Deluxe department stores like Neiman Marcus grab the headlines but even the cheapest goods can be bought in the center.

24-room mansion, designed by Houston architect John F. Staub, is filled with decorative American art from colonial times to the early part of the 20th century. The collection was left to the museum by Houston philanthropist Ima Hogg (yes, it was her real name), daughter of the state's first Texas-born governor, James Stephen Hogg. The 14 acres (6 hectares) of landscaped grounds are open to the public every day except Sunday and Monday.

Also not to be overlooked is the **Blaffer Art Museum** (3401 Cullen Boulevard; tel: 713-743-9521; Tue–Sat 10am–5pm; free) – described as a "laboratory for the visual arts and contemporary culture" – located in the Arts District of the campus of the University of Houston. Echoes of the Old West are preserved in the **American Cowboy Museum** (11822 Almeda; tel: 713-433-4441; www.americancowboymuseum.org; appointment only), and proof that Houston can be as weird as the best of them, the **National Museum of Funeral History** (415 Barren Springs Drive; tel: 281-876-3063; www.nmfh.org;

Tue–Fri 10am–4pm, Sat until 5pm, Sun noon–5pm), which has a collection of hearses, sarcophagi, and coffins, and memorabilia from the funerals of Michael Jackson, JFK, and others, always evokes curiosity from macabre-minded visitors.

Oak-shaded campus

The gentle Victorian Romanesque campus of **Rice University**, surrounded by giant oaks, abuts Hermann Park to the west. **Rice University Art Gallery**, displaying contemporary art, is open to the public (6100 Main Street; tel: 713-348-6069; www.ricegallery.org; Mon–Fri 10am–5pm; free). Beyond is the immense and highly regarded **Texas Medical Center ❶**, whose 700-acre (283-hectare) complex, renowned for its cancer treatments. The center's former cardiac surgeons include Michael deBakey, who was awarded the US Congressional Gold Medal for his work. Kings, world leaders, and presidents have come here for treatment. Rice, a pleasant retreat from the sterile towers of the Medical Center, has set up a monumental sculpture by Michael Heizer – three 70-ton (63.5-metric ton) blocks of pink Texas granite.

Eccentric architecture

The area around Rice is the most beautiful in Houston. **Rice Village ❶**, at Kirby and University, was Houston's first upscale shopping center and its 325 stores are still a major attraction today. Two stately streets, North and South boulevards, set the local standard for majestic oak tree canopies, and, behind Georgian Revival facades live the old moneyed classes of Houston eccentricity, as seen in a totally pink house at the corner of Hazard and Sunset streets. Everything, including the fence and garage, is painted tropical flamingo pink.

A comprehensive tour of Houston architecture would also have to include the unbelievable folk art building **Beer Can House ❶** (222 Malone Street, off Memorial Drive;

NEIGHBORHOOD DINING

Houstonians are said to eat out more than any other US community, and there are over 8,000 restaurants in the Houston area from which to choose. Reflecting the city's multicultural background, you'll find every cuisine here, from Chinese, Vietnamese, and Indian to Cajun, Italian, and Tex-Mex, plenty of casual fare, and some of the most inventive gourmet dining around. Neighborhood restaurants are constantly springing up, as Houston grows and new areas become hot destinations. In the West University/Rice area, **Goode Company Texas Bar-B-Q** (tel: 713-522-2530; www.goodecompany.com), is a nationally recognized Texas barbecue mecca. In the Museum District, **Green Seed Vegan** (tel: 713-487-VEGN; www.greenseedvegan.com) is considered to be one of the best vegan restaurants in the US. Award-winning chef-owner Hugo Ortega's **Hugo's** (tel: 713-524-7744; www.hugosrestaurant.net) in a beautiful dining space in Montrose is the place to push the boat. In the Galleria, you'll find popular **RDG + Bar Annie** (tel: 713-840-1111; www.rdgbarannie.com), a great place for inventive Southwest food. Meanwhile, in the Upper Kirby/Greenway Plaza neighborhood of Central Houston, you can enjoy casual Indian dining at **Pondicheri** (tel: 713-522-2022; www.pondichericafe.com), a sister restaurant to **Indika** (tel: 713-524-2170; www.indikausa.com) in Montrose. You'll eat well in Houston. Bring a big appetite.

tel: 719-926-6368; www.beercanhouse. org; Sat–Sun noon–5pm), constructed from 50,000 cans by John Milkovisch, a retired upholsterer for the Southern Pacific Railroad, near the extensive and lovely Memorial Park.

Art Deco tower

Heading out from the city center, US 59, also called the Southwest Freeway, carries a river of commuters every day, with rush hours lasting 6–9am and 2–8pm. At the point where it intersects with Loop 610 stands the ultimate in freeway architecture, the **Williams Tower**, formerly the Transco Tower, designed by Philip Johnson and John Burgee. The facade, inspired in part by the San Jacinto Monument, is the same on all four sides, in order to be admired from any direction, and its Art Deco lines can easily be taken in while driving at 55mph (88kmph). A beautiful nearby fountain rewards those who see it on foot.

Upscale shopping

Williams Tower is right next to the famous upscale **Galleria** shopping center, centered around Post Oak Road and Westheimer Road, near the West Loop (I-610). Here can be found a Who's Who of retailing – Neiman Marcus, Saks Fifth Avenue, Gucci, Tiffany, Cartier, and Versace, to name but a few. The area is marked by glamorous buildings designed by Cesar Pelli and Johnson and Burgee, and the enclosed Galleria itself is modeled on Milan's Galleria, but blown up to immense size. Every luxury store under the sun is represented, as well as an ice-skating rink and a jogging track around the roof.

In its early years, the Galleria was supported by the well-heeled from sections like River Oaks, around the 610 Loop, between Uptown and Downtown, one of America's first planned communities and a model for beautifully integrated homes and landscaping. River Oaks was established around a country club in the 1920s by brothers William and Michael Hogg (brothers of Ima Hogg) and is now the most expensive subdivision in Texas, with mansions costing between $1 million and $20

Rice Village.

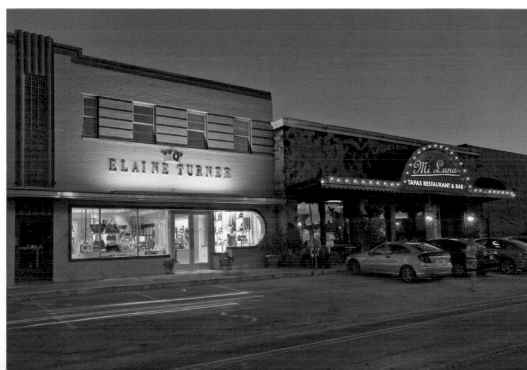

million. The mansions along streets like River Oaks Boulevard, Lazy Lane, and Inwood belong to captains of industry, oil and cattle barons, their descendants, and a few Arab sheiks. First-run foreign and independent movies can be seen at the 1939 vintage River Oaks Theatre (2009 W. Gray Street, near Shepherd; tel: 713-524-2175).

Fiesta Market

If you exit the Southwest Freeway at Hillcroft and head south toward the Bellaire intersection, you will come to the **Fiesta Market**, the ultimate ethnic grocery store. Advertising is in Spanish, Vietnamese, Chinese, Hindi, and English. Fiesta sells everything from cowboy boots to goat's milk. It is always jammed with shoppers, and the interior is ablaze with huge neon signs. It is an astonishing and hilarious store, now replicated at other locations. In another display of pure Texas culture – the culture of bigness – a huge piano on the Southwest Freeway alerts drivers to the presence of a piano store.

Heading north

Just north of the center of the city, and slightly west, is a mixed residential and industrial neighborhood called **The Heights**. The houses are older and more graceful, but one of the highlights of The Heights is the grave of Texas billionaire Howard Hughes in **Glenwood Cemetery**, off Washington Boulevard. Hughes's grave is as simply marked as those of his parents nearby. All three are completely overshadowed by the dramatic figure of a weeping angel embellishing an adjacent grave. This flamboyant monument was prepared by a local interior designer for himself.

Down south

In the southern part of the city is **NRG Park** Ⓦ (tel: 713-667-1400; www.nrg-park.com), which includes the famous Astrodome, built in 1968 and once nicknamed "The Eighth Wonder of the World." It is vast – large enough to fit an 18-story building inside. After the building was shuttered in 2008 due to numerous occupancy code violations, it fell into disuse. Plans to convert the

Goode Company Texas Bar-B-Q.

Astrodome into a luxury hotel, movie production studio, or convention center were rejected by voters. The Astrodome was added to the National Register of Historic Places in January 2014 but remains empty.

Nearby is NRG Stadium, home of the NFL American football team the Houston Texans, along with NRG Center (with 706,000 sq ft/7,061 sq meters of exhibit space) and NRG Arena, another event center. NRG Stadium has a retractable roof and seats nearly 70,000 spectators. NRG Park hosts the huge Houston Livestock Show and Rodeo, the world's largest event of its kind, featuring Western contests from bronco-busting to chuckwagon-racing, as well as soccer matches, an increasingly popular sport in the US.

Houston's Orient

Many of Houston's attractions are in the East End, beginning, on the other side of US 59, with **Old Chinatown**, whose major landmark is the **Sun-Young Taoist Temple** Ⓧ (1507 Delano Street). Here visitors can determine their fortune by shaking out numbered reeds. Be sure to visit the nearby **Kim Son** (2001 Jefferson Street; tel: 713-222-2461; www.kimson. com), a Vietnamese landmark and the largest Asian restaurant in the state. Across town, there's a burgeoning Vietnamese community operating other restaurants on Milam Street, just south of downtown, while Chinese immigrants and their descendants shop and eat in **New Chinatown**, located in Southwest Houston along Bellaire Boulevard, between Gessner and Wilcrest. New Chinatown is sometimes referred to as the Bellaire Corridor, or the Diho Area, after the **Diho Supermarket**, a large, Chinese food mart.

Ships and spaceships

The wealth Houston enjoys today derives not only from oil discovered elsewhere but the 50-mile (80km) **Ship Channel** that turned it into an inland port. Houston businessmen persuaded the government to pay for the shipping channel, which developed their city into one of the three busiest ports in the US, stealing the glory (and the trade) from coastal

Ice rink at the Galleria shopping center.

Galveston, after an apocalyptic storm wrecked the latter city's harbor in 1900. The channel's turning basin, off US 90A near Navigation Boulevard, is the site of free harbor tours, but a more rewarding trip is to visit the other end of the channel, where it enters Burnett Bay and ends its journey to the sea.

The way there, however, takes one through the **Pasadena–Baytown Industrial Corridor**, a district filled with every kind of petrochemical processing plant. The air smells like floor cleaner and plays havoc with the sinuses, although at night the industrial landscape assumes a beautiful, otherworldly quality. Pasadena also has a landmark: the vast **Armand Bayou Nature Center** (8500 Bay Area Boulevard; tel: 281-474-2551; www.abnc.org; Wed–Sat 9am–5pm, Sun noon–5pm; free). You can visit the center's Martyn Farm, which will take you back to farm life in the late 1800s.

There are two attractions at this end of the channel, in La Porte: the World War I dreadnought Battleship Texas **State Historic Site**, which served as

General Eisenhower's flagship during the 1944 D-Day invasion, and the 1,200-acre (486-hectare) San Jacinto **Battleground** State Historic Site (3523 Independence Parkway; tel: 281-479-2431; www.tpwd.tx.us/state-parks; open daily 10am–5pm, self-guided tours). The latter commemorates the Battle of San Jacinto on April 21, 1836, making it arguably the most significant monument in the state, as it marks the date on which Texas won its freedom from Mexico with General Sam Houston's defeat of Mexico's Santa Anna. Only weeks after the ignominy of the Alamo, revenge must have been sweet. The Art Deco monument offers an elevator ride 570ft (174 meters) to the top for a view of downtown Houston on one side and a spaghetti bowl of pipelines on the other.

Notwithstanding its varied other attractions, what has brought Houston to worldwide attention in recent decades has been the **Johnson Space Center** (see page 184), 25 miles (40km) southeast of downtown (take I-45, then NASA Road 1; tel: 281-244-2100; www.spacecenter.org; open daily).

Historic Queen Anne building on Heights Boulevard.

Tex-Mex

Tex-Mex is a homestyle border cuisine that emphasizes inexpensive spiced meats such as hot chili, beans and tortillas, salsa picante, guacamole, and cheese.

Visitors to Texas are guaranteed to encounter Mexican food – and plenty of it. But it's not exactly Mexican. What you will find is a Texan version of it called "Tex-Mex." These dishes are quite a bit hotter than California-Mex or Arizona-Mex, so keep plenty of yoghurt or rice handy.

Discussing what precisely constitutes Tex-Mex is a state pastime – so don't expect to discover any definitive answers. However, most Texans would probably agree that, in its most elemental form, Tex-Mex food consists of some preparation of flat cornmeal tortillas, beans, and tomatoes, onions, and chili peppers, the latter three items frequently chopped together in a picante (hot) sauce. They'd possibly also accept in the definition cheese and chili meat sauce, but beyond that they're likely to disagree.

Only in Tex-Mex

Texans are more unified in their definition of what Tex-Mex isn't. Any part of the States with a Mexican heritage will have its own related version of "Mex" cooking, but the cuisine of Mexico is not Tex-Mex. Neither is New Mexico-Mex, with its refined green *chile* (note the Spanish spelling) sauces and distinctive blue cornmeal; neither is California-Mex, rich with sour cream and lavish produce.

Tex-Mex food is not fancy. The meat it includes is usually inexpensive and tough, chopped or marinated into submission. The most famous, of course, is chili, which in Tex-Mex is a spicy meat stew without beans. Tex-Mex food is home fare, the food of the common people. But, most importantly, it is the supreme expression of the noble chili pepper, and as such it must be as hot as the hinges of Hell's Front Door.

Where to find the best Tex-Mex is a bigger debate than what it contains. Serious devotees contend that real Tex-Mex food can't be found north of Waco (mid-state), but all Texans agree on one thing – it doesn't exist outside the state.

Menu classics

Most Tex-Mex is eaten as Mexican restaurant fare.

The menu traditionally consists of the following: baskets of fried tortilla chips and bowls of *salsa picante*, accompanied by beer or iced tea, are offered while the order is prepared. Shortly afterward, a hot plate of several different specialties arrives.

These might include *enchiladas* – tortillas wrapped around cheese and onions and covered with meat or a spicy tomato sauce; *tacos* – tortillas folded, fried, and stuffed with ground meat, beans, cheese, and the above-mentioned vegetables; a guacamole salad of spiced mashed avocados; and *fajitas* – marinated and grilled bits of steak. The meal is served with rice and beans, hot tortillas, and, of course, several more bowls of *salsa picante* to spoon over everything. Dessert may be a token scoop of ice cream sherbet, or a praline candy purchased at the counter.

Tex-Mex cooking has recently absorbed some refinements – using better cuts of meat than its beloved *cabrito* (roast kid) and *menudo* (tripe stew) for example; and the "Tex-Mex cuisine" gaining popularity in the eastern US and Europe is a considerably cooled-down version of it. The more accessible it becomes, the less it resembles real Tex-Mex. To a certain extent this is necessary: every ethnic food has ingredients that appeal only to those who have been raised on them.

Colorful, spicy, authentic Tex-Mex dishes can only be truly savored in Texas itself.

HOUSTON'S SPACE CENTER

Houston, home base for NASA's Apollo lunar missions, was the most important and recognized city on Earth during the early era of space travel.

In the future, should aliens look back on man's first tentative steps beyond Earth, the name Houston will be on the tips of their tongues, tentacles, or whatever it is they use for speaking. Texas's biggest city never actually launched a man into orbit during the heyday of the space program, but US-manned space flights relied upon ground staff here to guide them on their way. Houston, or Mission Control, is the focus of all earthly activity when an astronaut is up there in the deep blue yonder. As well as guiding spacecraft during their missions, Houston is also the selection and training base for NASA astronauts, where they are put through their paces, physically and mentally, before being sent into orbit.

The Manned Space Center, renamed the Johnson Space Center, was opened by the NASA in 1962, as part of President John F. Kennedy's declared intention for America to land a man on the moon before the decade was out. The center played its part to perfection, and "Houston" was the first word spoken from the surface of the moon, by Apollo XI commander Neil Armstrong.

In 1981, NASA launched the Space Shuttle, the first reusable space exploration vehicle, and Houston was again central to its success. Much of NASA's current work revolves around the International Space Station – a cooperative venture between the US and Russia – and the Mars Rover program.

The men who made history – the crew of Apollo XI, the first mission to land on the moon: Neil Armstrong, Michael Collins, and Edwin "Buzz" Aldrin.

Space Center Houston, at the Johnson Space Center, has a fascinating collection of artifacts, including moon rocks, space capsules and an impressive collection of space suits.

From the air, the size of the Space Center's 1,625-acre (660-hectare) site is immediately apparent.

Originally known as the Manned Space Center, nasa's Houston site was later renamed to honor Texan-born President Lyndon B. Johnson.

SPACE-AGE FUN FOR ALL

NASA was established in 1958 as a US Government agency for research into aeronautics and space flight. Throughout the 1960s, it enjoyed substantial funding and plenty of glory, but times have become harder since, with both politicians and the public losing interest in the agency's work.

The fatal 2003 space-shuttle explosion cast further doubt on NASA, which has had to publicly justify every mission.

Part of the PR exercise has been the opening up to the general public of bases like the Kennedy Space Center in Florida and the Johnson Space Center in Houston.

With the help of the Walt Disney Corporation's creative genius, NASA developed a fascinating entertainment and educational exhibit. Now 1.5 million visitors a year come to see IMAX films, moon rocks, spacecraft, including a replica of Space Shuttle *Independence,* and other memorabilia, and to take tram tours of previously off-limits areas. Interactive exhibits allow them to simulate landing a space shuttle or retrieving a satellite.

The Prebreathe Reduction Program is a research study program at the JSC that is currently being developed to improve the safety and efficiency of space walks from the International Space Station.

In 1995, NASA opened a new Mission Control Center at the site. Costing around $250 million, it replaced the old Mission Control, which had monitored the Apollo and Space Shuttle crews.

One of the Center's biggest attractions is the 363ft (110-meter) long Saturn V rocket. The most powerful rocket of its day, it lifted the Apollo craft into space

EAST TEXAS

Dense woodlands, stunning lakes, and historic towns make this often ignored part of Texas a discovery; even the oil-producing cities of the "Golden Triangle" have much to interest the traveler.

There's a whole section of Texas that is larger than New England – and has more trees – and its un-Texas topography is certain to confuse most newcomers. **Piney Woods**, the timber country of East Texas, lies between Louisiana and Central Texas, the state's economic launch pad. It was here that industrial interests first wrestled with Mother Nature, raking timber off the land and squeezing oil from beneath it. A lot of scars remain, but this region is known as much for its natural beauty as for its oil and timber industries.

The economic significance of the Gulf of Mexico and the salt dome geological formations along the relatively unsettled coast mean that the region's largest metropolitan area is found at its southeastern corner, specifically around Beaumont, Port Arthur, and Orange. Practically located in Louisiana, and flanking I-10, the three cities, dubbed the "Golden Triangle," now have a metropolitan population approaching 389,000.

Good guess

Founded in 1835, **Beaumont** ❶, the state's first oil boomtown, sits 21 miles (32km) up from the Gulf of Mexico on a deep-water ship channel dredged from the Neches River. Geologists of the late 19th century had scoffed at the theory that oil reservoirs might

be tucked inside the salt domes, but a local real estate developer, Patillo Higgins, suspected the gaseous vapors and sulfurous water at nearby Spindletop Hill indicated a pool of the valuable liquid. Along with an Austrian immigrant, Anthony F. Lucas, he drilled several unsuccessful wells in 1900, before hitting the Lucas Gusher. After the Spindletop oil discovery on January 10, 1901, Texas was transformed from an agriculturally dominated economy into one that could tap very fast-flowing pockets of wealth.

Main Attractions

Texas Energy Museum, Beaumont
Museum of the Gulf Coast, Port Arthur
Caddo Mounds State Historic Site
Freeman Plantation, Jefferson
Sam Rayburn House Museum, Bonham
Eisenhower Birthplace State Historic Site, Denison
Big Thicket National Preserve

McFaddin-Ward House Museum.

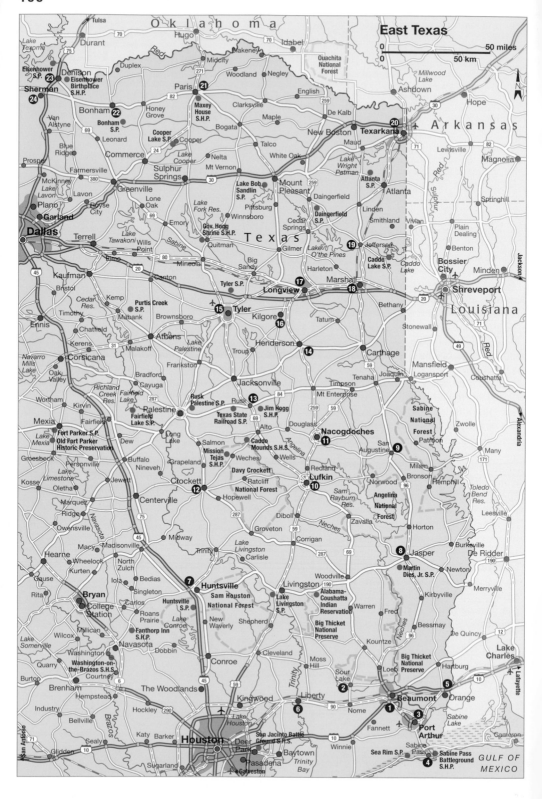

East Texas

0 _____ 50 miles
0 _____ 50 km

N

OKLAHOMA

Lake Texoma · Tulsa · Durant · Hugo · Midcity · Brakeney · Idabel

Ouachita National Forest

Millwood Lake · Ashdown · Hope

Eisenhower S.P. **23** · Denison · Eisenhower Birthplace S.H.P. · Duplex · Woodland · Negley · English · Millwood Lake

Sherman **24** · Bonham **22** · Honey Grove · Maxey House S.H.P. **21** · Paris · Clarksville · Maple · De Kalb · New Boston · Texarkana **20**

Van Alstyne · Leonard · Bonham S.P. · Cooper Lake S.P. **24** · Cooper · Nelta · Talco · White Oak · Maud

Arkansas

Blue Ridge · Commerce · 24 · Lake Cooper · Mt Vernon · Lake Wright Patman · Atlanta S.P. · Atlanta · Lewisville · Magnolia

Prospe · Farmersville · McKinney · Sulphur Springs · Lake Bob Sandlin S.P. · Mount Pleasant · Daingerfield · Springhill

Plano · Garland · Greenville · Lone Oak · Emory · Winnsboro · Pittsburg · Cedar Springs · Daingerfield S.P. **19** · Linden · Smithland · Plain Dealing

Texas

Dallas · Terrell · Wills Point · Lake Tawakoni · Quitman · Gov. Hogg Shrine S.H.P. · Gilmer · Lake O'The Pines · Jefferson · Bossier City · Benton

Kaufman · Canton · Mineola · Big Sandy · Harleton · Caddo Lake S.P. · Caddo Lake · Shreveport · Minden

Cedar Res. · Kemp · Brownsboro · Tyler S.P. **15** · Tyler · Longview **17** · Marshall **18** · Bethany · **Louisiana**

Ennis · Mabank · Kilgore · Henderson **16** · Tatum · Carthage · Stonewall

Corsicana · Athens · Troup · **14** · Mansfield · Logansport · Coushatta

Malakoff · Lake Palestine · Jacksonville · Tenaha · Joaquin · Zwolle

Palestine · Rusk Palestine S.P. **13** · Rusk · Mt Enterprise · Timpson · Sabine National Forest · Patroon

Fort Parker S.P. · Texas State Railroad S.P. · Jim Hogg S.H.P. · Alto · Douglass · Nacogdoches **11** · San Augustine **9** · Many

Old Fort Parker Historic Preservation · Long Lake · Salmon · Caddo Mounds S.H.S. · Weches · Wells · Redland · Angelina National Forest · Bronson · Hemphill

Mexia · Fairfield · Mission Tejas S.H.P. · Davy Crockett National Forest · Lufkin **10** · Norwood · Toledo Bend Res.

Groesbeck · Crockett **12** · Ratcliff · Hopewell · Sam Rayburn Res. · Leesville

Centerville · Diboll · Zavalla · Horton

Hearne · Madisonville · Midway · Trinity · Lake Livingston · Corrigan · Jasper **8** · Burkeville · De Ridder

Bryan · College Station · Huntsville **7** · Sam Houston National Forest · Livingston · Alabama-Coushatta Indian Reservation · Martin Dies, Jr. S.P. · Newton

Fanthorp Inn S.P. · Lake Conroe · New Waverly · Shepherd · Big Thicket National Preserve · Warren · Kirbyville · Merryville

Washington-on-the-Brazos S.H.S. · Conroe · Cleveland · Moss Hill · Kountze · Big Thicket National Preserve · Hartburg · Lake Charles

Brenham · The Woodlands · Kingwood · Liberty **6** · Sour Lake **2** · Beaumont **1** · Orange **5** · Lafayette

Houston · Deer Park · Baytown · Liberty · Nome · Port Arthur **3** · Sabine Lake

San Jacinto Battle Ground S.H.S. · Pasadena · Galveston · Winnie · Sea Rim S.P. · Sabine Pass Battleground S.H.P. **4** · Cameron

GULF OF MEXICO

In the space of two years, Beaumont's population swelled from 9,000 to 50,000, as East Texas became a get-rich-quick magnet. Oil derricks sprouted here as thick as the pines, and their furious pumping of the salt domes took its toll. At the appropriately named **Sour Lake** ❷, about 20 miles (32km) west of Beaumont on State Route 105, visitors can still survey the damage in the form of a 10-acre (4-hectare) sinkhole created in 1929 by three decades of drilling.

Among the many museums devoted to the industry's fascinating history are Beaumont's reconstructed **Spindletop-Gladys City Boomtown Museum** (5555 Jimmy Simmons Boulevard; tel: 409-880-1750; www.spindletop.org; Tue–Sat 10am–5pm, Sun 1–5pm) on the Lamar University campus, and the **Texas Energy Museum** (600 Main Street; tel: 409-833-5100; www.texas energymuseum.org; daily 9am–5pm).

The city's oldest home, the **John Jay French Museum** (3025 French Road; tel: 409-898-0348; www.jjfrench.com; Tue–Fri 10am–3pm, Sat 10am–2pm), depicts the life of the Connecticut-born trader, who settled here in 1845, while the elegant **McFaddin-Ward House Museum** (1906 Calder Avenue; tel: 409-832-2134; www.mcfaddin-ward.org; Tue–Fri 10am–3.30pm, Sat 10.30am–3.30pm, Sun 1–3.30pm) is a 17-room mansion owned by an early 20th-century oilman.

Among the city's other sights are the **Edison Museum** (350 Pine Street; tel: 409-981-3089; http://edisonmuseum.americommerce.com; Mon–Fri 9am–5pm; free), housed, appropriately, in a converted power station and devoted to the life of the great inventor; the **Fire Museum of Texas** (400 Walnut Street; tel: 409-880-3927; www.firemuseumof texas.org; Mon–Fri 8am–4.30pm; free), and the **Babe Didrikson Zaharias Memorial** (1750 I-10 East; tel: 409-833-4622; www.babedidriksonzaharias.org; open daily; free), which commemorates the state's most famous athlete, the Beaumont-born triple winner of

track and field events at the 1932 Los Angeles Olympics. The memorial also houses the Chamber of Commerce.

Lively Cajuns

Beaumont's sister city to the southeast is **Port Arthur** ❸. Home of the world's largest petrochemical complex, it is noted for its fleet of shrimp boats, its superlative seafood, and its Cajun nightclubs, with their fiddle music and rowdy atmosphere. "*Laissez les bon temps rouler!*" – Let the good times roll! – is a much-quoted Cajun saying, which the tourist board never tires of pointing out.

Port Arthur was the birthplace of the late rock singer Janis Joplin, whose birthday is celebrated every January 19, and is the kind of place where tourists can attend a genuine, music-filled Cajun wedding – of two alligators.

The city was founded in 1895 as the seaport terminus of his Gulf Coast Railroad by Arthur Stilwell, who ran out of money and lost ownership to a famous speculator, John "Bet-a-Million" Gates. But the glamorous mansions of what was once "Stilwells' Dream City"

Port Arthur is home to the world's largest petrochemical complex.

Caddo Lake State Park.

still remain along the white sandy shores of **Lake Sabine**, some 9 miles (14km) long and 7.5 miles (12km) across, and joined to the ocean by the Sabine–Neches Ship Channel, which flows right through the city.

The little town of **Sabine Pass** ❹, laid out by Sam Houston himself in 1836, was the site of a famous 1863 Civil War battle; today it is part of Port Arthur. **Sabine Pass Battleground State Historic Site** (6100 Dick Dowling Road; tel: 512-463-7948; www.visitsabinepassbattleground.com; daily 8am–5pm, until 8pm May–Sept) honors the 46 Confederates, led by a barkeep named Dick Dowling, who deployed half a dozen cannons to drive off a Union force at least a hundred times as large. The site features a stately bronze statue of Confederate Lt. Richard "Dick" Dowling, who led the men to victory, and an interpretive pavilion illustrating the story of the battle. Nearby **Sea Rim State Park** (19335 South Gulfway Drive; tel: 409-971-2559; www.tpwd.state.tx/sea-rim; open daily), along the gulf, is a great place to do some birdwatching.

The most famous house in Port Arthur is **Pompeiian Villa** (1953 Lakeshore Drive; tel: 409-983-5977; www.museumofthegulfcoast.org; Mon–Fri 10am–2pm), built in 1900 for barbed wire inventor Isaac Ellwood. He sold it to a fellow tycoon, Diamond Match Company president James Hopkins. When Hopkins's wife arrived to discover Port Arthur's oppressive heat, mosquitoes, and muddy streets she turned right around and returned to St Louis, so Hopkins traded the mansion to banker George Craig for 10 percent of the stock in the newly formed Texas Oil Company (which became Texaco). When teased later about why he'd given up his stock for what became known as "the billion dollar house," Craig replied: "Oil companies were a dime a dozen then. How did I know the Texas Oil Company would survive?"

Two other old Lakeshore mansions are worth visiting: **Rose Hill Manor** (100 Woodworth Boulevard; tel: 409-985-7292; Tue–Fri 11.30am–5pm, Sat by appointment only; donation) and **White Haven** (2545 Lakeshore Drive; tel: 409-984-6101; free guided tours by

The marshy areas of East Texas are alligator country – beware!

appointment). Port Arthur's heritage is further displayed in its **Museum of the Gulf Coast** (700 Procter Street; tel: 409 982 7000; www.museumofthegulfcoast. com; Mon–Sat 9am–5pm, Sun 1–5pm), where such celebrated locals as Janis Joplin, the Big Bopper, Harry James, Babe Didrikson Zaharias, and artist Robert Rauschenberg are honored.

Over the Rainbow

Rainbow Bridge, a 1.5-mile (2.5km) graceful arc over the Neches River, at a clearance height of 177ft (56 meters), is the tallest on the coast and joins Port Arthur with the city of **Orange** ❺. Here Farmer's Mercantile on Division Street, a funky store that opened in 1928, is not only still in business but carries some of the same items as when it began.

On Green Avenue, the **Stark Museum of Art** (712 Green Avenue; tel: 409-886 2787; www.starkculturalvenues. org/starkmuseum; Tue–Sat 9am–5pm) and nearby **W.H. Stark House** (tel: 409-883-0871; www.starkculturalvenues. org/whstarkhouse; Tue–Sat 9am–5pm) are eye-popping structures whose exteriors are almost as interesting as the furniture and artworks that they contain.

From Orange, fascinating airboat tours can be taken (Adventures 2000 Swamp and River Tours, 813 Lutcher Drive; tel: 409-988-9342; http://swamp andrivertours.com) of the alligator-infested swamps, salt marshes, and bayous that surround the area. The rice fields and marshlands, with their moss-laden trees and tropical palms, are a refuge for hundreds of thousands of migrating waterfowl, attractive alike to the birdwatcher and, alas, the hunter.

Farther north

Liberty ❻, on US 90 near the Trinity River, between Beaumont and Houston, traces its history back to the Spanish mission erected nearby and its downtown area created by the Mexican government in 1831. **Huntsville** ❼, 70 miles (113km) north of Houston, on US 75 and I-45 – which marks the western boundary of the East Texas

pioneer region – was founded in 1830 by settlers from Huntsville, Alabama. It has the state prison and Sam Houston State University, and claims added significance as the town where Sam Houston lived his later life. The site of Houston's grave is also here, along with a 67ft (20-meter) -tall statue of Houston as you approach Huntsville from the south on I-45. **Jasper** ❽, 100 miles (160km) to the east, where US 190 meets US 96 (which runs part of the way alongside Sabine National Forest), offers visitors another chance to view historic sites. Founded in 1824 beside the Angelina River, Jasper was the home of the Tavern Oak, a 250-year-old giant pine oak (connected to a tavern there in 1839 but unfortunately destroyed by a tornado in 1996). Several old historic houses, from around the middle of the 19th century, do, however, exist.

Almost in Louisiana, **San Augustine** ❾ is a town where, at one time or another, nearly every famous Texan in those early days walked the streets, including Davy Crockett who was given a feast here on the way to the

FACT

Mission Señora de los Dolores de los Ais (also known as the Dolores Mission) was founded in 1716 and abandoned in 1773. Nothing remains of the historic structure, but there is a visitor center with informative displays at the site.

The W. H. Stark House.

The Kilgore College Rangerettes have performed at 64 consecutive Cotton Bowl games since 1951.

Tyler Municipal Rose Garden.

Alamo. Historic places include Cullen House (205 S. Congress Street; tel: 936-275-5110), the 1839 house of the famous Texas judge; the site of the 18th-century Mission Señora de los Dolores de los Ais; and the Old Town Well, dug to a depth of 27ft (8 meters) by slaves in 1860 to serve travelers.

Wood wealth

After the political turmoil of the early 19th-century had been quelled, a new wave of boomtowns grew up in East Texas, built on another economic base: timber. **Lufkin** , on US 69, southeast of San Augustine, was founded in 1882 and was the home of the South's first paper mill. It remains the center of the state's timber industry. One main attraction in this city of 36,000 people is the **Texas Forestry Museum** (1905 Atkinson Drive; tel: 936-632-9535; www. treetexas.com; Mon–Sat 10am–5pm; free), built in a grove of Texas pines, with large glass windows bringing the forest right inside. A moonshiner's still and a blacksmith's forge are among the exhibits. Lufkin also stages an annual Forest Festival every September.

Nacogdoches ⓫, 20 miles (32km) farther north on US 259, was originally settled by the Nacogdoche branch of Caddo Indians, with evidence of settlement dating back 10,000 years ago. It claims to be the first incorporated town in Texas. Now a modern city of 33,000, with a solid economic base of manufacturing, agriculture, retail trade, and tourism, Nacogdoches, almost midway between Houston and Texarkana, makes a fine base for exploring the rest of East Texas.

Nacogdoches and the surrounding area have numerous historic sites, of which the most interesting, 26 miles (42km) west of town, in Alto, is **Caddo Mounds State Historic Site** (1649 US 21 West; tel: 936-858-3218; www. visitcaddomounds.com; open daily), the only significant prehistoric American Indian site in Texas. Built by the Hasinai branch of the Caddo Indians 1,200 years ago, the 397-acre (160-hectare) site was the southwesternmost ceremonial center for the powerful Mississippian Mound Builder culture, which spanned the Eastern Woodlands for 2,500 years. The site preserves two temple mounds and a burial mound as well as much of the village. A trail loops around this lovely site, and takes about 45 minutes to walk.

Just north of Nacogdoches is **Millard's Crossing Historic Village** (6020 North Street; tel: 936-564-6631; www.millardscrossing.org; Mon–Sat 9am–4pm, Sun 1–4pm). It comprises a dozen or more structures, including a church and schoolhouse, some dating back as far as 1820 and many stocked with original artifacts. **La Calle del Norte** (presently North Street) once linked the original American Indian settlement to villages in the north, and is said to be the oldest public thoroughfare in the United States.

At Pilar and Lanana streets is the **Sterne-Hoya House Museum and Library** (211 S. Lanana Street; tel: 936-560-5426; Tue–Sat 10am–4pm; free), built in 1828 by a pioneer merchant who helped found the state, and now occupied by a library. Here too, is the **Stone Fort Museum** (1808 Alumni Drive; tel: 936-468-2408; Tue–Sat 9am–5pm, Sun 1–5pm; free), a 1779 Spanish trading post reconstructed on the campus of Stephen F. Austin State University. The fort marks the site of four unsuccessful rebellions, and the museum features tribal artifacts along-side memorabilia from the eras of the eight flags that have flown above the fort – Spain, Magee-Gutierrez Expe-dition, Long Republic, Fredonian Republic, Mexico, Republic of Texas, Confederacy, and US.

El Camino Real

Nacogdoches is on one of the most historic routes in America: **El Camino Real de Tejas**, blazed by the Spanish as "The King's Highway," or the Old San Antonio Road. Travelers can follow that path today by taking US 21 out of Nacogdoches in either direction. El Camino Real de Tejas (now a designated National Historical Trail managed by the National Park Service) linked Span-ish Colonial Mexico with settlements in Texas and Louisiana by following American Indian trails, shallow fords, or rivers. Incorporated into the state highway system in 1929 as US 21, El Camino Real connects innumerable other historical sites. Not far to the west, for example, is **Crockett** ⓬, founded in 1837 on the spot where Davy Crockett camped en route to martyrdom at the Alamo. Davy Crockett Memorial Park's 35 wooded acres (15 hectares) are ideal for picnics and relaxing.

Trains and Confederate guns

Rusk ⓭, at the intersection of US 84 and US 69, between Lufkin and Tyler, was founded in 1846 and is home of the **Texas State Railroad State His-torical Park** (tel: 877-726-7245; www. texasstaterr.com; trains depart 11am and return at 3.30pm Mar–May Sat–Sun, May–Nov Fri–Sun), a train track that forms the nation's long-est and narrowest state park. Visitors

can climb aboard for an enjoyable 50-mile (80km) round-trip journey through the Piney Woods and across 30 bridges, one a 1,000ft (300-meter) crossing of the Neches River.

Historic Fifth Street features old homes and what is claimed to be the nation's longest footbridge, a 547ft (168-meter) span built in 1861, sepa-rating the business district from the old residential area. As an important Confederate Army conscription center, Rusk figured prominently in the Civil War. Look for the historical marker that denotes the Confederate Gun Fac-tory. Two miles (3km) west of town is the **Jim Hogg State Historical Park**, 178 acres (72 hectares) dedicated as the birthplace of the state's first Texas-born governor (1891–95).

Henderson ⓮, on US 259 in the center of Rusk County, is another find for visitors in search of old houses, with 44 historic properties on the National Register. Founded in 1843 on land owned by the Cherokee Indians, Hen-derson's attractions include **The Depot** (514 N. High Street; tel: 903-657-4303; www.hendersonmuseum.com; Mon–Fri

Farmland near Rusk.

Replica Eiffel Tower, Paris, Texas.

Draughon-Moore Ace of Clubs House, Texarkana.

9am–5pm, Sat 9am–1pm), an old railroad depot restored as a museum and children's learning center.

Metropolitan centers

Three other metropolitan centers – Tyler, Longview, and Marshall – are representative of East Texan urban life, with their oil and timber economic foundations.

Tyler ⑮ (pop. 99,000), the largest, is located about 100 miles (160km) east of Dallas on I-20 and is a petroleum production center. Also known as the "Rose Capital of America," the town markets more than 50 percent of the nation's rose bushes, maintaining a 14-acre (6-hectare) **Municipal Rose Garden** (420 Rose Park Drive; tel: 903-531-1212), containing over 30,000 bushes and more than 400 varieties. The garden is at its best from May through October.

The oil boom of 1900 at Beaumont proved a harbinger of things to come for the entire region, as wildcatters scattered throughout the Piney Woods prospecting for oil. The frenzy peaked in 1930 with the discovery of the biggest well of all, in Rusk County. This well,

known as the Great East Texas Oil Field, was a discovery that held the state's economic spotlight until the fields of West Texas surfaced after World War II.

The boom town associated more than any other with the 1930 strike is **Kilgore** ⑯, just off US 259, 25 miles (40km) east of Tyler. It lies in the center of the field, with more than 1,000 oil-producing wells. The "world's richest acre" was the description for a downtown block of Kilgore, where 24 oil wells once produced simultaneously. The town's **East Texas Oil Museum** (1100 Broadway Boulevard; tel: 903-983-8295) tells the story. Another attraction is the **Rangerette Showcase** (tel: 903-983-8295; www.easttexasoilmuseum.com; Tue–Sat 9am–4pm, Sun 2–5pm; free) at Kilgore College, which pays tribute to the college's high-kicking precision dance team, formed in 1940 to provide half-time entertainment at football games.

On I-20 is **Longview** ⑰ (pop. 81,000), 10 miles (16km) northeast of Kilgore, which enjoyed explosive growth in the oil-crazed 1930s. Thanks to a dynamic industrialization program begun after World War II, Longview considers its location – among the tall pines, near several well-stocked bass lakes – a magnet for industry as well as recreation. The town's **R.G. Le Tourneau Museum** (2100 S. Mobberly Avenue; tel: 903-233-3270; www.letu.edu/_Academics/library/museum; daily 8am–5pm; free), on the Le Tourneau University campus, displays patents and objects related to the man who became the world's foremost inventor of heavy earth-moving equipment.

Confederate base

Continuing east on I-20, next comes **Marshall** ⑱ (pop. 25,000), a oncewealthy city that supplied gunpowder and ammunition to the Confederacy, for which it became an administrative center. Originally a stagecoach stop, it achieved its prosperity after the arrival of the Texas and Pacific Railroad. A reminder of those early days is provided by the venerable **Ginocchio Hotel** (1896), which anchors the town's three-block historic district.

Historic homes

There's always debate about which town in East Texas has the best old homes. San Augustine usually wins great praise, but **Jefferson ⓳** (pop. 2,200) on US 59, just 58 miles (93km) south of Texarkana, is high on the list, too. It is a living museum of antebellum houses.

Laid out in 1842 as a river landing on Big Cypress Bayou, Jefferson grew into early Texas's primary river port, as steamboats from New Orleans brought settlers westward. With them came the plantation culture and architecture of the Old South. But decline began when the city refused a rail depot.

Many of the city's fine old homes are open during the Annual Historical Pilgrimage on the first weekend in May. Highlights include the **Freeman Plantation** (Highway 49 West; tel: 903-665-2320; tours by appointment), built in 1850 in Greek Revival style and embodying the grandeur of Louisiana plantation life.

Famous patrons

Jefferson's **Excelsior House Hotel** (211 W. Austin; tel: 903-665-2513; www.theexcelsiorhouse.com), dating from 1858, is the second-oldest hotel in Texas, a place patronized by US Presidents Rutherford B. Hayes and Ulysses S. Grant, as well as Irish playwright and novelist Oscar Wilde and the famous 19th-century industrialist Jay Gould. Still in operation today, it offers guests a chance to relax amid period furnishings, many of them acquired when the hotel first opened more than a century ago – and rumor has it some of the rooms are haunted.

Nearby is Jay Gould's well-preserved luxury railroad car, named the Atalanta (open daily). From **Jefferson Landing**, across the bridge from downtown Jefferson, visitors have the chance to take a 45-minute river tour along the old steamboat channel in 20ft (6-meter) handcrafted river boats.

Twice as nice

In the northeastern corner of the region is **Texarkana ⓴** (pop. 37,000), perched on the Texas-Arkansas state

The House of the Seasons, in Jefferson, built by Benjamin Epperson.

line and thus half in each state. Texarkana is an agribusiness center for farming, livestock, and timber interests in Arkansas, Louisiana, and Texas. Its slogan is "Twice as Nice," a phrase to describe the city's unique status, which is best illustrated by one of its most unusual landmarks – the Post Office Building, which straddles the state line.

In addition to the town's **Museum of Regional History** (219 State Line Avenue; tel: 903-793-4831; www.texarkanamuseums.org; Tue–Sat 10am–4pm; free), depicting 19th-century life in the region, there is the multi-faceted **Draughon-Moore Ace of Clubs House** (420 Pine Street; tel: 903-793-4831; www.texarkanamuseums.org; open Sat for tours, weekdays by appointment; free), built over a century ago by the winner of a poker game and still containing the original furnishings.

Pioneer towns

Another notable pioneer town is **Paris** ㉑ (pop. 25,000), on US 82 near the Oklahoma border. Founded in 1839, Paris became home to a notorious list of frontiersmen, including retired outlaw

Native fungi, Big Thicket National Preserve.

Frank James (brother of Jesse James) and bandit queen Belle Starr. Here (by appointment) visitors can tour the **Sam Bell Maxey House State Historic Site** (812 S. Church Street; tel: 903-785-5716; www.visitsambellmaxeyhouse.com; Tue–Sun 9am–4pm), an exquisite Victorian home built in 1868 by a Confederate general.

A lesser-known victim of the Alamo siege in 1836, James B. Bonham, had a town named after him the following year. It can be found on Highway 82 in the northern part of the state. **Bonham** ㉒ (pop. 10,000) was the home of Sam Rayburn, the Texas politician who served as Speaker of the US House of Representatives for longer than anyone else. The enjoyable homestead that comprises **Sam Rayburn House Museum** (890 W. State Highway 56; tel: 903-583-5558; www.visitsamrayburnhouse.com; Tue–Sun 9:30am–4:30pm), with the nearby Library, contains papers of the farmer's son from Fannin County who was House Speaker from 1940 until his death in 1961, apart from two brief interludes.

The **Fannin County Museum of History** (1 N. Main Street; tel:

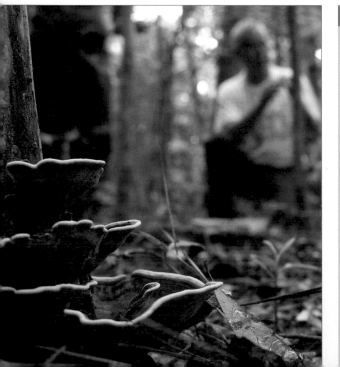

THE ALABAMA COUSHATTA

There are few signs in modern times of Texas's once-thriving American Indian population. The small Alabama-Coushatta Indian Reservation has existed since 1854, when Sam Houston established it as a reward to the two tribes for their neutrality during the war for Texan independence. The Alabama-Coushatta trace their ancestors to the historic Muscogee or Creek Confederacy in Alabama, east of the Mississippi, who were removed to this area in the late 18th century. They are one of six federally recognized tribes whose members are descended from the Creek Confederacy. The tribe is known for its annual powwow, which takes place in early June. It also runs a pleasant campground with tent sites, RV hookups, and cabins at Lake Tombigbee (tel: 800-926-9038 for reservations).

903-583-8042; Tue–Sat noon–4pm, from 10am Apr–Aug; free), in a restored railroad depot, is an absorbing collection of pioneer artifacts, ranging from ancient costumes to railroad tools. **Fort Inglish Park** (W. Sam Rayburn Drive; tel: 903-583-3441; www.traveltex. com/activities/fort-inglish-park; Apr–Sept Tue–Fri 10am–4pm, Sat–Sun 1–5pm) displays replicas of the blockhouse and stockade built by Bailey Inglish in 1837.

Eisenhower country

Denison ㉓ and **Sherman** ㉔ on the Oklahoma border near Lake Texoma – an impoundment of the Red River – are rich from farming and livestock industries. While it is well known that Texas produced President Lyndon Johnson, another president also came from the Lone Star State, and Denison takes pride in honoring that favorite son: Dwight D. Eisenhower. The **Eisenhower Birthplace State Historic Site** (609 S. Lamar Avenue; tel: 903-465-8908; www.visiteisenhowerbirthplace.org; Tue–Sat 9am–5pm, Sun 1–5pm), a two-story frame house, has been restored to its appearance in 1890, the year Ike was born. The adjoining visitor center depicts life during the years when he was president.

Diverse ecosystem

Big Thicket National Preserve (tel: 420-246-2337; www.nps.gov/bith; open daily; free) in East Texas is a fabulous counterpoint to West Texas's massive desert of Big Bend National Park. A dense and mysterious forest, it blankets much of southeast Texas and is bounded by the Neches and San Jacinto rivers and Pine Island Bayou.

Set aside during the Great Depression, when the federal government bought the area from hard-pressed timber companies, Big Thicket withstood challenges from the oil and timber industries for decades and finally, in 1974, environmentalists persuaded Congress to establish the preserve. Its 108,000 acres (43,706 hectares) and 15 units protect nine different ecosystems,

including forests of longleaf pine growing near yucca and cacti, and bald cypress-lined bayous next to southern magnolia trees. Since 1981, it has been a Unesco International Biosphere Reserve, and, in 2001, the American Bird Conservancy designated it a Globally Important Birding Area.

The preserve has 40 miles (64km) of hiking trails, from short boardwalk trails to longer hikes, but no campgrounds; however, primitive camping is allowed with a permit. Boating and kayaking are popular on the **Neches River and Village Creek**. Wildlife watching is the big draw. The preserve lies beneath two major bird migratory routes, and some 185 species of bird can be found living in or migrating through the preserve. Watch for the red-cockaded woodpecker and the brown-headed nuthatch on the Sundew Trail.

At **Big Thicket Visitor Center** (tel: 409-951-6700; daily 8am–4.30pm; free), located 8 miles (13km) north of Kountze, or 30 miles (48km) north of Beaumont via US 69/287, park rangers can help with trip planning and also offer talks and guided hikes daily.

TIP

When visiting any of the East Texas natural areas, don't forget your insect repellent. The mosquitoes can be ferocious!

Eisenhower Birthplace State Historic Site.

THE GULF COAST

The sea border of Texas runs from Louisiana in the east to Mexico in the south. Its sweeping arc encompasses countless unspoiled beaches, several wildlife sanctuaries, and two historic cities.

I t's been called a lot of different things – "funky," "scruffy," oddly even "Byzantine" – but one label has rarely been pinned on the Texas Gulf Coast: "chic." It just does not fit. It's not the Riviera, and it isn't Rio. Even Daytona and Malibu are very distant American cousins. But, from South Padre Island north to Bolivar Peninsula, the Gulf Coast ranks as one of Texas's most powerful magnets for travelers. It exudes history.

When the European explorers arrived, its shores were home to coastal tribes, some with a reputation for cannibalism. In keeping with its faded, once rather barbaric image, the coast sheltered early 19th-century pirates seeking refuge from the early US Navy, which established strongholds along the Gulf. From such a heritage sprang a prosperous trading culture in the late 19th century. The inheritors of that legacy are the present-day developers who have ventured cautiously onto its shores in order to build condominiums and professional buildings. They tread lightly with good reason because, within that legacy, lies a pattern of destruction that visits with clockwork regularity.

Nature's fury

Here on the Texas coast, nature has demonstrated its powers as it has nowhere else. Galveston is the site of the most celebrated catastrophe in US

history – the 1900 hurricane, which destroyed the city and killed thousands of people. The area was once again battered by a destructive hurricane in September 2008, when Hurricane Ike, a Category 2 storm with winds up to 110mph (178kph), made a direct hit on East Galveston, creating a massive storm surge that inundated Galveston and the nearby Bolivar Peninsula. The destruction on Bolivar was almost total, flattening 3,000 homes and businesses, destroying the historic lighthouse, and blowing debris into

Main Attractions

High Island, Bolivar Peninsula
Texas Seaport Museum, Galveston
Bishop's Palace, Galveston
Moody Mansion, Galveston
Art Museum of South Texas, Corpus Christi
Padre Island National Seashore
King Ranch

Galveston harbor.

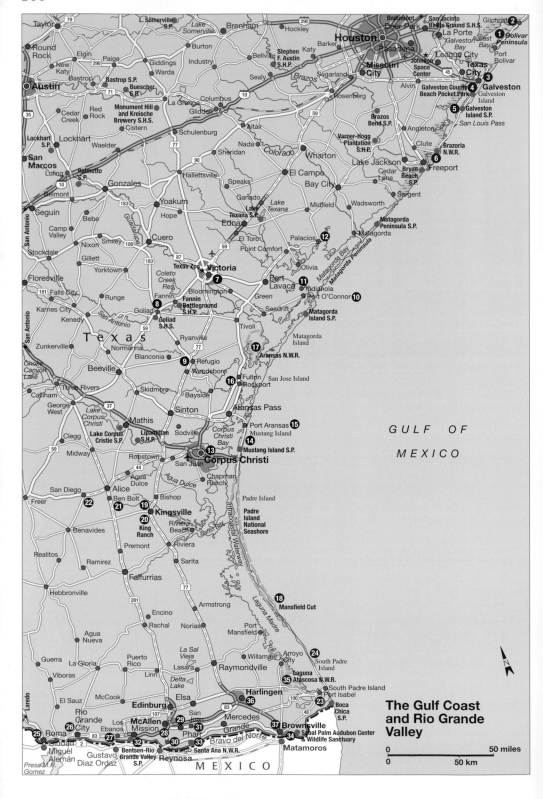

The Gulf Coast and Rio Grande Valley

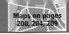

Galveston Bay. Years later, the Bolivar Peninsula is still rebuilding, but the community stands strong. People here are resilient.

The great escape

Whether or not the wind and rain are pounding from above, the Gulf of Mexico is always pulling from below, eating at the shoreline, and claiming the land. Engineers have predicted the eventual reclamation of beach homes at many points during the 21st century. Still, developers take their risks and beach visitors continue to seek that special relationship with the sea. Between storms, and in spite of their fears, coastal Texans have created an enchanting domain. The Gulf of Mexico in summertime is as warm as bathwater, and the hour's drive from Houston to nearby tranquil Galveston provides a contrast that can be felt as well as seen.

Less cluttered by neon and glitz than most modern coastlines, Texas's Gulf shore is a welcome escape hatch for city refugees. Visitors won't find the world's best surf, but they will find isolated beaches and sleepy villages with a lifestyle that is as surprising as it is charming.

The Texas coastline runs 367 miles (590km) in a great arc that forms the southeastern corner of the state. The land here does not end in the abrupt cliffs and rocky shores to be found in other parts of America. In Texas, the land surrenders gradually to the water, drifting from the region of rolling hills and pine forests known as the Coastal Plains into a grassy marshland called the Coastal Prairie. The Coastal Plains includes East Texas and the Rio Grande Valley; the Coastal Prairie is, more precisely, the Texas coast.

Starting at Bolivar Peninsula, just north of Galveston, the Texas shore forms the world's longest chain of barrier islands as it slips toward Mexico: 624 miles (1,000km) of tidewater coast, when you add the bays, lagoons, and swamps between the bayou marshland in the north and

coastal brush in the south. The region includes two cities – Galveston to the north and Corpus Christi to the south.

Bolivar peninsula

Unspoiled South Padre Island, to the south, is generally considered the tourist's best chance for a Caribbean resort-style vacation in this state. Compared with South Padre, **Bolivar Peninsula** ❶, a wild barrier island that has been developed, is a diamond in the rough, to the north. But it can be a true gem for those who appreciate a holiday uncluttered with glitz.

Extending like a long finger down the Texas Coast from Louisiana, the peninsula was named in 1815 to honor the Latin American revolutionary Simon Bolivar, during an era when the Gulf Coast and the Caribbean were aflame with anti-Spanish sentiment. A free 20-minute ferry carries cars and their passengers from Galveston's east end to State Route 87 on the peninsula, which provides the only convenient access to Bolivar's beaches. But this very remoteness has guaranteed splendid isolation for Bolivar's

Reddish egret, Bolivar Peninsula.

beachgoers, who go birding (334 species), crabbing, and camping near the surf. Beach houses – many on stilts and rebuilt following Hurricane Ike – can be rented at the main residential community on the west end of Bolivar, Crystal Beach. Reservations should be made in advance through one of Galveston's real estate companies.

Gilchrist ❷ is a small town about 20 miles (32km) north on State Route 87, and its main attraction is **Rollover Pass**, a channel that slices through the center of town, serving up some of the best bankside fishing in the state. Elsewhere along the peninsula, visitors will find an unpretentious montage of honky-tonk taverns, hamburger joints, and convenience stores.

The narrow Bolivar Peninsula runs for 27 miles (43km) along the shore and on its east end crosses bayous, marshes, barrier islands, and the Intracoastal Waterway as it heads north on State Route 124. **High Island** is celebrated for its birding. Its unique salt dome geography allows trees to grow that offer resting places for thousands of neotropical migrating birds during spring migrations. There are no less than four bird sanctuaries run by Texas Audubon here, including Smith Oaks Sanctuary on High Island, and on the other side of the Intracoastal Waterway, on East Galveston Bay, **Anahuac National Wildlife Refuge**, one of several national wildlife refuges along this section of the coast.

Historic Galveston

This island city of just under 48,000 residents has been described as the only part of the coast you'd want to visit on a rainy day. Visitors who head directly for the beach will miss plenty, because, in addition to the sea, recreational attractions and good shopping, **Galveston ❸** offers a unique historical perspective.

But for that 1900 hurricane, Galveston might have been today *the* industrial heavyweight, instead of its neighbor, Houston. After a roguish beginning as a seaport haven for the pirate clan of Jean Lafitte, Galveston was one of the South's most significant cities by the end of the 19th century.

The French-born Jean Lafitte and his brother, Pierre, were already

Tall ship Elissa, Texas Seaport Museum.

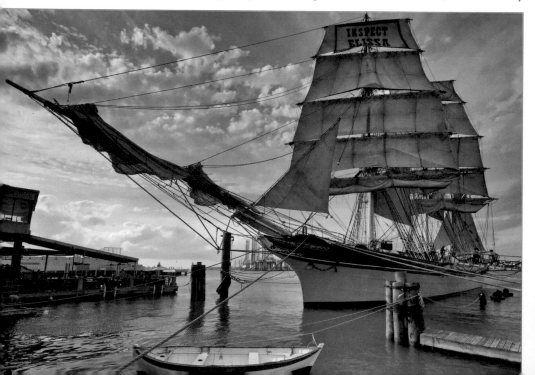

legendary smugglers in nearby New Orleans, when, in 1817, they founded a town called Campeachy on Galveston Island. Their fort, Maison Rouge, attracted a "navy" of over 1,000 men, who continually disrupted Spanish shipping in the Gulf of Mexico. Lafitte's pirate "den," as it has been called, was a wicked place: slaving, gaming, drunkenness, and whoring abounded. He sold all the blacks of Galveston, including freed slaves, in New Orleans. To some a romantic figure, Lafitte was the last of the pirates on the Gulf, until the US Navy forced him out of the area in the early 1820s. He sailed away to Mujeres Island off the Yucatan Peninsula in Mexico.

Galveston was then developed as a seaport during the Republic, and soon became the state's largest city. Blockaded during the Civil War, the city remained in Confederate hands, except for a few months in 1862. The Union Navy entered the harbor in October, landed on Christmas morning, and was expelled on New Year's Day 1863. They were back on June 19, 1865, to take over the city and proclaim the freedom of the slaves. "Juneteenth" has been celebrated by African-Americans in Texas ever since.

A hurricane for the ages

Galveston continued to grow, but its population was eventually surpassed by San Antonio and Houston. Much of Texas's cotton was exported through the city – ancient cotton warehouses and grain elevators survive today – and the water of the bay is still yellow from the shipping of sulfur. A hub of commercial activity between the 1870s and 1900, Galveston had Texas's first telegraph, electric lights, brewery, and medical college. Splendid mansions were erected, paid for with the profits from all the city's commerce.

The 1900 hurricane on September 8 and 9 dimmed Galveston's glow in a matter of hours. Winds sometimes in excess of 100 mph (160kmh) swept tides of 4–6ft (1–2 meters) across the island to produce one of the nation's worst natural disasters. There was nothing to break the hurricane's force: Galveston's highest elevation was a mere 8ft (2.5 meters). At one point the water rose

FACT

Galveston is an anglicized version of Galvez, the original Spanish name for the island settlement. It was named for Bernardo de Galvez, the Spanish Governor of Louisiana.

Aerial view of Galveston.

FACT

The stage of the Grand
1894 Opera House has,
in its time, played host to
the likes of actress
Sarah Bernhardt, singer
Al Jolson, and the Marx
Brothers.

4ft (just over a meter) in four seconds: 1,500 acres (600 hectares) of houses were completely destroyed. Death estimates have ranged from 5,000 to 8,000. So complete was the devastation that many wanted to abandon the place, but, stubbornly, Galveston refused to surrender. The people resurrected their demolished homes and constructed a 17ft (5-meter) seawall, protection against future ravaging by the waters of the Gulf. The present seawall is 10 miles (16km) long, 16ft (5 meters) wide at its base and 5ft (1.5 meters) wide at the top. Hurricane Ike also created damage in Galveston, too, but nothing compared to the great 1900 storm.

Meanwhile, its big rival, Houston, with more people and better rail connections, seized its opportunity and, with federal money, began dredging a ship channel in the Buffalo Bayou to the San Jacinto River and, from there, into the Gulf. So, Houston – 50 miles (80km) inland – became a port city while Galveston, although remaining a port, became less important and was frequently referred to as "that island city south of Houston."

Onto the island

Primary access to the island city is via I-45, a freeway that stretches from Dallas, through Houston, and over a bridge into Galveston. Once on the island, it becomes **Broadway** Ⓐ, Galveston's main street, which carries you through the oldest part of the city to **Stewart Beach** Ⓑ. A right turn on to 61st Street, before I-45 becomes Broadway, bypasses the central city and takes you to the island's most popular beach district, **West Beach**, on the south shore.

In Galveston, all other roads seem to lead eventually to **Seawall Boulevard** Ⓒ, a broad avenue along the waterline above the city's dramatic seawall, with an array of shops, restaurants, motels, bicycle rentals, arcades, and other amusements lining one side, and the Gulf of Mexico pleasantly filling the horizon on the other. The island's visitor information center is at 2328 Broadway Street (tel: 409-425-4753; www.galveston.com). Popular seafood restaurants on Seawall Boulevard include Gaido's, founded in 1911 and a good place to find gumbo, and the adjoining Casey's.

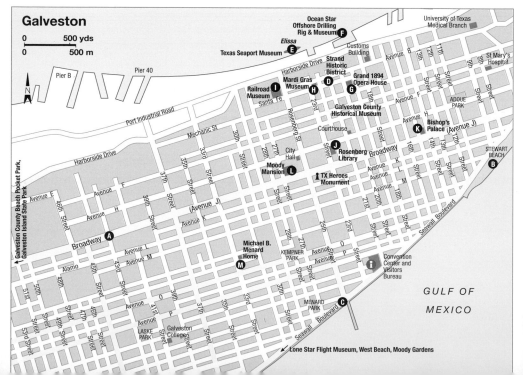

Buildings restored

There's a lot for families to do in Galveston. Start with a stroll along the **Strand Historic District** ⓓ, a 12-block area that parallels Broadway between 20th and 25th streets, which was once part of the city's warehouse district. Named for the street in London with all the famous shops, thanks to its profusion of great commercial houses, it was once renowned as "The Wall Street of the West."

The solid, iron-fronted Victorian structures have been refurbished with more than 90 shops and restaurants. Some highlights in the area include La King's Confectionery, home of old-fashioned ice-cream and candies such as saltwater taffy, Hendley Market (Victorian clothing, antique postcards), and the restored square-rigged tall ship Elissa at the **Texas Seaport Museum** ⓔ (Pier 21; tel: 409-763-1877; www.galvestonhistory.org/attractions/maritime-heritage/texas-seaport-museum; daily 10am–6pm). The museum also offers harbor tours with dolphin watching, a documentary on the 1900 hurricane, and a database of immigrants who disembarked in Galveston between 1846 and 1948. On board the **Ocean Star Offshore Drilling Rig and Museum** ⓕ (Pier 21; tel: 409-766-7827; www.oceanstaroec.com; daily 10am–5pm), three decks of equipment, exhibits, and interactive displays detail offshore oil and gas exploration, drilling, and oil production. Housed in a retired jackup drilling rig, the museum offers the rare opportunity to explore the rig floor and pipe deck of a massive, sea-going structure.

Another historic structure is the spectacular **Grand 1894 Opera House** ⓖ (2020 Post Office Street; tel: 409-765-1894; www.thegrand.com) where contemporary Broadway musicals are performed.

Mardi Gras in Galveston

The Strand's ambiance is reminiscent of Bourbon Street in New Orleans's French Quarter, and, like that colorful Louisiana city, Galveston makes a big thing of the Mardi Gras. The entire city turns out for the parade that marks Fat Tuesday. Beads and token coins fill the air as the Strand celebrates and rejoices. The **Mardi Gras Museum** ⓗ (23rd and Strand streets; tel: 409-763-1133; Mon–Fri 10am–8pm, Sat 10am–10pm, Sun 10am–6pm; free) is devoted to the subject, displaying costumes and other historic memorabilia. Two blocks farther, you will find the **Railroad Museum** ⓘ (2602 Santa Fe Place; tel: 409-765-5700; www.galvestonrrmuseum.com; Apr–Oct daily 10am–5pm, Nov–Mar Mon–Fri 9am–4pm, Sat–Sun 10am–5pm), with audiovisual displays and a collection of 35 old rail cars. It is in a looming early 20th-century skyscraper, the former home of the American National Insurance Company, founded by wealthy Galvestonian William Moody, Jr. Sculpted life-like figures sit optimistically in the waiting room.

The **Rosenberg Library** ⓙ (2310 Sealy Street; tel: 409-763-8854; www.rosenberg-library.org; Mon–Sat 9am–6pm), opened in 1902, was the

Sculpture carved from one of the thousands of trees felled by Hurricane Ike.

Seawall Boulevard, Galveston.

first library in the state. The library's history center holds a large collection of historic maps and materials relating to Galveston's early businesses, and is a useful archive for historians.

Historic homes

Galveston offers the pleasures of the seaside but is also enthralling for anyone interested in history. The best place to see some of the city's wealth of old mansions is in the delightful **East End Historical District**, bounded roughly by Broadway, Mechanic, 19th and 11th streets. Here, Victorian homes are intermixed with buildings that betray neoclassical, Renaissance, and Italianate influences. Bungalows rest in the shade cast by oleanders, oaks, maples, and palms, and are slightly raised from the ground out of respect for the Gulf. Post Office and Church streets are particularly lovely. Several of the town's best eateries are on 14th Street.

On the corner of Broadway and 14th Street is the pink granite, turreted Gothic fantasy that is the **Bishop's Palace ⓚ** (1402 Broadway;

Moody Gardens, near Galveston.

tel: 409-762-2475; www.galvestonhistory.org/attractions/architectural-heritage/bishops-palace; daily 10am–5pm, Sat until 6pm), the only building in Texas on the American Institute of Architecture's list of 100 outstanding structures in the US. It was built for the wealthy Gresham family from 1887–92, by famed Galveston architect Nicholas Clayton. Owned since 1923 by the Galveston-Houston diocese of the Roman Catholic Church, it served as the bishop's official residence until it was opened to the public in 1963.

The elaborate, four-story 1895 **Moody Mansion ⓛ** (2618 Broadway; tel: 409-762-7668; www.moodymansion. org; daily 11am–4pm) is the former home of powerful Galveston financier William L. Moody, who bought the home from the original owners following the 1900 hurricane. Moody made his money in cotton, then later ranching, banking, and insurance. The home remained in the Moody family until 1986, when it was donated to the city along with its contents. Today, visitors can tour 20 rooms of the restored home and view many 19th- and early 20th-century antiques and furnishings that belonged to the family and tell their history.

The oldest mansion in Galveston is the **Michel B. Menard Home** (1605 33rd Street; tel: 409-762-3933), built in 1838 in the elegant Greek Revival style. French-Canadian fur trader and land speculator Michel B. Menard was one of the founders of Galveston during the time of the Republic of Texas. His mansion has now been restored and is a museum housing remarkable period furnishings and other antiques.

Coastal mix

Between Galveston and Houston is the Kemah-Seabrook area, a region where visitors are certain to find a real mixture of Texas coastal dwellers, ranging from space scientists on their day off from NASA to old seadogs and fishermen swapping yarns at popular hangouts like Jimmy Walker's and Maribelle's. In the west, **Galveston County Beach Pocket Park** ❹ and **Galveston Island State Park** ❺ provide beach access with parking, for picnics, swimming, and sunbathing. Out here, just south of I-45, you will also find the sprawling **Moody Gardens** (tel: 800-582-4673; www. moodygardens.com), Galveston's major tourist attraction. Among the highlights in the 242-acre (98-hectare) educational complex are a 10-story glass rainforest pyramid packed with exotic flora and fauna, which thrive among waterfalls, cliffs, caverns, and forests; a Bat Cave; an MG 3D theater; an authentic reproduction of a 19th-century paddlewheel, which offers cruises along the bayou; a lazy river you can float down, and an aquarium. Other attractions here incude a rainforest pyramid and an MG 4D Special FX theater for a truly multi-storey experince. There is also a 300-room convention hotel. Not far from Moody Gardens, at Galveston International Airport, is the **Lone Star Flight Museum** (2002 Terminal Drive; tel: 409-740-7722; www.lsfm.org; daily 9am–5pm), a magnet for fans of vintage aircraft, with more than 40 restored planes on display.

TIP

Make a point of visiting Goliad State Park, just south of Goliad, off US 183. The huge park includes the reconstructed Mission Espiritu Santo, which was established in 1749. You can also camp, picnic, and fish.

Galveston's East End Historical District.

The Padre Island National Seashore offers some fantastic opportunities for horseback riding.

Texas State Aquarium, Corpus Christi.

Down the coast

Just down the coast, at the point where the Brazos River empties into the Gulf, is the **Brazoria National Wildlife Refuge** ❻. It was near here that Stephen F. Austin and his colonists first landed and also where the new government of the Republic of Texas held its first session. Today, it's a great place to view large flocks of snow geese and other migratory birds.

Between the cities of Galveston and Corpus Christi, on US 59, the **Texas Zoo** (110 Memorial Drive; tel: 361-573-7681; www.texaszoo.org; daily 9am–5pm) at **Victoria** ❼ features 150 species found in Texas, plus lions, tigers, and Texas black bears.

Another place of interest is historic **Goliad** ❽, at the crossroads of US 59 and US 77. Here, not far from the Fannin Battlefield, are the graves of Col. James Fannin and the 342 men who, in 1836, were massacred after surrendering to Mexican general Santa Anna. "Remember Goliad!" became a battle-cry of the Texas Revolution. At **Refugio** ❾, visitors can take haywagon rides and watch cowboys at work at the Dos Vaqueros Ranch Resort (tel: 361-543-4905).

Seashore towns

There are a number of relatively unspoiled little seashore towns close to State Route 35, among them **Port O'Connor** ❿, a focal point for serious fishermen and duck hunters. **Indianola** ⓫, now reduced to just a few fishing families living among stone foundations at the water's edge, rivaled Galveston as the top Texas port until September 17 1875, when a hurricane literally blew the place away. Farther up the coast, **Palacios** ⓬, with its down-home and very weather-beaten Luther Hotel (408 S. Bay Boulevard; tel: 361-972-2312), is worthy of note, as are Freeport and Surfside.

Corpus Christi

For fans of sparkling seaside development, **Corpus Christi** ⓭ has the flavor of a young Miami Beach. With a population of 312,000, it is the state's eighth-largest city, yet its semitropical climate and reputation as a recreation capital have created the image of tranquility.

"The isles of Texas" is the tourist department's description, and those visitors who experience the offshore beaches, deep-sea fishing, catamaran trips, and the sailboarding and Jetskiing might well remember it that way.

Corpus Christi's 2-mile (3km) **Seawall A**, 14ft (4 meters) high and 20ft (6 meters) wide, is an attraction in itself, having been designed by the famous sculptor Gutzon Borglum, who went on to carve the presidential heads on Mount Rushmore. Steps from the seawall down to the beach provide a popular resting place, while joggers, strollers and cyclists populate the top.

Driving in Corpus Christi requires a good map. Because it follows the curve of the bay, few of its streets run straight. The focal point for activity is the **Bayfront Arts and Sciences Park B**, beside the water at the north end of Shoreline Drive. In addition to a convention center and auditorium, the Harbor Playhouse, and a marina, the complex contains the 1972 **Art Museum of South Texas** (1902 N. Shoreline Boulevard; tel: 361-825-3500; www.artmuseumofsouthtexas.org;

Tue–Sat 10am–5pm, Sun 1–5pm), designed by Philip Johnson. Near here is the **Corpus Christi Museum of Science and History C** (1900 N. Chaparral Street; tel: 361-826-4650; www.ccmuseum.com; Tue–Sat 10am–5pm), which includes a fascinating display of shipwreck artifacts.

Another site worth viewing is the surprising **Texas State Museum of Asian Cultures D** (1809 N. Chaparral Street; tel: 361-881-8827; www.asianculturesmuseum.org; Tue–Sat 11am–5pm), home of a prize collection of treasures from Japan acquired by a Corpus native, Billie Trimble Chandler, during her 17 years as a teacher there.

North Beach

Corpus Christi first came to life as a tent city and shipping point for the US Army, when the annexation of Texas sparked a war with Mexico. In the 1920s, the US government sent in the dredgers to create what became the deepest port on the coast and one that has retained its military ties, with half of the US Navy's air training bases located in the area.

Corpus Christi.

Port Isabel lighthouse.

North Beach.

Just across the 620ft (191-meter) **Harbor Bridge** ❺ – at 250ft (77 meters) above the water, the state's second highest – is **Corpus Christi Beach** ❻. This area was famous for its casinos and amusement parks in the 1930s, but fell out of favor until a revival in the 1970s. Natives call it "North Beach," and it offers the city's most challenging surf. Also here are the **Texas State Aquarium** ❼ (2710 N. Shoreline Boulevard; tel: 361-881-1200; www. texasstateaqarium.org; daily 9am–5pm, until 6 Mar–Aug), and the World War II aircraft carrier **USS Lexington** ❽ (tel: 361-888-4873; www.usslexington. com; daily 9am–5pm). About a mile (1.6km) to the south is the much shorter **Magee Beach** ❾, attracting families with small children because of its calm and shallow bay waters.

Wild horses

From the crook of Corpus Christi Bay, the city allows excellent access northeast to Mustang Island, Port Aransas, and Aransas Pass, known as the "Shrimp Capital of Texas." **Mustang Island** ⑭, earning its name from the wild mustang ponies left behind by the Spaniards several hundred years ago, is a barrier between the bay and the Gulf of Mexico. It protects the city to some extent from hurricanes. Visitors will find one of the state's finest beaches at Mustang Island State Park, and, at the northern end of the island, they'll find one of the state's best fishing ports.

A (free) 24-hour ferry runs across from where US 361 ends to **Port Aransas** ⑮, home for hundreds of shrimp boats moored in Conn Brown Harbor. Among numerous places offering accommodations is the landmark Tarpon Inn (200 E. Cotter Avenue; 361-749-5555; www.tarponinn. com), an 1895 hotel once favored by President Franklin Roosevelt. Its lobby walls are covered with tarpon scales autographed by successful fishermen.

Whooping cranes

This whole seashore is a big draw for bird-watchers, who come to view the nearly 400 species of birds that either reside or migrate through here. The **Rockport-Fulton** ⑯ area attracts thousands of hummingbirds, which rest over for their 500-mile (800km) flight across the Gulf of Mexico on the return trip to Mexico each fall. Nearby, famous for the November migration of whooping cranes, is **Aransas National Wildlife Refuge ⑰** (tel: 361-286-3559; www.fws.gov/refug/aransas; daily sunrise to sunset). These protected birds arrive from Canada for the winter and evoke admiration in thousands of tourists on account of their 7ft (2-meter) wingspans, long black legs, and voracious appetites. The rescue of the whooping cranes from near extinction is a real success story. In 1941, there were only 16 known whoopers left in the US; now an estimated 304 birds turn up at Aransas. This is the only known wild flock of whooping cranes. They can be viewed through binoculars from an observation tower, or seen closer up on one of the frequent boat tours, many of which feature talks by professional ornithologists.

Padre Island

Farther south, **Padre Island National Seashore**, divided from South Padre Island by **Mansfield Cut ⑱**, and preserved from developers, is the finest stretch of natural beach in America. It was named for Padre Nicolas Balli, who bought it from the Spanish Crown for 400 pesos. In 1844, the last of the Balli family moved away and three years later John Singer and his family were shipwrecked on the island. They chose to build a home and stay here. Singer became rich from his shares in his brother's sewing machine company and reputedly buried treasure on the island before leaving. It has never been found and, after a century of storms disrupting the island's landscape, it is doubtful if it ever will be.

Ranch country

Inland, the closest you can get to the coast is along US 77 through ranch country and **Kingsville ⑲**. From here, make a diversion westward along US 141 to reach the visitor center of the famous **King Ranch ⑳** (2205 W. Highway 141; tel: 361-592-8055; www.king-ranch.com; open daily; tours Mon–Sat 11am and 1pm, Sun 12.30pm and 2pm). Visitors can watch a video and then take a 1-hour guided tour along

TIP

The first 9 miles (14km) of Padre Island have a paved roadway and another 5 miles (8km) can be driven by car. But the 55 rugged miles (90km) to Mansfield Cut demand four-wheeling. For beachcombers and shell collectors, however, this trip is mandatory.

Freshly caught red snapper, Padre Island.

TEXAS CITY Y SPILL

On March 22, 2014, Matagorda Island, part of Aransas National Wildlife Refuge was stricken by oil spilt when a ship collided with an oil tanker in Galveston Bay. The refuge is a winter home to many rare birds, including 11 pairs of nesting aplomado falcons and the only wild flock of whooping cranes in the country, as well as Kemp's Ridley sea turtles, which nest on the white sand beaches in spring. The Texas City Y Spill released 168,000 gallons of oil and affected 90 miles (145km) of Gulf coastline. Two million pounds of oily sand were removed, and 331 oiled birds, 39 dolphins, and 17 turtles were cleaned by volunteers. There are at least 275 oil spills in Galveston Bay annually, affecting vulnerable wildlife in the coastal areas.

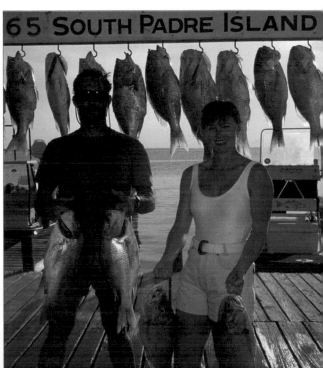

a 12-mile (19km) loop of the immense ranch, known for its wealth – worldwide holdings once covered almost 11 million acres (over 4 million hectares) in seven countries. It also developed a stable of Kentucky Derby winners and its own breed of Santa Gertrudis cattle.

Nearby, on State Route 281, is **Ben Bolt** ㉑ (a tiny place with about 100 inhabitants), where a legendary Headless Horseman is buried. This phantom-like figure, who terrorized the region in the mid-19th century with a head dangling from his saddlehorn, was actually a rustler who had been killed by a Texas Ranger, his head tied to a wild mustang as a warning to others.

Northwest of Kingsville, the town of **San Diego** ㉒, on State Route 44, was an important cattle shipping center that became so rowdy a special detachment of Texas Rangers was stationed there. Their task was to deal with the bands of rustlers who infested the backcountry.

South to the border

Between the coast and Padre Island, the Intracoastal Waterway continues all the way down to **Port Isabel** ㉓. Port Isabel Lighthouse (317 E. Railroad Avenue; tel: 956-943-2262; www.portisabellighthouse.com; open daily) on US 100 is irresistible to photographers. It was built in 1852 on a site used by General Zachary Taylor's army in the US War with Mexico.

The most unusual wildlife refuge around is **Sea Turtle, Inc.** (6617 Padre Boulevard, South Padre Island; tel: 956-761-4511; www.seaturtleinc.com; Tue–Sun 10am–4pm), a nonprofit organization that is helping restore the population of the endangered Kemp's Ridley turtle by protecting their nests and hatchlings on South Padre Island beaches. Through rehabilitation, research, and education, the group is actively involved in the survival of all sea turtle species threatened by harvest of their eggs and by hunting. Baby and adult sea turtles, either in rehabilitation or nonreleasable, are on view in large tanks.

South Padre Island ㉔, a 34-mile (54km) section of what is really just a 100-mile (160km) sandbar, or barrier island, is nowhere more than half a mile (0.8km) wide, yet it has become the state's premier beach resort, thanks to its windswept dunes, gorgeous beaches, and balmy tropical temperatures. Discovered by Spanish explorers in 1519, it was first named Isla Blanca for white sands whose purity has been preserved despite extensive development.

Only one paved road, Padre Boulevard, running up the center of the island, carries on beyond the city limits, but it peters out after a few miles amidst sand dunes, marshes, and birdlife.

Even after the island was joined to the mainland by a causeway in 1974, development barely took off, but, later, a real estate boom began when the causeway was widened and the Texas legislature passed laws forcing the insurance industry to provide coverage to coastal areas. The nearest airports are at Harlingen and the border town of Brownsville.

View from Port Isabel Lighthouse.

Oyster boat, Laguna Madre.

White-tailed deer.

RIO GRANDE VALLEY

Drab and downbeat to some, a warm winter
haven for others, the Rio Grande Valley looks
set to diversify from its citrus-growing past
and may well become the new Florida.

long the river, from the dusty Tex-Mex town of Roma to the sultry fishing village of Port Isabel, lies the Rio Grande Valley, a region packed with the history of border wars, steamboat navigation, and nomadic tribes who have long since disappeared. There are 38 communities scattered along 110 miles (177km) of alluvial plain, but most of the towns situated between Falcon Lake and the lower Rio Grande Valley are nothing but caution lights and an extra lane along the highway.

Roma ㉕, founded in 1765, might be considered the beginning of the Rio Grande Valley. Marlon Brando came to Roma in the early 1950s to film several scenes for *Viva Zapata*, a movie about the most romantic hero of the Mexican Revolution, Emiliano Zapata. (Much of the film was shot in the sleepy – and more picturesque – village of **San Ygnacio** farther up the river. The 1830 Jose Trevino house here was chosen because of its typical Mexican design.)

Roma is a border town in economic and architectural decline. There is some interesting old architecture, but the place is so dreary that one South Texas newspaperman declared sarcastically after Falcon Dam was built that a real opportunity had been passed up when Roma wasn't relocated to its middle. The 5-mile (8km) long dam, constructed in 1953 to control irrigation, was built jointly by the US and Mexico

and bears the seals of both countries at the international border line.

Joined by a suspension bridge across the river from Roma is **Ciudad Miguel Alemán**, a clean, modern, and uninteresting Mexican city named after a former president. Eleven miles (18km) northwest of Ciudad Alemán is the forgettable Mexican town of **Mier**. Mier was the site of the capture, in 1842, of the renegade Republic of Texas soldiers involved in the "black bean incident." After capturing Mier, the Texans had to surrender to the Mexican army. They

Main Attractions

La Borde House, Rio Grande
  City
Oblate Mission, McAllen
Santa Ana National Wildlife
  Refuge, Alamo
Laguna Atascosa National
  Wildlife Refuge, Hondo
Gladys Porter Zoo,
  Brownsville

Bentsen-Rio Grande Valley State Park.

were marched farther into Mexico to Saltillo where 17 of the 176 were executed. A lottery determined who was to die; those who drew one of the black beans from a pot were shot by a firing squad.

Roman hills

Along this stretch of the Rio Grande there are some tenuous connections with continental culture. Until the 1830s, Roma was called Garcia's Ranch. A visiting priest convinced himself, and the locals, that the hills here were like those of Rome. It still looks like Garcia's Ranch. In **Rio Grande City** ㉖, a Catholic priest built a replica of the Grotto at Lourdes in France, while, in the same town, a nostalgic François La Borde, in 1899, commissioned a Paris architect to design the family residence. Now the **La Borde House** (601 E. Main Street; tel: 956-487-5101; www.labordehouse.com), it has been restored as an inn.

Until the arrival of the railroads, the river was the valley's principal avenue of commerce, and Rio Grande City, complete with Victorian-era buildings, was an important riverboat terminal. The

Food stall, Rio Grande City.

buildings are still there, but the river has retreated to the south, leaving the town high and dry.

The Magic Valley

The region was nicknamed the "Magic Valley" by land developers in the early 1900s to entice farmers to the fertile irrigated fields, which are capable of producing two or three crops a year. The Magic Valley also lures about 130,000 "Winter Texans" annually. These fugitives from the mid-continental weather of Minnesota, Michigan, Canada, and Ohio head south in recreational vehicles to bask in the sun and eat just-picked oranges. Years ago, it was not uncommon to see citrus orchards doubling as seasonal trailer parks, but catering to Winter Texans is now big business. As with other farmers, citrus growers experience boom and bust years. While citrus acreage is shrinking, farm stands still sell fresh, fragrant fruit.

Rich soils

Centuries of flooding have deposited layers of rich alluvial soil along the Rio Grande's banks, helping to make

Hidalgo County one of the state's richest agricultural regions, with sugar cane, cotton, and vegetables – especially onions – grown year-round. The land produces numerous varieties of fruit and vegetables as well as most of the aloe vera grown in the US. But a series of unprecedented cold snaps has occasionally frozen not only the winter citrus crops but many of the trees themselves. Some of the growers of the famous Texas Ruby Red grapefruit have sold up rather than replant.

The valley's disastrous lockstep with the Mexican economy and peso has loosened in recent years. While more and more valley companies are supplying components and logistics for the dozens of brand-name automotive, electronic, and appliance manufacturers just across the border, the region's economic base has diversified. The healthcare, tourism, agriculture, and service industries have expanded enough to bring unemployment levels down. The University of Texas campuses in Brownsville (8,612 students) and Edinburg (18,744 students) are graduating educated adults; a lack of education in older generations has meant about 25 percent of valley residents have incomes below the poverty level.

The Rio Grande Valley now ranks among the fastest-growing regions in the nation, with a construction boom seen in new houses, businesses, and roads, propelled by a relatively young population and a lower than average cost of living. The overwhelming majority of the population is ethnically Hispanic. Although a significant number of the people whose families have lived here for generations do not speak Spanish at all, first-generation immigrants tend to speak only Spanish. But, like the three-car, hand-drawn ferry at **Los Ebanos** ㉗ – the last of its kind, running since 1954 – some things still move at a slow pace.

Our Lady of Lourdes grotto, Rio Grande City.

Bigger and better

Many consider **McAllen** ㉘ one of the livelier places in the valley. It is bigger (pop. 135,000), tidier, and a little more upbeat than most surrounding cities. There are adequate hotels and restaurants, though these are usually full during the September white wing dove hunting season. The city

Hand-drawn ferry at Los Ebanos.

TIP

For detailed advice
about crossing the
border into Mexico –
even just for a few hours
– and all the formalities
involved, see Travel Tips
at the back of this book.

also has large shopping centers and
chain restaurants. The ancient **Oblate
Mission** is where the fathers planted
the region's first citrus orchards, but
the valley's vast citrus industry began
with the McAllen estate of John Shary.
Although his estate is still privately
owned, the lush orchards can be
observed from the road, and, in spring,
the air is heavy with the fragrance of
orange and grapefruit blossoms.

East of McAllen, the little town of
Pharr ㉙ is home to the decidedly unas-
suming **Ye Olde Clock Museum** (929
E. Preston; tel: 956-787-1923; Mon–Fri
1–5pm; free), some of whose 2,000
exhibits are more than 200 years old.
For music machines, visit **Smitty's Juke
Box Museum** (116 W. State; tel: 956-
787-0131; Mon–Fri 9.30am–4pm). Used
clothing shops (*ropa usada*) are plentiful
in Pharr, and it's easy to find a bargain.

Hot spot

*United States Border
Patrol vehicle, on the
US–Mexico border
near McAllen.*

The Mexican border is a political hot
spot. Farm workers and growers here
will continue to square off across picket
lines. Mexicans and Central Americans
will continue to slip across the river to

work in a country where the streets may
not be paved with gold, but are at least
paved.

The river is 8 miles (13km) to the
south and here the International Bridge
connects the American settlement of
Hidalgo ㉚ – a cluster of freight-for-
warding houses – with **Reynosa**, a rapidly expanding Mexican city of 589,466.
Parking is available on the American
side of the bridge.

Within walking distance of the
bridge is Reynosa's Plaza Hidalgo and
an open shopping mall in the town's
zona rosa ("pink zone"). In addition to
housing tourist-oriented stalls, shops,
and restaurants, the zone features bars,
clubs, and hotels. Most of the men in
khaki uniforms are not policemen, but
cuidadores, public parking attendants
who, for a reasonable fee, will watch
your car and attend to the parking
meter while you roam.

Border trouble

This muddy stretch of the Rio Grande,
called the Río Bravo by Mexicans, is
shallow enough that undocumented
immigrants can tie their belongings

around their necks and hazard an illegal entry into the US. Sometimes they hire a "mule," or "coyote," who will carry passengers on his back. When the river is high, inner tubes or small boats shuttle the illegal immigrants – usually young men, hoping to find work – to the American side. US Border Patrol officers – *la Migra* – each year apprehend over half a million undocumented aliens in Texas – up to 10,000 a week – most of whom crossed here, and many of whom are young children traveling unaccompanied to escape persecution in their home countries. What discourages illegals from crossing farther north is the brutal, unforgiving desert, but, from here, Corpus Christi, San Antonio, or Austin can be reached within days. And once within a large American community, undocumented arrivals from Mexico and Central American can easily disappear into the largely Hispanic population.

Miraculous medicine

East of McAllen at **San Juan** ❸, on I-83, the reconstructed Basilica of Our Lady of San Juan houses a replica of a Mexican statue of the *Virgen de Los Lagos*. This local statue won an identity of its own in 1970 when it survived a plane crash that destroyed the original. *Curanderas*, or traditional healers, often invoke the Virgin Mary and are often a popular alternative to mainstream medication within the Hispanic community, particularly among elders. On the Mexican side of the river, Mexican doctors have established clinics that offer treatments not yet approved by the Food and Drug Administration (FDA). Even more popular are Mexican dentists and pharmacists, who offer goods and services at a fraction of US prices. Tiny Nuevo Progreso, south of Weslaco, has over 300 dentists.

Wildlife

The Rio Grande Valley is a bird-lover's paradise. Some 274 species are sighted in **Bentsen-Rio Grande Valley State Park** ❸. The subtropical woodland near Mission has been preserved as a wildlife habitat. Other wildlife can be observed at **Santa Ana National Wildlife Refuge** ❸ (3325 Green Jay, Alamo; tel: 956-784-7500; www.fws.gov/

FACT

The Rio Grande is the 21st longest river in the world, traveling 1,885 miles (3,030km) from its source in Colorado to its estuary on the Gulf of Mexico.

Basilica of Our Lady of San Juan.

CROSSING INTO MEXICO

Over 150,000 people safely cross the border (La Frontera) to visit Mexico each day – about 9.5 million a year – either traveling by car or walking across the pedestrian bridges over the Rio Grande linking the two countries. All citizens of other countries, including US citizens, need to have valid identity documents: a passport or proof of citizenship with photo, and a green card to reenter the US, if necessary. If you stay in Mexico more than 72 hours, or travel beyond the border zone, you'll need a Tourist Card, available at the border. You will also need auto insurance to cover any car travel in Mexico; US insurance policies do not cover travel south of the border. At this time, despite a drop in overall fatalities, travel in the border area of Mexico remains potentially dangerous, as a result of narcotic smuggling, gang violence, hostage taking, rapes, theft, and crossfire from gun fights. The US State Department has an advisory in place warning against travel in the border area. You are advised to be very cautious if you do cross into Mexico. Stay in tourist areas, travel in daylight hours, travel with others, and be low-key in your attire, jewelry, and attitude. Avoid using credit and debit cards, if at all possible, and ask your bank to limit amounts on spending when traveling over the border.

The painted bunting is often described as the most beautiful bird in North America.

Spanish moss draped over trees in Santa Ana National Wildlife Refuge.

refuge/santa_ana; daily 8am–4pm, tours Thanksgiving–Apr), south of Alamo, which includes more than 380 bird species, in addition to bobcats, coyotes, ocelots, and jaguarundis. Nature trails run through the preserve, and a tram takes visitors on tours with a skilled guide.

On FM 1419, south of Brownsville, is **Sabal Palm Audubon Center and Wildlife Sanctuary ㉞** (tel: 956-541-8034; www.sabalpalmsanctuary.org; daily 7am–5pm), an attractive preserve with self-guided trails. Also open to the public is **Laguna Atascosa National Wildlife Refuge ㉟** (tel: 956-748-3607; www.fws.gov/refug/laguna_atascosa; open daily). The refuge of open water, marshes, coastal prairie, cropland, and brushland in Rio Hondo is a sanctuary for deer, bobcat, and migrating birds, located on the coast south of Port Mansfield. Half an hour's drive west of the refuge is **Harlingen ㊱**, noted for its original working model of the famous Iwo Jima War Memorial (320 Iwo Jima Boulevard; daily 10am–4pm; free) at Arlington National Cemetery. It depicts the raising of the flag in World War II. At **Ramsey Nature Park**, native plants

have transformed a former landfill into a refuge for animals and people.

Brownsville

To the south, **Brownsville ㊲**, connected to the Gulf of Mexico by a 17-mile (27km) ship canal, is the largest American city on the lower border. Here, the **Gladys Porter Zoo** (500 E. Ringgold Street; tel: 956-546-7187; www.gpz.org; Mon–Fri 9am–5.30pm, Sat–Sun until 6pm) is a cageless habitat allowing endangered and other species to reside on mini islands; visitors can wander along ingenious water-fringed walkways. Nearby, the museum **Costumes of the Americas** (Dean Porter Park; tel: 956-547-6890; www.costumesoftheamericas musem.net; Tue–Sat 10am–5pm, Sun noon–4pm) displays an extensive collection of native garb of North and South American tribes and settlers

North of Brownsville, near the intersection of FM 1847 and 511, is where an artillery duel opened the US War with Mexico on May 8, 1846. At the Palmito Ranch, south of the city, on May 12–13, 1865, the last battle of the American Civil War took place, although Lee had surrendered at Appomatox a month earlier. Illustrations of such battles can be inspected in the **Historic Brownsville Museum** (641 E. Madison Street; tel: 956-548-1313; www.historicbrowns villemuseum.com; Mon–Sat 10am–4pm) in the old Southern Pacific Railroad Depot, and at **Brownsville Heritage Complex** (1305 E. Washington; tel: 956-541-5560; www.brownsvillehistory.org; Tue–Sat 10am–4pm).

Crossing the border

Thousands of people cross every day over the border between Brownsville and Matamoros on the Mexican side. Because of the need for Mexican automobile insurance, many visitors choose to park their cars near the Brownsville Civic Center on International Boulevard, or across from the Chamber of Commerce on Elizabeth Street, both of which are close to the Gateway International Bridge.

DEL RIO TO LAREDO

This well-watered stretch of the Rio Grande Valley has long been a magnet for colorful characters, attracted by the ease of crossing into Mexico and the trade the border region encourages.

Water has been the moving force in Del Rio's history, as in the history of all the Texas border towns. Around 1870, there was considerable development of San Felipe Springs, whose 90 million gallons (over 340 million liters) of water a day attracted farmers and ranchers, and provided agricultural and drinking water for the region. In more recent times, the damming of the Rio Grande and the Devils and Pecos rivers has created a massive lake with huge recreational potential.

Friendship Lake

Amistad National Recreation Area ❶ (tel: 830-775-7491; www.nps. gov/amis; open daily; free) – *amistad* means "friendship" in Spanish – protects Lake Amistad, a reservoir with more than 1,000 miles (1,600km) of shoreline created by damming the Rio Grande in 1969. It is now managed for recreation by the National Park Service, and boat rentals and scuba diving are available here in what is reputedly the state's best lake for bass fishing and also good for underwater visibility. Hunting licenses for deer, turkey, dove, quail, and the more exotic game found here are available on a daily or seasonal basis. American Indian cave paintings, some dating back 8,000 years, are also found along the shores of

Lake Amistad and, although many are inaccessible, others such as Panther Cave can be reached by boat if lake levels are high enough.

Sadly, hundreds of caves were inundated when the Amistad Dam was built, and many of the more accessible ones have been defaced by vandals. However, some of the better paintings are now protected by the State of Texas at **Seminole Canyon State Park and Historic Site ❷** (tel: 432-292-4464; www.tpwd.state.tx.us/state-parks.seminole-canyon; open daily), on the northern

Main Attractions
Amistad National Recreation Area
Seminole Canyon State Park
Langtry
San Agustín Plaza, Laredo
Lake Casa Blanca International State Park

La Posada Hotel, Laredo.

The Jersey Lilly Saloon, where where the self-proclaimed Judge Roy Bean held court.

extension of the lake. Camping is permitted in the national recreation area and in the state park. All 400 or so archeological sites on the lakeshore are owned jointly by the United States and Mexico.

Wine and rodeos

Del Rio ❸ (pop. 35,543), 13 miles (21km) south of the lake, remains free of the herds of tourists that frequent the towns of the Lower Rio Grande Valley. San Felipe Springs feeds the Horseshoe Park swimming hole and has kept the Qualia family prospering at the **Val Verde Winery** (100 Qualia Drive; tel: 830-775-9714; www.valverde winery.com; open daily for free tours and tastings) for more than 100 years. Texas's oldest vintner offers free tours and wine-tasting every day.

Del Rio's downtown area has a fine variety of 19th-century architecture. A taste of the cowboy past appears at the **George Paul Museum** (tel: 830-775-9595; open daily), saluting a champion bull rider from Del Rio with exhibits of rodeo gear and hosting the nation's largest bull-riding event in April.

The Val Verde Winery.

The city's **Whitehead Memorial Museum** (1308 S. Main Street; tel: 830-774-7568; www.whitehead museum.org; Tue–Sat 9am–4.30pm, Sun 1–6pm) houses a collection of reconstructed pioneer buildings put together by a local ranching family. Exhibits include a replica of the famous saloon and courtroom of the notorious Judge Roy Bean who, along with his son, is buried in the grounds.

Border Crossing

Across the river from Del Rio is the city named after the romantic, but ultimately suicidal, Manuel Acuña (1849–73), one of Mexico's most widely read poets. In order to reach **Ciudad Acuña** (pop. 144,669), drive out of Hudson or Las Vacas to the International Bridge. There is ample parking on the American side, and most of the shops offering typical souvenirs are clustered together on Hidalgo Street near the bridge. There is a second international bridge to Mexico at Amistad Dam.

Thousands of visitors cross into Mexico annually. However, the US

Del Rio to Laredo

0   20 miles
0   20 km

State Department warns you to be very cautious about travel in Mexico due to gang violence and crime. Be sure to have valid identity documents with you (see page 298). You will need Mexican auto insurance if you drive over the border into Mexico, so many people simply walk across for the day on the pedestrian international bridges in Del Rio and other towns along the border.

Langtry

Judge Roy Bean's original Jersey Lilly Saloon, named after Lily Langtry, the English actress whom he admired from a distance, still stands in tiny **Langtry** ❹ (pop. 76), northwest on US 90, near the Pecos River. Proclaiming himself the "Law West of the Pecos," the illiterate Judge Bean doffed his bar apron in favor of a waistcoat whenever court was in session, drafting a jury from drinkers at the bar. One example of his unconventional justice came during an inquest, when $40 and a pistol were found on the corpse. Fining the corpse $40 for having a concealed weapon, Bean pocketed the money.

Strangers from the east would drop off the train to drink beer at the saloon and buy a round for the judge's pet bear, Bruno. In 1904, the year after the 78-year-old Bean died after a drunken outing, Lily Langtry made her first visit to the town, admired her portrait (which still hangs in the saloon) and was given one of Bean's six-shooters. Today, 85,000 visitors a year call in on the Judge Roy Bean Visitor Center (tel: 432-291-3340) in the tiny hamlet to watch a video about the old judge. If you're headed west, take advantage of the store here to buy snacks and coffee as this is the only available sustenance in the 120 empty miles (193km) between Langtry and Marathon.

Farther downstream is the small town of **Comstock**, before the river runs into Lake Amistad and joins the Rio Grande.

Military times

56 miles (90km) south of Del Rio is **Eagle Pass** ❺ (pop. 27,000) and its Mexican neighbor, Piedras Negras (pop. 150,000). Other than Mexican political unrest that closed the International

FACT

A humble innkeeper by profession, Roy Bean was created a Justice of the Peace by the Texas Rangers when the new town, which Bean named Langtry, was founded in 1880. His novel law-keeping methods have been described as "creative," but suitable for the times.

The Pecos River near Comstock.

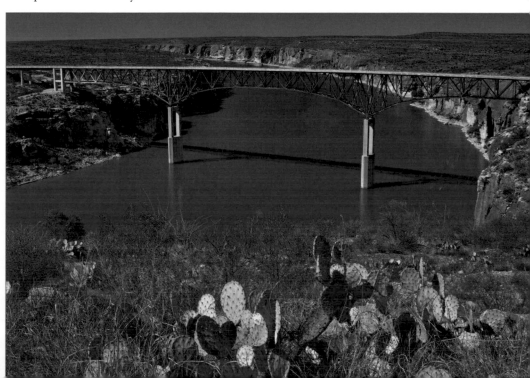

Hidalgo Street, Laredo.

Bridge on several occasions in 1985, not much has happened here since **Fort Duncan** was closed for the second and last time after World War I. It had been established by the US Army in 1849, and a detachment of mixed-race American Indian scouts, descended from runaway black slaves, served there after the Civil War. Many of the original buildings, now restored, comprise the **Fort Duncan Museum** (Bliss Street; tel: 830-758-1445; Tue–Sun 1–5pm), featuring military memorabilia and relics of mid-19th-century Texas.

Military history buffs may also want to hazard a guess as to the precise spot along the Rio Grande from which Confederate General Joseph O. Shelby, on July 4, 1865, ordered his Confederate flag weighted and lowered into the river. Shelby, in the romantic tradition of the South, also tore the plume from his hat and cast it into the water.

Black rocks and nachos

Eagle Pass is the seat of Maverick County, named after early rancher and signer of the Texas Declaration of Independence Samuel Maverick (see page 70). In October each year, the town organizes a nacho cook-off, attracting over 3,000 hungry visitors. Piedras Negras ("black rocks") and Eagle Pass (paso de águila) are regular stops for Kickapoo Indians who, under a US-Mexican agreement, are free to reside in either country. The Kickapoo sell handcrafted goods at the border, and at the **Kickapoo Lucky Eagle Casino** (7777 Lucky Eagle Drive; tel: 830-758-1936; www.luckyeagletexas.com), Texas's only casino. The flashing lights and bells of slot machines vie for attention with games of Texas hold 'em poker and roulette.

Piedras Negras remains a stop-and-shop Mexican town with a few good restaurants. Although it is now sadly closed, the most famous building in the area is the **Restaurant Bar Moderno** (Allende 407 Oriente), which, in its former guise of the Victory Club, claims to have invented nachos.

Twin Laredos

Laredo ❻ and its Mexican neighbor, Nuevo Laredo, together form a city of some 636,516, with 90 percent of the residents on the Texas side Hispanic. The cities were outposts in what was once the backwater of Spain's American colony, and retain little of what colonial charm they may once have had. Most of the culture here is commercial. Residents from each side of the border once lined for bargains on the other. Nuevo Laredo's current reputation for violence, reflecting drug gangs' heavy presence in the city, has destroyed its appeal for visitors unwilling to be targets of kidnapping or stray bullets.

Downtown Laredo caters to Mexican shoppers buying inexpensive clothing, various electrical items – often made in Asia – and some processed foods. This seedy area has been abandoned by many American shoppers, but competition for the Mexican buyer has lowered prices on portable TVs, stereos, and other electronic goods, and a variety of other appliances and clothing unavailable in Mexico. Away from the bridge, the downtown area improves.

San Agustín Plaza, where the Texas city began as a Spanish settlement in 1755, is flanked by **St. Augustine Cathedral** (built 1872); the attractive **La Posada Hotel** (1000 Zaragoza Street; tel: 956-242-7493; www.laposada. com), now one of the top hotels in Texas; and the **Republic of the Rio Grande Museum** (1005 Zaragoza Street; tel: 956-727-3480; Tue–Sat 9am–4pm). The Republic was a short-lived revolt led by disenchanted Mexican federalists who met in convention in what was still a Mexican city in 1840. Somewhere between the rapidly expanding Manifest Destiny of the United States and the rapidly receding border of Mexico, the Republic of the Rio Grande was lost. The museum's exhibits explain some of this history.

Two blocks north, at San Bernardo and Washington streets, is Bruni Plaza, named for Antonio Mateo Bruni, an Italian immigrant who died a politician and wealthy rancher in 1931. Engraved on a plaque here is part of his philosophy: "God has given us political power to be used for the welfare of the people."

San Bernardo Street shops overflow with Mexican pottery, clothing,

DJ Wolfman Jack.

RADIO HEALING

Driving at night, you may hear – even as far away as the Canadian border – the broadcast from XERF, one of the last Mexican border-blaster radio stations. In the 1960s, famed DJ Wolfman Jack worked at a border-blaster station and introduced a generation of Americans to rock 'n' roll. Nowadays, the standard radio fare is medication commercials and cassette-tape Christianity. These airwave evangelists suggest that to be saved and healed (via the US Postal Service and 200,000 watts of Christianity), all listeners need to do is put your hand on the radio and a check in the mail.

The American Medical Association had its reservations about the authenticity of the pills and elixir marketed by one early Del Rio citizen. The proximity of the Mexican border probably made Del Rio seem a favorable business climate to Dr Johnny Brinkley of Kansas, who made a career of peddling exotic cures. In 1933, Brinkley used his own border radio station, KFKB (Kansas First, Kansas Best) – on which he cranked the power up to 1 million watts – to sell goat-gland pills and extended virility to thousands of Americans. Despite spending time in jail for practising medicine without a license, he became wealthy and built the Dr John R. Brinkley Mansion, which still stands at 512 Qualia Drive in Del Rio. He died penniless, however, following a slew of lawsuits from former patients.

leatherwork, colonial-style furniture and curios mixed with the work of artisans. Texas A&M University's TAMIU **Lamar Bruni Vergara Planetarium** (5201 University Boulevard; tel: 956-326-2463; www.tamiu.edu/planetarium) brings the wide Texas skies into focus at sky shows and telescope nights.

Native plants and animals, such as alligators, cacti, and wildflowers, can be seen at the **Lamar Bruni Vergara Environmental Science Center** at Laredo Community College (1 West End Washington; tel: 956-764-5701; www.laredo.edu/cms; Mon–Thu 8am–6pm), a living laboratory containing representations of the Rio Grande ecosystem.

About two-thirds of the US trade with Mexico crosses the border here, a volume that has only increased since the passage of the NAFTA agreements. Laredo is now the nation's largest inland port. Immigration and Customs Enforcement offices are open 24 hours daily. On the US side, customs agents collect hundreds of millions of dollars in duties each year. *Casas de cambio*, or currency exchange houses, on both sides of the bridge, usually offer a fair exchange rate for pesos and dollars, and they are convenient. Check the banks (Mexican banks are generally open Mon–Fri 9am–1.30pm) before changing large amounts.

Across the border

Nuevo Laredo, a short walk across the old International Bridge, is something of a Texas Tijuana, with the usual plethora of tacky tourist souvenir shops. Nuevo ("new") Laredo is old, but not attractive. It is also very dangerous as drug cartels fight for power with shootouts on city streets, day and night. You may want to consider visiting other border towns rather than this one.

Surrounding Laredo are miles of the Texas one sees in movies. Ranches are enormous, since making a living on arid scrubland requires a enormous spread. When oil and gas were discovered, most of the region's wealth, although greatly increased, remained concentrated in the hands of a few people. Poverty is still the norm here, and many of the streets of Laredo remain unpaved.

Lake Casa Blanca International State Park ❼ (5102 Bob Bullock Loop; tel: 956-725-3826; www.tpwd.state.tx.us/lake-casa-blanca), off Highway 59, at the eastern edge of Laredo, offers swimming, boating, fishing, and camping. The park has a lovely lake and is home to abundant wildlife, including whitetail deer and ground squirrels. Some 78 miles (125km) south of Laredo is **Falcon State Park** ❽ (tel: 956-848-5327; www.tpwd.state.tx/stateparks/falcon; open daily), protecting Falcon Reservoir, a jointly owned American-Mexican impoundment.

This massive reservoir covers 87,210 acres (35,293 hectares) and has an international reputation for black bass and catfish, as well as deer and dove hunting in the surrounding countryside. Downriver, the landscape gradually changes from semi-arid, scrubby hills to the lush delta of the Lower Rio Grande Valley.

Falcon Reservoir.

EL PASO

Thanks to its American Indian roots, its proximity to Mexico, and its distance from other major towns, El Paso – the former haunt of Wild West outlaws – is quite unlike any other Texas city.

For some 1,200 miles (1,930km), the Rio Grande twists and turns, widens, then roars through tight places, all the while uniting Texas with the Mexican states of Chihuahua, Coahuila, Nuevo León, and Tamaulipas. In Spanish, it is known as la frontera – the border. La Frontera is a place apart, where you will find neither the best of Texas nor of Mexico. In a sense, it is one of the few places where the First World meets the Third World. On the Mexican side, maquiladoras – American-owned assembly plants – enjoy proximity to the border combined with Third World operating costs. American retail businesses sell Mexicans what their country can't or won't manufacture: TVs, stereos, medical instruments, and designer jeans. They capitalize on a widely held Mexican belief: Lo gringo es lo mejor – American-made is best.

The differences in lifestyle and economic status are striking. Outside a Zenith assembly plant in Reynosa, a 40-year-old man scratches out an existence selling salted pumpkin seeds, or *pepitas*. "*Semillas, semillas, semillas,*" he sings to passing workers. Mostly, he is ignored. A University of Texas professor in El Paso writes poetry describing the "trenchant sadness" of the Mexico framed in the window of his office. In the lower Rio Grande Valley, a Border Patrol officer quietly delivers three Salvadoran refugees, who

were apprehended an hour earlier, to a church-sponsored sanctuary house.

The final barrier

For Central Americans, the Rio Grande represents the last geographical obstacle in their struggle toward a better life here in *el Norte*. Most are only a few weeks away from a country ravaged by war and poverty. And most of them enter the US illegally. For the fortunate few who find their way to the sanctuary houses, the chances of remaining in the country usually improve. Nevertheless,

Main Attractions

El Paso Mission Trail
Magoffin House
El Paso Museum of Art
Franklin Mountains State
  Park
El Museo de Arte e Historia,
  Juárez

Chamizal Memorial mural.

FACT

The pictographs at Hueco Tanks are sacred to the Tigua Indians. One of the most revered sites is Speaking Rock – hence the name of the tribe's gambling center at Ysleta del Sur Pueblo.

many will spend their first, and last, night in *América* in one of the border detention facilities operated by the US Immigration and Customs Enforcement (ICE).

Despite the Rio Grande's length, fewer than 10 international cities straddle the river. In and around them has gathered a unique mixture of Texans and Mexicans, including a motley crew of international hucksters of low culture and high commerce. If you're looking for the cosmopolitan culture of Mexico City, or the quiet charm of San Antonio, it's unlikely that you'll find it here. But this place is worth a closer look: *la frontera*, if nothing else, is unique.

Much of what this border is about is people standing in line on one side to cross over for something on the other.

Border regulars start lining up before dawn: Mexican agricultural laborers wait for the contractor's bus to take them to their day's work. By seven it's too late; they've missed their ride. By 11, the lines are on the other side. The American day trippers are here – stereotypical tourists, out for an afternoon in the market, and dinner. Almost all will be home before dark, with a bottle of José Cuervo tequila, crepe flowers, and something for the kids. And so it goes. Dollars to pesos, pesos to dollars. You can usually spend both on either side. Money is the motor that moves this place.

Cash flow

Much of the history of the border in the late 20th century was tied to the exchange rate of the two currencies. For some 30 years, the peso was at a positive 12.5 to the dollar, which allowed most border towns to slouch toward prosperity. But with the first devaluation in 1976, then another devaluation in the early 1990s, the value of the peso fell precipitously and the economic climate on both sides of the river was, at best, cloudy. Mexican workers, with or without papers, found the lure of the dollar irresistible. And why shouldn't they? The federally fixed *daily* wage on the Mexican side is usually about the same as the *hourly* rate on the American side. For the American tourist, the lure has always been well-priced Mexican goods south of the border.

Although things are improving economically in Mexico – and, in theory, the border region – La Frontera has been beset by an even greater problem: a dangerous drug war operated by competing drug cartels, which has led to horrific violence, from shootouts with guns and grenades to rapes, hostage taking, and high levels of crime. Even though murders and crime figures are now lower for Mexico as a whole, and despite the best efforts of Mexican tourism officials to reassure travelers and promote their cities, La Frontera remains volatile, and Americans are advised by the State Department to either avoid the region or be cautious traveling there (see page 298 for advice on traveling into Mexico).

A far-out Texas city

It has to be said: to get to **El Paso** ❶ in extreme West Texas from most Texas cities requires driving from dawn to dusk. Politicians and cartographers claim that El Paso is part of Texas. Most Texans know better. About halfway between Houston and San Diego, California, El Paso's heart belongs to New Mexico, which borders the city, and speaks fluent Spanish.

Sprawling across the Valley of El Paso del Norte, **El Paso-Juárez** is an international city of 2.7 million people, regarded by some as the most diverse city on the border, with its mix of three cultures. The Tigua (or Tiwa) Indians were here first, followed by Norteño Mexicans and Southwestern Americans. Related to the Pueblo Indians of New Mexico, the Tiguas moved to the Spanish mission of San Antonio (later San Augustín) de la Isleta del Sur in 1680, during the Pueblo Revolt, when the Pueblos threw out their cruel Spanish overlords and took back New Mexico for native people until the Reconquest of New Mexico by Spaniard De Vargas in 1692.

Today, the Tiguas are farmers and live in **Ysleta del Sur Pueblo** ❷ (an archaic Spanish spelling of "little island"), the oldest community in Texas (1681) and one of the oldest continuously occupied pueblos in the Southwest (Taos and Zuni Pueblos in New Mexico also claim this title). The tribe operates the 850-seat Speaking Rock Casino (tel: 915-860-7777), just behind the mission. Ysleta is part of Tigua Indian Reservation, one of only three reservations in Texas.

Signs of an even earlier culture can be seen at **Hueco Tanks State Park**

The Ysleta Mission, in Ysleta del Sur Pueblo on the Tigua Indian Reservation, was built in 1681 and is the oldest mission in Texas.

Guided tour of Hueco Tanks State Park and Historic Site.

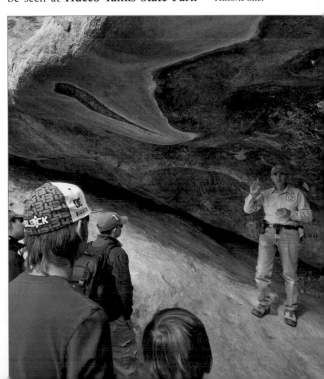

TIP

John Wesley Hardin is buried in the "Boot Hill" section of Concordia Cemetery near the west entrance to the walled Chinese section.

and Historic Site ❸ (6900 Hueco Tanks Road No. 1; tel: 915-857-1135; www.tpwd.state.tx.us/state-parks/hueco-tanks; open daily), 32 miles (51km) to the northeast, in the Franklin Mountains. With its thousands of prehistoric colorful and engaging pictographs of human, animal, and mythological figures, the site (also popular with climbers) is spiritually significant to the Mescalero Apache, the Kiowa, and Pueblos like the Hopi who trace their ancestors to the site.

El Paso Mission Trail

The Ysleta mission is still in use, as is the **Socorro Mission ❹** (tel: 915-851-1682), which was built in the same decade, the 1680s, and is the oldest continuously active parish in the US. El Camino Real, the royal highway that once linked El Norte to the capital of New Spain in Mexico, is today a quiet farm road that connects the Ysleta and Socorro missions with the **San Elizario Presidio Chapel ❺**. The presidio chapel was built in 1789, using a mixture of Spanish Colonial and native architectural styles, as a fortified base for the army. It

Wall mural on a Seventh Avenue store.

was reconstructed in 1877.

El Paso Mission Trail Foundation (tel: 915-851-9997; www.visitelpasomission trail.com) offers daily tours of El Paso's two restored Spanish missions and presidio chapel. They are located 9 miles (14km) apart.

Across the border, in Ciudad Juárez, the even older (1668) **Guadalupe Mission** is famous for the legend that its shadows point to the Lost Padre Mine in El Paso's Franklin Mountains, where Spanish gold is said to be hidden.

A slap-leather town

Ever since the Spanish explorer Juan de Oñate laid claim to El Paso del Rio Grande del Norte – a self-explanatory name – this city has been Hispanic, as are most of its residents. Far removed from the events of the Texas Revolution, El Paso for a long time shared a common religion, language, and history with Juárez, becoming a part of Texas a full five years after Texas became a state.

The overall impression of El Paso – at 674,333 souls, Texas's fourth largest city – is of "beige" – from the largely adobe buildings that are made from, and cling to, the pale caliche hills of this part of the Chihuahuan Desert.

The Old West lives on in this dusty and unprepossessing city. El Paso retains something of the ambiance of the slap-leather town it was in 1896, when gunman John Wesley Hardin was shot dead in the Acme Saloon. Hardin had been pardoned, reformed, and was practicing law in El Paso when a local constable ended his life. Along with other notorious gunslingers, he is buried in **Concordia Cemetery A**, east of downtown. Years after his death, the city remained a convenient place for outlaws to cross the river.

Campus Asian influences

El Paso has a small Chinese community – descendants of the "Chinamen" who laid the tracks for the railroad that reached here in 1881. It grew with Mexican revolutionary Pancho Villa's 1910 attacks on the Chinese living in the neighboring Mexican states of Chihuahua and Coahuila. You won't see too much evidence of this Chinese community, but one unusual Asian feature in El Paso is the Tibetan architecture

on display at the **University of Texas at El Paso B** (UTEP) campus.

It's not exactly what you would expect here, but the story is that Katherine Worrell, the wife of the dean at a time when UTEP was known as the Texas State School of Mines and Metallurgy, lifted the design from *National Geographic* after a 1916 fire destroyed almost half of the campus. The three oldest buildings are pure Bhutanese Eclectic, copied from a Tibetan monastery and fortress at Grag-Gye-Jong in the Himalayas. Most later buildings are variations on this style. While you are visiting the campus, check out the university's **Centennial Museum and Chihuahuan Desert Gardens C** (tel: 915-747-5565; Tue–Sat 10am–4.30pm; free), where displays include ancient pottery, dinosaur bones, and relics from the Ice Age.

UTEP, in the foothills of the Franklin Mountains, is a large four-year state university with 23,000 students that began life in 1914. Its 51,500-capacity stadium hosts college football on weekends during the season and is the site of the **Sun Bowl**, an annual

TIP

If you can't acquire tickets for the Sun Bowl, pack your binoculars and drag a blanket up the side of the mountain along with the locals and students.

View of downtown El Paso.

The El Paso county symbol above the entrance to the city courthouse.

Museo de Arte e Historia.

football classic, second only in age to Pasadena's Rose Bowl. The game is usually played in late December, but the weather is invariably fine: El Paso has more sunny days than almost every other city in the country. Occasional music events are also staged at the stadium. North of UTEP, **McKelligon Canyon**, popular with hikers, is the site of the summer-long outdoor dance extravaganza *¡Viva El Paso!* (tel: 915-534-0062; www.viva.ep.org) in a 1,500-seat amphitheater.

A unique feature of El Paso is "The Star on the Mountain" – a 460-by-280ft (140-by-85-meter) star erected by the local electrical utility in 1940. Illuminated by 459 white light bulbs, it can be dedicated by anybody to a friend or relative by the night, week, or month. The El Paso Times publishes the dedications daily, and sponsors get a star-shaped pin and certificate.

Downtown

San Jacinto Plaza marks the original city square and is the starting point for bus routes. Around here is what remains of the El Paso that has been documented, along with downtown Juárez, by Elroy Bode, the city's master of the *bosquejo*, or literary sketch. The city was once called Magoffinville, after one of its founding fathers, and until the 1960s, alligators were kept in the plaza.

El Paso Convention and Visitors Bureau ❶ (1 Civic Center Plaza; tel: 915-534-0600; http://visitelpaso.com; open daily) should be your first stop to pick up a walking tour brochure of downtown El Paso. Among the sights on the tour are the 1952 **El Paso Museum of Art** ❷ (1 Arts Festival Plaza; tel: 915-532-1707; www.elpasoartmuseum. org; Tue–Wed and Fri–Sat 9am–5pm, Thu 9am–9pm, Sun noon–5pm; free), which, in addition to its European collection and contemporary American works, possesses an unusually impressive collection of Mexican Colonial art and is well worth a visit. Nearby is the **El Paso Museum of** History (510 N. Santa Fe Street; tel: 915-351-3588; www.elpasotexas.gov/history; Tue–Wed and Fri–Sat 9am–5pm, Thu 9am–8pm, Sun noon–5pm; free), which has exhibits on the city's history in an attractive new building. The most surprising museum downtown is the **El Paso Holocaust Museum** (715 N. Oregon Street, tel: 915-351-0048, Tue–Fri 9am–4pm, Sat–Sun 1–5pm; free), which seems a bit out of place in this heavily Hispanic city, but offers some moving exhibits about the Holocaust.

While you are walking around the area, be sure to stop in at the spectacular historic **Camino Real Hotel** (101 S. El Paso Street; tel: 915-534-3000; www.caminoreal.com/elpaso). Reason enough to spend the night in El Paso, this handsome and sophisticated hotel has parts dating to 1912, including a simply amazing Tiffany glass-domed lobby, on a par with anything you might enjoy in Texas. At the very least, enjoy a drink at the bar or a gourmet meal in the elegant restaurant under the dome.

Another historic building in downtown El Paso that you should not miss is the **Magoffin Home State Historic Site ❻** (1120 Magoffin Avenue; tel: 915-533-5147; www.visitmagoffinhome.com; Tue–Sun 9am–5pm), an elegant 1875 adobe mansion, with walls 2.5ft (76cm) thick, that contains many of the original family furnishings and paintings.

Franklin Mountains

Northeast of downtown, off US 54, is Fort Bliss Military Reservation, the site of the largest air defense school in the free world. One curiosity here is the **Fort Bliss Replica Museum ❼** (tel: 915-568-4518; open daily; free), where history buffs can wander through the adobe pre-Civil War army outpost. It is a re-creation of what a frontier fort of the late 19th century would have looked like. Near here, in the Franklin Mountains, is Wilderness Park, home to El Paso Museum of Archaeology, Wilderness Park (4301 Transmountain Road; tel: 915-755-4332; Tue–Sat 9am–5pm, Sun noon–5pm), which interprets American Indian culture, from prehistoric times to the present and offers hiking on trails into canyons. Next door is the Border Patrol Museum (4315 Transmountain Road; Tue–Sat 9am–5pm; free), which chronicles the heritage of the Border Patrol force since its inception in 1924.

At 23,863 acres (9,657 hectares), **Franklin Mountains State Park** (1331 McKelligon Canyon Road; tel: 915-566-6441; www.tpwd.state.tx.us/

The Sun Bowl stadium.

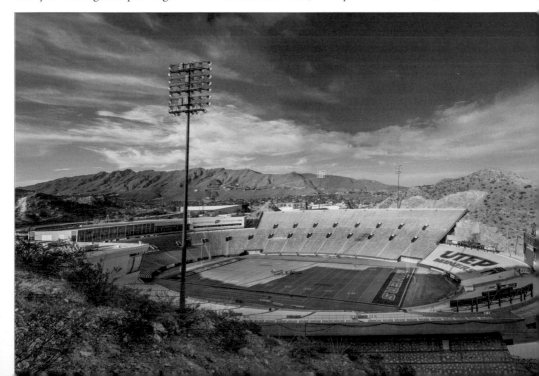

stateparks/franklin-mountains), home to North Franklin Peak, at 7,192ft (2,192 meters), the highest peak in El Paso, is the largest urban city park in the US, home to ringtail cats, coyotes, and other wildlife, and offers numerous places to explore, picnic, and relax. Ride the **Wyler Aerial Tramway** (1700 McKinley Avenue; tel: 915-566-6622) to Ranger Peak (5,632ft/1,716 meters) for views of Mexico and New Mexico. Northwest of the city, scenic drives across the Franklin Mountains, and especially along **Transmountain Road** (exit off I-10 West), provide spectacular views.

Across the border

Back in 1911, El Pasoans were able to gather on the flat roofs of their houses for "battle teas" and watch the Mexican Revolution unfold in **Ciudad Juárez** across the Rio Grande. For a while, Pancho Villa took refuge north of the border, acquiring a taste for ice cream and learning to ride a motorcycle here.

Political geography, as well as climate, shaped the character of this Mexican city. It was named for Benito Juárez, who fled here in the 1860s when Napoleon III made the Austrian Archduke Maximilian the Emperor of Mexico. Juárez, a Zapotecan Indian, fought as President to make Mexico a secular state.

Mexican bargains

Like most border towns, Juárez offers something for almost everyone. The **Museo de Arte e Historia**, on Avenida Lincoln, exhibits Mexican art by period, from pre-Hispanic to the present. The building's design is modern, unique and certainly worth a look. The museum is in a tourist-oriented commercial center that includes the government-sponsored FONART artisans' market. This is not as fecund as the *mercado central*, and there is no haggling with vendors, but it is interesting nonetheless. Along Lincoln, between FONART and the intersection of Avenida de las Americas, are a number of artisans' and curio shops, providing a good walking tour for shoppers.

Shopping is a popular pastime on both sides of the border. In El Paso,

A busy intersection in Ciudad Juárez.

the fly-and-buy tourist will find the boutiques of La Placita conveniently located near the airport, and, at I-10 and Hawkins is the Cielo Vista Mall.

Around El Paso, great bargains can be found at factory outlets for cowboy boots and Western wear. On the other side of the river, in the central *mercado*, Avenida 16 de Septiembre, you'll discover a variety of regionally manufactured goods – generally leather and textiles – and local produce.

Pedestrians can enter Mexico over the downtown **Stanton Street Bridge** , which is the closest approach to the Mexican Tourist Center, and walk back across the river by the **Santa Fe Bridge** . Most automobile traffic crosses via the **Cordova Bridge of the Americas** , off I-10, the largest bridge – and best avoided at rush hours.

Close to the bridge terminals, on both sides of the border, are parks named **Chamizal** , which memorialize the victims of the border war of a century ago and mark its peaceful settlement. Here the **Chamizal Memorial** (800 South San Marcial; tel: 915-532-7273; www.nps.gov/cham; open daily; free) records how the border has been surveyed over the centuries. Park entertainments – which take place in an art gallery, an indoor theater, and an al fresco amphitheater – vary from displays of local artworks and musical performances to films and temporary exhibitions. A fourth bridge, the **Zaragosa Bridge**, can be found on the far eastern side of El Paso.

Much of Juárez can be seen on foot, and most cab drivers speak English (but you should agree on a price before closing the door). Spanish and English are spoken in both towns.

The atmosphere in Juárez is a little more *picante* – spicy – than in El Paso, and so is the food (but don't drink the water here, or consume ice cream or ice cubes). There are lots of good and bad bars, and equally good and bad restaurants. Women are discouraged from visiting – and in some cases turned away from – *cantinas*, the traditional "men's bars." In fact, several working-class *cantinas* in downtown Juárez are best avoided by all tourists: size things up before you decide to hang around.

Pedestrians queue at the Cordova Bridge of Americas crossing.

IMPROVED SECURITY

El Paso and its sister city Juárez have been particularly hard hit by their reputation as being on the front lines of the drug war. A staggering 47,515 people died in drug-related violence between the time Mexican President Felipe Calderon took office in 2006 and 2012. But with improved cooperation between US and Mexico, and the arrival of thousands of troops in Juárez to quell problems, things have improved in the last couple of years. In 2012, homicides were at their lowest rate since 2007, when drug violence flared between the Sinaloa and Juárez cartels. That trend continued in 2013, with 497 homicides reported, the lowest amount since 2007, dropping Ciudad Juárez to the 37th spot of most-dangerous cities in the world.

An old movie set in Big Bend Ranch State Park.

BIG BEND COUNTRY

This arid region is as tough as it gets, a land dominated by unforgiving desert and a lack of drinkable water, but a land rich in minerals and natural beauty, with the highest peaks in the state.

In his classic novel, *West of the Pecos*, Zane Grey described this part of western Texas as "desolate, gray and lonely, an utter solitude uninhabited even by beasts of the hills or fowls of the air." The Spanish conquistadors who discovered it in the 16th century named the region *el despoblado*, the uninhabited place, and 300 years later a pioneer cattleman, Charles Goodnight, cursed it as "the graveyard of the cowman's hopes." General Sheridan summed up his impressions by saying that, if he owned Texas, he would "rent it out and live in hell."

The Pecos River

Beginning as a clear stream in the Sangre de Cristo Mountains north of Santa Fe, the Pecos flows 900 miles (1,440km) southward to the Rio Grande, entering "a flat, hellish desert of mesquite and greasewood" even before it reaches Texas. "Buzzards soar above the flat, torrid land," wrote Bryan Wooley in the Dallas Morning News about the Pecos region, "Dust devils dance across the plain like small brown tornadoes. Oil well pump jacks dot the landscape, many of them leaking. Quicksand forms below the river's banks and its water turns too salty for man or beast to drink." It was a major hazard to all who had to cross it, from the American Indian fighters marching to their West Texas forts to the

early 1850s immigrants on their way to search for gold in California.

The mythical Pecos Bill, legendarily reared by coyotes and who fed his horse barbed wire, stems from this region of tall tales and great accomplishments. Such an accomplishment was featured in Larry McMurtry's *Lonesome Dove*, which was inspired by the way that Goodnight and Oliver Loving expanded the range of the longhorn hundreds of miles north, driving a quarter of a million cattle across the Pecos. In that era – the 1860s

Main Attractions

Marfa
Museum of the Big Bend, Alpine
Fort Davis National Historic Site
McDonald Observatory
Guadalupe Mountains National Park

The Big Bend Saddlery store, Alpine.

– the river was 50–100ft (15–30 meters) wide, spreading to a mile (1.6km) after floods and leaving deadly lakes of poisonous alkaline water behind when the floods receded.

Spanish gold is said to be buried in the desert, though it would take unimaginable endurance to search for it. In the 1930s, Hollywood struck a rich vein of its own with a raft of titles such as *The Pecos Kid*, *The Stranger from Pecos*, *King of the Pecos* (starring John Wayne) and *Robin Hood of the Pecos* (Roy Rogers). "The Pecos river holds a fascination for people," Paul Patterson, a 90-year-old cowboy who has lived along the river most of his life, told the *Dallas Morning News*, "unless they have to stop and camp and drink the water." A local joke maintains that when a coyote drinks the water he immediately licks his behind to get the bad taste out of his mouth.

The fossil clock

Like the Grand Canyon, the history of the earth can be read clearly in arid West Texas, where vegetation has not scrawled its graffiti of decay. Nature's first attempts at complex creatures can still be seen in the 600-million-year-old remains of algal colonies in pre-Cambrian limestone, 2.5 miles (4km) north of Allamoore, 10 miles (16km) northwest of **Van Horn** ❻ (pop. 1,971). Van Horn is an historic crossroads of the old Bankhead Highway and the Old Spanish Trail, 150 miles (240km) southeast of El Paso, an area of West Texas dubbed Big Bend Country. US 90 and I-10 cross here today, and it's a good jumping-off point for explorations to this remote southwestern section of Texas.

It's worth stopping in Van Horn to view the ancient pictographs on dark red precambrian rocks and pink and purple cambrian formations on **Red Rock Ranch** (305 Broadway; tel: 432-283-7800 or 800-735-6911; tours by reservation, with at least one week's notice), north of town. The 3.5-hour tours take in the rock art, an 1880 ranch house, and an old movie set.

West of here, I-10 crosses the foothills of the Sierra Diablo Mountains before passing through **Sierra Blanca** ❼, with dramatic views of 6,950ft

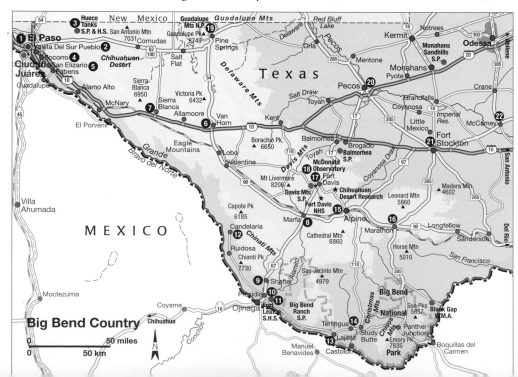

Big Bend Country

(2,120-meter) Sierra Blanca Mountain and "forests" of Spanish dagger yucca plant. This is where Chinese railroad workers from the west met Irish laborers from the east to complete the second transcontinental railroad.

Marfa

Beginning life in 1883 as a water stop and freight headquarters for the Galveston, Harrisburg, and San Antonio Railway, **Marfa** ❽ (pop. 1,900), 75 miles (120km) south of Van Horn, was named for a character in Fyodor Dostoevski's *The Brothers Karamazov*. The book was being read at the time by the wife of the chief railroad engineer. By 1885, when the impressive courthouse was built, poker bets in the saloons were being made with town lots. At 4,688ft (1,428 meters), in a semi-arid region, Marfa boasts a superb climate and, in summer, is one of the coolest places in Texas.

Marfa is celebrated as the location for the 1956 movie *Giant*, starring Rock Hudson, Elizabeth Taylor, James Dean, and other Hollywood stars who took over downtown's charming 1930 El Paisano Hotel (207 Highland Street; tel: 432-729-3669; www.hotel paisano.com) as a headquarters. The Pueblo Deco hotel, designed by Trost and Trost, has a decidedly faded air of glamor today, but its lobby is worth a look. You can still stay in one of the historic rooms the stars occupied, including the Rock Hudson Suite.

The Chinati Foundation

Spain had practically abandoned West Texas by the time it became a part of independent Mexico in 1821. As the Anglo frontier moved westward, the fierce mounted Comanche war parties began to prey on wagon trains and Mexican and Anglo settlements along the Comanche War Trail, especially during the late summer and early fall harvest season. To counter these depredations, a line of cavalry forts was established soon after the Republic of Texas joined

the United States in 1846. The old fort, just north of Marfa, has today been transformed into the **Chinati Foundation** (1 Cavalry Row; tel: 432-729-4362; www.chinati.org; Wed–Sat 9am–4.30pm; tours by reservation), a contemporary art museum founded by artist Donald Judd specifically designed to exhibit large-scale installations by a range of artists.

The New York sculptor Don Judd fathered the $4 million project, with Houston oil heiress Philippa de Menil Pelizzi Friedrich as reluctant mother. Judd needed isolation for himself and open spaces for his work, both of which Marfa offers in abundance. His variously permutated groups of large rectangular concrete structures are rhythmically arranged in an endless progression toward the far horizon; some 100 aluminum pieces are housed in a glass-walled gun shed. There are also works by other prominent contemporary artists on display in the fort, such as the crushed auto-body sculptures of John Chamberlain and the fluorescent sculptures of Dan Flavin.

The Prada Marfa art installation, north of Marfa.

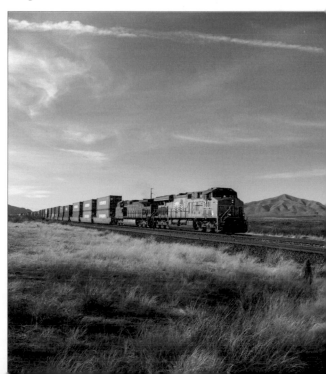

Eastbound freight train.

FACT

Big Bend Ranch State Park should not be confused with Big Bend National Park, although it is equally stunning in many ways. The land was acquired by Texas Parks and Wildlife Department in 1988.

Unlikely art and food oasis

Countless artists followed Judd to Marfa, and the town is now a haven for hip East Coast urban artists, many of whom have sensitively restored historic buildings as homes, art galleries, restaurants, a great hometown independent bookstore (with books on art, of course), and next door, a popular local public radio station. The wail of locomotives flying through town is often the only sound in this quiet West Texas backwater.

For its size, Marfa is spoiled for enjoyable places to stay and eat out on top of its novel attractions – it boasts a double-take fake Prada Marfa store beside the highway northwest of town, actually an art installation, and is also known for its Marfa Lights, nightly illuminations in the sky that can be viewed out beside the highway. Next to the train tracks, visit the small weekly farmer's market and line up for tasty Mediterranean food at the popular **Food Shark** food truck (it just opened a new bricks-and-mortar cafeteria-style eatery in downtown). For dinner, **Cochineal** (107 W. San Antonio Street; tel: 432-729-3300; www.cochinealmarfa.com; reservations recommended), owned by seasoned restaurateurs from New York City, is a chic eatery that gives any fine dining establishment in New York a run for its money.

Marfa attracts many visitors.

Down to the border

From Marfa, US 67 heads southwest to **Shafter** ❾, a ghost town in the Chinati Mountains, where millions of dollars of silver were mined and where stories persist about treasure buried in caves. Farther south, on the banks of the Rio Grande, is **Presidio** ❿ (pop. 4,266), described in the WPA guidebook to Texas in 1940 as "an old town of sunbaked adobe houses, squatting like an ancient hombre in the shade of giant cottonwoods." The town, which was founded by Franciscan missionaries in 1683, hosts an annual onion festival (May).

Fort Leaton State Historic Site ⓫ (tel: 432-229-3416; www.tpwd.state.tx.state-parks/fort-leaton; open daily), an interesting example of native adobe construction, southeast of town, was not a military outpost but a trading post operated in the mid-19th century by a certain Ben Leaton. Leaton had been among the first Anglo settlers to arrive in Presidio. In their fortified trading post, he and his wife outfitted and accommodated travelers who were somehow drawn to this backwater of civilization. The Texas Rangers had a base here when Pancho Villa was rampaging south of the border, but the post was abandoned in 1926. Most of the old outpost has now been restored.

Across the river from Presidio is **Ojinaga** ("o-hee-NAH-ga"), which lacks the touristy feel of most border towns. There are a few good restaurants, and at least one good hotel. Cautions for travel in Mexico apply here, as elsewhere along La Frontera.

The highest waterfall in Texas is on a private ranch near the tiny settlement of **Candelaria** ⓬, northwest of

Presidio. Capote Falls crashes 175ft (54 meters) on to the rocks below. Inquire locally about making a visit.

El Camino del Rio (Farm Road 170) follows the Rio Grande southeast from Presidio down to the tiny village of **Lajitas** ⓭, a spectacular drive with sharp curves, steep grades, and occasional wandering livestock. The village owes its origins to the 1915 US Army base established to protect settlers against Pancho Villa's border raids, and is a useful base from which to explore the area. The Cavalry Post, one of three motels in town, is built on the site of the trading post established by General Jack Pershing before he mounted his "punitive expedition" against Villa. This unsuccessful foray demonstrated the army's lack of experience in fighting on foreign terrain. A young lieutenant by the name of George Patton saw his first action here, as a member of Pershing's expedition, and killed two men and a horse. The hotels in Lajitas are part of a large upscale Western conference center that has a variety of recreational activities, including a nine-hole golf course, a pool, and a saloon/dance hall.

Several companies licensed by the National Park Service in nearby Big Bend National Park offer raft trips of 1–9 days' duration on the Rio Grande, through narrow 1,500ft (460-meter) deep canyons, or farther down in challenging rapids. Among them is Far Flung Outdoor Center (tel: 800-839-7238; www:bigbendfarflung. com) in Terlingua. Just east of Lajitas, on FM 170, is **Barton Warnock Environmental Educational Center** (tel: 432-424-3327; www.tpwd.state.tx.state-parks/barton-warnock; daily 8am–5pm), named after a local botanist. The center sits at the eastern entrance to **Big Bend Ranch State Park** (tel: 432-358-4444; www.tpwd.state.tx/state-parks/big-bend-ranch; open daily), a state park adjoining the national park to the east; the western entrance is at Fort Leaton State Historic Site.

Gem hunting

FM 170 continues onward to **Terlingua** ⓮ (pop. 58), now a collection of mostly abandoned stone and adobe ruins, but, at the turn of the 20th century, a prosperous mining town of 2,000 inhabitants. Here red cinnabar ore was mined and cooked to yield millions of dollars' worth of mercury. The 27 miles (43km) of tunnels and shafts – some as much as 900ft (275 meters) deep – of the abandoned mercury mines have yielded a treasure trove of rocks, fossils and mineral specimens cast aside by miners, as well as abundant specimens of cinnabar. This looks much like lipstick smears on the fissured surfaces of igneous rocks.

Views of the nearby peaks of the Chisos Mountains in Big Bend National Park (see page 253), and multicolored badlands on every side, form a surreal backdrop for rock hounds and cactus collectors, who can run amok here. Amber, the hard golden resin of prehistoric plants, is occasionally collected from cretaceous coal outcrops along Terlingua Creek, just west of Big Bend. The mountains in this region were

Terlingua's historic cemetery.

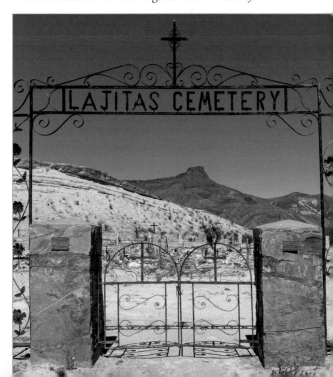

once the hideout of outlaws, renegades, and the like – especially the little settlement of **Valentine** (pop. 187) on US 90, northwest of Marfa. They now attract rockhounds, on account of the numerous minerals and gems they yield. An outstanding example is the famous Texas plumed agate, in which red flames and black feather shapes are captured in a translucent white matrix. It is most easily found near Marfa and Alpine.

Alpine

An attractive college town with a lot of art galleries, restaurants, and lodging options, **Alpine** ⓖ (pop. 5,800), the northeastern corner of the triangle made up of Marfa and Presidio, is the main center of activity in Big Bend Country. To someone arriving from the broiling flatlands, the town's 4,500ft (1,370-meter) altitude can indeed seem alpine. In the heart of cattle country, Alpine is a stop on AMTRAK's Sunset Limited, between Chicago and Los Angeles. Many people choose the town for their vacation headquarters and enjoy summer

Guests at the Holland Hotel, Alpine.

theater productions and museums at **Sul Ross State University**, which stages the annual Cowboy Poetry Gathering every March for a weeklong celebration of culture and art. Also on campus is the excellent **Museum of the Big Bend** (tel: 432-837-8143; www.museumofthebigbend.com; Tue–Sat 9am–5pm, Sun 1–5pm), which interprets the natural and cultural history of Big Bend.

Marathon

Less than one hour to the south of Alpine, at the junction of US 385 and US 90, the turnoff for Big Bend National Park, you'll find tiny **Marathon** ⓰ (pop. 430). Geologists are delighted by the diversity of rocks and minerals in the vicinity, while rugged nature photographers use Marathon as a jumping-off point for trips to **Black Gap Wildlife Management Area**, 58 miles (93km) away. Though 80 miles (129km) distant, Big Bend National Park is the next sign of civilization toward the south. If you're driving west along the Rio Grande route along the border, Marathon is the first main town after leaving Langtry and a good place to spend the night before heading down to Big Bend National Park.

The beautifully renovated **Gage Hotel** (tel: 432-386-4205; www.gagehotel.com), a national historical landmark, is just the ticket for weary travelers with a taste for backcountry luxury and the Old West. It was built as a private lodge by rancher Alfred Gage in 1927 and is set around a lovely courtyard and fountain, hacienda style. All rooms are furnished with antiques, American Indian artifacts, and Mexican furniture. The restaurant is an oasis for foodies, offering delicious New West dishes in a memorable setting. It is alone worth the trip.

Fort Davis

To the north of Alpine, at the intersection of highways 17 and 118, is **Fort**

Davis ⑰, named after the much-honored Jefferson Davis, who was president of the Confederate States of America but is remembered locally as the man who, as US Secretary of War, introduced camels to West Texas. The fort stands dramatically with its back to a wall of volcanic rock named Sleeping Lion Mountain. At 5,000ft (1,540 meters), the community is the highest in Texas and has some lovely artisan stores and lodging options.

At **Fort Davis National Historic Site** (tel: 432-426-3224; www.nps.gov/foda; daily), the life of the late 19th-century frontier soldier has been recreated. Actual buildings survive from the days when such soldiers mounted up to escort wagon trains on the Chihuahuan Trail, or stagecoaches on the Butterfield Overland Mail Route. This is considered the best-preserved US fort in the West. The fort adjoins **Davis Mountains State Park** (tel: 432-426-3337; www.tpwd.state.tx/state-parks/davis-mountains; open daily), a pretty valley that is a lovely place to hike and relax, with oak-shaded campsites in its campground.

The **Chihuahuan Desert Research Institute** (tel: 915-364-2499; Mon–Sat), on Highway 118 a few miles south of Fort Davis, is a popular port of call for those fascinated by native desert plants. Among its attractions is a cactus greenhouse. Visitors can also, in two hours, drive a scenic winding loop on highways 166 and 118 through the Davis Mountains, where gentle, weathered slopes belie their violent volcanic origins. From Wild Rose Pass on, one has the same view of Limpia Brook, as it runs between high cliffs, that the Apache and Comanche raiding parties had as they lay in ambush.

In this area, **McDonald Observatory** ⑱ (3640 Dark Sky Drive; tel: 432-426-3640; www.mcdonaldobservatory.org; daily 10am–5.30pm), perched atop Mount Lock, houses one of the largest astronomical telescopes in the world, the giant 433-inch (9.2-meter) HET optical telescope

The mountains

Interstates I-10 (which runs through Fort Stockton) and I-20 (through Pecos) meet to the west, on the edge of the Davis Mountains. This vast range (under different names) runs from the New Mexico border – aside from a gap between Fort Davis and Alpine – all the way south to Big Bend National Park on the Rio Grande. Islands of green – the forests and meadows of the high mountains – rise in the sea of brown.

Six of them soar to over 8,000ft (2,400 meters), including **Mount Livermore** at 8,206ft (2,525 meters). In these enclaves of pine, fir, maple, and oak, there are small populations of elk, black bear, bighorn sheep, and mountain lions, the reminders of better, wetter grazing times. A drying trend over the past 100 years, coupled with overgrazing by livestock, has depleted the grass and the steppe has become a desert hell.

The youngest ranges are the Franklin Mountains at El Paso and the Delaware Mountains north of Kent, which are part of the Rocky Mountain system and still rise at an average

A section of the Cleburne history mural, Alpine, by award-winning artist Stylle Read.

Desert highway near Marathon.

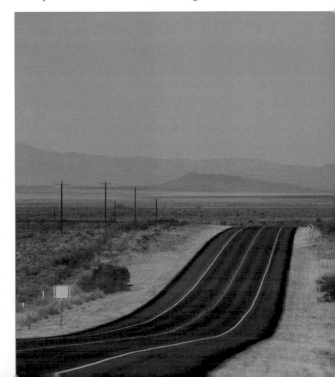

Desert Plantlife

Hardy survivors of the scorched earth, desert plants endure through cunning, thrift, and clever adaptations and emerge in spectacular springtime displays after wet winters.

The flowering plants of the Chihuahuan Desert perform a spectacular, although brief, extravaganza after the spring rains; but most of the rest of the year they are occupied with vegetative survival rather than reproductive exhibitionism. If you see a *lechuguilla* plant, you'll know where you are, since the habitat of this member of the amarillis family coincides perfectly with the boundaries of the Chihuahuan Desert.

Lechuguilla, which means "little lettuce" in Spanish, is easily recognized by its rosette of succulent bluish-green, spine-tipped leaves about 2ft (67cm) long and 1.5 inches (4cm) wide. In true desert plant fashion, it can inflict a painful wound on the unwary.

The yucca species are somewhat similar to agave but are actually members of the lily family.

There are over 100 native species of cactus in Texas.

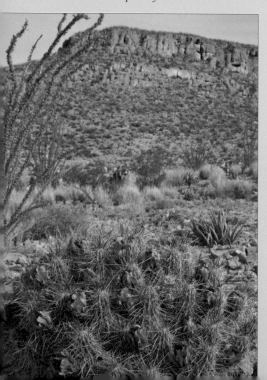

They have narrower, more flexible, and less succulent leaves, and flower annually. The torrey yucca grows almost to the height of a tree north and west of Van Horn, forming the only "forest" in the desert lowlands.

Desert cactus

The cactus family, that classic form of desert life, originated in the southwestern US and Mexico and has attained its greatest diversity there. Over 100 species of cactus are Texas residents.

Ocotillo is a cactus prevalent in the Far West. It looks like a naked spider on its back and its long 6–20ft (2–6-meter) legs, protected by stiff spines, are used as living fences by goat raisers. This cautious species puts out leaves only after rainfall and discards them as soon as drought returns.

Greasewood, or creosote bush, is, along with cactus, ubiquitous in North American deserts, taking its name from the thick resin on its small yellowish-green paired leaflets. Usually only around a meter in height, it has been used as fuel by the desert cultures for thousands of years. Its wide, even spacing and the general absence of competing species are the result of special adaptation to the limited availability of water, for greasewood secretes a poison that kills even its own seedlings.

Another plant particularly common on mesas and hillsides is sotol, or "bear grass," so called for its 4ft (1.25-meter) long, arching, narrow leaves with small claw-like spines along the margins. Its slender, 4–15ft (1.25–4.5-meter) brush-like, flowering stalk may persist for several seasons.

Native uses

All of these large plants were important to the American Indians who inhabited the area. Their leaves provided fiber for clothing and utensils, as well as soap, and the thick basal stems were baked in stone-lined fireplaces, of which the scattered remains can be seen.

The pea family is also well represented by thorny shrubs like the infamous cat claw acacia, or "wait-a-minute bush," from the automatic cry of "Wait a minute!" as hikers try to extricate themselves from this vegetable's clutches.

Devil's head cactus is an interesting plant about a foot (31cm) in diameter. It lurks, partially buried, ready to snare a hoof, paw, or sneaker with its four-pronged spines. On the whole, desert plants are best admired from a safe distance.

rate of more than quarter of an inch (0.65cm) per year. Many of the ranges in the basin-and-range area of Texas were formed during the tumultuous Tertiary period, approximately 60 million years ago. Massive uplifting and faulting led to intrusions of molten rock, like those in the Chisos Mountains of Big Bend National Park, and extensive lava flows that created the Davis Mountains.

These volcanic formations cover mountains from earlier periods, as well as marine sediments and coral reefs. Folding and overthrust faulting have left young rock strata covered by a layer 150 million years older in places – a picture puzzle complex enough to delight the most jaded structural geologist.

Texas's highest and most majestic mountains, the Guadalupes, at the Texas–New Mexico border, began as a massive coral reef, the Permian Reef, some 250 million years ago. Two periods of uplift have raised the reef to its current elevation of over 8,000ft (2,440 meters) – Carlsbad Caverns, just over the border in New Mexico, meanwhile,

protects decorated caves in that same formation beneath ground. The dominant feature in **Guadalupe Mountains National Park** ⑲ (tel: 915-828-3251; www.nps.gov/guad; open daily) is 8,749ft (2,667-meter) Guadalupe Peak, the highest point in Texas. Approached from the west on US 62/180, this giant wedge of limestone resembles an enormous ship moving over the desert. The cliffs of El Capitan Peak form the prow, towering above a white sea of salt. McKittrick Canyon is a major draw in fall foliage season, when its maples display brilliant hues. The park's small campground is a nice spot to relax, hike, and enjoy the desert, and is convenient for visiting nearby Carlsbad Caverns. Get there early to secure a spot.

Cantaloupes and rodeos

Pecos ⑳ (pop. 8,785) is the largest town along the river of the same name and famous for its cantaloupes. Here, in 1883, the world's first rodeo took place. The boys from the Hashknife outfit challenged boys from other ranches to horse-racing, bronc-busting, and calf-roping contests. The

Fort Davis National Historic Site.

tradition is carried on, with a major rodeo here around July 4 each year. The **West of the Pecos Museum** (120 E. Dot Stafford Street; tel: 432-445-5076; www.westofthepecosmuseum.com; Mon–Sat 9am–5pm, Sun 1–5pm) displays a century-old saloon in one of its 50 rooms.

North of Pecos, bordering New Mexico, is **Loving**, the most sparsely populated county in the US – 67 people with an average 10 sq miles (26 sq km) each. So despite the name and with such a small population, not a whole lot of loving goes on. Four hundred oil leases have been registered here, but there is no water – it has to be trucked in.

The only reservoir in Texas along the Pecos River is Red Bluff in Loving County, but it has only once been full in the past 60 years. New Mexico defended itself in court for 16 years against Texan charges that it was taking too much water out of the river. Finally, in 1988, the US Supreme Court ruled in Texas's favor and its neighbor was forced to pay $14 million in damages.

The first place of any size along the river south of Pecos is **Fort Stockton** ㉑ (pop. 8,535). By the mid-1880s, with no enemies left to fight, the fort was abandoned, but it has been restored to its earlier appearance. Four of the original fort's buildings, constructed in 1867, can be visited and a museum and visitor center (tel: 432-336-2400/800-336-2166; www.historicfortstocktontx.com; open daily) has been established in Barracks 1. Burrowing owls pop out of the earth of the parade grounds during the day. Other interesting local sights, including the world's largest roadrunner, are included on the self-guided tour map.

Forty miles (64km) east of Fort Stockton, at the junction of US 67 and US 385, is **McCamey** ㉒, an "instant town" on November 16, 1925, when the No. 1 Baker oil well blew in. Within months, there were 10,000 people in town and the solitary Texas Ranger – lacking a jail – was obliged to chain prisoners to a post. One group of tethered roughnecks uprooted the pole and took it to the nearest saloon. In 1936, McCamey was the scene of the world's first Rattlesnake Derby, with a $200 purse for the winner.

Rider at the West of the Pecos PRCA rodeo.

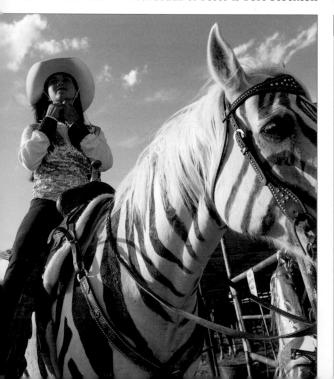

CHILI COOKOFF

If you're a fan of hot food, Terlingua is the place to make for on the first Saturday in November every year. Since 1967, this dusty little hamlet on the Rio Grande, west of Big Bend National Park, has been the venue for the Terlingua International Chili Cookoff. The cookoff attracts over 10,000 "chiliheads" for two annual chili cookoffs: the Chili Appreciation Society International and the Frank X. Tolbert/Wick Fowler World Chili Championships. Among the founders of the first chili cookoff in 1967 was car manufacturer Carroll Shelby, who owned a 220,000-acre (89,000-hectare) ranch nearby. Expect hotels to be fully booked around the time of either cookoff. For more information and a schedule of events, visit www.abowlofred.com.

The Marfa Lights

Alien spacecraft, atmospheric mirages, burning gases, desert reflections – no one knows what causes the famous nightly lights in the sky near Marfa.

Robert Reed Ellison, a young cowhand, was the first to report the Marfa Lights. Looking across to the Chinati Mountains in West Texas he saw them twinkling in the night and figured they must have been the campfires of Apache Indians. But when he went searching the next day he found no Apaches – nor even the ashes of any fires. This was 114 years ago and people have been watching the lights ever since, but still without being able to explain what they are and where they're coming from. As elusive as rainbows, they disappear as soon as you think you're getting up close.

According to one guidebook the lights "move about, split apart, melt together, disappear and reappear." In recent years they have become such a tourist attraction that the Texas State Highways Department has built a special parking area from which to view them along US 90, about 10 miles (16km) east of town. And at the Apache Trading Post, just west of Alpine, there's now a screening room, where visitors can view films and videotape of the lights.

Following the lights

During World War II, pilots training at the nearby army base conducted an aerial search but were no more successful than previous investigators: the lights remained a mystery. Superstitious locals tend to reflect the views of a Mrs W.T. Giddings who claims they are a friendly source that once saved her father from a blizzard by leading him to a cave. Other explanations have included: electrostatic discharge, St Elmo's Fire, swamp gas or other natural gases igniting, moonlight reflecting on veins of mica, and even the ghosts of conquistadors in search of gold. *A New Handbook of Texas* says the most likely explanation is that the lights are a mirage caused by atmospheric conditions, produced by the interaction of cold and warm layers of air that bend light so that it can be seen from a distance but not up close.

Enough theories for a book

The Desert Candle, the former local newspaper, which during its years of publication ran numerous reports of sightings, some of which were compiled in a book by editor Judith M. Brueske, suggested that the spaciousness of the Big Bend region and "the relatively low light contaminant," compared to more heavily populated areas, might make such lights easier to see. In the chapter titled *"The Marfa Light"* she offers several explanations, ranging from the phenomenon known as *ignis fatuus* (the spontaneous combustion of natural gases) or static electricity to the combination of moisture with bat guano phosphates (there are many bat caves in the mountains). And she, too, brings up the possibility that many of the sightings could be mirages, pointing out that, especially at sea, people have conjured up the vision of islands or villages.

What argues against this theory is the sheer ubiquity of the sightings. Usually they are small and seen at a distance, but occasionally lights as big as footballs have come close to people's cars. Nobody has ever reported being harmed.

Marfa Lights are visible every clear night between Marfa and Paisano Pass, in the direction of the Chinati Mountains.

Spectactors gather to watch the Marfa Lights.

BIG BEND NATIONAL PARK

Beautiful Big Bend, where the Rio Grande lurches to the northeast, has canyons, waterfalls, and hiking trails galore, but with far fewer visitors than you'll find at Yosemite or the Grand Canyon.

The state's largest park, Big Bend National Park, is most challenging to backpackers and nature lovers. The Chisos Mountains, the wide desert, the Rio Grande, and the magnificent canyons combine to form a true wilderness, sections of which are still relatively unexplored.

Big Bend National Park (tel: 432-477-2251; www.nps.gov/bibe; open daily) is one of those places you have to be going to in order to get there. The closest town is Alpine, about 65 miles (105km) to the northwest of the northernmost tip. The park encompasses a vast area of 801,163 acres (324,230 hectares) and varies in altitude from 1,850ft (570 meters) all the way up to 7,835ft (2,410 meters). It has hundreds of trails, 100 miles (160km) of paved roads, and 170 miles (272km) of dirt roads. There is a campground with hookups and shelters, a post office, and a gas station. **Panther Junction ❶** has the park headquarters and visitor center (open daily 8am–6pm), which should be your first stop on arrival. Year-round, Chisos Mountains Lodge (tel: 432-447-2291), at **Chisos Basin ❷**, provides camping and motel accommodations. RV and tent campsites are also available at **Rio Grande Village ❸**, near Boquillas, and at Cottonwood, near Castolon. Permits (free) are required for backcountry camping.

Cacti on an arid hillside.

Wild country

King of the air around here is the endangered peregrine falcon, whose concentration of aeries is the largest in the contiguous 48 states. Golden eagles are frequently seen in winter, near the mountains and over the high grasslands, but, as the clouds move across this desolate land, you may be reminded of the gargantuan pterosaur whose 51ft (15.5-meter) reptilian wings cast terrifying shadows on the lesser dinosaurs below. The remains of these cretaceous creatures, the largest animals ever to fly,

Main Attractions
Chisos Basin
Chisos Basin Trail
Rio Grande Village Nature Trail
Santa Elena Canyon
Castolon

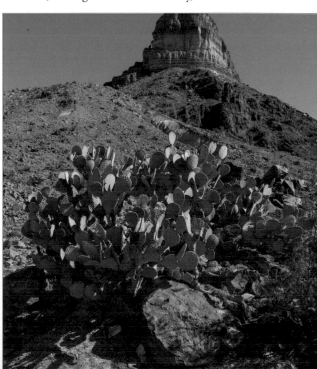

were found in the Big Bend area in the early 1970s.

The great outdoors

The real Big Bend is best seen from its hiking trails, or from a kayak trip on the Rio Grande. Extensive information about getting the best out of your visit through hiking, camping, kayaking, scenic hikes, and river rafting trips is available from the National Park Service. But Big Bend is wild country, and should be respected as such.

Hit the trail

Some of the 36 marked hiking trails are strenuous and treacherous; others are easy. Many are interpreted by self-guiding leaflets and trail signs. A number of trails take off from near Chisos Basin.

During the summer, a hike down the easy, 1.5-mile (2.5km) **Chisos Basin Trail** is guided by a park naturalist. At the overlook about halfway along the trail, the major features of the Chisos Basin stand out against the sky: towering Emory Peak, at 7,825ft (2,400 meters) the highest in the park; Ward Mountain; Carter Peak and The Window; Vernon Bailey Peak and Pulliam Ridge; Casa Grande and Toll Mountain. This trail provides a good introduction to the major features of the Big Bend park.

Halfway between The Basin and Panther Junction, the **Pine Canyon Trail** explores a wooded canyon for 4 miles (6km). At trail's end, a waterfall pours down the 200ft (60-meter) cliff after a heavy rain.

Just north of The Basin, the moderately difficult 5-mile (8km) Lost Mine Trail follows the north slope of Casa Grande and leads to a point high on the west side of Lost Mine Peak. It affords beautiful views of the surrounding mountains and canyons. A very difficult trek up the 7,500ft (2,300-meter) Casa Grande Peak takes off from the Juniper Canyon Overlook along the Lost Mine Trail.

The 5-mile (8km) **Chimneys Trail** lies southwest of The Basin and leads to a group of high rock outcroppings, or "chimneys," the southernmost of which contains ancient American Indian pictographs.

Two groups of trails into the Chisos lie south of The Basin: the High Chisos Complex trails and the Outer Mountain Loop trails. The High Chisos trails are some of the most beautiful, but they require serious hiking and climbing. The panorama from the South Rim Trail includes Santa Elena Canyon 20 miles (30km) to the west, Emory Peak to the north, and the mountains in Mexico to the south. Various trails branch off from this one and, for instance, lead up Emory Peak into Boot Canyon – the summer home of the Colima warbler, found nowhere else in the United States.

While the High Chisos trails are strenuous, they are, at least, well marked. The Outer Mountain Loop trails, on the other hand, are not so well marked and hardly flat at all. Among these, Blue Creek Trail is known for its colorful balanced rocks and pinnacles. However, these two series of trails can be combined for a lengthier expedition into the Big Bend wilderness.

Spectacular canyons

Another popular trailhead is the Rio Grande Village area, near the river in the eastern part of the park. The very easy **Rio Grande Village Nature Trail**, just under a mile (1.2km) long, interprets several plant habitats, including the lush river floodplain and the arid desert. An overlook at trail's end gives breathtaking views of Mexico, the river, the Chisos Mountains, and Boquillas Canyon.

Boquillas, the longest canyon in the park, is also accessible along the 1.5-mile (2.5km) **Boquillas Canyon Trail**. For

TIP

Water can be a real problem on both long and short hikes. Dehydration comes on quickly in Big Bend's dry air, and springs and streams are not reliable for drinking. Make sure you bring at least a gallon of water per person per day and drink it frequently, along with salty, nutritious foods that help balance electrolytes in the body.

One of the 36 marked hiking trails in the park.

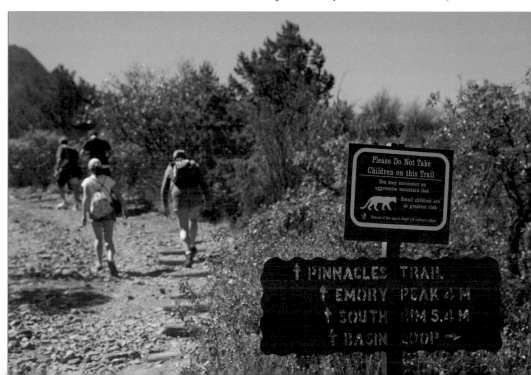

the more adventurous, a three-day trip covering 17 miles (27km) in the canyon and 8 miles (13km) on the Rio Grande can be a wonderful experience, with all the side canyons there are to explore on both banks, in Texas and Mexico.

The most spectacular of the Big Bend canyons, **Santa Elena**, can be seen on an easy 1.5-mile (2.5km) trail that crosses Terlingua Creek and wanders through the magnificent 17-mile (27km) canyon to the river.

If you decide to run the waters, bear in mind that the river is very tricky, especially in high or low water. Eleven miles (18km) of scenic river precede the canyon entrance, but watch for strong currents over hidden rocks. The most dangerous part of the canyon is the rockslide about a mile (1.6km) beyond the entrance. Running the slide is always difficult, and downright dangerous at high and low water levels. Portaging it is socially acceptable and no blemish whatsoever on anyone's manhood. After the slide, navigation is more tranquil and boaters can enjoy colorful canyon walls and also explore the jewel-like Fern Canyon.

Relaxing in the Hot Springs bathing pool, along the Rio Grande in the south part of the park.

Mariscal Canyon, the most isolated of the three major canyons, is accessible on a strenuous, unshaded 6.5-mile (10km) hike. The rim affords a wide view of the canyon 1,500ft (460 meters) below – a fine reward for the persevering hiker.

By car

Even from a car, Big Bend visitors can see the wild country. The River Road traverses the 51 miles (82km) between the Boquillas–Rio Grande Village road and Castolon. The road can be traveled by most high-clearance vehicles, but its side roads usually require four-wheel-drive. Old ranches and fishing camps occasionally appear along the road, and it passes the ruins of Mariscal Mine, an old mercury working at the foot of Mariscal Mountain. The ruins are fun to explore, but beware of open, unmarked mine shafts. Farther west lie the remains of the Johnson Ranch House, probably the largest adobe ruin in the park. The road ends at **Castolon** ❹, a 19th-century farming settlement and early 20th-century US Cavalry and Texas Ranger post.

Boquillas Canyon.

WILDLIFE IN TEXAS

You don't need to venture deep into the Texas countryside to discover the state's weird and wonderful wildlife. But, if you do, take care.

As you wander the civilized streets of Dallas or Houston, catching your reflection in a glass skyscraper, it's easy to forget that this is still the Wild West – "wild" in the sense that the animals that call Texas their home remain as unfazed by progress as they were in the days of the frontier pioneers.

The scurrying armadillo is a familiar sight in many parts of the state. Other creatures are more regionalized, preferring the marshy wetness of East Texas or the unrelenting dryness and heat of West Texas. Some Texas wildlife is continually on the move – winging, crawling, or grubbing its way into new corners of the state.

The comical antics of the prairie dog, the elegance of deer grazing in the Hill Country. or the smiling dolphins off the Gulf Coast should not lead visitors into a false sense of security. Like the prickly desert plants, native Texan beasts must be met on their own terms, if met at all. They can bite, they can sting. They can annoy, they can maim. The rule is: Don't mess with them. If you leave the animals to themselves, the chances are they'll keep well away from you. Be sensible. Follow all warning signs and don't tempt danger. But, for all the cougars, black bears, rattlesnakes, alligators, and coyotes, there are also stunning birds, majestic buffalo, thriving longhorns, languid sea turtles, and exotic fish you won't find anywhere else.

And with scores of natural wildlife refuges for safe viewing, the beautiful creatures of Texas can still charm and enthrall.

The Prairie dog, a member of the squirrel family, lives in colonies of thousands. Its name is derived from its cry, or "bark."

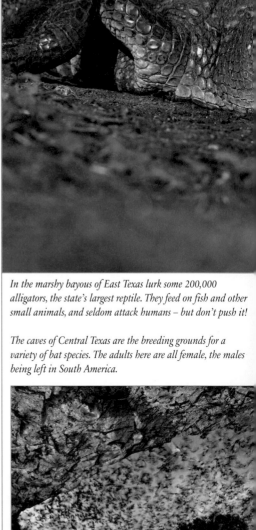

In the marshy bayous of East Texas lurk some 200,000 alligators, the state's largest reptile. They feed on fish and other small animals, and seldom attack humans – but don't push it!

The caves of Central Texas are the breeding grounds for a variety of bat species. The adults here are all female, the males being left in South America.

A western diamondback rattlesnake ready to strike.

SNAKES IN THE GRASS

The statistics tell the truth: there is more chance of being killed by a lightning strike in Texas than from a snake bite. Nevertheless, the thought of a venomous rattler is enough to panic many Texas visitors.

The state is home to more than 100 species of snake, but less than 10 percent are a danger to humans. The rattlesnake (actually 11 varieties) is the most feared. It can be found in most parts of Texas, but is prevalent in the Big Bend region. The coral snake is also a nasty little wriggler and may be encountered in areas from Central Texas south. The same territory is inhabited by the copperhead, equally dangerous if provoked, while the cottonmouth is semi-aquatic and lives mostly around rivers in Central and East Texas.

Cougars are found in the mountains of Big Bend Country. They can be aggressive towards humans and should not be approached. Smaller cats live elsewhere in the state: lynx-like bobcats in East Texas and ocelots in South Texas. Look out for wild dogs, too, particularly coyotes and wolves.

Despite being armed with tusks and musk, the near-sighted javelina, a cousin of the South American tapir, is not dangerous.

The prickly looking horned lizard, often mistakenly referred to as the "horny toad," can shoot a stream of blood from its eyes.

The Big Texan Steak Ranch, Amarillo, home of the "free" 72-oz steak.

WEST TEXAS

Dusty West Texas has ridden coal and oil booms and boasts a tough, independent character that has fostered ranchers, presidents, and early rock and roll.

West Texas, as a geographic region, takes in the whole western part of the state. It's a huge area, not easily defined except by generally being in the Chihuahuan Desert. People in the far western desert portions of Texas, from El Paso and Big Bend Country to Amarillo and the Panhandle Plains, call themselves West Texans, but so, interestingly enough, do the people of the southern parts of North Central Texas.

The latter do so not out of geographical ignorance, but out of a sense of history and place. After the Civil War, their ancestors from southern states, knowing no place else to go to begin a new life, headed west, where they encountered a foe more relentless than General Sherman: the slow-yielding, tightfisted land itself, ruled by distance, drought, and the most ferocious aboriginal army ever to ride horseback: the Comanche. Thus, mile after uncertain mile was conquered by people who were not searching for wealth, but for a place to survive. They did survive, and left their descendants with the knowledge that anything is possible if one is self-reliant and looks toward the horizon.

Travel in this relatively featureless landscape can become an agonizingly slow unfolding of geography, if you expect to be constantly entertained by the fluff and fanfare of tourist

A Texas icon: the oil pump.

extravaganzas. However, if you adopt the easy-going friendliness of its people, and attune yourself to the voices of its heroic past, West Texas will be an unforgettable experience.

Fort Worth to El Paso

West of Fort Worth, where I-20 drops down from rough-cut juniper- and oak-covered hills on to the fitful beginning of the Panhandle Plains, are the ruins of **Thurber** ❶, a coal-mining town better suited to northeastern Pennsylvania or the Ruhr Valley than

Main Attractions
Old Jail Art Center, Albany
Permian Basin Petroleum Museum, Midland
Palo Duro Canyon State Park, Canyon
National Ranching Heritage Center, Lubbock
Buddy Holly Center, Lubbock

post-frontier Texas. Where 10,000 people from 17 countries lived between 1880 and 1922 – making it the biggest coal mining town in Texas at the time – there now exist only 48 residents, a tall brick smoke stack, a restaurant-museum, the remains of a great brick factory, and a service station. The rest of the town has been sold brick by brick, down to the last utility pole.

As one looks across the now empty valley to the conical piles of black coal spoil and "red dog" cinders, it is difficult to imagine the wealthy, cosmopolitan city that stood here on the near side of frontier times. Thurber is where the Metropolitan Opera of New York performed, where Miss Wallis "Wildcat" Warfield (later the Duchess of Windsor) grew up in one of the mansions along Silk Stocking Road on New York Hill, and where a World War I clothing drive netted no fewer than four dozen mink coats.

In 1895, Thurber was one of the first completely electrified cities in the world. After a long, bitter strike presided over by Texas Rangers, Thurber became the first and perhaps the only 100-percent unionized town in America. The 100 million tonnes of coal mined here powered the belching locomotives of Jay Gould's Texas and Pacific Railroad as they trundled across the prairie. In 1881, the last 595 miles (958km) of the T&P mainline were completed between Fort Worth and Sierra Blanca in a phenomenal 11 months, by a crew of 300 hard-drinking Irishmen.

The railroad's role in the rapid demise of the frontier is dramatically demonstrated by the almost simultaneous founding of Abilene, Big Spring, Midland, Odessa, and the other major cities of the region. They were shipping points for cattle, eliminating the long trail drives to Dodge City and Abilene in Kansas. The change from coal- to oil-powered locomotives led to the dismantling of Thurber and helped set the stage for the meteoric emergence of **Ranger** ❷, 13 miles (21km) to the west and the most rip-snorting boomtown of all.

Oil boom doom

Derricks and pump jacks are still in evidence, but the quiet streets of modern Ranger fail to suggest the frenzy of the weeks in 1917, after oil rig McClesky No. 1 blew in with 1,700 barrels a day. At World War I prices, a good well yielded $250,000 a week. The 10 trains that rolled into Ranger every day were filled with speculators, jacklegs, riffraff and ruffians, ambitious men and loose women. The town exploded from a village of 1,000 to a seething city of 40,000 in a matter of months. Streets turned into a sea of mud, traversed on sleds or the backs of men in hip boots. Guests in those days paid luxury hotel rates to sleep in armchairs. The evangelist Billy Sunday went in search of souls to saloons called the Grizzly Bear, the Blue Moose, and Oklahoma, where as many as five people a day met their oil boom doom. Small wonder there was violence when, for example, one lease changed hands three times on a Friday, increasing in value from $150 to $15,000. Everyone in the trade but the middle man must have felt taken. Talk to some of the old-timers for more details of the years when Ranger's oil produced more wealth than the California gold rush at its peak.

Rest In Peace

A few miles west lies **Eastland** ❸, another boomtown gone bust. Today its principal claims to fame are the Post Office mural, a montage of 11,217 stamps, which depicts the history of the communications service; the restored 1920s Majestic Theatre;

Shackelford Country Courthouse, Albany.

Remote farmhouse.

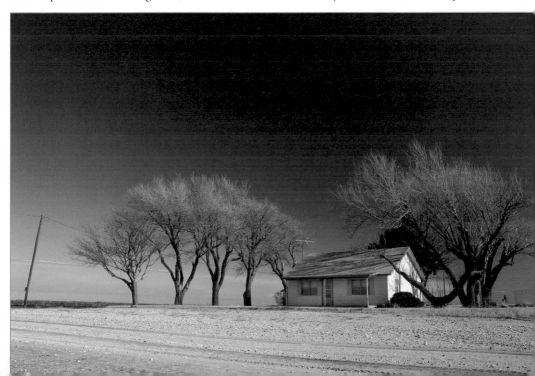

Horned toads like Rip, an Eastland celebrity, are not actually amphibians but lizards. Although the little critters are unable to cause warts, they do shoot a thin stream of blood out of the corners of their eyes, to a distance of up to 4ft (1.2 meters).

The restored St. Barbara's Catholic Church, Thurber.

Outdoor Art's reproductions of 41 masterpieces, such as Andy Warhol's Campbell's soup can, on a round building; and a horned toad named Rip (Rest in Peace), which was sealed into the cornerstone of the old courthouse in 1897 and found to be alive when the new courthouse was built some 28 years later. The creature died a year later, after achieving national fame. His stuffed body was then placed in a glass case in the new building. In his miniature coffin, he resembles a rather flat and very prickly pin-cushion, about the size of a child's hand.

Today, one approaches **Albany ❹**, northwest of Cisco, over the same rolling red plains the cowboys covered on the trail to Dodge City in the 1870s. Due to overgrazing, however, the lush prairie grasses they found here are gone. There is only the eroded soil and lacy-leaved mesquite trees. Although mesquite steals precious moisture from the soil, it puts back nitrogen, because it is a leguminous plant. Its protein-rich beans were ground into a flour by the nomadic Plains Indians and are still eaten today by cattle in times of drought. More importantly, its wood is considered by many Texans to be without parallel for cooking barbecue.

Only in Albany

At first sight, Albany is as unimposing as the mesquite "forests" that surround it, but this prairie town of just over 2,000 possesses an exceptional collection of 20th-century art, displayed in the **Old Jail Art Center** (201 S. Second Street; tel: 325-762-2269; www.oldjailartcenter.org; Tue–Sat 10am–5pm, Sun 2–5pm; free), a place where drunken cowboys and assorted desperados were once detained. The limestone building itself (*c.*1878) is a good example of frontier architecture, with its decoratively routed and scored casements and cistern out front. Alongside pre-Columbian displays, among the many artists represented in the large permanent collection are Matisse, Rouault, Picasso, Modigliani, Miró, Henry Moore, and Giacometti. The center aims to be the primary cultural resource for the region.

Albany's **Fort Griffin Fandangle** (tel: 325-762-3838; www.fortgriffin fandangle.com) is the oldest outdoor musical in Texas. The historical pageant is staged during the last two weeks in June. The roles of American Indians, cowboys, buffalo hunters, soldiers, bandits, and settlers are sung and acted, as they have been since 1938, by the descendants of those who originally occupied the Texas frontier.

Stop at the Albany Visitor Center (2 Railroad Street; tel: 325-762-2525; www. visitalbany.com; Tue–Fri 10am–5pm), in the depot at the corner of Railroad and Main, to pick up a walking tour map of Albany's historic buildings. One to look out for is the **Ledbetter Picket House** (24 S. Main Street; hours vary; free), a restored "dog run cabin" 1880s frontier ranch house with many authentic furnishings that was built near Fort Griffin and moved to this location in the 1950s. A similar ranch house served as the commandant's headquarters in the early days of what is now **Fort Griffin State Historic Site ❺** (1701 US 283; tel: 325-762-3592; www.visitfortgriffin. com; daily 8am–5pm), 15 miles (24km)

north of Albany. Established in 1867, Fort Griffin belonged to the outer line of frontier defenses. The first line, which swung in a wide arc southwest from Fort Worth to San Antonio, was established in the late 1840s on the edge of Comanche territory. Its line of forts was a buffer between the Plains Indians and white colonies. The renovated fort has one of the state herds of longhorns, managed by Texas Parks and Wildlife and now numbering 250 head in several parks, and also a campground.

The roughest town in Texas

From its hilltop, the stone ruins and partially reconstructed wooden remains of the fort look down on what was possibly the roughest, most brawling and iniquitous town in the history of Texas: "The Flats." Never has a lustier mixture of manhood been stirred in one pot. Imagine them bellied up to the same bar: bitter, defeated southern veterans of the Civil War alongside the blue-jacketed conquerors and the Buffalo Soldiers, as the American Indians called freed slaves who were part of the US Army. As if

TIP

Take advantage of the fact that Palo Duro is one of America's more accessible canyons. A spectacular 10-mile (16km) drive by car can be made year-round across the canyon floor.

Replica frontier cabin, Fort Griffin.

A scissor-tailed flycatcher, also known as the Texas Bird of Paradise.

they were not enough, add buffalo hunters flush from selling hides, plus the professional gamblers and bandits who preyed on them, and the bounty hunters who, in turn, preyed on them. Ironically, one of the few original buildings remaining in "The Flats" was far more respectable: it served as the church, school, and Masonic lodge.

Cowboys still exist here. You can find them at the Texas Cowboy Reunion (tel: 325-773-3138; www.tcrrodeo. com) in **Stamford** ❻ on the Fourth of July. This is no slick, professional production in an air-conditioned coliseum. This is where "good ol' boys" risk their necks, not for love of money – or even the love of their girls, who perch on the top rail of the arena fence – but for love of their favorite activity: roping horses.

Farther west, 14 miles (22km) north of Abilene, is **Fort Phantom Hill** ❼. The very name has the chill of desolation to it. Loneliness still lingers about the tall, solitary chimneys, the empty commissary, guardhouse, and powder magazine, especially in the dim red light of dusk. From its founding in

Buffalo Gap Historic Village.

1850, to protect the region from hostile Comanche Indians, there were frequent desertions from this post, where boredom alternated with the raids. After its abandonment in 1854, the hated fort was burned by one of the withdrawing soldiers. Later, it became an overnight stop for mail coaches on the Butterfield Trail.

In making your way through the scrub oak and mesquite to Abilene, you will probably see the silver-and-salmon flash of the scissor-tailed flycatcher. In excited flight, the graceful tails, which are twice as long as the bodies, almost seem to flitter like a carnival bird on a stick.

God's glorious city

Abilene ❽ (pop. 117,000) likes to promote itself as "The Defining City of West Texas" but might more aptly be described as the "Glorious City of God," being the home of three religiously affiliated institutions of learning – McMurry University, Abilene Christian University, and the Southern Baptists' Hardin-Simmons. Round-the-clock prayer meetings for rain didn't bring an

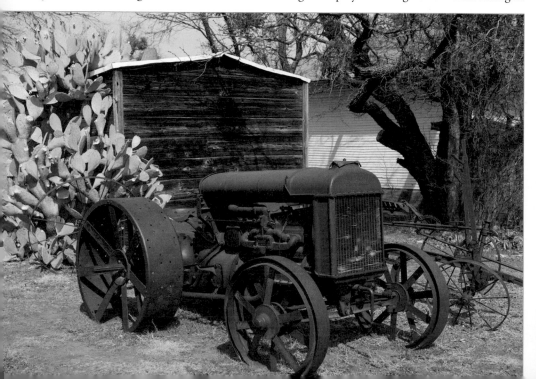

end to the drought of the early 1950s, but they must have made an impression, the region has been blessed with oil discoveries ever since. A rig was set up on the **Taylor County Expo Center** (Highway 36 at 11th Street) grounds here for demonstration and, of course, it struck oil. Rodeos are held here each spring and fall.

The extensive **Grace Museum** (102 Cypress Street; tel: 325-673-4587; www.gracemuseum.org; Tue–Sat 10am–5pm, Thu until 8pm) has history exhibits relating to Camp Barkeley, the World War II army base and prison camp, whose ruins can still be seen on US 277, south of town. There are other sections in this attractive complex that are devoted to children and fine arts.

Buffalo Gap

An authentic taste of the Old West is to be had 10 miles (16km) southwest of town, where the low, dark juniper-covered hills of the Calahan Divide are broken abruptly at **Buffalo Gap Historic Village** ❾ (133 N. William Street: tel: 325-572-3365; www.tfhcc.com; June–Aug Mon–Sat 10am–6pm, Sun noon–6pm; Sept–May Mon–Sat 10am–5pm, Sun noon–5pm). A mix of authentic frontier buildings and tourist attractions is found at this site operated by the Texas Frontier Heritage Cultural Center. An old courthouse, jail and log cabins are among the old buildings. A doctor's office, a barber shop and a print shop are modern reconstructions.

Twice a year, in the 19th century, buffalo passed through the mountain gap here, indelibly etching a permanent trail. When this brown, woolly group flowed between these ancient hills, Tonkawa and Comanche Indians still camped in the cool shade of the native pecan groves and made arrowheads, traces of which can still be found. Charles Goodnight, one of the most celebrated of early longhorn ranchers out west, described the main buffalo herd as being 125 miles (200km) long and 25 miles (40km) wide. The trail they blazed was later the one he used to drive his own cattle to the Kansas railheads.

When the area was settled by whites in the 1870s, this natural funnel

FACT

The Texas High School Rodeo Finals take place in Abilene in June. Tel: 325-603-8086.

A cowboy snake-handler at the World's Largest Rattlesnake Roundup in Sweetwater.

through the hills continued to be a focus for the region. Today, over 20 of the original buildings have been restored, including the limestone courthouse and jail. In the Buffalo Gap Cemetery, gravestones of Civil War veterans and others tell the history of the settling of West Texas in a few poignant words.

Frontier Texas (625 N. First Street; tel: 325-437-2800; www.frontiertexas.com; Mon–Sat 9am–6pm, Sun 1–5pm) is a hands-on, multimedia immersion in early Texas, with buffalo stampedes and saloon shootouts. Great fun for the kids.

Gypsum deposits

The town of **Sweetwater** ❿, 40 miles (64km) west of Abilene on I-20, was well named in an area where so many of the streams are tainted with gypsum. Gypsum, otherwise known as Epsom salts, is fine for soaking tired feet but, as a drink, keeps one on the run. The rich, local gypsum deposits have been put to constructive use in the manufacture of wallboard by two large factories.

One of the few towns in West Texas to predate the coming of the railroad, Sweetwater began in 1877 as a general store for buffalo hunters, dug into the banks of Sweetwater Creek. The world's largest rattlesnake roundup is held here during the second weekend in March, at the Nolan County Coliseum (tel: 325-658-6757). It is a bring-em-back-alive affair in which the snakes are milked for their venom and prizes are given for the longest, shortest and heaviest (by the pound). A record 14,000 lbs (6,350kg) were delivered in 1985. If you have ever had a hankering to eat a fried 6ft (2-meter) long western diamondback, or buy a transparent toilet seat with a rattler coiled in it, here is such an opportunity.

A few moments on the weed-broken tarmac of the Old Sweetwater Army Airfield will resurrect memories of the 1940s, when the Women's Airforce Service Pilots (WASPS) received their flight training here. Farther west, past Colorado City (locally pronounced Cah-la Ray-da Ciddy), is the town of **Big Spring** ⓫, a site important in another war. American

Downtown Midland.

Indian occupation of this natural oasis goes back to Folsom Indian times, 10,000 years ago, and it served as a major rest stop for the tribes on the Comanche War Trail, halfway between their home on the High Plains to the north and the white settlements in Texas and Mexico to the south. They shared its precious water with antelope, buffalo, and wild mustangs. This ancient oasis is still very appealing in late afternoon among the trees of Comanche Trail Park or at **Big Spring State Park** (tel: 432-263-4931; www.tpwd.state.tx.us/state-parks/bigspring; open daily), which provides a view of the entire area from a 200ft (60-meter) mesa within the city limits.

Southbound travelers along US 87 from Big Spring will pass through **San Angelo** ⑫, a modern city of lakes and rivers on the edge of the Texas Hill Country. Like San Antonio, it has a River Walk, winding its way past landscaped gardens, parks, and beautiful homes by the Concho River. **Fort Concho National Historic Landmark** (630 S. Oakes Street; tel: 325-481-2646; www.fortconcho.com; Tue–Sat 9am–5pm, Sun 1–5pm), the best preserved of the Indian War stockades, is filled with exhibits from frontier times.

The Permian Basin oil field

At the midway point of the 600-mile (965km) drive from Fort Worth to El Paso, a mirage of civilization rises out of the endless illusion of water over the highway ahead. The small city of **Midland** ⑬ (pop. 124,000), the hometown of President George W. Bush, is dominated by glass-and-steel towers, containing the offices of more than 650 companies dedicated to coaxing crude oil from the bottom of a 250-million-year-old inland sea, now buried tens of thousands of feet below the desert sand. The city is a vibrant, modern haven with an active cultural scene. It has weathered the roughest historic and economic storms.

The city was in the thick of battles between Comanches and settlers

when the oil boom arrived and prosperity flooded the region. Consequently, when Texas oil went bad, the city faced rough times. The **Permian Basin Oil Field** is the second-largest in the world, and the price of a barrel of Texas Permian Intermediate Weight Crude is the standard against which the prices of all other US oils are determined. The nodding, hobbyhorse-like pump jacks seem to repeat as they suck at the earth: "Fiftydollars, fiftydollars, fiftydollars…" Not only have their rhythms enriched many a slouch-hatted rancher, but the University of Texas as well. In the 19th century, having virtually no funds to offer the fledgling institution, the state legislature apologetically proffered 2.2 million acres (890,000 hectares) of sand and desert scrubland. That these holdings coincide with the outlines of the Permian Basin is a happy coincidence that has bequeathed the University around $2.5 billion.

The science and technology of oil are brilliantly explained in the **Permian Basin Petroleum Museum** (1500 W. I-20, exit 136; tel: 432-683-4403; www.

A crew working at an oil rig in the Permian Basin.

petroleummuseum.org; Mon–Sat 10am–5pm, Sun 2–5pm), where visitors can stroll along the bottom of the ancient sea where deposits eventually trapped oil for later wealth. Another educational site is the **American Airpower Heritage Museum of the Commemorative Air Force**, near the airport (9600 Wright Drive; tel: 432-563-1000; www.airpowermuseumorg; Mon–Sat 9am–5pm, Sun noon–5pm) with a collection of World War II aircraft and an Aviation Art Gallery.

Midland's other claim to fame is that it is the "Tumbleweed Capital of the World." In the scorching 100+°F (38+°C) days of summer, when all else turns brown, legions of prickly green tumbleweeds (in actual fact Russian thistle, an introduced species) crowd the roadside and abandoned fields. These tumbleweeds resist the heat as they grow up to 8ft (2.5 meters) tall, awaiting the moment in the fall when they break free of the earth to rush pell-mell down the road. Since Bob Nolan and the Sons of the Pioneers immortalized this common nuisance in the song Tumbling Tumbleweed,

Monahans Sandhills State Park.

the plant has become a symbol for the spirit of movement that led to the development of the West Texas frontier, especially in the person of the drifting cowboy.

Odessa

Traveling on to **Odessa** ⓴, expect to encounter the authentic West Texas "redneck." Midland is the business center of the Permian Basin, and Odessa is the home of the oil field worker or "roughneck." "Oil field trash and proud of it," say bumper stickers often seen on huge pickup trucks, with loaded rifles hung in racks across the back window. No need to search farther for the modern counterpart of the frontier cowboy.

Odessa does hold a few surprises, though – none of which have anything to do with oil. For example, on the Odessa College campus you will find the **Globe of the Great Southwest Theatre** (2308 Shakespeare Road; tel: 432-332-1586; www.globesw. org; tours available by reservation), a replica of Shakespeare's Globe Theatre in London, plus a replica of Anne

Hathaway's Cottage, complete with a Shakespeare library. A professional repertory company produces the classics and an annual Shakespeare Festival. There is also a Permian Playhouse Theater and a symphony orchestra.

At 622 N. Lee Street is the **Presidential Museum and Leadership Library** (tel: 432-363-7737; www.thepresidentialmuseum.org; Tue–Sat 10am–5pm), an interesting but blaringly patriotic museum dedicated to the US Presidency, including campaigning memorabilia and First Lady dolls. The restored homes of Presidents George H.W. and George W. Bush, who lived in Odessa for a while, are on the grounds here.

To visit a natural wonder, take a drive out to the **Odessa Meteor Crater ⓯**, just west of town, off Farm Road 1936. The nation's second largest meteor crater, it has a diameter of 500ft (152 meters). The crater was formed when some 2 million lbs (907,200kg) of extraterrestrial iron crashed into the earth during the last Ice Age.

West of Odessa, at the western edge of "West Texas," the great Chihuahuan Desert begins and continues across Big Bend Country into Mexico. The best vantage point for any sort of sandy "desertscape" is **Monahans Sandhills State Park ⓰** (2500 E. I-20, exit Park Road 41; tel: 432-943-2092; www.tpwd.state.tx.us/state-parks/monahans-sandhills; daily), 24 miles (38km) west of Odessa, where naked dunes tower up to 70ft (21 meters) high and stretch north and south for 200 miles (320km).

America's most bizarre forest grows along the margin of this desolation. The Havard oak forms a dense, at times almost impenetrable growth that is easily overlooked, because the mature trees stand only about 3ft (1 meter) tall. West Texans call the trees "shin oak" and the forest the "shinnery." These plants are marvelously well adapted to drought, with roots that can reach a depth of 90ft (27 meters).

Amarillo

In the northern Panhandle sections of West Texas, the landscape stretches in an unbroken line, with perhaps an occasional pump jack or farmhouse on the horizon. The sunsets

TIP

For a taste of old fort life, visit Fort Concho on the first weekend in December, when an 1880s-style celebration is held, reenacting a Christmas holiday from that era.

Presidential Museum and Leadership Library, Odessa.

A Route 66 sign on
Fifth Street, Amarillo.

Big Texan Steak
Ranch chef.

can be breathtaking: with nothing to obscure the view, the sky blazes with oranges, yellows, and reds, and fades to soft pinks and purples. Driving at night, you can see the lights of many small towns in all directions. Because of the relatively high altitude, the air is very clear and dry. And, after the sun sets in the summer, the evening brings cool breezes.

Amarillo ⓱ (pop. 195,250), which means "yellow" in Spanish, is a major center for cattle distribution. This dusty town claims to have the world's largest private cattle auction, and it certainly smells that way as you get near town, when you encounter enormous feedlots of cattle destined for market – the **Amarillo Livestock Auction** (100 S. Manhattan Street; tel: 806-373-7464; www.amarillolivestockauction.com; tours daily, auctions Tue; free) sells over 100,000 head a year. At the eye-catching American Quarter Horse Hall of Fame and Museum (2601 E. I-40; tel: 806-376-5181; www.aqha.com/museum/explore/halloffame; Mon–Sat 9am–5pm), perched roadside along one of the major cross-country routes

in the US, visitors learn why this particular breed was the cowboys' favorite mount. Amarillo is headquarters for the Working Ranch Cowboys Association, which organizes the World Championship Ranch Rodeo every November.

Visitors to the **Don Harrington Discovery Center** (1200 Streit Drive; tel: 806-355-9547; www.dhdc.org; Tue–Sat 9.30am–4.30pm, Sun noon–4.30pm) can enjoy the experience of an interactive science and technology attraction, as well as daily laser and planetarium shows.

Route 66 and steaks

The city's one-way system can be a bit confusing to travelers. But if you follow signs for the US Route 66–Sixth Street Historic District, west of Amarillo's central business district, you'll encounter a section of historic Route 66 that is still very much alive, with antiques stores, gift shops, and great little eateries in restored historic buildings. On Sixth, look for the Natatorium (604 S. Georgia), built as an indoor swimming pool in 1922 and later converted into a ballroom, Taylor's Sixth Street Gas Station, built in 1937; and the Golden Light Café, a landmark that has been serving home-style food since 1946 and now offers live music in its cantina.

The Big Texan Steak Ranch (7701 E. I-40; tel: 806-657-7177), now located near the Quarter Horse Hall of Fame just north of I-40, used to be located on Route 66 and, with its famous beckoning cowboy, was one of its most distinctive landmarks. After the interstate was built in the 1970s and Route 66 fell by the wayside for most travelers, the owners decided to relocate the kitschy restaurant and adjoining hotel, famous for its Texas-shaped pool, along the freeway. This roadside attraction is a lot of fun and worth a stop to enjoy a good steak (they even serve bison and rattlesnake). Its famous 72-ounce (2kg) steak is free if you can down the whole thing, along with all the trimmings, in an hour. Fans of barbecue will be delighted to know that some of the best mesquite-smoked ribs and brisket in the state can be found at Tyler's Barbecue (2014 Paramount Boulevard; tel: 806-331-2271; www.tylerbarbecue.com). Expect a line at both these restaurants; they are hugely popular.

Texas's O'Keeffe country

South of Amarillo is the town of **Canyon** ⑱, home of West Texas A&M University and the sprawling Panhandle-Plains Historical Museum (2503 4th Avenue; tel: 806-651-2244; www.panhandleplains.org; Mon–Sat 9am–5pm, until 6 June–Sept). This state history museum contains an art collection, geological exhibits, and a reconstructed pioneer town of a century ago. One wing is devoted to the oil-boom years of the Texas Panhandle during the 1920s and '30s, displaying equipment from that period. One exhibit, People of the Plains, relates 14,000 years of man's occupation of the Southern Great Plains.

Canyon is also notable for the tenure from 1912–18 of Georgia O'Keeffe. As a young woman, the celebrated artist came to teach art in Amarillo, then at West Texas State Normal College in Canyon. While there, she produced a striking series of watercolors of the plains, sunrises, and night skies. She said, "Texas is my spiritual home."

Search for gold

Here at Canyon, 16 miles (29km) south of Amarillo, the flat plains come to a dead halt. What lies ahead is a vast chasm. At 60 miles (96km) long, up to 20 miles (32km) wide, and with 800ft (245-meter) walls, Palo Duro Canyon gives the Grand Canyon a run for its money. Spanish conquistador Francisco Vasquez de Coronado, head of the first Spanish expedition to make an entrada into El Norte from New Spain, is believed to have come upon Palo Duro in 1541 while searching for Quivira, the richest of the mythical cities of gold – a tall tale told by survivors of an earlier Spanish expedition who shipwrecked in the Gulf of Mexico

Palo Duro Canyon State Park.

and wandered west, eventually returning to Mexico City.

In the 19th century, the canyon was a Comanche stronghold. The Comanche suffered their final defeat in 1874, when they were surprised by a cavalry force commanded by General Ranald Mackenzie, who drove 1,500 horses and mules out of Palo Duro and slaughtered them. Without their horses, the Comanche were helpless. They were removed from their homelands to reservations in Oklahoma. Geologists say over 240 million years of erosion by creeks and streams, abetted by incessant wind, formed this majestic canyon. Palo duro means "hard wood" in Spanish, and refers to the juniper trees found in the area.

Enchanting **Palo Duro Canyon State Park** ⑲ (11450 Park Road 5; tel: 806-488-2227; http://tpwd.texas. gov/state-parks/palo-duro-canyon; open daily). The state park covers 16,400 acres (6,600 hectares) and offers hiking and horse trails, scenic overlooks, and camping options that range from primitive to developed; you can also book one of several extremely rustic Civilian Conservation Corps (CCC) cabins right on the rim or nearby. In summertime, there are nightly (except Sundays) performances of the spectacular, rousing musical drama Texas (reservations tel: 806-655-2181). With a canyon wall as a backdrop, a cast of 60 brings to life Pulitzer Prize winner Paul Green's play about the settling of West Texas.

The great ranches

The legendary figure of Charles Goodnight, the first rancher to move into the Panhandle in 1876, is closely associated with Palo Duro Canyon and with the beginning of the cattle drives. Goodnight designed the first chuckwagon. Backed by the British financier John Adair (their cattle were branded with "JA" and the ranch was christened "The JA"), Goodnight built up his herd to as many as 100,000 head in 1889. For a while in the 1880s, theirs was the largest ranch in Texas – more than 1,325,000 acres (536,000 hectares). Then in 1885, the XIT Ranch was established in the far

BUDDY HOLLY

Charles Hardin Holley, better known as Buddy Holly, was born in Lubbock, Texas, on September 7, 1936. As a child he played piano, then accompanied himself with guitar on favorite country songs, particularly those of Hank Williams who, along with Bill Monroe was to influence his early singing style. But seeing Elvis Presley perform changed Buddy's style forever, prompting him to distill a blend of pop, blues, and country.

In 1955, a Nashville recording agent saw Buddy and his group and, the following year, invited him to Nashville, where he recorded "Blue Days, Black Nights," his first single release. With a country melody, but a blues inflection, the track was difficult for some reviewers to categorize. In February 1957, Buddy, along with Jerry Allison, Niki Sullivan, and Larry Welborn as The Crickets, recorded "That'll Be the Day" at Norman Petty's studios in Clovis, New Mexico. "That'll Be the Day" topped the charts in September 1957, followed by "Peggy Sue." Its innovative "Holly sound" included steady guitar strumming, rapid, accented drumming, and his famous vocal "hiccup." With "Words of Love" (also recorded in 1957) Buddy introduced another

innovation – overdubbing. In 1958, the same year the Crickets released "Not Fade Away" and "Oh Boy!," they released "Rave On," Think It Over," and "It's So Easy." They toured widely, appearing for the second time on the top-rated Ed Sullivan Show. On February 3, 1959, a few weeks into a tour with singers Ritchie Valens and J.P. Richardson (the "Big Bopper"), Holly's plane crashed in a snowstorm near Clear Lake, Iowa, killing all on board.

It's hard to overstate Holly's and the Crickets' importance to the development of rock 'n' roll. Holly was among the first – if not the first – to use his own band in the studio. They were among the first to generate their own material for release as singles; among the first to work outside the established studio system and to use overdubbing and other soon-to-be-common effects in their recordings. Holly cast a long shadow over The Beatles, The Rolling Stones, Bob Dylan, Bruce Springsteen, and generations of other rock performers. Holly's statue stands outside Lubbock's Civic Center and visitors from all over the world pay homage at his grave in the City of Lubbock Cemetery on East 34th Street, near Quirt. The city also has a museum in his honor.

northern Panhandle on over 3 million acres (1.25 million hectares), which the State of Texas had traded for the new State Capitol building in Austin. In order to stock the XIT Ranch, British and Midwestern investors were again brought in. An XIT reunion is held at Dalhart, 80 miles (130km) north of Amarillo every year, in the first full week of August. The amateur rodeo and enormous barbecue attract thousands.

Chuckwagon breakfasts at the working cattle ranch of Elkins Ranch (tel: 806-488-2100; www.theelkinsranch. com; Apr–Oct Tue–Sun; Jeep tours; reservations required) always draw plenty of dudes. They begin with a chuckwagon breakfast on the rim of Palo Duro, to which visitors are carried in a horse-drawn wagon from the Elkins Ranch near Claude, off US 217 east of Canyon, next to the Palo Duro State Park entrance.

Lubbock

Even though singer Mac Davis claims "Happiness is Lubbock, Texas, in my rear-view mirror," most residents of

Lubbock ⑳ (pop. 236,000) would live nowhere else. Even Mac concedes at the end of his song that now "Happiness is Lubbock, Texas, getting nearer and dearer." A center for cotton growing that also ships grain and livestock, Lubbock is on the South Plains, at one of the southermost tips of the Llano Estacado, or "Staked Plains." The Staked Plains, from the name early Spanish explorers gave the immense plains that sweep for 1,600 miles (2,560km) through America's center, all the way up to Canada, produce a substantial proportion of the country's grain, meat, and fiber. A plaque marking the Llano Estacado's eastern boundary sits on US 84, southeast of town.

Texas Tech University, at 4th Street and Indiana Avenue, is one of Lubbock's main attractions. Its full sports agenda entices enthusiastic crowds. The university's teams are known as the Red Raiders and are members of the Big 12 Conference.

The university has established the Museum of Texas Tech University (3301 4th Street; tel: 806-742-2490;

The Buddy Holly Center.

www.depts.ttu.edu/museumttu; Tue–Sat 10am–5pm, Sun 1–5pm; free) and the **National Ranching Heritage Center** (3121 4th Street; tel: 806-742-0498; www.nrhc.ttu.edu; Tue–Sat 10am–5pm, Sun 1–5pm; free), a 30-acre (12-hectare) area through which winds a trail past more than 38 buildings, including a schoolhouse, a blacksmith's shop, homes, barns, and windmills, representing ranching's early days. The museum offers a mixed bag of paintings of the American West, along with European art, sculpture, ceramics, and lithographs. Changing exhibitions narrate the story of the region from prehistoric times through the Spanish explorations and the settling of the region by ranchers and farmers.

The museum also contains the **Moody Planetarium** and operates an archeological site beside Lubbock Lake Landmark (2401 Landmark Drive; tel: 806-742-1166; guided tours Sat 10am and 1pm, Sun 2pm), northwest of the city, near US 84 and Loop 289. This site has yielded artifacts and tools from all known cultural groups who once lived in the Southwest, from the mammoth hunters 10,000 years ago to the Comanches of the 19th century. No other New World site houses such a complete chronological record.

A museum dedicated to Lubbock's most celebrated musical son is housed in the Historic Depot District. The **Buddy Holly Center** (1801 Crickets Avenue; tel: 806-775-3560; www.buddy hollycenter.org; Tue–Sat 10am–5pm, Sun 1–5pm) honors the rock 'n' roll pioneer.

An offbeat monument to another Lubbock musical icon lies on East Broadway across from the South Plains Fair grounds. A larger-than-life bronze of the late C.B. Stubblefield stands on the site of his former Stubb's BBQ restaurant and club. "Stubbs" was a mentor and friend of many of the 1970s generation of Lubbock musicians, including Terry Allen, Joe Ely, and Butch Hancock.

Off University Avenue, 3 miles (5km) south of town, is **Science Spectrum** (2579 S. Loop 289, No. 250; tel: 806-745-2525; www.sciencespectrum.

The National Ranching Heritage Center.

org; Mon–Fri 10am–5pm, Sat 10am–6pm, Sun 1–5pm), a hands-on science, nature, and technology museum. It has an OMNI theater and a movie theater with a 58ft (18-meter) domed screen (tel: 806-745-6299; shows daily).

The **Canyon Lakes Project** is a string of five lakes in Lubbock's Yellowhouse Canyon, where man-made waterfalls, fishing piers, camping and picnicking areas, and hike and bike trails, attract fans of the outdoors. Part of the canyon is devoted to Mackenzie State Park, where one of the few remaining colonies of prairie dogs resides. These amusing, squirrel-like creatures proved such a pest at one time that farmers did their best to exterminate them. Living in giant underground colonies, their "towns" covered thousands of square miles under the prairie grass before civilization overtook them.

The region's soil and climatic conditions have proved to be excellent for most of the California-type wines. There are several vineyards, among them the **Llano Estacado** Winery ㉑, 3 miles (5km) east of US 87, on FM 1585. Here, free daily tours and wine tastings are offered (tel: 806-745-2258).

Post

Fifteen miles (24km) southeast of Lubbock, at the foot of the dramatic Caprock escarpment on US 84, is **Post** ㉒ (pop. 5,340), named for cereal magnate Charles W. Post. He founded it in 1907, after an extended stay in the Kellogg brothers' Battle Creek sanitarium for his health. Noting that the Kelloggs had devised for their patients food substitutes made from grain, Post blended wheat, bran, and molasses to create a coffee substitute called Postum. In the decade beginning in 1902, he spent $60 million to advertise Postum and such other products as Grape Nuts and Toasties. Long after his death in 1914, the Postum cereal company became General Foods Corporation which was later acquired by American multinational Philip Morris Companies. A spin-off company was created called Post Foods.

The famous Cadillac Ranch.

CADILLAC RANCH

Millionaire rancher Stanley Marsh 3 (never III) once said that he envisioned art as "a series of unanticipated rewards." If so, then his Cadillac Ranch, alongside I-40, west of Amarillo, is art of the highest order. Who, after all, could anticipate a row of 10 long-finned luxury cars (dating from 1949–63) buried nose down in a field in the plains at, it is said, the exact same angle as the Great Pyramid of Cheops? A San Francisco art collective called The Ant Farm, which specialized in art as public spectacle, built the 1974 creation at Marsh's behest.

Marsh, the proverbial eccentric Texas tycoon, made his money in television stations and decided to spend it having some fun. The much-photographed and graffiti-adorned Cadillac Ranch is his love letter to the promise of the open road. Be sure to stop and bring with you a can of spray paint to add your own graffiti to what is already there. Due to westward sprawl from burgeoning Amarillo, Cadillac Ranch has already had to be relocated once, and will probably have to be relocated again soon. But be sure to stop: this is a modern American roadside attraction – a counterpoint to the Big Texan Steak Ranch, the old Route 66 roadside attraction on the northside of I-40, east of Amarillo. Cadillac Ranch is on the south side of I-40, between exits 60 and 62 (daily during daylight hours; free).

N.C.A.   National Conservation Area
N.H.P.   National Historic Park
N.H.S.   National Historic Site
N.M.   National Monument
N.P.   National Park
N.R.A.   National Recreation Area
N.W.R.   National Wildlife Refuge
R.A.   Recreation Area
S.P.   State Park
S.H.P.   State Historic Park
S.H.S.   State Historic Site

New Mexico

M E X I C O

Texas Parks

	0		100 miles
0		100 km	

Texas bluebonnets along a path by Inks Lake.

TEXAS PARKS

Camping, fishing, and water sports are major attractions in the state's many parks, but these well-tended sites also provide fascinating lessons in geography, history, and natural science.

Parks in Texas are as varied as the people and the landscape. There are very large areas, like massive Big Bend National Park (see page 253), while, at the opposite extreme, the most intimate one is probably the grave of Davy Crockett's wife in **Acton State Historic Site ❶**, near Granbury, in the heart of the Cross Timbers region. Parks planned around lakes and rivers are especially plentiful, testifying to the Texan love affair with water, historically a rare, almost mystical commodity in much of the state.

Tent and trailer camping, hiking, picnicking, birdwatching, horseback riding, golf, and all manner of zoos are found in parks throughout the state. Best of all, Texas parks showcase the natural features of their region, whether they are the moss-laden cypresses of Caddo Lake in East Texas, the cliffs of Palo Duro Canyon in the Panhandle, or the lonely shell-strewn beaches of Padre Island.

Thirteen parks are managed by the National Park Service as part of the National Park System, 131 are state-owned, and there are countless roadside parks. At least one park is found in every Texas town or county and beside every lake. Amenities and standards of maintenance vary, but all these parks exist because of Texans' strong attachment to the outdoors. Many parks were developed by the

Civilian Conservation Corps (CCC) in the 1930s, as part of Roosevelt's New Deal program.

Many Texas parks are built around water. Large lakes are found in various parts of the state. Although mainly for power generation and flood and drought control, they are the basis of some of the best park fun in the Lone Star State, and especially sports such as waterskiing, boating, and fishing. While most lakes are artificial, the parks on Texas rivers are notable for their natural scenery and features. And

Main Attractions
Big Thicket National Preserve
Lost Maples State Natural Area
Aransas National Wildlife Refuge
Guadalupe Mountains National Park
Palo Duro Canyon State Park
Big Bend National Park

Palo Duro Canyon State Park.

TIP

Spring and fall are the prettiest times of the year to visit parks in East Texas; summertime, as in the deep South, is hot, humid, and bug-ridden. Remember to bring a good insect repellent.

the many miles of Texas beaches are just plain fun-in-the-sun.

National Forests

Angelina National Forest, one of four national forests in Texas, lies on both sides of the Sam Rayburn Reservoir, a 115,000-acre (47,000-hectare) lake east of Lufkin, 160 miles (256km) northeast of Houston. This is Texas's largest reservoir, and its surrounding recreation areas provide a wide variety of boating, hiking, and camping activities in the towering pine forest and along the lake branches. Backpacking and primitive camping are permitted throughout the 153,000-acre (62,000-hectare) forest, unless otherwise posted.

West of Angelina, **Davy Crockett National Forest** covers more than 160,000 acres (65,000 hectares) along the Neches River. A second-growth forest, it has made a remarkable comeback since logging stopped in the 1920s. The 4-C Trail, a scenic 20-mile (32km) trek, connects Ratcliff Lake Recreation Area with Neches Bluff. It is best to travel along it in the fall, winter, or spring,

Great Blue Heron, Caddo Lake State Park.

when the climate is more hospitable and the bugs are less numerous. Basic camping is allowed along the 4-C Trail, but be suspicious of the water. Carry your own or use water purifiers.

Sabine National Forest, with 160,000 acres (65,000 hectares), stretches along the Texas side of the Toledo Bend Reservoir on the Louisiana border. It includes a historic battleground where a 47-strong band of Confederates prevented a Union invasion of Texas. There are amenities for hikers, campers, boaters, and anglers. Catfish, bass, and crappie are the major fish to be found in the smaller lakes, but be sure to have a current fishing license and observe all bag limits.

Hiking in the east

In East Texas, **Sam Houston National Forest** offers excellent hiking and camping between Huntsville and Lake Livingston. Its highlight is **Lone Star Trail**, the longest developed hiking route in the state, at 129 miles (208km). The forest's Double Lake and Stubblefield recreation areas have extensive camping and picnicking, and

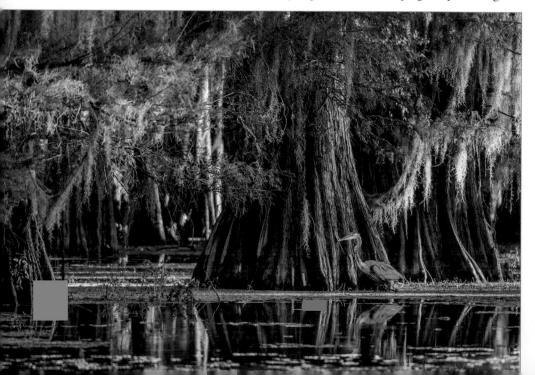

scrvc well as trailheads. Camping is also permitted along the trail and in designated areas. Hikers are advised to tote their own water in and garbage out. But beware: from mid-November until January 1, hiking can be dangerous, because the hunting season is open.

On the water

Martin Dies, Jr. State Park ❷, on Steinhagen Reservoir, lies 15 miles (24km) east of the town of Woodville. The trees are gorgeous in the fall and, in addition to water sports, there is a wide variety of birdlife along its trail.

Lake Livingston State Park ❸, 75 miles (120km) northeast of Houston, occupies the east shore of the 85,000-acre (34,000-hectare) lake. Ninety-eight species of birds have been spotted along its 4 miles (6km) of trails.

Just 15 miles (24km) east is the **Alabama-Coushatta Indian Reservation**, established in 1854, when the state legislature gave 1,280 acres (520 hectares) to the Alabama Indians, who had settled in East Texas 40 years before. Additional land has since been added to this densely forested region. An area along the Neches River, to the east of the reservation, has been set aside as **Big Thicket National Preserve ❹**, a unit of the National Park System, protecting an area of immense biodiversity, where desert and swamp sit cheek by jowel. Gourd dancing predominates at the tribe's annual pow-wow held the first weekend in June.

Mossy cypresses

Caddo Lake State Park ❺, near Marshall to the northeast of here, is the largest natural lake in the state. Spanish moss drapes its ancient cypress trees. Waterskiing is possible on sections of the lake, but drifting along in a canoe is better suited to its peaceful nature.

In the northeast corner of Texas, **Atlanta State Park ❻** sits on the banks of Lake Wright Patman, in a forest of oak, pine, and dogwood. Near the town of Daingerfield, 30 miles (50km) to the southeast, **Daingerfield**

State Park ❼ surrounds a small lake often filled with blooming water lilies. Its trails reward hikers with glimpses of wildlife, including deer and raccoons.

Tyler State Park ❽, just north of the city of Tyler, is a large park where swimming areas and a good fishing lake can be found. When the dogwood blooms in spring, Tyler Park is at its best.

Lake Somerville State Park and Trailway ❾, on the western edge of East Texas near Brenham, 85 miles (135km) northwest of Houston, consists of two units on either side of the lake. They are connected by a 13-mile (21km) trail, along which some of the campgrounds are especially for equestrians. There is also a wildlife management area in the park.

On the Brazos River, less than 70 miles (110km) south of Houston, **Brazos Bend State Park ❿** has 3.5 miles (5km) of river frontage. The alligator and hundreds of bird species are stars here, and migrating waterfowl lure so many visitors in the fall that reservations are necessary for its overnight facilities.

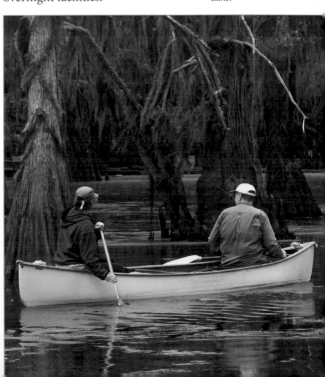

Canoeing on Caddo Lake.

TIP

If you plan to visit several Texas state parks, invest $70 in an annual Texas State Parks Pass, which allows unlimited admission to the state's more than 90 parks. Contact Texas Parks and Wildlife Department at 512-389-8900.

New lakes

Drought and flood control projects of the 1950s and '60s created a multitude of new lakes in the central and western parts of Texas. There are no pine forests surrounding these lakes, but they often have their own special appeal.

About 100 miles (160km) west of Fort Worth is **Possum Kingdom State Park ⓫**, its 10 miles (16km) of shoreline shaded by deciduous oaks and juniper trees, which many westerners call "cedar." Waterskiing and scuba diving are popular here. About 55 miles (89km) southeast, **Lake Mineral Wells State Park ⓬** sits in a pretty valley with an equestrian trail and small boats for rent.

Down the road, **Lake Whitney State Park ⓭**, 75 miles (120km) south of Fort Worth, is excellent for waterskiing and bass fishing. Its numerous facilities include an airfield for campers who fly in with the herons and geese.

Anglers in search of a good fishing lake with a lot of variety will enjoy **Fairfield Lake State Park ⓮**, 90 miles (145km) southeast of Dallas, noted for

Preparations for a cliff-diving competition on Possum Kingdom Lake.

redfish, large-mouth bass, crappie, catfish, bluegill, and drum.

On the Red River border separating Texas and Oklahoma, Lake Texoma is popular with sailboaters and water skiers. Anglers go after the native Red River white bass and the black and striped bass. **Eisenhower State Park ⓯** lies on the cliffs above Lake Texoma, offering plenty of room for campers, fishermen, and boaters, and even a protected cove for swimmers. There are campgrounds along the lake's 15-mile (24km) Cross Timbers Trail, but water is not available, except in the developed areas, and the presence of snakes requires caution. Five miles (8km) southeast, in Denison, is the restored two-story birthplace of President Dwight D. Eisenhower.

Less crowded

Four parks in North Central Texas, more or less along the Fort Worth–Waco corridor, are very pleasant, have good amenities, and are not often crowded. **Cleburne State Park ⓰**, near the town of the same name, was built around a small lake, while **Meridian**

State Park ⓱, 70 miles (110km) southwest of Fort Worth, also has a small lake with a hiking trail around.

Mother Neff State Park ⓲, 128 miles (206km) south of Fort Worth, was the first Texas state park, the first 6 acres (2.5 hectares) being donated by Governor Pat Neff's mother. The governor gave an additional 250 acres (100 hectares) in 1933. Developed by the CCC in the 1930s, it is a fitting tribute to early park pioneers. Fort Parker State Park ⓳, on Fort Parker Lake, near Mexia, provides waterskiing and fishing; the grounds incorporate the now-dead town of Springfield – only its cemetery remains.

Hill Country

Large lakes and cypress-shaded rivers in the Hill Country, between Austin and San Antonio, host a wide array of water activities. There are six large lakes on the lower section of Texas's Colorado River alone, all dotted with informal camping and fishing areas, and with private marinas and resorts, while the Guadalupe River feeds Canyon Lake, about 40 miles (65km) southwest of

Austin, as well as six smaller lakes. The most popular lake park is probably Inks Lake State Park ⓴ near Burnet, offering waterskiing, scuba diving and fishing, as well as a nine-hole golf course and a 7-mile (11km) hiking trail. Reservations are essential.

Garner State Park ㉑, on the Frio River, 30 miles (50km) north of Uvalde, although now enlarged, still tends to be crowded, with reservations necessary year-round for the picturesque cabins. Frio means cold in Spanish, and this river usually is. The scenery is at its best when the spring wildflowers make their show. One of the best ways to see the beautiful river canyon is from a rented pedal boat or inner tube.

Guadalupe River State Park ㉒ is a favorite spot for canoeing, which is a growing sport in Texas. Thirty miles (50km) north of San Antonio, the park's four rapids have excited enthusiasts of all skill levels. Deer, coyotes, raccoons, and gray foxes can often be spied directly from the hiking trails, and bird-watching enthusiasts will find golden-cheeked warblers nesting

Alligator, Brazos Bend State Park.

The Lighthouse Rock, Palo Duro Canyon State Park.

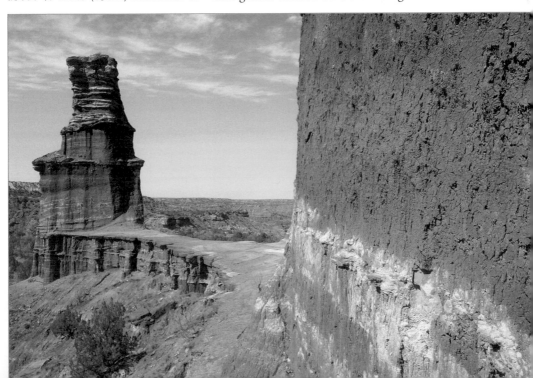

in a stand of Ashe juniper from March to late summer.

Within an hour's drive north of San Antonio, **Blanco State Park** ㉓ straddles 1.5 miles (2.5km) of the Blanco River, near its namesake town. Its small size seems to discourage crowds. The park's main activities are swimming, fishing, and watching the river go by.

The diversity of the Hill Country is especially evident at **Pedernales Falls State Park** ㉔, about 45 miles (70km) west of Austin. Along parts of the Pedernales River, one finds lush vegetation and armadillos among the scrub cedar. The Pedernales, like a lot of Texas rivers, floods when it rains, but is otherwise a peaceful stream running over a rock bed into calm pools. Watch out for flash floods and an occasional treacherous waterfall or whirlpool, especially when the river is rising. The 7-mile (11km) Wolf Mountain Trail is rewarding to skilled backpackers and hardy novices alike.

Lake Brownwood State Park ㉕ is 22 miles (35km) west of Brownwood, where the Hill Country segues into West Texas. Its many facilities include picturesquely situated stone cabins. The 7,300-acre (3,000-hectare) lake imposes no limit on boat size.

Granite and cool forests

Several parks within easy reach of Austin are very popular. **Enchanted Rock State Natural Area**, 18 miles (30km) north of Fredericksburg, centers around a billion-year-old granite mountain. Its prominence in the landscape made it a source of American Indian ghost tales and a traveler's landmark. While most trails around the rock are taxing, one trail to the top is manageable by most healthy hikers.

A large stand of big-tooth maples, 35 miles (55km) southwest of Kerrville, is the focus of **Lost Maples State Natural Area**. One of the few remnants of the large maple forests of a less arid time in Texas, these trees provide glorious color in October. Most of the trails here are challenging, but a short one along the Sabinal River is easy. The park is pleasant at all times and is particularly popular with birders. Golden and bald eagles can often be seen in winter.

In a relic pine forest less than 30 miles (45km) southeast of Austin, rustic **Bastrop State Park** ㉖ gives another glimpse of an earlier Texas. Its picturesque cabins were built by the CCC. Reservations are necessary for these and for the park's campgrounds.

Farther south, **Palmetto State Park** ㉗, 60 miles (95km) east of San Antonio, near Gonzales, has hiking trails that show off the plant and animal life and the extensive bird population. Its Ottine Swamp contains a tropical forest of palmettos (low-growing palms native to Texas) and other exotic flora. Spring and fall are the best times to visit; summer can be humid and stifling.

Keeping cool

Perhaps nowhere in the state are water sports more appreciated than in South Texas, a pretty dry place that can get very hot in summer. Spring and fall are the most enjoyable seasons for

Blanco State Park.

both locals and visitors. **Lake Texana State Park** is well stocked with catfish, large-mouth bass, and striped bass, with early spring being the best time for fishing. Additional campsites are available at the nearby Lavaca-Navidad River Authority's Brackenridge Campground.

Although **Lake Corpus Christi State Park** was developed by the CCC in the 1930s, most of its amenities are more modern. Fishing, especially for catfish, is good. Because of its mild climate and proximity to Corpus Christi, 35 miles (55km) to the south, the park is popular all year round and can be crowded.

Up the Rio Grande, near Del Rio, **Amistad National Recreation Area** provides facilities all along the American side of Lake Amistad for watersports. Scuba diving is especially good because the water is so clear. Deer (with bow and arrow only) and bird hunting are allowed in certain areas during the season.

One of the largest lakes in Texas, Falcon Lake, is also on the US–Mexican border. **Falcon State Park ㉘**, 15 miles (24km) north of the historic border town of Roma, has comfortable accommodations. Birders here are rewarded with a variety of rare species, including the green kingfisher.

Bentsen–Rio Grande Valley State Park ㉙, on the river near Mission, is most popular in the winter, when its subtropical climate attracts many wintering tourists. Its nature trail interprets the hundreds of rare birds, animals, and plants in the area.

Wildlife refuges

Aransas National Wildlife Refuge, on San Antonio Bay near Rockport, has a visitor center and miles of trails for viewing the refuge wildlife, including the rare and endangered whooping cranes that winter here. Sixteen miles (26km) of roads give glimpses of the many deer, alligators, and javelinas, as well as other birds that live here year round. Probably the surest way to see the whoopers is to take the boat that goes out from the Sea Gun Inn, near Fulton, from October to early April. Campgrounds are handy at nearby **Goose Island State Park**.

TIP

On the Guadalupe and other rivers in the state, the water levels are unpredictable and are subject to rapid rises and falls. Be forewarned.

Lake Amistad.

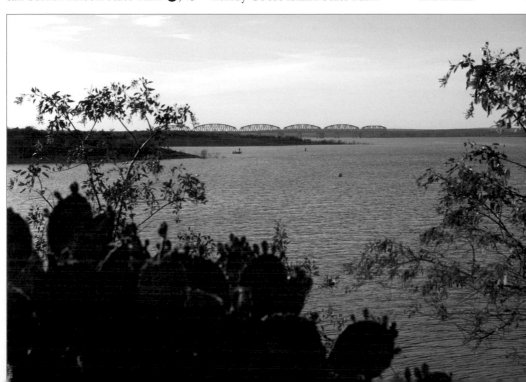

TIP

The most popular time to visit Lost Maples is late October/early November, when the leaves turn stunning colors. If you want to visit at this time, make it a weekday, when the crowds aren't so pervasive.

Laguna Atascosa National Wildlife Refuge is just north of Port Isabel on the Laguna Madre. When ducks and geese fly south for the winter, this is where many of them come. Camping is not allowed, but there are auto and walking trails.

Santa Ana National Wildlife Refuge, on the Rio Grande near McAllen, has 12 miles (19km) of hiking trails through its 2,000-acre (800-hectare) subtropical forest. It is the northern limit of many Mexican birds' migration. One of the forest's ebony trees may be the oldest and largest in the United States.

At the beach

The beaches of the Gulf of Mexico are the site of some of the state's best-developed and most popular parks. **Sea Rim State Park** ③⓪, on the coast near the Louisiana border, is one of the more tranquil. The greater part of the large park is an extensive marsh inhabited by a multitude of alligators, nutria, mink, raccoons, and wintering waterfowl.

Galveston Island State Park ③①, on the west end of the island, has well-located beach campgrounds and picnicking areas. Occupying 5.5 miles (9km) of Gulf beach, down the coast, is **Mustang Island State Park** ③②, with hundreds of campsites and picnic sites. About half of the beachfront is undeveloped. At both parks, reservations are advisable, especially in the summer.

Fourteen miles (23km) farther south is **Padre Island National Seashore** ③③ America's largest designated national seashore. Its camping facilities stretch along a 66-mile (106km) white sand beach strewn with seashells – the prettiest beach in Texas.

The most remote beach park has to be **Matagorda Island State Park and Wildlife Management Area**. Accessible only by ferry across Aransas Bay or private boat, the park has no drinking water, no electricity, and no telephones. Whooping cranes winter on the island. Make sure you contact park headquarters in Port O'Connor prior to a visit.

To the mountains

Guadalupe Mountains National Park ③④ straddles the New Mexico–Texas border, about 100 miles (160km) due east of El Paso. These mountains are actually an uplifted Permian era fossil reef, the largest in the world (and also home to all that Texas oil). Over the border, in New Mexico, an underground section of the reef has been eroded by groundwater into the famous stalactites and stalagmites protected in Carlsbad Caverns National Park. In this lovely location, the Chihuahuan Desert rises to spectacular evergreen forests more reminiscent of the Rocky Mountains in Colorado than flat and dusty West Texas. The highest point in Texas, Guadalupe Peak, at 8,749ft (2,667 meters) can be found here, along with the sheer cliffs of El Capitán, which tower 2,000ft (610 meters) high. The varied landscape supports a great deal of flora and fauna. Greasewood and lechuguilla give way to lush ferns in the protected canyons, and more

Riding along Padre Island beach.

than 170 species of bird and over 50 different reptiles and amphibians live in the park, as well as elk, mule deer, gray foxes, coyotes, and a mountain lion and black bear or two.

McKittrick Canyon, with its historic cabins and famous maple fall foliage, is one of the highlights of Guadalupe Mountains National Park. The canyon displays a rare and varied collection of vegetation. High sheltering walls and year-round streams ensure the right conditions for ferns, big-tooth maples, and little-leaf walnuts to grow. The marked trail into it is not difficult, but stay on the trail to avoid disturbing the fragile ecological system. Permits are required for backcountry camping; the park's lovely little campground is a popular spot. Get there early to secure a spot – the nearest lodging is in Carlsbad, New Mexico.

Rugged landscapes also characterize **Palo Duro Canyon State Park 35**, in the Panhandle, spectacular from every angle. Smaller canyons can be found at **Caprock Canyons State Park 36**, 60 miles (100km) southeast of Palo Duro.

Hunting and boating

As in South Texas, where large lakes make summer more acceptable, way up in West Texas's Panhandle Plains, 35 miles (56km) east of Amarillo, **Lake Meredith National Recreation Area** cools the arid Llano Estacado. Deer and bird hunting is permitted in certain parts of this park during the season. There is usually a good wind for sailing, but storms are unpredictable and boaters of all types should always be very cautious on this stretch of water.

Not as heavily developed as Lake Meredith, other West Texas lakes still give welcome recreational relief to many Texans and tourists. **Lake Colorado City State Park 37**, between Big Spring and Abilene, and **Lake Arrowhead State Park 38** near Wichita Falls, are both on good-sized lakes and are popular with motor boaters and waterskiers.

Abilene State Park 39 about 20 miles (30km) southwest of town, is just across the road from Lake Abilene, and not far from an area once rife with wild buffalo. The park's campgrounds

A rare sight: a whooping crane in Aransas National Wildlife Refuge.

Guadalupe Mountains National Park.

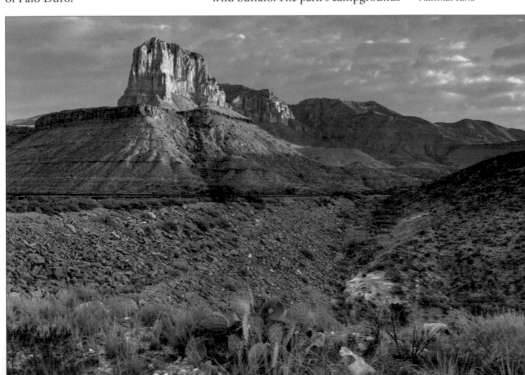

FACT

Alibates flint, found in Alibates Flint Quarries National Monument, north of Amarillo, was named for Ali Bates, a one-time local cowboy.

and swimming pool are set in a historic pecan tree grove.

Cultural past

A large and growing class of parks protect and display the cultural heritage of the state. The historical and recreational are often combined in these parks, providing fun flavored with a little education.

Dinosaur Valley State Park ❹ exhibits the tracks made by the Pleurocoelus and Acrocanthosaurus dinosaurs, prehistoric reptiles that walked around in the mud of a shallow sea that covered Central Texas during the Cretaceous era, more than 100 millions years ago. The interpretive center explains the tracks, and a trail leads right to them. Camping, hiking, and picnicking are also provided in this park, which is 60 miles (95km) southwest of Fort Worth, near Glen Rose.

Remnants of other prehistoric Texas cultures are preserved in several parks. **Alibates Flint Quarries National Monument** ❹, on the red bluffs above the Canadian River north of Amarillo, in the Panhandle of West Texas, was the source of flint used by prehistoric tribes for thousands of years. Of particular interest is the **Waco Mammoth Site** ❷, in Central Texas, where paleontologists have uncovered the fossils of 24 Columbian mammoths and other mammals from the Pleistocene Epoch.

Caddo Mounds State Historic Site ❸ clear across the state in East Texas, 30 miles (50km) west of Nacogdoches, protects three ceremonial mounds built by the Caddo, the westernmost branch of the Missippian Mound Building culture, a branch of the eastern Woodland culture. The site was inhabited from the eighth to the 14th centuries and is the best-preserved ceremonial site in Texas. Interpretive exhibits and a self-guided tour explain as much as is known about the early Caddo people. During summer, archeological digs sometimes take place, and visitors are invited to watch.

Recreational and camping facilities are convenient at **Mission Tejas State Park**, 8 miles (13km) down the road.

Pictographs

Close to Del Rio, on the border in South Texas, is another site with striking evidence of inhabitants 2,000–8,000 years ago. These ancient nomadic people painted the walls and ceilings of their cave dwellings, in what is today **Seminole Canyon State Park and Historic Site** ❹, with fanciful animals and other images whose meaning is now lost. One pictograph-covered shelter is open to visitors on a guided tour. The trail leading to it takes stamina, particularly in the summer heat. An award-winning exhibit at the visitor center interprets the prehistory and history of the park. Campsites with water are available.

Rock art is also found at **Hueco Tanks State Historic Site** ❹, 32 miles (51km) northeast of El Paso in West Texas. Tribes may have come through the area as long as 10,000 years ago.

Freshly caught bass.

Water held in the depressions of the rocks made it a popular place for travelers in the surrounding desert. Pueblo rock art dating from AD 1000 and Mescalero Apache images from the 18th century can be seen on a self-guiding tour. Wildlife watching is also fruitful here, and campsites and picnic areas are both available.

Spanish colonial

The first colonizers of Texas, the Spanish, have left substantial reminders of their presence. **San Antonio Missions National Historical Park** (see page 168) includes four 18th-century mission churches, a dam, and an aqueduct along the San Antonio River. All are managed by the National Park Service; the remains of a fifth mission, the Alamo Chapel in downtown San Antonio, is owned by the state of Texas.

The Spanish mission of Nuestra Señora Espiritu Santo de Zuniga is the centerpiece of **Goliad State Park** ❹❻, just south of the historic town of Goliad. The mission was reconstructed by the CCC on the ruins of the 1749 church. The park has a scenic campground on the river and exhibits in the church and granary. The nearby Presidio La Bahia gained notoriety in 1836 when it was the site of Santa Anna's execution of Fannin's men during the Texas Revolution – hence "Remember Goliad!" The old presidio (garrison) has been reconstructed and is open to the public.

Independent Texas

Washington-on-the-Brazos State Historic Site ❹❼ is the site of the proclamation of the Texas Declaration of Independence on March 2, 1836. Nothing much remains of the bustling 1850s town, but a replica of Texas's Independence Hall and the home of the Republic's last president have been reconstructed. Reenactors bring 19th-century life to present-day visitors. The Star of the Republic Museum, operated by Brenham's

Blinn College, sits in the park grounds and has a number of good exhibits about life in early Texas. The park's riverside picnic area is on a bluff above the Brazos.

Six weeks after the declaration of Texas Independence, Sam Houston's small band of Texans routed Santa Anna in the marshes of Buffalo Bayou, now commemorated by **San Jacinto Battleground State Historic Site** ❹❽. In La Porte, just east of Houston, San Jacinto Monument rises in the midst of the battleground and houses a museum. The park provides picnic areas but no campgrounds.

Although the Texas Republic was established by the April 1836 battle at San Jacinto, it struggled against continued Mexican incursions for the next 10 years. **Monument Hill State Historic Site** ❹❾, in La Grange, 70 miles (115km) east of Austin, honors the Texans who died in two responses to such attacks, the Dawson and Mier expeditions. **Kreische Brewery State Historic Site** is contiguous and contains the ruins of a mid-19th-century brewery, at one time the third largest

A pictograph of Tlaloc, a rain deity, in Hueco Tanks State Historic Site. The Jornada Mogollon people (450–1400 AD) drew many symbols associated with water, which was vital for growing corn in the desert.

LOCAL HERITAGE

Like much of the rest of the United States, Texas has gradually become more aware of its cultural heritage over the past 40 years, particularly the Victorian period after Texas became part of the United States and new communities were founded. Almost every city and town has at least one historic house museum that local folks point to with pride. Some are large groupings of houses with a paid staff and long opening hours, like **Sam Houston State Park** in Huntsville, which has assembled buildings associated with Sam Houston, hero of the Texas revolution, including two homes, a gazebo, and a blacksmith's shop.

Others are smaller and either run by the city or privately, and often manned by dedicated volunteers. They include places like French's Trading Post, now the **John Jay French Museum**, in Beaumont, the city's first two-story house; the **Annie Riggs Memorial Museum**, a former hotel in Fort Stockton that once accommodated passengers on the Butterfield Overland Mail stage coaches; the gothic **Bishop's Palace** in Galveston (listed as one of the top 100 significant historic buildings in the US), which was built for the Gresham family and later used as the bishop's official residence; and the **Charles Stillman House** in Brownsville, built in 1851 by Charles Stillman, founder of the city. Individually and collectively, these fine sites and structures skillfully illustrate life during that colorful era.

in the state. The sites share a well-developed picnic area and grand views of Texas's Colorado River. No camping is available.

Frontier forts

Fortifications of many types are scattered around the state and represent battles of various sorts fought on Texas soil. The most famous of all, of course, is the Alamo in San Antonio. **Old Fort Parker Historic Preservation** ❺⓪, about 35 miles (55km) east of Waco and now owned by the City of Groesbeck, commemorates another famous battle of 1836, the Apache attack on Parker's Fort and the capture of little Cynthia Ann Parker. The "Fall of Fort Ceremony" each May vividly recounts the story of this family fort and the lives and deaths of its inhabitants.

After annexation by the United States in 1845, the Texas frontier stretched long and wide and was poorly protected. Settlers in the most remote areas had to create their own defense systems against hostile American Indians and outlaws. **Fort Leaton**

Battleship Texas, San Jacinto Battleground State Historic Site.

State Historic Site ❺⓵, on the Rio Grande near present-day Presidio, was built by a border trader (some called him a smuggler), Ben Leaton. The federal government also built forts to cope with American Indian threats to the advancing settlers, and a group of fort parks represents the 40-year struggle. **Fort Lancaster State Historic Site** ❺⓶, **Fort Davis National Historic Site** ❺⓷, and **Fort McKavett State Historic Site** ❺⓸ were all built before the Civil War.

Fort Lancaster's adobe ruins lie about 70 miles (115km) east of Fort Stockton, and are interpreted in the visitors' center and via a self-guided tour of the old parade field. At Fort McKavett, about 40 miles (65km) northwest of Junction, and Fort Davis, in the Davis Mountains 25 miles (40km) north of Alpine, little is left of their earliest incarnations, but they have been restored to their post-Civil War state. More forts were built after the war, when American Indian hostilities reached their height. **Fort Richardson State Park and Historic Site** ❺⓹ in Jacksboro, 100 miles

(160km) northwest of Fort Worth, and **Fort Griffin State Park and Historic Site** ⑤⑥, 50 miles (80km) north of Abilene, have been developed with pleasant camping and picnicking adjuncts. Highlights of visits to all the forts are occasional military reenactments: check individual parks for details.

Parks of another kind

Some parks defy the usual categories. **Texas State Railroad State Park** ⑤⑦ runs for 25 miles (40km) between Rusk and Palestine, and is one of the most popular parks in East Texas. The turn-of-the-20th-century rolling stock gives an authentic flavor to the scenic ride along the historic route. The round trip takes three hours. There are picnic sites at both ends to round off the journey.

Battleship *Texas* State Historic Site, a memorial to Texans who fought in World War II, is moored at San Jacinto Battleground State Historic Site in La Porte. Commissioned in 1914, it is the only surviving Navy ship that served in both wars, notably in D-Day operations off the coast of Normandy in 1944 and in the Pacific at Iwo Jima and Okinawa in 1945. Open to the public seven days a week, the ship features a self-guided tour and interesting displays about ship life.

It is not the only warship to be named after Texas. More recently a nuclear submarine was named after the city of Corpus Christi, which is the home of a naval air station. The name had to be changed when complaints about the implications of its Latin meaning (Body of Christ) were voiced.

Beyond words and pictures

There are, of course, many excellent parks in the state that have not been mentioned here, through lack of space. But the list is also incomplete in that no words or pictures can ever fully capture the beauty and spirit of the Texas landscape like a campout in the East Texas Piney Woods, a hike through a dusty, rugged canyon, or a quiet afternoon's sailing on a placid lake on a late fall afternoon.

Hiking through McKittrick Canyon.

The Armadillo Palace, Houston.

INSIGHT GUIDES TRAVEL TIPS
TEXAS

TRANSPORTATION

GETTING THERE AND GETTING AROUND

GETTING THERE

By Air

There are four airports in Texas classified as international: Dallas–Fort Worth, George Bush Intercontinental Airport in Houston, Austin-Bergstrom in Austin, and San Antonio. Air passengers to Texas usually arrive at Dallas–Fort Worth Airport or George Bush Intercontinental Airport in Houston, but now that British Airways operates a service from London to Austin, that airport is becoming popular. Many flights touch down in El Paso for passengers to board or change planes.

A network of smaller airports serves the state, with scheduled flights to over 30 cities. Connections are easy to arrange, even between different carriers, and there are frequent shuttles between major cities all day.

Airline Companies

More than two dozen airlines fly in and out of Texas airports, including major carriers such as Fort Worth-based American Airlines (and its regional off-shoot, American Eagle), as well as United, Continental, British Airways, and Delta.

Air fares change frequently, as do schedules and discount rates. Check the internet regularly for specials, or contact airlines directly by telephone for information and reservations. Local or toll-free central numbers can be obtained either from directory assistance (in Texas, dial 1-411) or the Yellow Pages of the local telephone directory.

By Train

Two Amtrak lines run through Texas: the Eagle from Chicago to San Antonio, with a Dallas–Houston connection; and the Sunset from Los Angeles to Orlando. The trains stop at 19 passenger terminals in the state: Alpine, Austin, Beaumont, Cleburne, Dallas, Del Rio, El Paso, Fort Worth, Houston, Longview, Marshall, McGregor, Mineola, San Antonio, Sanderson, San Marcos, Taylor, Temple, and Texarkana. Accommodations include coach and sleeping facilities. There are lounge and dining cars. Outside North America, you can purchase a USA Rail Pass from travel agencies, which allows unlimited rail travel within specified dates.

For reservations and information inside the US, call 1-800-USA-RAIL or 1-800-872-7245 toll-free, or visit www.amtrak.com.

By Bus

Greyhound buses (tel: 800-231-2222; www.greyhound.com) connect Texas with all major US cities. Buses are always air-conditioned, with toilets on board and free Wi-fi.

GETTING AROUND

On Arrival

Dallas–Fort Worth Airport

The airport (tel: 972-973-3112; www.dfwairport.com) is 18 miles (29km) northwest of Dallas and within four hours of most cities in the US. The third busiest airport in the world, it handles approximately 2,000 domestic flights per day and 500 international flights per week.

The Trinity Railway Express (TRE; www.trinityrailwayexpress.org), a train system that connects Fort Worth to Dallas, stops near the airport (you must take a Remote South bus to reach it) at least once an hour on weekdays; one zone costs $2.50. Allow at least an hour's travel time. A taxi ride downtown takes around 35 minutes and costs about $45. SuperShuttle Dallas (tel: 800-258-3826), which transports passengers to all areas by van or minibus, costs less at $25, but can take up to 90 minutes, depending on destination.

Love Field Airport

The hub for Southwest Airlines, Love Field (tel: 214-670-6080; www.dallas-lovefield.com) is 7 miles (11km) northwest of downtown Dallas, but within the city limits. Buses that leave from a stop outside the terminal run at least once an hour for a 40-minute ride to the West Transfer Center in downtown Dallas and cost $2.50. A taxi takes about 20 minutes to get downtown and costs about $15. SuperShuttle shared-van service (tel: 800-258-3826) is approximately $20 and can take over an hour, depending on destination.

George Bush Intercontinental

Located 23 miles (37km) north of downtown Houston, Bush Intercontinental (tel: 281-230-3100; www.airport-houston.com) has daily services to 119 US cities and 65 international destinations, and is a hub for United Airlines.

Houston's METRO bus system has a route that runs from Intercontinental Airport to downtown Houston every 15 minutes, from

6am to midnight Mon–Fri, and once an hour on weekends for $1.25. Taxis to downtown cost about $52.50 and take around 30 minutes. The SuperShuttle shared-van service is approximately $25 and can take 90 minutes, depending on destination.

William P. Hobby Airport

Serving as a hub for Southwest Airlines, Hobby (tel: 713-640-3000; www.fly2houston.com) is 7 miles (11km) southeast of downtown Houston.

The METRO bus system goes from Hobby to downtown Houston every 15 minutes from 6am to midnight Mon–Fri and at least once an hour on weekends for $1.25. Taxis downtown cost about $30 and take around 20 minutes. The SuperShuttle shared-van service (tel: 800-258-3826) is approximately $20 but takes an hour or more, depending on destination.

Austin-Bergstrom International Airport

Recently upgraded to international status, ABIA (tel: 512-530-ABIA; www.austintexas.gov/airport) is 8 miles (13km) from downtown Austin.

The METRO bus from ABIA to downtown Austin takes 30 minutes and leaves on the hour and half hour, Mon–Fri 5.30am–11.30pm, with slightly adjusted hours on weekends; fare $1.50. Taxis downtown cost from $12.85 plus mileage and take around 20 minutes. The SuperShuttle shared van service (tel: 800-258-3826) is approximately $20 but takes an hour or more, depending on destination.

Public Transportation

By Air

Within Texas, Southwest Airlines has the largest number of flights and usually the lowest fares; Express Jet offers discount-rate flights between Austin and Houston.

By Bus

All cities and most towns have some form of local bus service at very low rates. Contact the local tourist office for listings (see page 312) or call the main office of the bus company listed in the telephone directory. Major cities like Dallas, Fort Worth, Austin, San Antonio, and Houston offer other bus services well suited to visitors, such as the 'Dillo (armadillo) "trolleys" in Austin and CITRAN (City Transit Service) in Fort Worth.

By Train

There are 62 stations on the popular light-rail DART system (Dallas Area Rapid Transit) (tel: 214-979-1111; www.dart.org) serving downtown Dallas and 12 surrounding cities. The new DFW Airport Station has greatly improved access to the metroplex for travelers who do not wish to rent a car. The Orange Line extension from Belt Line Station to the newly built Terminal A at DFW Airport is now the longest light rail in the nation, at 90 miles (145km). Each station has ticket machines with clear instructions for use. There are also special services for people with disabilities. For further information, tel: 214-979-1111. A two-hour pass costs $2.50/$5.00 for a day pass.

DART stops at Union Station, from which Amtrak trains connect Dallas with Chicago and Houston. The station is connected by pedestrian tunnel to the Hyatt Regency Hotel (beside Reunion Tower). See page 296 for information on Amtrak services.

Houston's METRORail (tel: 713-635-4000; www.ridemetro.org) connects downtown, midtown, the Museum District, the Texas Medical Center, Reliant Park, and the South Fannin Park & Ride lot.

By Taxi

Taxis can be a convenient way to get around cities. However, unlike those in major cities like New York and London, Texas taxis do not cruise around looking for people hailing them from the curb. To get a taxi, you must call the cab company (look under Taxicabs in the Yellow Pages of the local telephone directory). Ask what the rates are, as they vary from city to city (but not from cab to cab). A 15 percent tip is appreciated if you are satisfied with the service provided, and especially if you need help with luggage.

Driving

The size and climate of Texas are good reasons to drive, since walking between attractions, even in a city, requires more time than most people have while on their vacations; for much of the year, it is simply too hot to walk around.

Interstate highways 10, 20, 27, 30, 35, 37, 40, and 45 crisscross Texas, providing direct and relatively hazard-free routes to major cities. For anyone interested in a closer look, however, there is a variety of US highways, state routes, and backroads (marked on the maps as FM or "Farm to Market", RM or "Ranch to Market", and RR or "Ranch Road") interconnecting all the major cities, smaller communities, and even ghost towns. Buy a map and plan a tour, but allow plenty of time to reach your destination since some of these Texas roads get quite winding and pot-holed.

Be aware, as well, that leaving the main track means fewer gas stations and convenience stores. However, if you remember to fill the tank and allow plenty of time to get where you're going, especially after dark, these secondary roads (dubbed "blue highways") may prove the most enjoyable way to travel since you'll be able to enjoy the countryside without having to worry about heavy traffic.

The Texas Department of Transportation (TDOT) runs 12 information centers offering advice on trip planning, road conditions, and other travel matters. For information call 800-452-9292; www.txdot.gov.

Anyone spending a significant amount of time driving US highways is strongly advised to join the **Automobile Association of America** (tel: 800-874-7532; www.aaa.com). Benefits include emergency breakdown service, excellent road maps, travel literature, and personalized trip planning, as well as discounts at motels like Best Western and other chains. Premier level offers towing up to 200 miles (320km) from breakdown site – important if you are in the middle of nowhere – and lockout, refueling, and jumpstart service. Insurance is also available through the association, which has a reciprocal arrangement with some of the automobile associations in other countries.

Car Rental

Cars can be rented in most cities. This is often done at the local airport since much of the rental business is with customers who have arrived by air. Choose the best rate available from one of the side-by-side booths or better, book a car in advance as, quite often, certain levels of vehicle are unavailable.

You must be at least 21 years of age to rent a car. Most companies require a credit card or debit card, although some do not accept debit cards, so be sure to inquire ahead of time. Be sure to arrange auto insurance if you do not have US coverage of your own. Even with your own coverage, you may be required to cover any damages upfront and be reimbursed later.

Some rental agencies expect the car to be returned to them. If you want to drive to another city and fly on from there, inform the rental agent at the time you arrange the terms. There are branches of the main rental companies across the state. There may be a charge to drop the car at their branch in another city. Check ahead because the cost can be prohibitive.

Interstates

Interstates (motorways) bypass most towns. They do get you to your destination fast, but when you are driving from Austin to Dallas or from San Antonio to El Paso, even fast can mean 4–10 hours. Along the interstates there are rest stops with restrooms and picnic areas, as well as restaurants and gas stations.

Highway Patrol and Hitchhiking

The Highway Patrol cruises these highways, not just monitoring speed limits but also looking for drivers in trouble. If you have any emergency that won't allow you to continue the trip, signal your distress by raising the hood. Be sure to keep a current driver's license and a certificate proving you have liability insurance with you at all times because you will be required to show them to the law enforcement officer who stops your car for any reason. It is illegal to drive in Texas without these items.

Motorists are often warned that they are safer staying in the car with the doors locked until a patrol car stops to help, rather than leaving it and trying to hitchhike. Hitchhiking is not considered safe, whether you are on the giving or the receiving end.

Rules of the Road

Speed limits for roads and highways are posted on white signs to the right, as are all other road signs. Some roads are for one-way traffic only and are identified by a black and white sign with an arrow pointing in the permitted direction of travel. At an intersection where each corner has a red stop sign with a smaller sign below it that says "4-Way" or "All-Way," motorists must completely stop and then proceed across the intersection following the order in which they arrived at the stop.

The official highway speed limit is 70mph (112kph); some highways are now 75mph (121kph). Although everyone passes you, resist the temptation to accelerate. If caught in

a "speed trap" by the Highway Patrol, whose black-and-white cruisers have radar, you will get a speeding ticket that has to be paid in a nearby (or sometimes not so near) town before continuing your trip.

The same advice should be followed when driving through towns and cities. Be sure to notice the white signs warning that, upon entering the town, you will be in a different "Speed Zone Ahead." Be prepared to slow to the lower speed you will soon see posted on upcoming white signs. Some very small Texas towns are notorious for catching and fining drivers who have not slowed down quickly enough from the highway speed to the in-town 30mph (48kph) speed limit. You may not notice the local (variously colored and lettered) police car parked surreptitiously in an alley until it is too late.

Pay attention to other drivers flashing their lights at you; probably either an accident or speed trap is ahead. Some Texas motorists ask the gas station attendants if there are Highway Patrol cars ahead but they cannot always be relied upon.

Parking fees vary from town to town, with rates higher in larger cities and nonexistent in smaller towns.

A state law requires every passenger in a car to use a seatbelt, and there are also requirements that small children and babies be secured in youth or infant seats that have been fitted into the car seat. In Texas, a traffic ticket is a criminal offense. Penalties run from $200 for an expired registration all the way up to $1,000 for passing a school bus.

Texas state law requires that all drivers carry auto insurance policies. Auto rental companies offer insurance that runs from $10 to $25 per day, depending on coverage.

It is legal to talk on your cell phone without a hands-free device in Texas, although for travelers unfamiliar with the area that may not be a good idea, particularly in busy urban areas. The exception is during school zone hours, when the use of cell phones is illegal, unless the vehicle is stopped or you are using a hands-free device. There are local ordinances about texting while driving.

Down Mexico Way

Current US State Department advisories caution against travel in Mexico due to ongoing drug war violence and crime in border areas. Recently, murders in the major flashpoint area of El Paso-Ciudad

Juárez have dropped considerably, after Mexico government crackdowns and a heavy military presence, and Mexican tourism officials are keen to encourage visitors to cross and enjoy all that the country has to offer. This is entirely a matter of informing yourself and exercising personal judgement, and keeping your wits about you. Thousands of people cross the border every day, with few problems.

You can cross into Mexico at 14 border crossings in Texas; the main crossings are El Paso, Eagle Pass, Laredo, and Brownsville. Under new Homeland Security rules, both US and non-US citizens must carry a valid passport to visit Mexico and to reenter the US by air or by sea (some US state-issued enhanced driver's licenses with embedded microchips are permitted, but don't rely on it) and, if applicable, an alien registration card (green card) to reenter the country. Be sure you have these on hand before making the trip to avoid big headaches at immigration. Short trips into the border zone (La Frontera), which extends approximately 25 miles (40km) south, are permitted.

If you're traveling deeper into the country or staying longer than 72 hours, a Mexican tourist card, or *forma migratoria turista* (FMT), is required. These are free from immigration officials at the border and also from Mexican consulates, Mexican government tourist offices, and travel agents. Drivers must also obtain automobile permits, valid for 180 days, when venturing beyond the border region. These cost $30 from Mexican immigration officials on production of a tourist card.

It is mandatory to obtain Mexican insurance because in the event of an accident vehicles are usually impounded, regardless of fault. Sanborn's Mexican Insurance (www.sanbornsinsurance.com) is a reliable company that specializes in this insurance. They have offices in most large border towns, and also in San Antonio. At the border you will be given a temporary import permit after you show proof of ownership (photocopy of title will do), or the hire contract in the driver's name if you are driving a rental car, and the insurance policy. Keep these handy, as 12 miles (19km) into Mexico, every car without Mexico tags is stopped at the border checkpoints.

Further information is available on 800-262-9128 or www.visitmexico.com.

ACTIVITIES

FESTIVALS, THE ARTS, NIGHTLIFE, SHOPPING AND SPORTS

FESTIVALS

Dallas Arts District hosts several free outdoor festivals throughout the year. Visitors can enjoy the Jazz Concert Series Live on the Lawn in Klyde Warren Park in June, the Art in October month-long arts festival, and the Dallas Dance Festival in November.

Houston's many ethnic celebrations include an International festival, an Asian American festival, and a Greek festival, all held in May, and a Chicano festival held in October.

San Antonio's celebrations center on the River Walk throughout the year, and include a glorious Battle of Flowers and Boat Parade to celebrate the Battle of the Alamo in April and 6,000 Southwest-style *luminarias* (candle lanterns in brown bags) along the riverbank at Christmas.

Austin's South By Southwest (SXSW) multimedia conference and showcase is now a creatively cross-pollinated event in March, for musicians, film makers, and interactive technology. Nearby Hill Country has delightful Old Country festivals all year, including a pageant marking the founding of Fredericksburg in April that involves lighting bonfires on surrounding hills.

See Spectator Sports (see page 305) for stock shows and rodeo listings.

January

AT&T Cotton Bowl Classic (Dallas). Found in Dallas at the Texas State Fairgrounds, this major college football game is part of the new College Playoff System begun in 2014, which includes the Peach Bowl.

It's nationally televised; www.cotton bowl.com.
Gulf Coast Music Hall of Fame Show (Port Arthur). This fun celebration of Gulf Coast musical talent grew out of the annual Janis Joplin Birthday Bash, a party for the famed Port Arthur singer held at the Gulf Coast Music Hall of Fame at the Museum of the Gulf Coast. Good music is guaranteed; www.museumof thegulfcoast.org.
Texas Citrus Fiesta (Mission). Since 1932, this fiesta in Mission has celebrated the Texas ruby red grapefruit and other citrus fruits. Highlights include the crowning of a King and Queen of Citrus and a parade featuring costumes made from citrus, as well as a ball; www.missiontexas.us/life-in-mission/attractions/texas-citrus-fiesta.

February

Charro Days Fiesta (Brownsville). A lively, four-day, pre-lenten cross-border festival in Brownsville celebrating Mexican culture. Among the highlights are parades and a traditional Mexican rodeo; www.charro daysfiesta.com.
Mardi Gras (Galveston). Giving Louisiana's New Orleans a run for its money, this legendary Mardi Gras celebration in Galveston has 20 krewes participating in 15 parades and includes more than 50 events, including the traditional bead throwing from floats; www.mardigras galveston.com.
Washington's Birthday Celebration (Laredo). Taking place over nearly a month, and with 400,000 attendees the largest event of its kind, this celebration of Washington's birthday offers various events, including a

Martha Washington Pageant and ball, a Princess Pocahantas Pageant and Ball, parades, a carnival, an air show, and a citywide prom where all the kids dress up in colonial attire; www.wbcalaredo.org.

March

Fulton Oysterfest (Fulton). This festival sponsored by the fire department in Fulton has rides, games, an oyster-eating contest, and live music, all to celebrate the local bivalve – the oyster; www.fultontexas. org.
Rattlesnake Roundup (Sweetwater). The world's largest rattlesnake roundup features rattlesnake hunts, tours, and demonstrations, as well as a Miss Rattlesnake pageant, sampling of fried rattlesnake, and a chili cookoff; www.sweetwatertexas/rattlesnake-round.
Buffalo Bayou Regatta (Houston). Texas's largest canoe race takes place in Houston's Buffalo Bayou waterway development with boat races, food, and music; www.buffalobayou.org/regattabayou.
South by Southwest (Austin). This famous Texas-sized arts networking conference and festival has grown from an industry event for creatives showcasing music and media into a huge festival with 2,200 local and national acts on over 100 stages, befitting Austin's claim as Live Music Capital of the World. It has expanded now to include film and interactive technologies in its offerings; www.sxsw.org.

April

Easter Fires Pageant (Fredericks-burg). A very popular Easter Saturday celebration in Fredericksburg that celebrates its German heritage and involves burning 22 bonfires on surrounding hills to mark Christ's resurrection. At the appointed hour, church bells ring, lights are extinguished, and the bonfires burst into flames; www.visitfredericksburg tex.com/easter-fires-of-fredericksburg-pageant.

Denton Arts and Jazz Festival (Denton). This music-rich college town north of Dallas comes alive each April with a panoply of musical performances, dance, choral music, drama, and visual arts events; www.dentonjazzfest.com.

Bluebonnet Trail Spring Celebration (Burnet). A celebration of the arrival of theTexas state flower on the hillsides of Hill Country takes place each spring in Burnet, designated "Bluebonnet Capital of Texas." Parades, a carnival, an air show, a classic car parade, and live music enliven the little town; www.lakesandhills.com/bluebonnet.htm.

Fiesta San Antonio (San Antonio). Celebrated for more than a century, this heavily attended event began as a festival to commemorate the Battle of the Alamo and grew into a fiesta. Events include a River Boat Parade, a Battle of Flowers Parade, events at the Mercado, and music and food celebrating the city's multicultural heritage; www.fiesta-sa.org.

Germanfest (Muenster). A celebration of everything German in Texas, including polka music, strudel, and sausage, along with a fun run and bike rally to keep the pounds off. www.germanfest.net

Scarborough Faire (Waxahachie). Jousting, juggling, living chess games, and folkcraft are the order of the day at this Medieval extravaganza; tel: 972-938-3247.

May

Cinco de Mayo celebrations Hispanic communities throughout Texas and the Southwest celebrate the battle at Puebla on May 5, 1862, when the Mexican army was victorious over the French. Mexican culture is on parade, including mariachi music, food, and folkloric dancing. Various communities, including Goliad, host enjoyable celebrations; www.goliadcc.org.

National Polka Festival (Ennis). One of Texas's unique cultural activities is polka, a result of its Czech heritage. This festival has plenty of polka music and dancing, a fun run, a crowning of the King and Queen of Polka, a parade, food (Ennis is known for its barbecue sausage), and a horseshoe tournament; www.nationalpolkafestival.com.

Mayfest (Fort Worth). This big family festival beside the Trinity River hosts a variety of events, including a fun run, music and theater on several stages, a petting zoo, carnival rides, duck races, and food booths. www.mayfest.org

Columbus Folk Fest (Columbus). A spring festival that includes historical reenactments, a celebration of Texas's live oaks, a Dead Folks Cemetery Tour, home tours, a Magnolia Belle presentation, and Miss Columbus Pageant, along with exhibits, food and beer booths, art vendors, and kids's games; www.columbustexas.org.

June

Chisholm Trail Roundup (Lockhart). The biggest event of the year in Lockhart includes a rodeo and a big-deal Texas chili cookoff; www.chisholmtrailroundup.com.

Juneteenth (Galveston and other communities). Marks the emancipation of Texas African-Americans on June 19, 1865. Celebrations in various cities across the state; www.juneteenth.com.

Texas! (Canyon). A musical pageant celebrating Texas Panhandle history takes place in the spectacular setting of Palo Duro Canyon. Nightly Tuesday through Saturday from early June to mid-August; www.texas-show.com.

Luling Watermelon Thump (Luling). A four-day celebration of the watermelon, including watermelon eating, the World Championship Watermelon Seed Spitting Competition, watermelon judging, a beer garden, and arts and crafts; www.watermelonthump.com.

July

Great Texas Balloon Race (Longview). Competing hot-air champions take to the skies in a big balloon race. www.gtbr.net **Houston Shakespeare Festival** (Hermann Park). Free nightly performances of Shakespeare's plays in repertory by the University of Houston in Miller Outdoor Theater in Hermann Park; www.uh.edu.

August

Gillespie County Fair (Fredericksburg). The oldest county fair in Texas does not disappoint, with horse races, a stock show, and food booths serving fair favorites like sausage-on-a-stick and funnel cakes; www.gillespiefair.com.

Hotter 'n Hell Hundred Bike Ride (Wichita Falls). Begun as a way of marking Wichita Falls's centennial – a 100-mile-long bike race in 100-degree heat to celebrate 100 years – the race now attracts over 12,000 peddlers as an endurance test; www.hh100.org.

Houston International Jazz Festival (Houston). This outdoor jazz festival in early August attracts numerous international headlining acts. It serves as a fund-raiser to support enrichment programs for kids at risk; www.jazzeducation.org.

De Leon Peach and Melon Festival and Tractor Pull (De Leon). This classic down-home festival has been celebrating the harvest for 100 years and also includes carnival rides, lots of watermelon and peaches, an exciting tractor pull competition in the dusty stadium; Error! Hyperlink reference not valid.

September

Grapefest (Grapevine). This annual wine celebration, the biggest in the Southwest, takes place north of Dallas, in the historic downtown of well-named Grapevine. Tastings of wines from many of Texas's 200-plus vineyards, as well as elsewhere; www.grapevinetexasusa.com.

National Championship Indian Pow Wow (Grand Prairie). Held at Trader's Village in Grand Prairie, this powwow attracts tribes from all over the US for drumming, fancy and social dances, arts and crafts demonstrations, traders, teepees, and costume competitions; www.tradersvillage.com/grand-prairie/events.

State Fair of Texas (Dallas). Held at historic Fair Park since 1886, Texas's huge state fair is a classic early fall treat for fair goers, with big name musical acts, rides, a stock show, arts and crafts, and classic fair food, like funnel cakes, all over 24 days. Begins September and ends in October; www.bigtex.com.

October

Cottonwood Art Festival (Richardson). An annual art show in Cottonwood Park in Richardson that showcases emerging regional artists, along with music and food booths; www.cottonwoodartfestival.com.

East Texas Yamboree (Gilmer). A charming East Texas institution for the last 100 years, the Yamboree includes a barn dance, a bike ride, a yam-pie contest, fiddlers, an antique car show, and a livestock show; www.yamboree.com.

Halloween on Sixth St (Austin). Definitely "Keeping Austin Weird," this is the place to be on Halloween night, when everyone strolls Sixth in their costume and parties the night away; www.6street.com.

Rockport-Fulton Seafair (Rockport). This terrific Gulf Coast event, now celebrating 40 years, features a gumbo cookoff, music, arts and crafts, a boat race, and a crab contest amid the soft sandy beaches of the Gulf; www.rockportseafair.com.

November

International Chili Championship (Terlingua). For many people, the dusty town of Terlingua on the Rio Grande in Big Bend Country is synonymous with its famed chili cookoff. At this time of year the heat is in the chili not in the desert; www.chili. org/terlingua.html.

Annual Heritage Syrup Festival (Henderson). A festival in East Texas highlighting pioneer activities in the piney woods, such as boiling down ribbon cane for syrup, lace making, rope making, basketry, quilting, woodcarving, and blacksmithing; www.texasforesttrail.com/events.

International Quilt Festival (Houston). Held in the convention center, this is a huge juried exhibition of hand-made quilts of many styles that attracts people from all over the world. In cooperation with the Texas Quilt Museum in La Grange; www.quilts.com.

Wonderland of Lights Festival (Marshall). Downtown is all illuminated during this festival of lights, which may be the granddaddy of them all. The courthouse is at the center of nightly son et lumière shows.

December

Campfire Christmas (Richmond). A wonderfully old-fashioned Christmas celebration that revisits Christmas in the 1830s Victorian period and 1930s Depression era at George Ranch State Historical Park. Historic dances and dining and hayrides; www.georgeranch.org.

Candelight Tour of Homes (Jefferson). A tour of charming

homes in historic Jefferson, featuring choral music, handbell ringers, brass bands, and trolley rides; www.jeffersoncandlelight.com.

Dickens on the Strand (Galveston). A Victorian Christmas celebration worthy of Dickens and old London (the Strand was named for that famous London Street), this delightful holiday street festival features costumed performers, choirs, handbell ringers, puppets, and lots of Christmas cheer on the shores of the Gulf; www.galveston history.org.

Fiesta de las Luminarias (San Antonio). Magical at any time of year, the River Walk is spectacular lit up for the holidays the first weekend in December with 6,000 luminarias (candles in brown paper bags weighted with sand used in Spanish communities at Christmas to help light the way for the Christ Child); www.thesanantonioriverwalk.com.

Zweite Weihnachten (Fredericksburg). Boxing Day celebrations on December 26, known in German communities as Zweite Weihnachten, or Second Christmas, is hosted by Fredericksburg's German Club and includes gluhwein, stollen, and lots of good cheer; www.visitfredericksburgtx.com.

THE ARTS

Music and Dance

The Dallas/Fort Worth cultural calendar is crowded with events. The Morton H. Meyerson Symphony Center in the burgeoning arts district is home to the Dallas Symphony Orchestra (tel: 214-670-3600; www.dallassymphony.com). The Dallas Opera (tel: 214-443-1043; www.dallasopera.org) performs in the Margot and Bill Winspear Opera House in the Arts District, between November and February. The opera house is part of AT&T Performing Arts Center (2403 Flora Street; tel: 214-880-0202; www.attpac.org), a new complex with theaters used by Dallas Theater Center (tel: 214-526-8210; www.dallastheatercenter. org); Dallas Black Dance Theatre (tel: 214-871-2387; www.dbdt.com); Texas Ballet Theater (tel: 817-763-0207; www.texasballettheater. org); and Anita N. Martinez Ballet Folklorico (tel: 214-828-0181; www.anmbf.org)

Further performing arts listings include:

Ticket Agents

Tickets for a wide variety of theater, dance, and other arts performances are available through Ticketmaster (tel: 800-982-2787; www.ticketmaster.com). Half-price tickets to some events on the day of the performance may be available. Call tel: 214-696-HALF or 972-263-1061 for further information. Front Gate Tickets (tel: 888-512-SHOW; www.frontgatetickets.com) is an Austin-based ticket company that sells tickets to events in Texas and some parts of the South and Midwest. For schedules consult local paper listings.

The Fort Worth Symphony, tel: 817-665-6000; www.fw symphony.org
The Dallas Chamber Orchestra, tel: 214-321-1411; www.dallaschamber orchestra.org.
The Greater Dallas Youth Orchestra, tel: 214-528-7747; www.3gdyo.org.
Concerts and festivals are staged at the Gexas Energy Pavilion (tel: 214-421-1111; www.gexaenergypavilion.net), in Dallas's historic Fair Park; the Music Hall in Fair Park stages an annual series of Dallas Summer Musicals, tel: 214-691-7200; www.liveatthemusicalhall.com).
In Houston, the spectacular Wortham Theater Center (tel: 832-487-7000; www.houstonfirsttheaters. com/worthamcenter), situated northeast of downtown, is home to the Houston Ballet (tel: 713-227-2787; www.houstonballet.org), and Houston Grand Opera (tel: 713-546-0200; www.houstongrandopera. org), as well as a variety of other activities. Nearby is Jones Hall for the Performing Arts, home to the Houston Symphony (tel: 713-224-4240; www.houstonsymphony.org) and the Society for the Performing Arts (tel: 713-227-4772; www.spa houston.org), which presents world-class orchestras, dance companies, and solo artists. The newly formed Houston First is a cooperative venture between the performing arts community and the city to promote performing arts in Houston.
Houston's Rice University has its share of cultural activities, with music and drama performances at the Miller Outdoor Theatre (tel: 832-487-7102; www.milleroutdoor theatre.com) in Hermann Park in

summer, and other venues, including the university's Hamman Hall.

It's also well worth making the relatively short trip to Galveston for a performance at the glorious Grand 1894 Opera House (tel: 409-765-1894; www.thegrand.com).

As befits a college town (especially one famous for its live music), Austin is also rich in classical music events, with regular performances by the **Austin Symphony Orchestra** (tel: 512-476-6064; www.austinsymphony. org) and the **Austin Chamber Music Center**, tel: 512-454-0026, www.austinchambermusic.org.

Theater

Notable theater events in the Dallas–Forth Worth area include the **Shakespeare in the Park Festival** (tel: 214-559-2779; www.shakespearedallas.com), held in the Samuell Grand Amphitheatre in Addison Circle Park in Addison in summer through fall. Also worth a visit is the Dallas Children's Theater (tel: 214-978-0110; www.dct.org).

Houston's **Wortham Theater Center** (tel: 832-487-7000; wwwlhoustonfirsttheaters.com/ worthamcenter) is the centerpiece of the city's compact Theater District, which also includes the 50-year-old award-winning **Alley Theatre** (tel: 713-220-5700; www.alleytheatre. org), which has earned a national reputation for original drama. Broadway shows are regularly presented by **Theatre Under the Stars** at the Hobby Center for the Performing Arts (tel: 713-315-2400; www.hobbycenter.org) on Bagby St in Houston.

NIGHTLIFE

Dallas/Fort Worth

Much of Dallas's liveliest nightlife is centered around Deep Ellum, the former industrial neighborhood in the 3500 block of Elm, just east of the central Expressway, where the live music action is both cutting edge at places like the hip Club Dada (2720 Elm Street; www.dadadallas. com) but there's also plenty of good ol' Texan country and western music, cold beer, and two-stepping at honky tonks like Adair's Saloon (2624 Commerce Street; tel: 214-939-9400; www.adairssaloon.com). The converted Granada Theater (3524 Greenville Avenue; tel: 214-824-

9933; www.granadatheater.com) is famous as the best live music venue in town.

These days, you'll find a lot of action in the Uptown and Knox-Henderson neighborhoods. The Old Monk Pub (2847 N. Henderson Avenue; tel: 214-821-1880; www.oldmonkdallas.com) is a popular Irish-owned bar/restaurant on Henderson with upscale pub food and a great ambiance. Not far away are JR's Bar and Grill (3923 Cedar Springs Street; www.jrsdallas.com) and Sue Ellen's (3014 Throckmorton Street; www.sueellensdallas.com), the city's two top gay bars. If you really must ride a mechanical bull (you are in Texas after all), then visit Gilley's (1135 S. Lamar Street; tel: 214-445-5397; www.gilleysdallas.com), which has a bull, live music, and food, and was immortalized in the movie Urban Cowboy.

For authentic Old West ambiance, your best bet is to head to Fort Worth's Stockyards district, where the **White Elephant Saloon** (106 E. Exchange Avenue; tel: 817-624-1887; www.whiteelephantsaloon. com) is among the spots offering live entertainment.**Billy Bob's** Texas (2520 Rodeo Plaza; tel: 817-624-7117; www.billybobstexas.com) is the world's biggest honky tonk. **Sundance Square** (tel: 817-255-5700; www.sundancesquare.com) in downtown Fort Worth has numerous restaurants, some outdoors with music.

Houston

As Houston has grown, and neighborhoods have become more defined as destinations, nightlife has shifted to a variety of venues around the city and new hip spots are always emerging. In the River Oaks section near the Galleria, you'll find **Elan** (526 Waugh Drive; www. elanhouston.net), an upscale dance club that specializes in 1980s dance music and nearby, **Local Pour** (1952 Gray Street; www.localpourhouston. com), a trendy bar that specializes in Texas microbrews on tap. The area around Rice University has a few nice bars to hang out with the college crowd, and those with a taste for the old and venerable may enjoy Downtown venues like **La Carafe** (813 Congress Street), which, in a dark-paneled1860 building, is the oldest bar in Houston, and **Warren's Inn** (307 Travis Street; tel: 713-247-9207), known for excellent jukebox selection and strong drinks.

Houston has a large gay population centered on the district of **Montrose,** which has become a major destination for entertainment – gay or straight. Check out **South Beach** (810 Pacific Street; tel: 713-529-7623; www.southbeachthenightclub.com), which has dancing to techno music; next door is the Houston branch of **JR's Bar and Grill,** which tops many best of lists. **Cezanne** (4100 Montrose Boulevard; tel: 713-522-9621; www.cezannejazz.com), located above the Black Labrador, one of Houston's most attractive English pubs, is the best place in Houston to hear live jazz on Friday and Saturday nights. Farther west, off I-10, is **The Usual** (5519 Allen Street; http://the usualpub.com), Houston's most popular lesbian bar, known for its karaoke and city views.

San Antonio

As with most things in San Antonio, the city's best nightlife can be found near downtown's River Walk. There's dancing and karaoke at the **Republic of Texas Nightclub** (526 Riverwalk; tel: 210-226-6256), in the restaurant of the same name, and rowdy sing-alongs taking place at **Durty Nelly's Irish Pub** (200 S. Alamo; tel: 210-224-3343; www.durtynellyspub.com) below the Hilton Palacio, which claims to hand out one ton of peanuts each week. The **Rivercenter Comedy Club** (tel: 210-229-1420) is a showcase for old and new performers. The historic **Menger Bar** (204 Alamo Place; tel:

210-223-4361), in the hotel of the same name, is de rigueur for history buffs (even if it is a bit touristy): it's here where Teddy Roosevelt rounded up his Rough Riders at the start of the 20th century. The bar is a replica of the House of Lords Pub in London.

The city's gay nightlife is concentrated just north of downtown, and includes clubs like Heat (1500 N. Main Avenue; tel: 210-227-2600), which has techno music and dancing, and the huge **Bonham Exchange** (411 Bonham Street; www.bonhamexchange.net), housed in an 1892 building with five bars spread over three floors.

Of interest if you are out and about in the area is **Gruene**, near New Braunfels, is famed for its century-old **Gruene Hall** (tel: 830-606-1281; www.gruenehall.com), the oldest dancehall in Texas and still a good place for boot-scootin'.

Austin

Austin, the burgeoning state capital and home of UT, calls itself the Live Music Capital of the World, a title it earned after popularizing live music concerts by well-known and emerging musician's on PBS's *Austin City Limits* TV concert series beginning in the 1970s. Back in the day, outlaw country musicians like Waylon Jennings, Jerry Jeff Walker, and Willie Nelson played at the old Armadillo World Headquarters, next to **Threadgills** in downtown, before they became famous and put the city on the map. Today, hundreds of acts, performing everything from country and bluegrass to rock and roll and comedy routines, play around around town in over 200 live music/entertainment venues, so you'll be spoiled for choice and really can't go wrong.

In downtown, near the state capitol, you'll find famous **Scholz Garten** (1607 San Jacinto Boulevard; tel: 512-474-1958), which has been serving German beers in a biergarten since 1866 (writer O.Henry frequented this watering hole).

The area around **Sixth Street** is popular with college kids and tourists and is more of a drinking and party scene. Among the better club venues to check out here is **Continental Club** (1315 S. Congress Avenue; tel: 512-441-0202; www.continentalclub. com), a Fifties style lounge with dancing to some of the best acts in Austin. Farther east along 6th, in the Red River area, you'll find a more local scene at Casino El Camino (517

E. 6th Street; tel: 512-469-9330), famous for its burgers and beers and good jukebox.

Heading west into the **Warehouse District**, hip bars and clubs known for salsa and martini, can be found, such as **Lucky Lounge** (209a W. 5th Street; tel: 512-479-7700; www.theluckylounge.com), a good place for an early music show. Austin's gay scene is primarily found in this area. Check out **Rusty's** (405 E. 7th St; tel: 512-482-9002; www.rustysaustin.com), which has country music and boot scootin', poker, and karaoke.

Highly recommended for country and western lovers is the veteran **Threadgill's World Headquarters** (301 W. Riverside Drive; tel: 512-451-5440; www.threadgills.com), where diners share long tables and stomp their feet to a never-ending stream of live country music.

If you're headed out into the Texas Hill Country, be sure to visit tiny **Luckenbach**, the ghost town popularized by country stars like Willie Nelson. They have regular concerts, and there are usually several musicians jamming in the little post office if you happen to stop by. Austin is renowned for its funky dives. In a league of its own is **Ginny's Little Longhorn Saloon** (5434 Burnet Road; tel: 512-407-8557), north of Austin, home to live music and Sunday night Chicken Shit Bingo, where you can bet on, yes, which number the chicken will poop on. Only in Texas.

Look for special events such as **Jerry Jeff Walker's Annual Texas Bash** (March, at the Paramount Theatre, Austin, and Gruene Hall, New Braunfels), celebrating the singer's birthday, and the summer outdoor concert series in **Zilker Park** (www.zilkerpark.org), also the venue for the big Austin City Limits Music Festival (www.aclfestival.com), a music festival featuring headliners like Pearl Jam and others, which takes place in fall.

SHOPPING

Where to Shop

Dallas

Dallas boasts that it has more shopping centers per capita than any other US city. Not only is it home to the internationally recognized specialty store **Neiman Marcus** and the retail department store giant

J.C. Penney but it is also the site of America's oldest shopping center, **Highland Park Village**, a high-end shopping mall sporting the likes of shoe maven Jimmy Choo and avant-garde designer Todd Oldham, who is a Dallas native.

Most of the major names in retailing are represented in Dallas, many in the four-level **Galleria** (LBJ Freeway & Dallas Parkway), with 200 stores, including Saks Fifth Avenue and Macy's, in a dramatic glass atrium supplemented by an ice rink and a Westin hotel.

Other huge malls include **NorthPark Center**, which also has a Macy's, as well as Nordstrom and Neiman Marcus. **Love Field Antique Mall**, behind the Mobil station at the entrance to Dallas's Love Field Airport, has 350 shops in addition to a collection of classic cars.

As with everything else, there are a number of specialty stores. **The Englishman's Furniture and Design,** founded in England in 1968, has a vast array of Staffordshire pottery, Welsh dressers, and other European furniture. Uncommon Market has a nice selection of English and French antiques.

Fort Worth

Sundance Square, in downtown Fort Worth, is fun to visit with its collection of antique and western shops, restaurants, and museums set among red-brick sidewalks and charming courtyards. Fort Worth is the place to buy western attire, of course. You can get fitted for a pair of classic roper boots at Justin Boots Outlet Store or a Stetson hat at Peter Bros. Hats. Be warned, stores in the Stockyards Historic District tend toward souvenir shops and kitsch.

Austin

Austin's biggest mall is **Highland Mall**, but there are also numerous little specialty stores, such as the **Turquoise Trading Post**, (Burnet Road at Koenig), which displays a large selection of American Indian jewelry, including Zuni fetishes, Navajo kachina dolls, medicine wheels, and dreamcatchers.The more macabre-minded will enjoy the selection of skulls, hides, and trophy mounts available at the **Corner Shoppe** on Lamar Street.

In the heart of Austin, you'll find many unique local boutiques in the Second Street District, including favorites like Heritage Boot, where owner Jerry Ryan designs each pair of his artsy footwear. The 23rd

Street Renaissance Market, across from UT, is a good place to pick up handicrafts. Waterloo Records is renowned for its knowledgeable staff and extensive selection of recordings by Texas musicians. Less than 30 minutes from Austin and an hour from San Antonio is **San Marcos Premium Outlets**, the largest factory outlet center in Texas, and one of the state's most popular travel destinations, with more than 145 stores offering big discounts on brand names such as Coach, Hugo Boss, Kate Spade, and more.

San Antonio

Visitors to San Antonio's **North Star Mall** (Loop 410 between San Pedro and MacCullough) are invited to begin their browsing with a visit to the information booth to pick up a free shopping bag and a coupon booklet offering discounts at many of the 200 stores. These include such big names as Saks Fifth Avenue, Marshall Field's, Guess, Williams-Sonoma, and Gap.

There are other malls, of which the most attractive architecturally is **Rivercenter**, 849 E. Commerce, adjoining the restaurants and IMAX theater in the heart of downtown. **La Villita**, the recreated Mexican village on the site of the original town, and **El Mercado** (514 W. Commerce), with 32 specialty shops, both offer Mexican arts and crafts.

San Antonio is home to **Luchese Boots**, maker of fine hand-tooled cowboy boots. You'll find unique gifts at the **San Antonio Museum of Art,** and in other museum shops.

Houston

There are more than 30 malls in the Houston area. In the city's southwest section, **Rice Village** draws the crowds with more than 300 stores ranging from familiar names to fashionable designer boutiques and funky mom-and-pop shops. There are also art and craft galleries and spas. Even bigger is the **Galleria** in the River Oaks area Uptown, which has 375 big-name stores, including Neiman Marcus, Tiffany, Hermes, Marshall Fields, and Saks Fifth Avenue. It claims to draw 10,000 visitors per day.

Three blocks east, the **Highland Village Shopping Center** also features upscale stores. For hard-to-find antiques and arty treasures, check out **The Heights,** whose streets (between 11th and 19th) are lined with Victorian structures and Craftsman-style bungalows. You'll

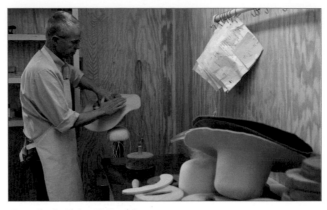

Hat-maker in Alpine, Big Bend Country.

find classic western wear at **Rick's Ranchwear** and **Cavender's Boot City**, which has 11 separate locations in Houston alone.

El Paso

Shopping in El Paso runs the gamut, given its proximity to both Mexico and New Mexico: gift shops and boutiques stand shoulder to shoulder with major department store chains in large malls. The name of the game in El Paso, though, is cowboy boots. Not for nothing does it proclaim itself Boot Capital of the World. It's home to 12 cowboy boot manufacturers, including **Tony Lama**, which has three factory outlets in the city. If you decide to treat your feet to a pair of custom handmade boots (starting at around $1,000 and hand lasted to your unique foot specifications for comfort), check out **Rocketbuster Boots**. Owner Nevena Christi is boot designer to the stars, and has custom designed and made boots that are pieces of art for everyone from Dwight Yoakum to Julia Roberts.

SPORTS

Participant Sports

Water Sports

Canoeing, tubing, and rafting take place on the Guadalupe River in Gruene. Contact **Gruene River Company** (tel: 830-625-2800; www.gruenerivercompany.com) or **Rockin R River Rides** (tel: 830-629-9999; www.rockinr.com). These companies are located next door to each other on Gruene Road, New Braunfels. Similar activities are also available on the Rio Grande. Contact

Far Flung Outdoor Center (tel: 800-839-7278; www.bigbendfarflung.com) in Terlingua. If you're a foodie and you're interested in pushing the boat out, consider taking one of the three-day fall gourmet raft trips with Swiss-born Francois Maeder (www.bigbendfarflung.com/river-trips/gourmet-on-the-rio-grande), chef-owner of the romantic fine dining restaurant Crumpets in San Antonio. Food really does taste better outside.

Cycling

Austin-based **Planet Earth Adventures** (tel: 800-923-4453; www.planetearthadventures.com) has a reputation for well-organized, multi-day cycle tours of the Davis Mountains, the Texas Hill Country, and Bandera.

Golf

The Dallas/Fort Worth area has over 200 golf courses, including: **Bridlewood Golf Club** (4000 W. Windsor Drive, Flower Mound; tel: 972-355-4800; www.bridlewoodgolf.com). A 7,000-yard (6,400-meter) course with lakes and a meandering creek. **Bear Creek Golf Course** (3500 Bear Creek Court, Dallas; tel: 972-456-3200; www.bearcreek-golf.com). Trees line the fairways of two 18-hole courses at this Dallas favorite at the DFW/Fort Worth Airport. **Hank Haney Golf** (2791 S. Stemmens Freeway, Lewisville; tel: 972-315-5300; www.hankhaney.com). Illuminated four-hole course, mini courses, and driving range next to the Dallas Market Center in Uptown. **L.una Vista Golf Course** (11223 Luna Road, Dallas; tel: 214-670-6322; www.lunavistagolf.com).

Formerly LB Houston, this par 72 municipal golf course has been transformed by the City into an attractive course for all skill levels. In San Antonio:

Hyatt Regency Hill Country Resort and Spa (9800 Hyatt Resort Drive; tel: 210-520-4040; www.hillcountry. hyatt.com).

Westin La Cantera Golf Club (16641 La Cantera Parkway; tel: 210-558-4653; www.lacanteragolfclub. com). A popular and very challenging Palmer golf course that was once used for the Westin Texas Open every fall.

Horseback Riding

Horseback trail riding can be found 2 miles (3km) north of downtown San Antonio in **Brackenridge Park** (3700 N. St Mary's Street; tel: 210-207-3000; www.sanantonio.gov/ parksandrec/directory_directory.aspx). Also try **Fredricksburg Western Adventures** (tel: 830-997-0288), a dude ranch that offers guided and unguided trail rides, camera tours, and ranch experiences of real cowboy life.

Other centers include: **Skyline Ranch** (1801 E. Wheatland Road, Dallas; tel: 972-224-8055; www.skylineranch.com) and **Texas Rose Horse Park** (14078 State Highway 110N, Tyler; tel: 903-882-8696; www.texasrosehorsepark.com).

Many Texas state parks have equestrian trails and campsites, but you will have to bring your own steed. However, in West Texas, Old West Stables (tel: 806-488-2180; www.oldweststables.com) offers horseback trail rides inside Palo Duro Canyon State Park from March to November, a wonderful way of seeing this beautiful park.

com), in October, and the **Valero Texas Open** (tel: 201-345-3818; www.valerotexasopen.com), in March, are held at the AT&T Oaks Course at TPC San Antonio Golf Club. And in Houston, the Shell Houston Open (5810 Wilson Road, suite 112, Humble; tel: 281-454-7000; www.shellhoustonopen. com), is played in the first week of April on the Golf Club of Houston Tournament Course.

Motor Racing

NASCAR racing goes on at San **Antonio Speedway** (14901 State. Highway 16, tel: 210-628-1499; www.sa-speedway.com) and at **Texas Motor Speedway** (3545 Lone Star Circle, Fort Worth; tel: 817-215-8500; www.texasmotorspeedway. com).

ACTIVITIES FOR CHILDREN

Houston's **Johnson Space Center** (2101 NASA Parkway; tel: 281-483-0123; www.nasa.gov/centers/ johnson), is one of the biggest family attractions, with its interactive exhibits, IMAX films about being an astronaut (shown on a screen five stories high), a moon rock display, space shuttle replica, information on NASA research, and behind-the-scenes tour by tram. Another giant screen can be found in the Wortham IMAX Theatre at the **Houston Museum of Natural Science** (5555 Hermann Park Drive; tel: 713-639-4629; www.hmns.org), which also includes a planetarium and a butterfly garden. Houston has a **Children's Museum of Houston** (1500 Binz St; tel: 713-522-1138; www.cmhouston.

org) with hands-on exhibits and mockups of ethnic villages.

The Dallas–Fort Worth area has a variety of amusement parks and attractions including the huge theme park **Six Flags Over Texas** (tel: 817-640-8900; www.sixflags.com/ overtexas) and adjoining **Six Flags Hurricane Harbor Water Park**, a family park featuring a plunging raft ride, whirlpools, wave pools, rain tunnels, and a sandy beach. Both of these are in Arlington. The **Sandy Lake Amusement Park** (1800 Sandy Lake Road; tel: 972-242-7449; www.sandylake.com) in Carrollton features paddleboats, miniature golf, and a giant swimming pool. The five-mile journey on Fort Worth's **Forest Park Miniature Railroad** (2700 Trinity Park Drive; tel: 817-336-3328; www.fpmt.us) is a pleasant way to slow the pace.

San Antonio has two theme parks: **Sea World of Texas** (10500 Sea World Drive; tel: 210-523-3000; www.seaworldparks.com/seaworld-sanantonio), a 250-acre (100-hectare) park with killer whales (orcas), a shark-infested coral reef, and a park with waterslides and exotic birds; and **Six Flags Fiesta Texas** (W. I-10 & Loop 1604; tel: 210-697-5050; www.sixflags.com/fiestatexas), with all the familiar attractions.

The **Austin Visitors and Convention Bureau** (602 E. Fourth Street; tel: 512-478-0098; www.austintexas.org) has information on family things to do in Austin, including activities such as watching the peacocks in Mayfield Park, shopping in a tiny grocery store in the Children's Museum, taking a miniature train ride in Zilker Park, or trying computer animation at the Dougherty Arts Center.

Spectator Sports

Horse Racing

Retama Park (1 Retama Parkway, Selma, just north of San Antonio on I-35; tel: 210-651-7000; www.retamapark.com).

Lone Star Park at Grand Prairie (1000 Lone Star Parkway, Grand Prairie; tel: 972-263-7223; www.lonestarpark.com).

Golf

The **AT&T Byron Nelson Championship** (tel: 972-717-0700; www.hpbnc.org/byronnelson) brings world-class golfers to Irving every May. Both the **AT&T Championship** (tel: 210-698-3582; www.attchamp.

Who Plays Where

The Dallas Cowboys play football in the AT&T Stadium in Arlington (tel: 972-556-9900; www.dallas cowboys.com).

The Dallas Stars play hockey, Sept– Apr, at Dallas's American Airlines Center (tel: 214-467-8277; www.stars.nhl.com).

The Texas Rangers play baseball April–October in Rangers Ballpark in Arlington (tel: 817-273-5100; www.texasrangers.com).

FC Dallas plays soccer at FC Dallas Stadium in Frisco (tel: 469-365-0000; www.fcdallas.com).

The Dallas Mavericks play basketball at the American Airlines

Center (tel: 214-747-6287; www.mavs.com).

The Houston Astros play baseball at Minute Maid Park (tel: 713-259-8000; www.houston.astros. mlb.com).

The Houston Texans play football at the NRG Stadium (tel: 832-667-2002; www.houstontexans.com).

The San Antonio Missions play baseball at Nelson Wolff Stadium (tel: 210-625-7275; www.samissions.com).

The San Antonio Spurs play basketball at the Alamodome (tel: 210-444-50550; www.nba.com/ spurs).

TRANSPORTATION

ACTIVITIES

A – Z

A – Z

A HANDY SUMMARY OF PRACTICAL INFORMATION

A

Accommodations

Hotels

Whatever your budget, you should be able to find a suitable place to spend the night in Texas for between $50 and $150 per night. In addition to independently owned hotels and motels in every price range, even the many chains operating in Texas reach into some of its smallest towns.

At the expensive end of the scale there are Sheratons, Hiltons, Marriotts, and Hyatt Regencies. A more moderately price choice would be the Holiday Inns, La Quintas, Ramada Inns, and Drury Inns. Quality Inns and Best Westerns are reasonable; the Motel 6, Days Inn, Rodeway Inn, and Travelodge chains are at the budget end of the market.

Bed and Breakfast

Bed and breakfast rates in Texas are generally reasonable; plan on spending $100–150 per night. In historic districts or towns, there is not much of a distinction made between "bed and breakfast" and "historic inn," since they are much the same. For information and reservations at many Texas's B&Bs contact or visit the website of **Texas Bed and Breakfast Association**, PO Box 1647, Brenham, TX 77834-1647; tel: 979-836-5951; www.texasbb.org.

Campgrounds

There are hundreds of state, federal, or privately owned campgrounds throughout Texas – over 400 privately owned campgrounds alone. Federally managed campgrounds in national parks and national recreation areas (National Park Service), national forests (US Forest Service), and the 20-plus impounded lakes administered by the US Army Corps of Engineers, are all now on a central reservation system. Reserve at www.recreation.gov or call 888-448-1474. Reservations may be made up to six months in advance. Note: If you have not made a reservation (advisable during the busy summer season), most NPS and USFS campgrounds have a number of first-come-first-serve sites, but these go fast, so be sure to arrive early in the day to get a spot.

Around 70 Texas parks and recreation areas managed by the state allow camping within their boundaries. **Texas Parks and Wildlife Division's Central Reservations** (www.tpwd.state. tx.us/business/park_reservations; tel: 512-389-8900) can reserve sites anywhere within the state park system. A useful free booklet, *Texas Public Campgrounds*, available from the Travel and Information Division can be downloaded at http://ftp.dot. state.tx.us/pub/txdot-info/trv/camp grounds.pdf, or contact the State Department of Transportation, PO Box 5064, Austin, TX 78763.

The *RV Travel and Camping Guide to Texas*, a booklet listing about half the total number of private campgrounds in Texas can be downloaded at www.texascamp grounds.com. It is published by the **Texas Association of Campground Owners (TACO)**. In addition, the **Texas Kampground Owners Association (KOA)**, www.koa.com, can provide a list of 20 member campgrounds around the state.

Vacation Rentals

Condominiums and beachfront/ bayfront homes are available to rent in some areas, particularly on Galveston and South Padre islands. Check the Yellow Pages under "Realtors," or contact: **Century 21 Bay Reef Realty**, 12200 FM 3005, Galveston, TX 77554; tel: 409-737-2300; www.bayreef.com; or **Island Services**, 1700 Padre Boulevard, South Padre Island, TX 78597; tel: 800-926-6926; www.pirentals.com.

Admission Charges

Some of Texas's most famous sights – the **Grassy Knoll** in Dallas, **the Alamo** in San Antonio – are free, and so are many museums in this wealthy state. Otherwise, most museums charge $5–10 per adult, although many have free entry days during the week.

The **Museum of Fine Arts, Houston** is free on Thursdays, while the **Dallas Museum of Art** is free on Tuesday nights and on the first Tuesday of every month. The **Lyndon B. Johnson Library and Museum** on the UT Campus in Austin is free all the time. At the other extreme, the **Johnson Space Center** in Houston charges $22.95 (with a $5 discount if you buy your tickets ahead of time online).

B

Budgeting for Your Trip

Texas has options both cost-conscious and luxurious in accommodations, food, and transportation. At one end lie budget motels for around $50 a night and national restaurant chains where dinner is less than $10. Conversely, the major cities all have swanky restaurants and luxury hotels with penthouse suites whose daily rate runs up to $2,500. The average lies somewhere between. Travelers can expect to spend $100–150 per night for a room in a decent hotel or bed-and-breakfast; prices and selection drop in less urban areas. Allow $20–25 per meal, although Texas's excellent "home-cooking" restaurants, barbecue joints, and food trucks are cheaper. Dinner at a big-city restaurant with fine dining starts at around $60 per person.

Rental cars cost approximately $350 per week, including unlimited mileage, Texas tax and license, and a vague surcharge called a "facility fee." In addition, Texas applies higher add-on fees for cars rented from the airport than any other state, with mark-ups averaging more than 50 percent.

Greyhound is the major bus line, with routes to and from all of Texas's largest cities. Tickets range from $30 (Austin–San Antonio) to $45 (Dallas–San Antonio); to ride from Dallas to Houston is $52.

C

Climate

What To Wear

For clothing, fabrics such as cotton, linen, and wool provide the best comfort in the Texas climate. Go particularly light in summer, but because of varying altitude and cool breezes, a sweater may be needed in the evening. The midwinters of

Sightseeing in summer calls for lightweight clothing.

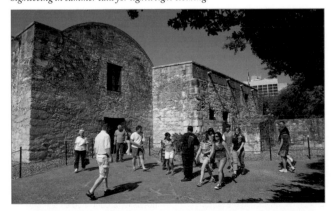

Central and East Texas, the Coastal Prairie, and the Rio Grande Valley usually require only a lightweight coat. In the mountains, High Plains, and Panhandle, winters can be so severe that you need layers of warm clothes.

Texans are very casual dressers and away from the office blue jeans are the norm. They are worn almost anywhere, anytime of the day, dressed up or down by changing a shirt, sweater, jacket, or accessories. People in Dallas and Houston dress formally for some evening events, but casual pants and dresses for women and shirt-sleeves or tieless shirts and jackets for men are acceptable almost anywhere you go.

With few exceptions, Western dress is informal and geared toward practical clothing for enjoying the outdoors. A pair of jeans or slacks, a polo or button-down shirt, and cowboy boots or shoes are appropriate at all but the fanciest places and events. Shorts and light shirts are suitable for most situations in the warmer months, though.

Year round, wear sunscreen with a SPF of at least 30, polarized eye protection, a broad-brimmed hat (cowboy hats are optional but very useful) to protect head and neck, layered clothing with sleeves and legs that can be rolled down as sun protection, and sturdy hiking footwear that secure the foot for walking on rough ground – flip flops are fine at the beach, but you won't want these when you are doing a lot of walking, wherever you are.

If you're hiking, a thin, inner polypropolene sock and a thick, outer sock will help keep your feet dry and comfortable. Blisters or sore spots can develop quickly. Cover them with moleskin or surgical tape, available

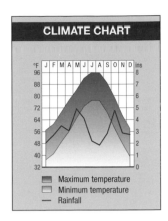

at most pharmacies or camping supply stores. Bring a warm coverup and rain shell; even in summer, the high country weather can be cool and suddenly rainy.

When To Go

A uniform description of either winter or summer weather in Texas is impossible: while it's snowing in the Panhandle, people wintering on the Gulf Coast may be getting a tan at the beach; Central Texas may be baking in the late-summer heat while the Guadalupe Mountains feel the early-fall chill.

Average temperatures of 30–50°F (around 0–10°C) in winter and 70–90°F (20–30°C) in summer do not vary greatly around the state, but the humidity factor and elevation affect the comfort level considerably. Central Texas, East Texas, the Coastal Prairie, and the Rio Grande Valley are humid and close to sea level, so it is usually very hot and sticky in the summer, often exceeding 100°F (38°C) between May and October.

Although it doesn't usually snow or freeze in these areas, occasionally it does so in a big way. It is not unknown for cities as far south as Austin and San Antonio to be blanketed with snow, shutting down businesses and roads completely for the duration. In the Panhandle and the higher elevations of the Davis Mountains, the Guadalupe Mountains, and the Big Bend area, where fall comes earlier than in the southern part of the state, there is little humidity except snow, which is common in the winters, sometimes causing roads and mountain areas to be closed to the public.

"Tornado Alley" runs through the state, and peak twister season lasts from late spring to early summer.

Annual rainfall ranges from 8–16 inches (20–40cm) in the dry Big Bend region, to over 48 inches (122cm) in the wettest parts of the state, such as Houston and East Texas.

The best time for statewide travel is late Oct/Nov, March and April, and late May/early June. This will avoid, for the most part, Texas's hottest and coldest temperatures and the heaviest rainfall.

Crime and Security

While most people go about their business safely, the fact remains that like any large American cities, Houston, Dallas, San Antonio, and El Paso have their incidences of crime and violence. Do not walk a long way after dark in strange or deserted parts of town. Keep a watchful eye on your belongings. Do not leave your car unlocked in parking lots, and never leave your children alone. Smaller towns in Texas have much lower crime rates, but use the same precautions everywhere as you would in a big city. Be especially mindful in border regions that see a lot of undocumented migrant activity, both in border towns and rural areas many miles inland. Due to heavy policing and international cooperation, the incidences of drug war crime have started to drop substantially in places like El Paso/Juárez, which used to be one of the most violent cities in the US. Other border crossings away from urban areas may not be as safe, however, so be careful.

Hotels usually warn you that they will not guarantee the safety of belongings left in your hotel room. If you have any valuables, you may want to lock them in the hotel safe.

To reach the police in an emergency dial **911**. For police non-emergencies dial **311**.

Customs Regulations

Everyone entering the United States must go through US Customs, often a time-consuming process. You may bring in duty-free gifts worth up to $100 ($800 for returning US residents). Visitors over 21 may bring in 200 cigarettes, 4.4lbs (2kg) of smoking tobacco, and 50 cigars (not Cuban); quantities permitted are higher for US residents. Those over 21 may bring in 1 quart (1 liter) of alcohol. Travelers with more than $10,000 in US or foreign currency, traveler's checks, or money orders must declare these upon entry.

Among prohibited goods are meat or meat products, illegal drugs, firearms, seeds, plants, and fruits.

For a breakdown of up-to-date US Customs and Border Protection regulations, contact US Customs Service, PO Box 407, Washington, DC 20044; tel: 877-227-5511; www.cbp.gov.

D

Disabled Travelers

The 1995 Americans with Disabilities Act (ADA) brought sweeping changes to facilities across America. Accommodations with five or more rooms must be useable by persons with disabilities (where possible). Older and smaller inns and lodges are often wheelchair accessible, but always ask. For the sight-impaired, many hotels provide special alarm clocks, closed-captioned TV services, and security measures. To comply with ADA hearing-impaired requirements, many hotels have begun to follow special procedures; local agencies may provide text telephone (TTY) and interpretation sevices.

Check with the hotel when you make reservations to ascertain the degree to which the hotel complies with ADA guidelines. Ask specific questions about bathroom facilities, bed height, wheelchair space, and availability of services.

Many attractions have wheelchairs for loan or rent; most parks today also offer barrier-free or accessible trails. Some provide special visitor publications for disabled visitors and interpreters and visitor guides. The Society for Accessible Travel and Hospitality (tel: 212-447-7284; www.sath.org) publishes a quarterly magazine on travel for the disabled.

E

Electricity

Standard electricity in North America is 110–115 volts, 60 cycles AC. An adapter is necessary for most appliances from overseas, with the exception of Japan.

Embassies and Consulates

Australia 4623 Feagan Street, Houston, TX 77007; tel: 713-782-6009.

Canada 750 N. St. Paul Street, Suite 1700, Dallas, TX 75201; tel: 214-922-9806.
5847 San Felipe Street, Suite 1700, Houston, TX 77057; tel: 713-821-1440.
106 South St. Mary's Street, Suite 800, San Antonio, TX 78205; tel: 210-299-3525.
United Kingdom 2911 Turtle Creek Boulevard, Suite 940, Dallas, TX 75219.
254 Spencer Lane, San Antonio, TX 78201; tel: 210-738-1704.
Wells Fargo Plaza, (19th Floor), 1000 Louisiana Street, Suite 1900, Houston, TX 77002, tel: 713-659-6270.

Emergency Numbers

For all emergencies requiring police, fire or ambulance dial 911.
Road conditions on state highways, tel: 1-800-452-9292.
Information on evacuation routes, shelters and special-needs transportation, tel: 211
Poison, tel: 1-800-764-7661 (Texas), 1-800-222-1212 (national).
American Red Cross, tel: 1-888-568-3318.
Roadside assistance, tel: 800-525-5555.
Texas crime stoppers, tel: 800-252-8477.
To report a missing person, tel: 800-346-3243.

Etiquette

The key word here is "relaxed." Openness and natural friendliness rule. Don't be surprised when strangers smile broadly at you and ask how you are doing as you pass them in the street. You can expect almost everyone with whom you come into contact to ask how you are feeling, where you come from, where you are going and, if you prove to be a foreigner, whether you are married, how many children you have, what your job is, and why you are here. Or they may just ask how you're "doin'."

This is not inappropriate behavior, personally invasive, or presumptuous, not even an attempt to begin a long, intimate conversation. It is natural friendliness and goodwill that prompts these genial greetings and enquiries from passersby, waiters, and salespeople who suddenly become new Texas friends. Don't even be surprised at a congenial slap on the back to emphasize a point, or – particularly in South Texas – a friendly embrace in greeting.

Health regulations prohibit all animals, except seeing-eye dogs, in public eating places in Texas.

G

Gay and Lesbian Travelers

Texas's urban centers, especially Dallas, Houston, San Antonio, and Austin, have large gay and lesbian populations, with corresponding businesses and services. In particular, Houston has the sixth largest gay population in the country, and has just become the largest US city to elect an openly gay mayor, Annise Parker. Both Dallas and Houston have gay neighborhoods around which the community is centered: Oak Lawn in Dallas, and the Montrose district in Houston.

Dallas has a weekly publication that comes out every Friday called *The Voice* (www.dallasvoice.com). Houston has a magazine called *OutSmart* (www.outsmartmagazine. com); Austin has *Q Monthly* Magazine (www.qmonthlyaustin. com). In addition, Houston has a comprehensive online guide at www.houstongayguide.com.

In September, Dallas hosts the annual Dallas Pride **Alan Ross Texas Freedom Parade** (www.dallaspride. com), while Houston and Austin both have parades in June, called **Houston Pride** (www.pridehouston.org) and **Austin Pride** (www.austinprideparade. org). Austin is home to the annual **Gay & Lesbian International Film Festival** every fall (usually in late September; www.agliff.org), while Dallas has **Out Takes**, an annual lesbian and gay film festival in November (www.outtakesdallas.org/index.asp).

Dallas's **Cathedral of Hope** (www.cathedralofhope.com) is said to be the largest gay and lesbian church in the world.

H

Health and Medical Care

Depending upon the country from which you are traveling or through which you have just come, you may need an international vaccination certificate. Many types of over-the-counter (OTC) medications are readily available, but if you're using prescription medication, it's best to

Bat colonies are an impressive sight, but direct contact with these creatures should be avoided.

bring extra, along with a spare pair of prescription glasses if you use them. Tap water is fine to drink, but if you're out camping in the more remote parts of some of the state's national parks or national forests, it is best to bring your own or use purifiers.

Emergency Medical Services

In the event of an emergency, **dial 911** (the operator will put you through to the police, ambulance, or fire services). The call is toll free anywhere in the US, including on cell phones. If you can't get through, **dial 0** for an operator. In national parks, it's best to contact a ranger.

Most cities have 24-hour pharmacies (drugstores), urgent care clinics, hospitals with emergency rooms, and poison control centers. Look in the Yellow Pages or the inside cover of the telephone book, or dial 411 for telephone operator assistance.

Precautions

Much of Texas is made up of wide open spaces (that is, all its small and sprawling cities together occupy only a tiny portion of the state), so anyone who spends much time exploring it has a good chance of coming into contact with a poisonous insect or snake. Don't forget: you are in their home territory, so avoidance is always the best strategy. If you are walking in a field, for example, cover up with loose clothing secured at neck, ankles, and wrists to discourage ticks and chiggers from finding a spot in which to embed themselves. Tall, thick boots help protect against stinging ground insects and reptiles. Watch out for loose mounds of dirt

in grassy areas, which could house fireants. Once disturbed (test the area with a long stick), they will swarm at great speed and can be all over your legs in no time. Be careful with children as they may not think fast enough to brush off the ants once attacked.

Rabies: Raccoons, skunks, bats, and squirrels can all be found in Texas, but should not be touched; they are potential carriers of rabies, which is easily transmitted to people.

Insects: The bite or sting of a spider, ant, or scorpion is not usually fatal, but it can cause a lot of pain and itching and the area around it may swell. In most cases, discomfort gradually subsides. If extreme symptoms such as numbness, tingling, shooting pain, high temperature, low blood pressure, abdominal cramps, spasms, breathing difficulty, or problems focusing the eyes occur, see a physician at once. Remember that bringing the insect with you greatly aids the doctor.

In Texas, chiggers are often referred to as "red bugs." A salve from the drugstore may help relieve the itching, but you will just have to wait for it to go away. The same is true of the bite of the mosquito, found by the million around water in low-lying areas. Try to avoid getting bitten by mosquitoes as out in the American West, they carry West Nile Virus.

Snakes: Snakes are not quite the omnipresent menace that strangers in Texas fear. They usually remain in fields or sand dunes and often hide under logs or in holes, waiting to hunt at night or early in the morning. In addition, most snakes in Texas are harmless and only strike in self-

TRANSPORTATIO
ACTIVITIES
A – Z

defense. Just entering a snake's territory and standing too close can agitate it enough to strike, so be cautious: walk in the open when possible, proceed with caution among rocks, sweep grassy areas with a long stick before entering, avoid dark or overgrown places where snakes might lurk, and shake out bedding or clothing that has been lying on the ground.

Coral snakes are abundant in Texas. Because of their beauty and relatively small size, youngsters frequently pick them up, so be sure to discourage children from picking up strange animals. Rattlesnakes and coral snakes have very different toxins: the toxin of the former attacks the nervous system, while the latter primarily affects the respiratory system. Treatment consists of injecting very different antivenins, so identification is extremely important.

If you are bitten, at least try to see what the snake looked like. A positive identification is extremely important for the physician making a treatment decision. Do not attempt any first-aid treatments such as freezing the limb, tourniquets, or the outdated cut-and-suck method. Instead, go to the emergency room of the local hospital at once.

Jellyfish: Portuguese man-of-war jellyfish are found in their hundreds on Padre Island. Washed ashore, their blue balloon-like forms with long tentacles continue to pulsate for a while. If you are stung by their tentacles – either on shore or in the water, where they are harder to avoid – you may develop rashes and red welts. A few sensitive victims go into shock or endure fever, cramps, and nausea. Some lifeguards treat these stings with meat tenderizer; others wash the area with sodium bicarbonate, boric acid, lemon juice, or alcohol. If symptoms are severe, you should see a physician.

Insurance

It's vital to have medical insurance when traveling. Athough hospitals are obligated to provide emergency treatment to anyone who needs it, regardless of whether they do or don't have insurance, you may have to prove you can pay for treatment of anything less than a life-threatening condition. Know what your policy covers and have proof of the policy with you at all times, or be prepared to pay at the time service is rendered. Your travel insurance should cover both

yourself and your belongings. Your own insurance company or travel agent can advise you on policies, but shop around since rates vary. Make sure you are covered for accidental death, emergency medical care, repatriation, trip cancellation, and baggage or document loss.

L

Lost Property

Texas is too big and too hands-off organizationally to have a central repository for lost items. The best you'll find might be a form you can fill out such as the one offered by the Dallas Police Department (www.dallaspolice.net/content/11/66/uploads/lostpropformenglish.pdf).

M

Maps

Mapsco (www.kappamapgroup.com) is the big map company of Texas. It publishes thick, complex binders of most major Texas cities, much like London's A-Z. At approximately $36, they're not cheap, but their level of detail is useful for those who will be driving around a city and need an explicit, page-by-page street guide. The Roads of Texas is a more practical, one-volume set of detailed maps that covers Texas's entire road system.

The **Automobile Association of America** (see page 297) provides excellent road maps and personalized trip planning for its members.

The **Insight Fleximaps** to Dallas/Fort Worth, Houston, and San Antonio are laminated and immensely durable.

Media

Print

In this rapidly expanding era of electronic publishing and free information on the world wide web, print media has undergone a massive contraction. Yet most communities still publish print editions of newspapers, as well as electronic versions, and the opinions and endorsements of columnists and editorial boards continue to play an important role in community life. Dallas and Houston have more than one daily newspaper, covering local, national, and international

Local Dialing Codes

Abilene 325
Amarillo 806
Austin 512
Corpus Christi/Padre Island 361
Dallas 214, 469, 972
Del Rio 830
El Paso 915
Fort Worth 682, 817
Galveston 409
Lake Jackson 979
Laredo/McAllen 956
Lufkin/Huntsville 936
Houston 281, 713, 832
San Antonio 210
Tyler 903
Waco 254

news. There are also several weekly newspapers in most cities that cover local and, sometimes, statewide news. Local newspapers include: *Dallas Morning News, El Paso Times, Fort Worth Star-Telegram, Galveston Daily News, Houston Chronicle, San Antonio Express-News, and Waco Tribune-Herald.*

In addition, Texas has some interesting and worthwhile alternative free newspapers, which usually offer a good source of information on local culture, politics, and community in each city. These include the *FW Weekly* (Fort Worth), *Houston Free Press* (Houston), *Austin Chronicle* (Austin), *Dallas Observer* (Dallas), *Texas Observer* (Austin), and *San Antonio Current* (San Antonio).

The Texas Department of Transportation (125 E. 11th Street, Austin, TX 78701; tel: 800-558-9368; www.txdot.gov) publishes the state's official monthly travel magazine, *Texas Highways* (www.texashighways.com), an attractive color magazine, as well as a weekly online newsletter. *Texas Monthly* (www.texasmonthly.com), a great way to tap into the pulse of Texas, is available at most newsstands.

There are also magazines dedicated to a particular city, such as *D Magazine* in Dallas. Bookstores display a wide array of books about Texas, from the *Texas Almanac* – covering every conceivable subject – to comprehensive bed-and-breakfast listings and cycling trip guides.

Radio and Television

There are over 70 television stations and at least 550 AM and FM radio stations in Texas. Thanks to cable, satellite, or pay television, programs from all over the world can be seen almost any hour of the day or night.

Some rental cars also come with commercial-free satellite radio. The installation of cable in most hotels and motels and many homes means that how a particular station is found depends on where it appears on the cable to which they subscribe. Consult the newspaper for television listings. Radio listings are sometimes given in Sunday supplements of newspapers.

Money

Foreign visitors are advised to take US dollar travelers' checks to Texas, since exchanging foreign currency – whether as cash or checks – can prove problematic. An increasing number of banks offer foreign exchange facilities, but this practice is not universal. Some department store chains offer foreign currency exchange.

Most shops, restaurants, and other establishments accept travelers' checks in US dollars and will give change in cash. Checks can also be converted into cash at the bank.

Credit cards and debit cards are very much part of daily life in Texas. They can be used to pay for pretty much anything, and it is also common for car rental firms and hotels to take an imprint of your card as a deposit. Rental companies may oblige you to pay a large deposit in cash if you do not have a card.

You can also use your credit card to withdraw cash from ATMs

Public Holidays

Banks, federal, state, county, and city offices and private businesses often close during public holidays. Many stores remain open during weekends and holidays.

New Year's Day 1 January
Martin Luther King Jr.'s Birthday 15 January, although observed the third Monday in January
Presidents' Day Third Monday in February
Easter Sunday Late March/early April
Memorial Day Last Monday in May
Independence Day 4 July
Labor Day First Monday in September
Columbus Day Second Monday in October
Veterans Day 11 November
Thanksgiving Day Fourth Thursday in November
Christmas Day 25 December

(Automatic Teller Machines). Before you leave home, make sure you know your PIN and find out which ATM system will accept your card and whether a daily limit applies. The most widely accepted cards are Visa, American Express, MasterCard, Diners Club, Japanese Credit Bureau and Discovery. This is often the safest and easiest way to get cash when traveling.

Restaurant bills do not usually include a service charge unless you are in a group of five or more, when a gratuity of 15 percent may be added to the total and unless the service is dreadful, you are obligated; otherwise, tips of 10–20 percent are expected.

Fifteen percent is a good rule of thumb when tipping for any service, including taxi rides and haircuts, although some Texans have not got used to tipping barbers. Bellhops and parking attendants expect a dollar per bag or vehicle, shoeshiners more. If you stay more than a couple of nights in a better hotel, it is usually suggested to tip chambermaids a small amount for making up the room. Staff are low paid and generally rely on tips.

O

Opening Hours

Offices: Mon–Fri 8am–5pm.
Banks: Mon–Fri 9/10am–3/4pm (although most have drive-through facilities that stay open longer). Some banks are open on Saturday morning.
Retail shops: Mon–Fri 10/11am–5/6pm, except in large shopping malls, when hours are extended to 8, 9 or 10pm and weekends. A few retail stores are always open.
Museums: many are closed on Mondays.

P

Passports and Visas

A machine-readable passport, a visitor's visa, proof of intent to leave the US after your visit and (depending upon your country of origin) an international vaccination certificate, are required of most foreign nationals for entry into the US.

As part of the visa waiver program (VWP), visitors from the UK staying less than 90 days do not need a visa; however, it is compulsory

for non-US residents from VWP countries to submit information about themselves online to the Department of Homeland Security and register via the website of Electronic System for Travel Authorization (ESTA) (www.esta. us/travel_authorization.html) to be preapproved for travel to the US at least three days before they travel.

Vaccination certificate requirements vary, but proof of immunization against smallpox or cholera may be necessary.

US citizens traveling by air between the US, Canada, Mexico, the Caribbean, and Bermuda must present a current passport; a birth certificate and photo ID are no longer valid proof.

Due to increased security, the precise regulations for entry to the US change often, and vary for citizens of different countries. It's a good idea to check on the current situation before you travel, on the US State Department website (www.travel.state. gov) or via a US Embassy or Consulate in your home country. Any non-US citizen wishing to extend their stay should contact US Immigration and Naturalization Service at 425 I Street, Washington DC 20536; tel: 202-501-4444 or 800-407-4747.

Postal Services

First-class postage and priority mail are the same anywhere in Texas, or in the US, and bills arrive just as quickly in tiny Cut-and-Shoot as they do in big-city Dallas. Post offices open at 7, 8, or 9am and usually close at 5pm, Mon–Fri. Many of them are open for at least a couple of hours on Saturday mornings, but they are all closed on Sunday.

There may also be coin-operated machines that dispense stamps whether the office is open or not. Rates are usually listed nearby. There are US Post Office Information numbers in the phone book, or call 411 and ask the operator.

Visitors can receive mail at post offices if it is addressed to them, care of "General Delivery," followed by the city name and (very important) the zip code. You must pick up this mail in person within a week or two of its arrival and will be asked to show some form of valid personal identification.

Public Restrooms

You will rarely find public restroom facilities. Stores, malls, restaurants, and gas stations are your best bet.

R

Religious Services

Texas's population is primarily Protestant in the North, Central, and East sections (with Baptists in the majority) and Catholic in the South and West. Other religions and ethical systems represented in the state include Baha'i, Buddhism, Hinduism, Islam, and Judaism. Consult the Yellow Pages or ask at the desk of your hotel for the nearest place of worship.

T

Taxes

There is no state income tax in Texas, but the state charges a sales tax of 6.25 percent on most purchases, from clothing to electronics to dining out. Individual cities then apply their own percentage, usually totaling approximately 2 percent. The only major nontaxable exception is food purchased from a grocery store.

Telecommunications

In this era of cell phones, you'll find fewer public telephones in hotel lobbies, restaurants, drugstores, garages, roadside kiosks, convenience stores, and other locations. The cost of making a local call from a payphone for three minutes is 25–50 cents. 800 numbers and 911 calls are free. To make a long-distance call from a payphone, use either a prepaid calling card, available in airports, post offices, and a few other outlets, or your credit card, which you can use at any phone: dial 800-CALLATT, key in your credit card number, and wait to be connected. In many areas, local calls have now changed to a 10-digit calling system, using the area code.

To call from city to city in Texas, you must first find out the area code. The state's size requires that it be divided into different three-digit codes. The numbers of people moving to Texas and the proliferation of cell phones in recent years has resulted in more and more areas being assigned new area codes, often not long after they have been changed, so don't be surprised if an area code has changed from the one currently published. To call from one area to another, dial 1 before the three-digit area code and the local seven-digit telephone number.

There are Western Union cablegram offices in most Texas cities. Look in the local telephone directory in the white pages (for major cities, there may be separate books for businesses and residences). Messages and money can be sent over the wires immediately. You must have identification, such as a driver's license, to receive money.

Watch out for in-room connection charges, especially in more upscale hotels; it costs less to use the payphone in the lobby, although some hotels may offer free local calls. Likewise W-fi access is frequently free in hotel lobbies, but there is often a charge for it in guest rooms.

Time Zones

Texas spans two time zones: Central Standard Time (Greenwich Mean Time minus six hours) and, in the extreme western corner of the state, Mountain Standard Time (Greenwich Mean Time minus seven hours). Daylight Saving Time is observed in almost every part of the state and begins at 2am on the first Sunday in April when clocks are advanced one hour, and ends at 2am on the last Sunday in October.

Tourist Information

Most cities in Texas have a Convention and Visitors Bureau (CVB), where staff will provide you with brochures and maps. Elsewhere you must rely on the local chamber of commerce. They are oriented toward business people, but the staff is usually happy to help, particularly in tourist areas.

The Media section (see page 310) gives details of Texas periodicals containing useful information for visitors to the state. To request a free *Texas Travel Guide* and other Texas travel information, contact the Tourism Division, Texas Department of Commerce, P.O. Box 141009, Austin, TX 78714-1009, or visit www.traveltex.com. Most information is now available online.

Travel Information Centers

Texas has 12 Travel Information Centers operated by the Texas Department of Transportation (125 E. 11th Street, Austin, TX 78701; tel: 800-558-9368; www. txdot.gov), and offering state and highway information, trip planning, information on scenic wildflower trails, and so on. They are located off the interstate at the main state entry

points and other key points around the state: Amarillo, Anthony, Austin, Denison, Gainesville, Langtry, Laredo, Orange, Rio Grande Valley, Texarkana, Waskom, and Wichita Falls. You can download most of their publications from their website.

Main Tourist Offices

Austin, 201 E. Second Street, TX 78701; tel: 512-474-5171; www.austintexas.org.
Dallas, 1201 Elm Street, TX 75270, tel: 214-571-1000; www.dallascvb. com.
El Paso, 1 Civic Center Plaza, TX 79901; tel: 915-534-0696; www.elpasocvb.com.
Fort Worth, 415 Throckmorton Street, TX 76102; tel: 817-336-8791; www.fortworth.com.
Houston, 901 Bagby Street, TX 77002, tel: 713-437-5200; www.houston-guide.com
San Antonio, 203 S. St Mary's Street, (2nd Floor), TX 78205, tel: 210-207-6700; www.sanantoniocvb.com

Tour Operators

Gray Line bus tours are available in all the main Texas towns and cities, and also include specialty tours, such as a Hill Country Wine Tour by wine experts. For information tel: 800-472-9546, international direct 303-394-6950; www.grayline.com.
Specialty tour companies include:
Big Bend Far Flung Tours (tel: 800-839-7238; www.bigbendfarflung. com. This Terlingua-based company offers rafting trips on the Rio Grande through Big Bend National Park and Jeep tours.
Hill Country Wine Tours (tel: 830-329-9463; www.hcwinetours.com). Limousine tours from Fredericksburg to Hill Country wineries, hosted by experts.
Padre Island Safaris (tel: 361-937-8446; www.billysandifer.com). Natural history tours of Padre Island National Seashore by well-known fisherman and naturalist Billy Sandifer.
Artist Boat Kayak Adventures (tel: 409-770-0722; www.artistboat.org). Ecotours of Galveston Island using art and natural history to teach about the wild shore ecosystem.

W

Weights and Measures

Despite efforts to convert to metric, the US still uses the imperial system of weights and measures.

FURTHER READING

FICTION

Lonesome Dove by Larry McMurtry. Life in a frontier Texas town is explored in this romantic Western novel, part of a tetralogy.

Woman Hollering Creek and Other Stories by Sandra Cisneros. The Mexican-American author's childhood in San Antonio comes to life in these vivid border tales.

Texas by James Michener. After moving to Austin to research his fictionalized account of Texas history, Michener liked it so much he stayed.

All the Pretty Horses by Cormac McCarthy. A gritty tale of the border country and its harsh realities by the El Paso-born writer.

Two for Texas by James Lee Burke. Known for his Dave Robicheaux Louisiana detective tales, Burke's historic novel is set during the Texas War for Independence.

The Devil Went Down to Austin by Rick Riordan. Fast-talking and hard-living P.I. Navarre, the detective with the PhD in literature, untangles dirty goings on in the state capital in this popular series.

Thyme of Death by Susan Wittig Albert. Small town New Age herbalist shop owner Chyna Bayles solves more mysteries than Miss Marple in this popular series by the prolific Hill Country writer.

All the Land to Hold Us by Rick Bass. An extraordinarily visionary novel by the petroleum geologist turned natural history writer. Set in West Texas's dusty oil country as the community and the landscape fall apart and unlikely alliances are made.

CULTURE AND CURRENT AFFAIRS

The Tex-Mex Cookbook by Robb Walsh. The Austin food writer brings to life the cuisine and colorful characters of border country.

The Wine Roads of Texas by Wes Marshall with forewords by Robert Mondavi and Fess Parker. This look at Texas's emerging wineries by wine expert Marshall with two celebrated vintners inspired the PBS series of the same name.

Kinky Friedman's Guide to Texas Etiquette by Kinky Friedman. The Jewish humorist offers his take on Texas do's and don'ts.

Friday Night Lights by Bud Bissinger. The true story of the high school football team that united a small town in Texas.

An Unreasonable Woman: A True Story of Shrimpers, Politicos, Polluters, and the Fight for Seadrift, Texas by Diane Wilson. A Texas Erin Brockavich, Wilson recounts the amazing story of her fight against pollution in the Gulf.

Molly Ivins Can't Say That, Can She? by Molly Ivins. The famed humorist rakes the Texas legislature (and

Send Us Your Thoughts

We do our best to ensure the information in our books is as accurate and up-to-date as possible. The books are updated on a regular basis using local contacts, who painstakingly add, amend and correct as required. However, some details (such as telephone numbers and opening times) are liable to change, and we are ultimately reliant on our readers to put us in the picture.

We welcome your feedback, especially your experience of using the book "on the road". Maybe we recommended a hotel that you liked (or another that you didn't), or you came across a great bar or new attraction we missed.

We will acknowledge all contributions, and we'll offer an Insight Guide to the best letters received.

Please write to us at:
Insight Guides
PO Box 7910
London SE1 1WE
Or email us at:
hello@insightguides.com

others) over the coals.

The Liar's Club by Mary Karr. The first of a two-part memoir about the gritty childhood of this Texan writer.

The Tennis Partner by Abraham Verghese. Written by the well-known AIDS researcher (and author of the best-seller *Cutting for Stone*), this memoir poignantly captures his experiences caring for AIDS patients as a young doctor in El Paso in the 1980s.

As Texas Goes: How the Lone Star State Hijacked the American Agenda by Gail Collins. The humorous New York Times columnist explores the impact of Texan politics on national culture.

Chinati: The Vision of Donald Judd by Marianne Stockebrand. A look at how New York artist Donald Judd transformed Marfa.

Texas Towns and The Art of Architecture by Richard Payne. A lovely photographic tour of the buildings in the Texan landscape.

HISTORY

Gone to Texas: A History of the Lone Star State by Randolph (Mike) Campbell. An engaging history of the last 10,000 years of Texas history through its waves of immigrants.

The Longhorns by J. Frank Dobie. This classic book about the history of Texas longhorn cattle helped save the breed.

The Men Who Wear the Star by C.M. Robinson. An engaging look at the storied Texas Rangers.

Oil in Texas: The Gusher Age 1845–1945 by Diana Davids Olien and Roger M. Oliens. How oil has made Texas wealthy.

The Big Rich: The Rise and Fall of the Greatest Texas Fortunes by Bill Burrough. An entertaining account of Texas's Big Four oil tycoons: Roy Cullen, H. L. Hunt, Clint Murchison, and Sid Richardson.

The Years of Lyndon Johnson: The Path to Power by Robert A. Caro. The accomplishments of LBJ are explored by the famed political biographer.

TRANSPORTATION
ACTIVITIES
A – Z

TRAVEL

Journey Through Texas by Frederick Law Olmsted. Essays by the celebrated landscape architect about his 19th-century travels through Texas.

Goodbye to a River by John Graves. The author and his dog float the river before it is dammed and reflect on its natural history.

A Field Guide to the Birds of Texas by Roger Tory Peterson. An invaluable handbook by the famed ornithologist.

Roadside Geology of Texas by Darwin Spearing. A look at how Texas's oil-rich geology has helped make it rich and has created interesting landmarks.

Wildflowers of Texas: A Field Guide by Geyata Ajilvsgi. A perfect companion for spring wildflower travels.

OTHER INSIGHT GUIDES

Insight Guide titles cover nearly every major travel destination in North America, from Alaska to Arizona. City titles include Boston, *New York*, *Chicago*, and *San Francisco*. Regional and state titles include *Arizona and the Grand Canyon*, *California*, *Florida*, *Colorado*, *New England*, *Alaska*, and *USA on the Road*.

CREDITS

Photo Credits

123RF 205T, 235, 277
Alamy 28, 56, 57, 130, 185BR, 187, 189B, 218, 222, 229, 271
AP/Press Association Images 4BR
AWL Images 8/9, 12/13, 14, 44/45, 62, 72, 90/91, 92
Bigstock 129, 238, 264
Bruce Bernstein, Courtesy of Princeton Library, NJ 24, 30
Carol M. Highsmith/Library of Congress 1, 4BL, 5BR, 6T, 7ML, 29, 46, 47, 48, 49, 52, 53, 54, 55, 63, 65, 66, 67, 70, 73, 78, 79, 80, 82, 83, 97, 98, 99, 114, 119T, 125, 149T, 154, 156, 168/169T, 168BR, 169ML, 169BL, 184/185T, 189T, 191, 192T, 193, 194B, 194T, 195, 217T, 217B, 219, 220B, 224T, 231, 233T, 236T, 240, 243B, 243T, 245, 247T, 252, 253, 263T, 265, 266B, 267, 272T, 281, 288, 291, 298/299
Corbis 50, 59, 86/87, 230
DVCB 5MR, 102, 104, 105T, 105B, 106, 107B, 107T
Fort Worth CVB 112B, 112T, 115
Getty Images 5TL, 10/11, 16, 17, 20, 21, 33, 35, 38, 40, 41, 42, 51,

60, 61, 68, 76, 77, 88/89, 96, 100, 108, 116, 118, 119B, 120, 122, 128, 132, 133, 134, 136, 140B, 141, 149B, 152B, 157B, 186, 190, 196, 199, 202, 203, 205B, 207, 209, 210B, 211, 212, 213, 214, 215, 216, 223, 225, 227, 228, 234, 239, 244, 251, 256, 257, 258/259T, 258BR, 259ML, 259BR, 259TR, 269, 270, 284, 293
Greater Houston Convention and Visitors Bureau 4MR, 5TR, 43, 170, 171, 173B, 174, 175, 176, 177B, 177T, 179, 180, 181, 182, 294
iStock 2/3, 4ML, 5ML, 5BL, 7TR, 7TL, 15T, 15B, 18, 22, 23, 27, 32, 36, 37, 39, 75, 85, 93T, 93B, 109, 121, 123, 126B, 127, 131T, 135, 138, 139, 140T, 144, 151, 155, 157T, 159, 164, 168BL, 169TR, 173T, 197, 201, 220T, 237, 248, 249, 258BL, 259BL, 261, 263B, 266T, 268, 280, 282, 283, 285B, 285T, 289T, 289B, 290, 292, 306, 309, 313
Jim Turner/Lady Bird Johnson

Wildflower Center/The University of Texas at Austin 142
Library of Congress 25T, 26B, 26T, 58
NASA 184BR, 184BL, 185ML, 185BL, 185TR
Public domain 25B, 34
Robert Harding 6B
SuperStock 71, 131B, 198, 226, 233B
Texas Highway Department 31
Texas Tourism 19, 69, 74, 84, 101, 111T, 111B, 113, 117, 126T, 137, 143, 145, 148, 150, 152T, 153, 158, 163, 165, 183, 192B, 206, 208T, 208B, 210T, 221, 224B, 236B, 241, 246, 247B, 255, 260, 272B, 273, 275, 276, 286, 287, 296, 304, 307
The Art Archive 64
TopFoto 169BR
Visit San Antonio 147, 160, 161, 162T, 162B, 166
Visit San Antonio/Carol Barrington 167
VisitHouston 81

Cover Credits

Front cover: Big Bend National park *Getty Images*
Back cover: (top) Austin *iStock*; (middle) oil well *iStock*
Front flap: (from top) Padre Island horse ride *Carol M. Highsmith/LOC*;

Salt Lick BBQ *Carol M. Highsmith/ LOC*; musicians in Terlingua *Texas Tourism*; cowhands *Carol M. Highsmith/LOC*
Back flap: West Texas country road *iStock*

Spine: Neon sign *Carol M. Highsmith/LOC*

Insight Guide Credits

Distribution
UK
Dorling Kindersley Ltd
A Penguin Group company
80 Strand, London, WC2R 0RL
sales@uk.dk.com

United States
Ingram Publisher Services
1 Ingram Boulevard, PO Box 3006,
La Vergne, TN 37086-1986
ips@ingramcontent.com

Australia and New Zealand
Woodslane
10 Apollo St, Warriewood,
NSW 2102, Australia
info@woodslane.com.au

Worldwide
Apa Publications GmbH & Co. Verlag
KG (Singapore branch)
7030 Ang Mo Kio Avenue 5
08-65 Northstar @ AMK
Singapore 569880
apasin@singnet.com.sg

Printing
CTPS-China
© 2015 Apa Publications (UK) Ltd
All Rights Reserved

First Edition 1986
Fifth Edition 2015

www.insightguides.com

Project Editor
Rachel Lawrence
Author
Nicky Leach
Picture Editor
Tom Smyth
Map Production
Original cartography Colourmap
Scanning Ltd, updated by
Apa Cartography Department
Production
Rebeka Davies

Contributors

This new edition was commissioned by **Rachel Lawrence**, Insight Guides' North America editor. Santa Fe writer **Nicky Leach** has worked with Insight Guides for nearly 20 years, creating and updating guides on Florida and the American West, including *Arizona and the Grand Canyon, Colorado*, and *USA on the Road*. This edition builds on earlier editions produced by **Helen Bryant**, **John Davis**, **Eileen Mattei**, **Ann Mills**, **Ed Proctor**, **John Wilcock**, and **Christopher Walters**. The text was proofread and indexed by **Penny Phenix**.

About Insight Guides

Insight Guides have more than 40 years' experience of publishing high-quality, visual travel guides. We produce 400 full-colour titles, in both print and digital form, covering more than 200 destinations across the globe, in a variety of formats to meet your different needs.

Insight Guides are written by local authors who use their on-the-ground experience to provide the very latest information; their local expertise is evident in the extensive background historical and cultural features. All the reviews in Insight Guides are independent and carefully selected; we strive to maintain an impartial view.

Legend

City maps

	Freeway/Highway/Motorway
	Divided Highway
	Main Roads
	Minor Roads
	Pedestrian Roads
	Steps
	Footpath
	Railway
	Funicular Railway
	Cable Car
	Tunnel
	City Wall
	Important Building
	Built Up Area
	Other Land
	Transport Hub
	Park
	Pedestrian Area
	Bus Station
	Tourist Information
	Main Post Office
	Cathedral/Church
	Mosque
	Synagogue
	Statue/Monument
	Beach
	Airport

Regional maps

	Freeway/Highway/Motorway (with junction)
	Freeway/Highway/Motorway (under construction)
	Divided Highway
	Main Road
	Secondary Road
	Minor Road
	Track
	Footpath
	International Boundary
	State/Province Boundary
	National Park/Reserve
	Marine Park
	Ferry Route
	Marshland/Swamp
	Glacier Salt Lake
	Airport/Airfield
	Ancient Site
	Border Control
	Cable Car
	Castle/Castle Ruins
	Cave
	Chateau/Stately Home
	Church/Church Ruins
	Crater
	Lighthouse
	Mountain Peak
	Place of Interest
	Viewpoint

INDEX